Visions of Japanese Modernity

The publisher gratefully acknowledges the generous support of the Ahmanson Foundation Humanities Endowment Fund of the University of California Press Foundation.

Published with the assistance of the Frederick W. Hilles Publication Fund of Yale University.

Visions of Japanese Modernity

*Articulations of Cinema, Nation,
and Spectatorship, 1895–1925*

AARON GEROW

University of California Press

BERKELEY   LOS ANGELES   LONDON

University of California Press, one of the most distinguished university presses in the United States, enriches lives around the world by advancing scholarship in the humanities, social sciences, and natural sciences. Its activities are supported by the UC Press Foundation and by philanthropic contributions from individuals and institutions. For more information, visit www.ucpress.edu.

University of California Press
Berkeley and Los Angeles, California

University of California Press, Ltd.
London, England

Library of Congress Cataloging-in-Publication Data

Gerow, Aaron Andrew.
  Visions of Japanese modernity : articulations of cinema, nation, and spectatorship, 1895–1925 / Aaron Gerow.
      p.   cm.
  Includes bibliographical references and index.
  ISBN 978-0-520-25672-9 (cloth : alk. paper)
  ISBN 978-0-520-25456-5 (pbk. : alk. paper)
    1. Motion pictures—Japan—History—19th century.   2. Motion pictures—Japan—History—20th century.   I. Title.

  PN1993.5.J3G45   2010
  791.430952'09041—dc22   2009030995

Manufactured in the United States of America

19 18 17 16 15 14 13 12 11 10
10 9 8 7 6 5 4 3 2 1

This book is printed on Cascades Enviro 100, a 100% post consumer waste, recycled, de-inked fiber. FSC recycled certified and processed chlorine free. It is acid free, Ecologo certified, and manufactured by BioGas energy.

To my parents

Contents

Illustrations

Acknowledgments

Many years have passed since I embarked on the road to writing this tome, a path that at times seemed interminable, with many detours and not a few potholes. Many individuals and institutions helped me reach my destination, and I am immensely grateful for their support. There are too many to name here, but I would like to at least touch the tip of the proverbial iceberg and mention some of the most prominent.

Kudos go first of all to my first two advisors, Professors Dudley Andrew and Iwamoto Kenji. The former first taught me the way of a good scholar and then valiantly endured the last frantic months of my writing the initial manuscript; the latter took me under his gentle wing and introduced me to the world of film research in Japan. To both men I am eternally grateful.

My research for this book was made possible financially by several organizations. I initially went to Japan on a very generous grant from the Japan Foundation. Film viewing at the Library of Congress, which provided a start to this research, was supported by funds from the Northeast Asia Council of the Association for Asian Studies. Yano Kazuyuki and the Yamagata International Documentary Film Festival helped me stay in Japan while also providing the wonderful opportunity for me to program films and edit *Documentary Box*. My universities, Yokohama National University, Meiji Gakuin University, and Yale University, helped me further develop my ideas while teaching, and my students deserve recognition for their penetrating questions and illuminating responses. At Yale, the Morse Junior Faculty Fellowship in the Humanities gave me time to polish the manuscript, the Frederick W. Hilles Publication Fund helped subvent publication, and the A. Whitney Griswold Faculty Research Fund helped prepare the text for publication in Japanese at the University of

Tokyo Press. My editor there, Hasegawa Hajime, and my translators, Hase Masato, Yamamoto Naoki, and Shimura Miyoko, all contributed to clean-ing up the English text as well. I especially thank Mary Francis, Jacque-line Volin, and Bonita Hurd of the University of California Press, and the anonymous readers for their direction and comments.

Along the way, I had the opportunity to publish sections of this work in Japanese and publish related research in English. I thank the editors of *Yuriika, Eizōgaku, Eigagaku, Iconics, CineMagziNet,* and *Screening the Past,* as well as Alan Tansman, Roland Domenig, Jeannette Paulson, Car-ole Cavanaugh, and Dennis Washburn, for the opportunity to present my work and for their comments and suggestions along the way. I have also presented aspects of this research at many universities and conferences, and I express my gratitude both to those who invited me and those who attended and asked questions.

Many individuals and institutions assisted me during all stages, from researching to writing. Saiki Tomonori, Sasaki Yoriaki, Okajima Hisashi, Okada Hidenori, Tochigi Akira, and Irie Yoshirō of the National Film Cen-ter of the Museum of Modern Art, Tokyo; Tajima Ryōichi of Nihon Uni-versity; and everyone at the Kawakita Memorial Film Institute and the Tsubouchi Memorial Theater Museum—all were invaluable in helping me collect materials for this study. I also received generous support in Japan from Satō Tadao, Takeda Kiyoshi, Kondō Kōjin, Thomas Rohlich, Katō Mikirō, Yomota Inuhiko, Komatsu Hiroshi, Iijima Tadashi, Tsu-kada Yoshinobu, Ueno Toshiya, Murayama Kyōichirō, Mizuguchi Kaoru, Yoshimi Shun'ya, and Sugawa Yoshiyuki. Tom Gunning and Donald Kirihara offered detailed comments on sections of this manuscript, and I also recognize friends such as Abé Markus Nornes, Noriko Aso, Alan Christy, Darrell Davis, and Mitsuyo Wada-Marciano for their selfless input. Heidi Kenaga and Michael Raine were godsends in their cheerful willingness to collect materials from across the ocean. And I salute the other members of my original dissertation committee, Kathleen Newman, Lauren Rabinovitz, Stephen Vlastos, and Mitsuhiro Yoshimoto, for their patience and support. Tom LaMarre, Joanne Bernardi, Charles Musser, John MacKay, Jennifer Robertson, Edward Kamens, Chris Hill, and John Treat are some of my other colleagues whom I offer deserved thanks for their assistance.

Finally, I offer deep and eternal thanks to a man whose contribution to my research was both special and unending: Makino Mamoru. Beyond selflessly offering up his collection and his food, he shared with me his vast knowledge of such topics as prewar censorship and magazine publishing,

Introduction

Takada Tamotsu, a reporter for the late-teens Japanese film magazine *Katsudō no sekai* (Movie World) once gave an account of the first press screening for *Sei no kagayaki* (The Glow of Life), Kaeriyama Norimasa's revolutionary 1918 film often cited as marking a major historical shift in film form in Japan. According to Takada's recollection, Yamamoto Yoshitarō, business director of the Tennenshoku Katsudō Shashin Kabushiki Kaisha—a leading 1910s film company called Tenkatsu for short—introduced the film with the following words: "The moving picture you are about to view is not a moving picture: It is a film, something which is completely different."[1] The Japanese word he was using in the first sentence was *katsudō shashin*, literally "moving photographs," the accepted Japanese name for the medium since its importation into Japan about twenty years earlier. Yamamoto, however, was attempting to mark a distinction between *Sei no kagayaki* and previous Japanese cinema by calling the film something different: an *eiga*, the two ideographs that make up the word signifying "projected pictures." While this term was used in the nineteenth century to denote the slides in magic lantern shows, it was not applied to the cinema until, the story goes, Kaeriyama himself, in his activities as a film critic, used it to signify those films (mostly American and European) that fulfilled the essence of the motion picture medium.[2] In the linguistic strategy employed by first Kaeriyama and then Yamamoto, *katsudō shashin* was redefined from designating the entire medium to denoting only those "uncinematic" Japanese works that Kaeriyama's groundbreaking *eiga* would relegate to the past, the term *eiga* itself signifying the kind of motion pictures advocated in Kaeriyama's cinematic revolution, a

Figure 1.   A still from Kaeriyama Norimasa's *Sei no kagayaki* (The Glow of Life), which signified the beginning of a discourse on *eiga,* or new cinema. (Courtesy of the Kawakita Memorial Film Institute)

loosely aligned front of critics, filmmakers, and public officials later called the Jun'eigageki Undō,[3] or Pure Film Movement.

Although Kaeriyama clearly intended his first directorial feature to speak for itself, exemplifying and justifying the conception of cinema he had outlined in film journals such as *Kinema Record,* it is impossible to separate his film from the discourses enunciated either at the press screening or by Kaeriyama himself and his journalistic compatriots. Their discourse was an effort to redefine cinema, not simply through promoting the practical application of formal and narrative devices deemed properly cinematic, but also, as the shift in terminology exemplifies, through the rearticulation of cinema. Cinema itself would be transformed through the ways people spoke about it, described it, and defined it in words and statements. That *eiga* would by the late 1920s supplant *katsudō shashin* as the generic appellation for film in the discourse of many Japanese is as much a sign of the effect of the Pure Film Movement as the proliferation of its favored formal techniques within Japanese film grammar.

Most histories of the Pure Film Movement or of this period concentrate on the transformation of film style. Deeply influenced by foreign cinema, pure film reformers countered a static, often theatrical Japanese film with a new definition of the cinematic that included the use of close-ups, analytic editing, actresses (until then, Japanese works featured *onnagata,* or female impersonators), and detailed screenplays. Although later foreign movements such as French Impressionist film in the 1920s also sought to perfect a pure cinema (and were often supported by critical writing), the Japanese case was less an effort to establish the motion picture as a pure art form in opposition to commercial cinema than to introduce the filmic innovations of Hollywood and European production, considered to be the best examples of the cinematic medium, into the Japanese industry. Since these changes were imbricated in transformations not only in style but also in the way such concepts as narrative, the spectator, and textuality were conceived, it is possible to trace a broad history of Japanese film in the shifts and breaks in the way the motion pictures were talked about and articulated in discourse.

A discursive history of cinema is necessary, because in reality discourse assumed an important role in molding the direction of the motion pictures in Japan. This is first exemplified by the Pure Film Movement, which began in the early 1910s precisely as a series of statements on the cinema, a revolution in film journalism and criticism that, as with the word *eiga,* sought to transform the meaning of Japanese cinema through formulating new ways of speaking about it. Importantly, this development in criticism long preceded any effort to mold the "thing" cinema itself by producing films in light of the movement's theoretical models (Kaeriyama's *Sei no kagayaki,* made in 1918 and released in 1919, is usually cited as the first "pure" film). In a sense, cinema was written in early Japanese film history before it was filmed. On a broader scale, the effect that speaking about cinema had on the film medium itself in Japan is best reflected in the example of the institution of the *benshi,* in the long-lasting practice of having a person in the silent era narrate films for the audience, one that made speaking about and explaining the cinema a central part of experiencing the medium. As I argue in this book, such narrations were seen to greatly influence the meaning of cinema not only for spectators but also for society at large, as they affected definitions of cinematic textuality and its place in modernity.

This history of discourse has yet to be fully told: existing histories of Japanese film, both by Japanese and non-Japanese, tend to focus on textual or auteurist analysis to the detriment of the role of other factors—the spectator, the industrial structure, criticism—in producing the cinematic experience.[4] The major histories of Japanese film by Tanaka Jun'ichirō, Satō Tadao, Okada Susumu, and other prominent Japanese scholars have always included an effort to historicize the text, but usually on the level of a limited *sesōshi* (history of social conditions) that merely notes apparent correspondences between historical events and filmic content, occasionally citing such conditions as an explanation for why spectators enjoyed these works or why a filmmaker tended to treat certain themes.[5] By offering a reflectionist model of the relationship between cinema and its historical context, a model that assumes a unified synchronic totality encompassing film and society, such histories have failed to delve into the historical construction of cinema itself in the Japanese social sphere and inquire into how relationships between cinema and history are mediated through various ideological, institutional, and discursive structures.

Influenced by structuralist and poststructuralist theory, Noël Burch attempted to make the discursive context the center of his history of Japanese cinema, *To the Distant Observer: Form and Meaning in the Japanese Cinema*. Burch even asserts that it is "this *presence of the context* [that] is a permanent feature of the Japanese *difference*, in both Heian literature and modern film practice,"[6] and emphasizes that Japanese cultural production features a unique intertextuality in which all film texts purposively refer to and rely on other texts to be understood, either through the body of traditional textual conventions or, in the case of silent film, the benshi who stood next to the screen and narrated the film's content. While modern Western texts hid their intertextuality in myths of originality and the individual author, Japanese culture, Burch claims, made the intertexts a visible aspect of both signification and pleasure for the reader and viewer. His emphasis on intertextuality in Japanese cinema is instructive, but it is often based on a binary distinction between Japan and the West in which Japanese tradition is figured as producing the level of intertextuality desired in poststructuralist thought. Beyond noting the Orientalism implicit in this position, we can question the historicity of Burch's claim that the traditional intertext "still bears the unmistakable stamp of three centuries of standardization."[7] He fails to ask some of the basic questions in considering the discursive formation of prewar cinema culture: Who spoke, and with what authority? Where or in what socioeconomic conditions was cinematic discourse being spoken, and to whom was it directed? What relations of power were imbricated in the relations between discourses? What were statements being made against, and what was their concrete political import? What was assumed or left unsaid in these enunciations? How were they articulating not just cinema but also those whom discourse was speaking of and the modern culture they inhabited? Simply, Burch does not interrogate the actual contemporary discourses on tradition, modernity, or intertextuality, instead assuming a figure such as the benshi to be a traditional object with a given meaning or effectiveness and never exploring how that might have been mediated in the intense debates over the relationship between the benshi and the text. Unable to divide discourse into various levels or oppositions, marking its fissures and contradictions over time, Burch pictures a Japanese cinema that is unified by a Japaneseness that discourse, in the end, only comes to reflect.

In contrast, David Bordwell, in his studies of the films of Ozu Yasujirō and 1930s Japanese cinema, stresses the importance of historicizing this cultural context. Countering Burch's assertion that Japanese tradition is fundamentally other to that of the West and has remained largely unified and unchanged over the centuries, Bordwell argues:

> Such a position ignores the fact that in most respects most films from Japan are comprehensible according to Western protocols for viewing. Because of this, I would argue that there are several distinct Japanese aesthetic traditions, undergirded by significantly varying assumptions about the nature and roles of art. (Indeed, the Heian tradition is at least partly a construct of later centuries.) Moreover, I would argue that representational conventions of form and address are mediated through post-Meiji modernizations (not least the popular urban culture of this century's first decades). There is evidence that by the time such features show up in films, they are not unreflectingly assimilated but are knowingly cited to achieve particular formal ends.[8]

Bordwell thus stresses the processes of change that occurred starting in the Meiji era (1868–1912), ones that produced both a plurality of options for representation and a distance between the filmmaker and "tradition" which made the past only one choice among many. Referring to discussions of Ozu, he emphasizes that "an appeal to 'tradition' often conceals a loose, untheorized, and imperialistic approach to 'Japaneseness.' The danger is the sort of ahistoricity . . . which is very common in studies of Japanese culture."[9] Bordwell tries to reinsert historicity into his discussion of Japanese film by emphasizing the historical mediation between tradition and cinema, one in which the unity of the social context itself comes into question. With imperfect access to Japanese-language materials, however, Bordwell's own analysis of these mediations can at best be called limited. Relying on the categories of a poetics of cinema that are equally applicable to Ozu and Bresson, Bordwell also fails to interrogate how the concepts of "norm," "understanding," "spectator," or even "cinema" were articulated. I will show how those concepts were shaped by various discourses in a certain historical conjuncture and imbricated with developing relations of social and cultural power.

The problem in writing a history of discourse, as Michel Foucault emphasized, is precisely in theorizing the relationship of the object of discourse to discursive history. Foucault stresses in *The Archaeology of Knowledge* that "the object does not await in limbo the order that will free it and enable it to become embodied in a visible and prolix objectivity; it does not pre-exist itself, held back by some obstacle at the first edges of light."[10] Especially since cinema was an imported medium, the "cinematicity" of cinema was not pregiven in the history of Japanese film; a primary question is how the object cinema appeared not only on Japanese soil but also in discourse, molded and defined by the operations of those talking and writing about it. The failure to address this issue undermines other studies in English of the Pure Film Movement.

Peter B. High's short history of 1910s reform is a colorful, flamboyantly written account of dedicated young fans battling an entrenched and conservative old guard, a drama of the heroes of progress and modernity triumphing over the evil forces of political reaction; his argument, however, contains some clumsy errors. Although he admits that the reformers may have been too elitist, High aligns himself so much with their cause that he more often reproduces their discourse than analyzes it, thereby failing to see the more complex politics involved in the project of reform. He assumes cinema to be an art and assesses good and bad according to which position individuals take on that issue. Typical is the point at which he berates an early Nikkatsu cameraman for being "a somewhat reactionary tyrant who refused to acknowledge the rights and responsibilities of the director":[11] never discussed is that, not only in Japan, but also in many other cinema cultures as well, the institution of the director, with its "rights and responsibilities," had not yet been named, let alone formulated and recognized, before at least the late 1910s. In this way, High writes history from his position in the present, projecting the values of his film culture back onto a time when such notions had not yet been discursively articulated.

Joanne Bernardi's research on the development of the screenplay by such individuals as Kaeriyama, Kurihara Tōmasu, and Tanizaki Jun'ichirō is an important contribution to the study of screenwriting in Japan (previously a neglected topic), especially as it was developed within the discourse of the Pure Film Movement. Her thorough research stands in counterpoint to the theoretical abstractions of Burch, although her analysis does not always pursue the conceptual implications of pure film reform, especially with regard to issues of class, power, modernity, and nationhood. While wonderfully outlining the positions of Kaeriyama and others on the cinema, Bernardi does not sufficiently dissect their notions to see how the cinematic truth or historical teleology they proffer worked to exclude other interpretations of cinema, or how such knowledge itself produced relations of power with other discourses and their speakers (or with those who were silent).[12]

This book focuses on the statements about motion pictures that both preceded and helped mold a new form of Japanese cinema within a field complexly structured by conflicts of class, power, and modernity. However, it is not a history of how well the discursive definitions were manifested in practice, analyzing how film style embodied or deviated from the critical ideal. Such a narrative would not be without merit, but it is neither desirable nor possible from the standpoint of this study. It is one of the bitter tragedies of studying early Japanese film history that only a handful of films before the mid-1920s exist; there are simply not enough extant works to do justice to a history of Japanese film style before 1925. It is partly out of necessity that this book does not analyze many of the filmic texts themselves, but it is also a matter of choice. Remember that Foucault argues, "What, in short, we wish to do is dispense with 'things'. . . . To substitute for the enigmatic treasure of 'things' anterior to discourse, the regular formation of objects that emerge only in discourse. To define these *objects* without reference to the *ground*, the *foundation of things*, but by relating them to the body of rules that enable them to form as objects of a discourse and thus constitute the conditions of their historical appearance."[13] Certainly Foucault does not intend a writing of a history without texts, but in a perhaps ironic way his form of discursive history allows us to still talk about early Japanese film history even though many of the "things," the motion pictures themselves, are not present for us to examine and analyze. Maybe it is better this way: until now, it has been the privileging of such works that has led most scholars of later Japanese film history to focus only on the texts and authors at the expense of understanding either the ways in which they first appear "only in discourse," or the conditions in which they emerged as the objects of people's understanding. That has also led to the downplaying of research on periods like that of early cinema, where there are few films. While certainly not a desirable situation, perhaps the absence of films from the 1910s and early 1920s permits us to pay more attention to the discursive basis on which they would have been created, watched, understood, and discussed.

The particularity and importance of such a study is reflected partly in the definition of discourse that Foucault offers, in which he does not treat "discourses as groups of signs (signifying elements referring to contents or representations) but as practices that systematically form the objects of which they speak. Of course, discourses are composed of signs; but what they do is more than use these signs to designate things. It is this *more* that renders them irreducible to the language *(langue)* and to speech. It is this 'more' that we must reveal."[14] I am interested, then, in not just the things discourse describes but also the historically grounded sets of rules and practices that, never reducible to things or words, do not simply name an already present reality but work to mold and create objects of understanding and knowledge. Concretely, this study is mostly concerned with discourse embodied in speech and writing, and focuses on statements about cinema that appeared in newspapers, magazines, and even legal regulations, spoken or written by institutions such as film journalism, the general press, education, literature, the film industry, and the law. I keep the definition of discourse open and loose, however, first to allow for such factors as architecture and geography to enter into consideration, and second, in recognition of the fact that the definition of discourse on cinema itself was an object of debate in Japan in the 1910s. As I show, some of the discourse on film in Japan concerned itself with what defines a legitimate statement on cinema and even the possibility of talking about the medium. It is especially the perceived conflict between the word and the image that forms one of the central contradictions defining much of early Japanese film.

TOWARD A SPECIFIC HISTORY

The point of this study is to show how the discourse of the Pure Film Movement marked a significant shift in statements about cinema in Japan. The moment of this break is hard to locate, and as a result the period covered by my research is somewhat open. The core of the discussion focuses on the 1910s and the early 1920s, but to establish a background I also outline how cinema was discussed in the first fifteen years after the apparatus was imported in late 1896. It would be hard to call early statements a discourse on film, since the object itself had not appeared: there was little to distinguish discussions of the motion pictures from those on any other fairground entertainment. It was only around 1910 that a more unified discourse specific to the cinema began to appear, but mostly through a series of negations that initially marked the medium as a problem: first, as a social predicament (a cause of either crime among juveniles or unsocial behavior among adults); and second, as a new problem revolving around the definitions of the cinematic (in which, in particular, certain forms of film experience became to be called uncinematic) and modernity (the struggles over how to define and shape new forms of social relations, subjectivities, identities, and cultures). It is perhaps at this point that the Pure Film Movement can be said to have started, commencing with the discursive effort to locate and study the sources of these problems and define a form of cinema that would be both true to its cinematic essence and socially acceptable in a new, modern Japan.

Especially by reviewing the work of Gonda Yasunosuke, who largely left it up to different spectators to determine the significance of cinema, I stress the existence of multiple options for defining the cinematic in discourse at the time. The history of discourse on film in the 1910s was often one of excluding and silencing these other possibilities, entailing a struggle over the meaning of the cinema that was intimately linked to relations of power in the social and cultural fields. I sketch the field of film culture in Japan in light of Pierre Bourdieu's sociology of culture, in which positions taken within a cultural field, while relatively autonomous of economically based hierarchies, create their own hierarchies founded on the economics of culture: the possession of cultural capital, the ability to get a return (in the form of prestige) on one's investment, and so forth. As Bourdieu states in relation to literature, "The field of cultural production is the site of struggles in which what is at stake is the power to impose the dominant definition of the writer and therefore to delimit the population of those entitled to take part in the struggle to define the writer."[15] I in fact argue that the field of cinema in the 1910s was such a site of struggle, in which what was at stake was the definition of cinema and the restriction of who could speak about the medium. Knowledge as power intersected with distinction as power, with young intellectuals striving to improve their status within the cinematic field by constructing a dominant version of film knowledge that valorized their own role. Contrasting their understanding of the medium with that of people considered ignorant and lower class, their position was in the end relational, depending "for its very existence, and for the determinations it imposes on its occupants, on the other positions constituting the field."[16] Such hierarchical relations were not always homologous to the class or political structure of the larger social field, since film reformers often took an ambivalent position toward the industry, presenting at times a vision of film culture that would be as independent of economic interests as the pure arts, while also offering proposals for a more socially responsible—and economically modern—industry. Yet in its alliance with both state authority, embodied in censorship, and "respectable" social values, the Pure Film Movement was often conjoined with structures of power in the larger—and shifting—social field of the 1910s and 1920s.

Kaeriyama and his fellow reformers, in attempting to delimit the field of cinema and who could talk about it, were focused on negating a particular form of cinematic production they felt was represented at the time by

Japanese film. Attempting to define a pure film, they also tried to discursively fix a variety of texts under the rubric of noncinema. This a-cinema was blamed for not clearly distinguishing itself from fairground entertainments or theater, for being vulgar and lacking in the values inherent to the motion pictures. Showmanship, the mode of presentation typical at temple fairs, when applied to film, was said to reveal only an ignorance of the truth of cinema that prevented the medium from advancing. The worst crime was precisely failing to distinguish the cinema, refusing to mark off the motion pictures as unique and instead presenting film as if it were low-class theater. The space of the theater itself interfered in the enjoyment of the film, as benshi were blamed for devoting more attention to their verbal effusions than to ensuring that spectators would understand the film. In the end, film producers were the ones cited as most responsible for this situation: first, by ceding the power over the medium to showmen exhibitors, and second, by creating films that ignored all the unique qualities of the medium—speed, realism, close-ups, editing, and most of all, illusionism: the creation of a diegetic world.

Into this situation stepped intellectual reformers who, after delineating the above problems in their written discourse, sought to make their revolution a reality by making films themselves, motion pictures that embodied the definition of cinema they had produced, and that manifested a difference in shot-length, camera distance, editing, and narrative process. While the films themselves, by all accounts, were different from the normal Japanese fare, a stylistic comparison would be insufficient to explain the complexity and breadth of the transformations under way. Only an analysis of the larger discursive field reveals that new conceptions appeared, not only of cinema, but also of narrative, the spectator, understanding, textuality, semiosis, the screenplay, criticism, exhibition, and production, and even of the image and the word. Japanese film culture in the 1910s and early 1920s witnessed a major shift in the basic understanding and social definition of cinema that exceeded changes in film form.

One can align these transformations with larger shifts in Japanese society, because modernization and mass culture were themselves advancing in an increasingly urban society. Industrialization was beginning to mold a new urban proletariat who would help found forms of urban culture and nascent leftist movements. In the realm of work, bureaucratic and corporate rationalism was on the rise at the same time there was an increase in leisure time. Department stores were being remolded at the end of the 1910s as the centers of a new consumerism that would be spread by forms of mass communication created by cinema and the publishing industry.

With advertising experiencing a boom, culture itself became increasingly commodified and everyday life more and more Westernized. Karatani Kō-jin has spoken about the shifts in Japanese literature in the 1890s during the *genbun itchi* movement (the effort to bring the spoken and written languages together), in which the discovery of landscape (a form of the Other) led to the formation of interiority, an enunciative subject that internalized language as something natural and expressive.[17] In some ways, the Pure Film Movement represented the effort to introduce such modern forms of subjectivity into a mass medium, a project that would later be advanced through the development of popular literature in the mid-1920s.

Considering the Pure Film Movement in this way as a form of epistemological break in early knowledge about cinema, it is possible to draw analogies between Japanese film culture in the 1910s and early 1920s and American and European cinema before and after approximately 1906, when developments in editing and other narrational techniques enabled a new form of narrative cinema to emerge, one best exemplified by the work of D.W. Griffith. In this sense, it might be useful to apply the insights of work on early cinema by such scholars as Burch, Tom Gunning, Miriam Hansen, Lee Grieveson, and André Gaudreault to explain the Japanese case. As summarized by Gunning, such scholars have tried to overturn the presumption dominant in most film histories that early cinema was either an "initial error" that failed to see what constituted essential cinematic value (e.g., reproducing theater instead of seeking more filmic modes and stories), or a mere "preparatory period" in the teleological evolution toward narrative motion picture art.[18] Instead, this scholarship rejects the sense of continuity between early and late cinema and considers the former on its own terms as a qualitatively different form of film; it uses new historiography to attempt to locate in social, economic, and ideological conditions the sources for a transformation in narrative cinema that is less evolutionary than marked by rupture and abrupt transitions that completely change the meaning and role of the motion pictures—the "paradigmatic shift" Hansen mentions.[19] In the case of Burch, early cinema is even valorized as a model of alternative film practice that reflects the values of its lower-class, immigrant audience, one that can oppose the operations of the dominant bourgeois narrative cinema.[20] Gunning himself stresses the affinity between the avant-garde and an early "cinema of attractions"—a mode of film experience that emphasized theatrical display over narrative, and direct address to the spectator over molding a diegetic world.[21] Focusing more on the spectator than on the text, Hansen speaks of the shift to classical narrative cinema as "gentrification," in which the appreciation of film as a local, live performance gave way to absorption in the text and suppression of the theater space, the heterogeneous, "relatively autonomous public sphere of the nickelodeons" becoming linked to "the more comprehensive, less class-specific public sphere of an emerging consumer culture."[22] Both Hansen and Gunning underline the desire by the film industry to create a more socially respectable product that was also compatible with efforts to standardize production and, in effect, create a culture industry. In his study of the censorship of early cinema in America, Grieveson shows, using a methodology that shares much with my research on the Pure Film Movement, how much the policing of the motion pictures became an essential component in defining the medium in society early on.[23]

To the degree that, up until recently, histories of early Japanese cinema have been written from the perspective of the Pure Film Movement (or even by its participants, like Iijima Tadashi) and have uniformly characterized pre-1918 Japanese film as "uncinematic" and in error, my work shares in the effort of recent scholars to revise historical assumptions, the emphasis being not on how the Pure Film Movement helped advance the evolution of cinema in the Japanese context but on how one model of cinema was in part replaced in discourse by a very different model. The rupture I describe shares elements with the changes observed in early American and European cinema, particularly the transformation from a film experience based in a local, live performance to a narrative system centered in the text created at the point of production. Cinema in Japan was also deeply imbricated in consumerism and the issue of class, as the Pure Film Movement can be considered one factor in a larger effort to raise the social status of film and eliminate the markers of class difference to create a mass and homogeneous consumer public. Industry organization was as much a problem in Japan as the United States: film reform in the late 1910s and early 1920s coincided with the establishment of new studios like Shōchiku that hoped to modernize and rationalize the industry. Perhaps such analogies can be made because Japan was undergoing some of the same problems of modernization, urbanization, consumerism, and nation building that Western countries were. It is also important to underline how much Japanese cinema culture itself was influenced by American and European films: the Pure Film Movement approximates many developments elsewhere in early cinema because the intellectuals championing reform were thorough scholars of foreign cinema and avid readers of American film magazines and how-to books. Even when discussing Japanese articulations of cinema, we must keep in mind how much the nation was interlaced with more global determinations.

I have chosen, however, not to make this a study of influence in hopes of avoiding a certain form of comparative analysis. First, there is already too much of a tendency to define research on non-Western cinemas through binary contrasts. Following the efforts by film theorists in the 1970s to define a cinema alternative to the classical Hollywood mode, a form of practice both radical and different, many studies of Asian or Third World cinemas have been pressed to locate in such bodies of texts instances of this alternative mode. Burch's work is an example of such a trend. One difficulty is that many who have made studies of national cinemas within the Western fold have not been subject to this demand to the same degree: they, in a sense, have been freer to concentrate on local specificities without perpetually comparing these other cinemas to the Hollywood dominant. Work on non-Western cinemas, by being structured by a desire to find an alternative to the West—an ideal Other—has too often been affected by the dynamics of Orientalism, in which the non-West functions as the mirror or dreamscape for the Western intellectual imagination, and in which local differences that fit neither the "alternative" image nor the conception of "Hollywood colonization" are considered irrelevant. The resulting binary worldview tends to posit a homogeneous West against a homogeneous non-West, each essentialized to a certain degree, effectively effacing the differences *within* each of these terms. It may in part be a result of this structure that Burch remains oblivious to many of the manifest contradictions within Japanese cinema and culture and sees instead an "integration of taste" between classes supposedly resulting from a lack of class conflict in Japanese history.[24] Such conflicts, however, have been very apparent in the discourse on early cinema in Japan, and it is imperative for historical studies to consider such differences within the Japanese sphere before contrasting them to Hollywood cinema.

Japanese film studies have focused increased attention on the issue of "national cinema," but even those that recognize that motion pictures are not the manifestation of some age-old national essence, and that they in fact participate in the modern construction of national identity, seem to be compelled to reduce films to the singular nation, even if that nation is constructed or inherently engaged in transnational systems of difference. By making the national the central category, even supposedly to deconstruct it, many studies have nonetheless made the cinema revolve around the question of the nation, effectively homogenizing it. I have published several works detailing how the supposedly "national" cinema of Japan was rife with contradictions and crisscrossed by transnational vectors,[25] but here, in refraining from pursuing a comparative study or focusing exclusively on the question of the nation, I am, in a strategic move, declaring that I am not interested in how "Japanese cinema" (a problematic term) is "similar" to or "different" from "Western cinema" (also a problematic concept); it is not my concern how Japanese early film may or may not be an "alternative" to cinematic practices in Hollywood. In resisting this binary, I hope to focus more attention on the fissures and contradictions within Japanese film history itself—by considering categories such as class, subjectivity, and modernity that may not be coterminous with the category of the nation.[26]

This attention to particularity is important given the significantly different conditions in which early cinema existed in Japan. One of the main topics of debate among recent scholars has been the role of narrative in early cinema. Charles Musser, for instance, has objected to the broad use of Gunning's concept of the "cinema of attractions"—which states that early films were less concerned with telling stories than with displaying views—and has reasserted the primacy of narrative in cinema after at least 1903.[27] Janet Staiger has echoed this point from a different perspective, underlining that it was spectators themselves who, in their reading strategies, rendered early cinema as narrative, and not the films that did this.[28] Such contentions are certainly worthy of more debate when considering cinema in the United States, but they do not easily translate to the period in Japan that I discuss. The shift I describe is less involved with the issue of narrative, because the benshi, in particular, were clearly supplying narratives for Japanese films that were, by the late 1910s, feature length; the telling of stories already occupied a dominant position in film culture, so narrative or its lack was not one of the central issues of the Pure Film Movement. Rather, the point of concern was *how* stories were being told, *where* narration took place, *what* the subject of narrative enunciation was, *how* narrative understanding should be defined, *how cinematic* that narrative was, and what alternatives existed to narrative. Changing the benshi's mode of narration, and altering their relation to the text, became one of the primary sources of debate throughout the period I discuss.

Scholarship on American and European early cinema can help us raise issues and questions with which to approach Japanese film, but we should remember to sift our answers through local forms of appropriation— local forms defined less in terms of a historically transcendent national essence or tradition than of concrete and geographically particular historical conjunctures, which may include the transversing of global forces. In the Japanese case, one example is the state. When considering issues of power, research on American early film, which the exception of perhaps

Grieveson's, usually centers on problems of self-censorship and rarely focuses primarily on the state (although much work has been done on the pressure for censorship applied by progressive or religious reform movements, for instance). This is perhaps legitimate, given that no nationalized censorship system was created in the United States, but that is not the case in Japan.[29] National state censorship was instituted in 1925, following a long series of efforts by local authorities to not only corral and regulate the industry but also control forms of spectatorship and reading. There has been a tendency in some histories of modern Japan, especially those influenced by modernization theory,[30] to romanticize the Taishō era (1912–1926) as an opening up of liberalism and free expression, a period of "Taishō democracy" typified by elected party cabinets that was interrupted by the fascist late 1930s and early 1940s. While it is important to understand the proliferation of possibilities inherent in that historical conjuncture, I tend to share the social historian Takemura Tamio's opinion that the basis for the mass mobilization for war should be sought precisely in this era.[31] One of my central concerns throughout this book is on how discourse on cinema has served to define the relation between the state and the motion pictures, especially given the often close alliance between film reformers and state censors. More than in the case of American cinema, the study of early Japanese film must consider how the definition of the motion pictures itself helped mold not only a film culture but also a populace compatible with an authoritarian state.

Just as I wish to avoid binary generalizations comparing Japan with the West, I refrain from drawing a map of the discursive field of cinema in Japan simply divided into two camps: the reformist intellectuals and the lower classes. There are figures like Gonda Yasunosuke who complicate this vision, who represent much more polyvocal fissures in the film culture, other possibilities that were not always pursued; Tom LaMarre has offered similar arguments with regard to Tanizaki Jun'ichirō.[32] Even if the narrative I write seems to flow toward a cinematic culture of domination, I listen to voices of resistance, to dissonance and hybridity remaining in a field increasingly univocal on the surface. In a discursive history of Japan, however, this is not always easy: almost by definition, the persons producing the most written discourse were intellectuals aligned with the reformist cause. The conditions of production of discourse reveal both a consensus of opinion and a curious silence: even though all seemingly agree there is a need to transform Japanese cinema, one rarely hears the voices of those perpetually cited as the "ignorant" and "vulgar," who mistakenly patronize the bastard forms of film. Yet it is in this silence that one can discern alternative visions. Faced with the same problem, Hansen notes, "Even if there were no empirical traces of autonomous public formations, they could be inferred from the force of negation, from hegemonic efforts to suppress or assimilate any conditions that might allow for an alternative (self-regulated, locally, and socially specific) organization of experience."[33]

While the object of reform can be as much imaginary as real, discerning other visions of cinema from that which is negated by the discourse of the Pure Film Movement itself—as well as locating the contradictions within that discursive project—can offer us a story more dramatic than the construction of a monolith. Yet it is important not to simply seek out forms of resistance merely for their own sake: not all forms of difference are "resistance" against a dominant form, and not all resistance succeeds against the forces of authority. As Foucault suggested, many forms of power create or enable the forms of resistance against them, but it is important to historicize the (im)balance between domination/resistance and the struggle over power and forms of difference. No matter how much we may wish to settle on hybridity as a persistent issue in early Japanese cinema, we must recognize that the dominant discourse, precisely by attempting to create a pure cinema, made every effort to eliminate such hybridity and efface traces of cultural difference within cinema and the film culture. The insistence on purity in the face of difference, as I have argued in relation to wartime film culture, often led to even more oppressive forms of management that were as complex and contradictory as they were restrictive. We must recognize the level of force applied to the cinema, as well as appreciate the persistently multiple forms of cinema that, at least to their detractors, necessitated that increasing institution of power.

THE PROBLEM OF BEGINNINGS AND BORDERS

The literature focusing on the specificity of early film in different national cinemas has increased in the last decade or so.[34] Some studies, like Heidi Schlüpmann's, have provocatively argued for the particularity of certain film cultures, thoroughly examining the contradictions constitutive of the local conjuncture without subsuming them in a binary comparison with a monolithic other, the United States; others, unfortunately, devote more time to elaborating a one-to-one opposition between a certain national cinema and the case of either American early cinema or the emerging classical mode.[35] Questions arise when researchers attempt to delineate when their histories begin, what their boundaries are, and what defines the mechanism of local appropriations of cinema or modernity. Ana M. López, for instance, in an important piece on early cinema in Latin America, rightly stresses that early cinema outside the United States and Europe did not develop linked "to previous large-scale transformations of daily experience resulting from industrialization, rationality, and the technological transformation of modern life," and argues that the relations between film and modernity must be conceived differently.[36] While she convincingly contends that "every nation and region created, and creates, its own ways of playing with and at modernity," her stress is still on "addressing impulses and models from abroad," especially regarding a "cinematic apparatus—a manufactured product—[that] appeared, fully formed, in Latin American soil a few months after its commercial introduction abroad." Although López might have reason for proceeding in this manner when discussing Latin America, in the case of a discursive history of Japanese cinema it still effectively presumes a preexisting object, one that, by being preformed in an external space, still gives that space a privileged position. By in effect affirming boundaries of time and space, where motion pictures are born on the other side, such a history leaves Japanese film figures with the role of merely reacting to what was imported from abroad.

Especially as a medium whose history is shaped by moments of importation, in terms of the introduction of both the technology and modes of filmmaking, cinema can easily be described through narratives of foreignness, of absence (being outside) changing to presence (being inside Japan), or of starts (when cinema or its modernity "began" in Japan) and stops (when a style of cinema, such as early film or even the Pure Film Movement, ended or became dominant). Those who, like Isolde Standish, subscribe to a degree of technological determinism, or to a strict ideological profile of certain technologies, tend to write histories that begin with the introduction of such devices.[37] Such boundaries, both temporal and spatial, can play an important role in Japanese film historiography, but I advise caution in constructing similar histories precisely because these boundaries should not be taken as given. They were themselves subject to discursive struggles at the time. Considering the historical discursivity of such borders has implications for how cinema is defined in relation to the nation and modernity and vice versa.

Take, for instance, the view that the Pure Film Movement was a form of Americanization imported from abroad. The few histories in English that discuss the movement are generally ambivalent if not negative about its lasting influence. Joseph Anderson and Donald Richie, while emulating Japanese accounts of cinema that effectively mark the trend as the start of Japanese cinema, nonetheless call it a failure, citing the fact that most of the important filmmakers in the crusade, like Kaeriyama, Kurihara Tō-masu (Thomas Kurihara), and Henry Kotani, had stopped making films by around 1923:

> The invasion from America, which was over by 1923, had failed not only because the Japanese audience continued to prefer the *benshi* films, but also because subject and treatment of the new-style films were considered "too American," the Japanese crews plainly disliking all of these foreign connections and much preferring to work in a "pure Japanese" style. This anti-foreignism held little political implication, but has always been a definite part of the Japanese film world. Thus after the artistic and commercial failure of both Thomas Kurihara and Henry Kotani, the drive to modernize the Japanese film was in the hands of those inclined to a more original Japanese approach.[38]

In making a similar point, Burch is much less equivocal, refusing to use quotation marks around such loaded terms as "Japanese": "The new-style producers and directors shortly before and after 1920 failed . . . to gain acceptance for their ideas among the Japanese movie-going public, failed to transform the Japanese cinema according to the canons of Hollywood and its European emulators. This failure is imputable to the fact that this need for a linearization, a re-ordering of the 'primitive' image in terms of a pseudo-linguistic montage, was meaningless to the Japanese. It was anti-thetical to Japanese art, literature and language."[39]

Such claims are open to debate. Peter B. High, for one, has asserted that the influx of American films to the Japanese market during the First World War constituted "a full-scale invasion destined to change forever the tastes of filmgoers and the methods of filmmaking in Japan."[40] I tend to side with his argument. It is difficult to deny that cinema drastically changed in Japan from 1915 to 1925 partly as a result of processes the Pure Film Movement helped set in motion: modes of cinematic narration were altered, *onnagata* (female impersonators) disappeared in favor of actresses, the star system was solidified, the institution of the author-director formed, the screenplay was established and codified, the genres of *shinpa* and *kyūgeki* were replaced by *gendaigeki* and *jidaigeki*,[41] censorship was rationalized and codified, and most important for this study, new ways of speaking about cinema were founded, ones that would dominate discourse on film until long after World War II. Anderson and Richie, on their part, recognize these changes yet assert they went too far and required a more "Japanese" adjustment. In light of Bordwell's account of Ozu, it would be difficult to claim, as Anderson and Richie do, that the Japanese industry has been possessed by antiforeignism. Ozu, supposedly the most

Japanese of all directors, loved Hollywood films and worked at a studio, Shōchiku, that consciously studied Hollywood methods and exhibited the influence of American cinema. Burch's claim that other cinemas failed to affect Japanese film is also problematic. Yamamoto Kikuo, in probably the most detailed comparative study of Japanese and foreign cinema so far, has devoted a book of more than six hundred pages to elucidating the influence of the latter on the former in just the prewar era. As Yamamoto stresses, this influence is not simply the product of ex post facto scholarly analysis: spectators and critics at the time were overwhelmingly conscious of it and used it as a mode of understanding and defining Japanese cinema.[42]

Some of the claims about the failure of Hollywood-influenced modes in the Japanese context verge on the illogical. While it is true that some of the canonical works of the Pure Film Movement (such as Kaeriyama's) were commercial and critical failures, it is difficult to assert that this was due to their being "un-Japanese" or "too American." Some films were criticized for flaunting a superficial Westernism (for being too *batā kusai*), but the same critics claimed that they had *not gone far enough* to reach the level of American films.[43] It also makes little sense to argue that these "Westernized" films could not succeed with audiences bearing Japanese tastes, given that the majority of films on the market until the mid-1920s were foreign, ones Japanese spectators apparently had no problem enjoying. It is thus untenable to argue that Hollywood montage was, as Burch claimed, "meaningless to the Japanese." One could assert that the audiences for Japanese and for foreign films differed in composition and taste (even though most film programs featured a mix of both Japanese and foreign fare), but this only shows how problematic it is to construct an entity like "the Japanese moviegoing public." Viewers could have mobilized different desires when watching Japanese and foreign films (demanding, for example, self-confirmation from the former and exoticism from the latter), but this situation would still demand a much more complicated and differentiated vision of audience taste than that produced by Burch and others.

The problem in many cases stems from asserting a clear border between Japan and the West when narrating a history of cinema rife with border crossings. Burch cannot fully appreciate the transformations resulting from the Pure Film Movement because he can only categorize it as "Western" and thus as foreign to the Japanese alterity he desires. Even Anderson and Richie, who seem to recognize the problem enough to place the terms *Japanese* and *American* in quotation marks, nonetheless argue for a "more original *Japanese* approach" to modernizing film without clarifying what that might mean. One could cite here the larger history of the impurities and hybridities that hide behind these supposedly clear cultural demarcations. By the late 1890s, Japan, in response to the Meiji government's official policies of "civilization and enlightenment" *(bunmei kaika)* and "national wealth and military strength" *(fukoku kyōhei)*, had significantly "Westernized." The dominant trend up until then was often to reject things "Japanese" and embrace those Western technologies and concepts that would enable Japan to free itself of its feudal backwardness and secure equal status with the European and American powers. This tendency was best expressed by Fukuzawa Yukichi's call to "leave Asia and join Europe" *(datsu-A nyū-Ō)*. The 1890s, with Japan's victory in the war against China in 1895, saw a return of Japanese national pride, manifested in the cultural realm with a reappraisal of pre-Meiji forms of art led by Okakura Tenshin and others. Yet as the literary critic Karatani Kōjin emphasizes, this resurrection of tradition to define the nation presupposed an influx of Western ideas: those central in forming the Japanese version of Benedict Anderson's "imagined community," the Japanese nation-state, were "the group opposed to the state, the people who for a time cut themselves off from all kinds of tradition."[44] This moment of severing oneself from the heritage of the historical past by grasping the Other was central to the nineteenth-century Japanese discovery of the national self, just as the "discovery of landscape," in Karatani's terms,[45] or externality, was an important step in the construction of internality in literature. Okakura Tenshin, after all, wrote his appreciation of Japanese art in English for foreign audiences.[46] The attempt to deny such paradoxes by resurrecting bifurcated purities such as "Japanese spirit, Western knowledge" *(wakon yōsai)*, which some in Japan have mobilized to posit a national soul untouched by a history of involvement with the West, often functioned ideologically to obscure the historical fact, pointed out by Kang Sang-jung among others,[47] that formulations of the idea of a pure *kokutai* (national polity), ranging from those by Motoori Norinaga to *Kokutai no hongi (The Cardinal Principles of the National Entity of Japan)*,[48] were invariably based on the presence of those foreign things that were supposedly being excluded from the pure nation. I have argued that the presence of foreign-made movies set in Japan in the 1910s helped spark the formation of a Japanese cinema, not just as an Orientalist object that Japanese filmmakers were attempting to oppose, but also as an object of desire that reformers adopted by displacing the crime of such "theft" onto fans of an existing Japanese cinema that was considered a national disgrace.[49]

Claiming hybridity, however, is insufficient to solve the problem of reified borders. The film theorist Okada Susumu, for instance, in his work on the image and Japan, succeeds in creating nationalism through hybridity.

The Japanese, he argues, while quickly adopting any technology, still remain Japanese because they use technology without being affected by it, separating it from their subjectivity such that the latter never changes. Such subjectivity, however, is never positive: the Japanese continually change with the ages, so much so that Okada says, "Being 'hybrid' is perhaps the purity of Japanese cultural identity." His use of the term *purity* is not ironic, even as he maintains the existence of racial, linguistic, and cultural homogeneity. His hybridity is one that never violates an essence: when he declares that "the origin of the Japanese is neither technology, thought, nor culture, but a simple fact: the point that more than anything one is Japanese, that one is nothing but Japanese,"[50] it is clear his Japaneseness is just another example of the "hybridism" that Koichi Iwabuchi has argued "essentialized hybridity and hybridization as an organic and ahistorical aspect of Japanese national/cultural identity."[51]

The best means to avoid these pitfalls when approaching the changes in early Japanese cinema is to problematize the division between Japan and the West by historicizing its role, formation, and meaning. A discursive history is strategically useful for this because it refuses to take things or their borders as given, but considers instead how they are defined and redefined at crucial conjunctures through the words and meanings attached to them. The transformations represented by the Pure Film Movement, then, are not simply instances of "Americanization" so much as a complex set of discursive enunciations and influences that cannot be reduced to an East/West binary. A discursive history of early Japanese cinema complicates narratives of importation, especially any history that spatially divides Japan from the West and states that cinema (and its discourse), being essentially Western, did not exist in Japan before it arrived from abroad. One version of this story features cinema as a carrier of Westernized discourse, invading Japan with foreign modes of seeing and experiencing that begin to spread among the populace through the power of the medium itself. This kind of narrative was utilized in 1930s Japan in complaints about "Americanization," when authorities, beginning to mobilize the citizenry for war, worried about the potential harm that popular foreign films had on the national spirit. This was not merely a question of the content of Hollywood films but of the essence of the medium itself, as even the novelist Tanizaki Jun'ichirō, in wondering in *In'ei raisan (In Praise of Shadows)* what the cinema would have been like if Japan had invented it, ascribed a particular Westernized discourse of light and shadow to the existing technology itself.[52]

While such stories of cultural invasion and imperialism cannot be ignored as long as significant imbalances remain between East and West,

North and South, or center and periphery, their assumptions often give the nature of discourse and the processes of importation short shrift. If a history of cinema in Japan focuses on the influence of a foreign object, one whose essence to a greater or lesser degree determines its effects (either a Westernized or cinematic essence, or both), then that history assumes that meaning has a univalent quality, which is problematic from the standpoint of poststructuralist semiotic and cultural studies. It also threatens to reproduce such geopolitical imbalances by depriving receivers of the ability to shape, interpret, and appropriate these discourses from abroad. Even if the technology of cinema was foreign, could one not argue that its articulation or even construction in discourse was at least partly a local affair, if we conceive of the local as porous and crisscrossed by, but never reducible to, the global? And can we not also say that some local articulations may predate the arrival of this "foreign" technology, establishing the cinema before it arrives?

Another narrative of the discourse on cinema in Japan could offer a tale of the "domestication" or the "vernacularization" of the motion pictures in the local sphere. Joseph Tobin has proposed the term *domestication* as a way of focusing on the productive aspect of how Western things are "re-made in Japan."[53] Tobin believes the concept of domestication rectifies the tendency of such notions as imitation and cultural imperialism to paint Japanese use of foreign objects as passive and morally suspect, and instead identifies what is really an active process of appropriation in more neutral terms. In a similar vein, Miriam Hansen has used the term *vernacular* to focus new attention on the status of modernism and the classical Hollywood style, not just as universalist imperial modes of production, but also as flexible horizons that were open to translation and creolization in specific local contexts of reception. Filmmakers and spectators in many countries used Hollywood form in a way similar to the way it functioned in America: as a means for varied populations to come to grips with the tumultuous transformations of modernity.[54] Using Hansen's schema in the Japanese case, domestic appropriations of cinema can then be said to form a "vernacular modernism" that, on the level of mass culture, helped Japanese to both appropriate the movies for themselves and use that medium to confront modernity.

I am sympathetic to such narratives, which share much with the work of López and others. My study similarly seeks out both the Western influences and the local inflections of the effort to create a pure, more "classical" film in Japan, all within a larger struggle over how to define the modernity making itself known in Japan. Yet I must qualify these accounts by questioning the boundaries they sometimes assume. The difficulty with the term *domestication,* for instance, is its assumption of a "domestic" that the object can become. The subject of the act of appropriation, and the sphere in which it operates, remains inadequately interrogated in Tobin's scheme, even though what is often a matter of conflict in "domestication" is where to draw the line between domestic and foreign. Hansen's notion of the vernacular does much to cure us of the notion of an overly monolithic Western cinema, especially the classical Hollywood style, overwhelming passive producers and spectators in other countries. Yet by discussing these appropriations as a form of "cultural translation,"[55] she may be unwittingly reinforcing the idea that Hollywood occupies the center, and that it is the one to be translated. She emphasizes the active process of appropriation, but pays insufficient attention to how articulations of modes of cinema such as the classical style are shaped not just by the process of coming to grips with modernity but also by struggles over the power to determine meaning and draw boundaries, from both inside and outside.[56] One of the problems with many conceptions of appropriation is that the ability to appropriate is taken as a given, is seen as inherent in the semiotic process; a notion such as this elides the often-contentious history of conflict over the extent and possession of that ability. If Japanese spectators or cinema producers have the power to discursively appropriate the motion pictures, that power is always subject to a tug of war—between domestic and foreign interests, imperial or neocolonial power and the nation-state, producers and spectators, different classes in society, and so on—over who has the ability to declare what is (Japanese) cinema and what is not. This, I believe, is aligned with what Stuart Hall meant when he placed "class struggle in and over culture" at the center of considerations of popular culture.[57]

A discursive history can focus on these struggles. It is certainly possible to point to hybridity or engage in a deconstruction of the nation or national cinema, to argue, as Homi Bhabha has done,[58] about an *inter*nationality inherent in the nation that is homologous to the inherent intertextuality of any text, but what is important here is less the deconstructive logic of finding the supplement (the excluded, the foreign) that supplants the original (the nation) and more the complicated historical processes by which hybridity or internationality, for instance, is articulated and contested. It is through these processes that terms like *domestic* and *foreign* are molded and take on real, though often contradictory, force. Tessa Morris-Suzuki has compellingly described how shifting international relations, and the domestic discourses of law, politics, and culture that responded to them, could in short periods of time in the late Edo and early Meiji eras drastically reconfigure conceptualizations of the borders of the Japanese nation, particularly conceptualizations of who was included in them and who was not.[59] Things brought into Japan, including the cinema, were thus not merely "domesticated" but also played an intimate part of this process of defining the domestic itself. The motion pictures, as I have argued elsewhere, were a special but complicated part of this modern construction of Japan.[60]

Any discursive territory one could call "Japanese" in the late Meiji already had mobile, porous, and sometimes ambiguous boundaries. Even items or concepts that seemed "originally foreign" had become so much a part of everyday discourse that it would be difficult to term them alien. Moreover, they had become central to the discursive operation of defining the Japanese national sphere itself, of delineating what was Japanese and what was not. It thus becomes difficult to conceptualize such technologies as cinema as originally external to the Japanese discursive sphere for the very reason that it was partly through their importation that Japanese borders were molded. It would not be problematic, in fact, to claim that cinema was not in part "already Japanese" even before it was planted on Japanese soil (though that statement, of course, complicates what "Japan" then could mean). In these cases, it is necessary to consider how the global defines the local, and vice versa, but in a way that is particularly sensitive to the fluidity of the specific, of the particular historical manifestations of cinema that are reducible neither to generalizations about transnational or national culture, nor to a universal process of semiotic deconstruction. To not do so, in fact, would make it difficult to understand a fascinating aspect of one of the early Japanese cinematic modernisms I discuss: the play with and enjoyment of combinations of texts, codes, and practices that by themselves could be regional, national, or international, local or universal, but which became specific to a site and time when mixed. If this modernism, we could speculate, constituted a form of resistance to or avoidance of the universalizing pretensions of modernity, it is incumbent upon us to finesse the borders of time and space to allow for such combinations to speak.

In approaching the discursive history of the arrival of cinema in Japan, I focus not on the discovery of the essence of cinema or its domestication in an existing Japan but on the ways in which cinema was dialectally accommodated within the field of discourse of post-1890s Japan and helped transform that field. While some of the discursive constructions may be analogous to those found in other situations, it is important to ground them in the historical conjuncture specific to the late Meiji. I argue that a definition of cinema was not created initially; film, while being discussed in then-contemporary journalism within a discernible set of patterns, did not yet exist as a unique problem that demanded a particular discursive solution. It was only around 1910, with a series of debates symbolized by the furor over the film *Zigomar* (which I analyze in chapter 1), that cinema, finally defined as an issue requiring a response, began to accumulate a set of meanings that would distinguish it from other media.

NARRATING A MODERN HISTORY
WITHOUT A BEGINNING

A discursive history would complicate not only the spatial borders of a history of early Japanese cinema but also its temporal limits, a development that would pose interesting issues for the narration of modernity in Japanese film history. This book focuses on the period between 1895, around when cinematic apparatuses first arrived in Japan, and 1925, when censorship was nationalized and the changes proposed by the Pure Film Movement had largely been realized, but at the same time it complicates those bookends. It may be tempting to narrate a history of discourse on cinema in Japan as a tale with an origin, as a story that definitely begins with the arrival of Edison's Kinetoscope in Kobe in November 1896 or with the first showing of the Lumières' Cinématographe in Osaka on February 15, 1897. In this narrative, cinema, as a foreign technology, comes from outside the Japanese discursive sphere, appearing as a fully formed, material, nonlinguistic obstacle that requires a language to name, appropriate, or in some cases obfuscate its presence so as to accommodate it within that sphere. Discourse on film arrives with that original moment and not before it, developing over time but still containing within it an essence that marks it as discourse on *film* from the start.

Making the history of discourse on film in Japan commence with the importation of the apparatus implies that no cinematic discourse existed before that point. Yet offering such a temporal demarcation between cinematic and noncinematic discourse aligns a historical narrative with a cinematic ontology (assuming an cinema has an essence before questioning if or how it has been historically formed), as well as confines discourse to the role of revealing this ontological essence. In such a historiography, history begins with the sprouting of the kernel of cinema and grows to its fruition (as, for instance, in André Bazin's historical ontology of film). Ways of speaking about film only progressively illuminate that developing ontological presence, following in its wake as a secondary effect. As with many teleological histories, the present conception of cinema is often read onto the past, and when this involves a Western medium entering Japan, Japanese film discourse becomes doomed to follow the foreign lead.

Such presumptions make it difficult to delineate the specific operations by which film was molded in various localities. It can be argued that many of the ways of writing and speaking used to discuss the motion pictures existed in Japan before 1896, with cinema first appearing in discourse only as a sign substitutable by other media, and being inserted into an only ill-defined subfield within a larger field (such as the *misemono*, or sideshow entertainments) in which all the components were largely equivalent. The question is whether film as a sign did in fact possess meaning from the start, or at least a definition capable of fully delineating it as a unique and separate medium. Without such semiotic demarcation, it becomes difficult to temporally and spatially corral the history of discourse on film, since we cannot clearly label one discourse cinematic and another not. In this state of semiotic ambiguity, which is in reality unavoidable, the history of discourse on cinema becomes less a reflection of the evolution of cinema's essence than a narrative of how the motion pictures formed, and in turn were formed by, the concrete struggles over the definition of the medium. This is the point of Michel Foucault's emphasis on the emergence of the object of discourse over the appearance of the "thing" itself. Amid a wide variety of crisscrossing and conflicting discourses, cinema was created as some of those discourses dropped off, others remained, new ones appeared, and others merged, forming conglomerations around a particular nexus that remained intimately connected to other discursive nodes. As we shall see, what constitutes discourse on film, and when that discourse started, became a subject of ideological conflict and debate.

One could, as Eric Cazdyn has done, narrate a history of cinema in Japan that is closely linked with definite events in Japanese capitalist modernity, such as the *genbun itchi* movement or the consolidations of the monetary system.[61] These can provide helpful analogies for re-perceiving Japanese film history, ones that can make us think about the larger implications of cinematic transformations within Japan's complex history of colonialism, capitalism, and war, but we should be careful when narrating the temporality of these conjunctures. Even if we can see the Pure Film Movement as the cinematic equivalent of *genbun itchi*, it occurred some twenty to thirty years after the latter, a disjuncture due in part to the different class dynamics within literature and cinema, particularly the stakes different audiences and readers had in transforming textuality and subjectivity. That reminds us that events in other fields, while possibly influential, are themselves subject to complex articulations within the particular power relations traversing film culture. It is the concrete struggle over meaning and influence—which can delay or alter the temporality of effect—that must be considered if we are to avoid adopting allegories of colonialism or capitalism as abstract narratives with a life of their own.

Given this temporal ambiguity, one could argue that the history of discourse on cinema in Japan started long before the apparatus itself arrived on Japanese shores. Some discourses on film grew out of discussions on such protocinematic devices as *gentō*, the Japanese version of the magic lantern (related forms were called *utsushi-e* or *kage-e*).[62] Just as research on early cinema in the United States and Europe has pointed to toys such as the Zoopraxiscope, or to the popularity of magic lantern shows, as a way of relocating the beginning of the formation of motion picture culture to a point before the apparatus was completed,[63] so too it is possible, as the anthropologist Yamaguchi Masao has argued, to cite *gentō* as the "shadow culture [*eizō bunka*] that prepared the way for image culture [*eizō bunka*]."[64] *Gentō*, first arriving from abroad in the early 1800s, quickly developed into a highly skilled narrative art that took advantage of some of the same cognitive operations as film to produce remarkable motion effects in dark theaters. Quickly changing between slides, or flipping portions of slides, expert Japanese *gentō* artists could use portable handheld lanterns to create an illusion of motion that, some have claimed, surpassed anything created by their Western counterparts and rivaled the magic of early motion pictures. The scientist and film essayist Terada Torahiko reports his first experience of watching film as "the sort of experience of 'not believing until you see it, but once you see it, you are surprised yet at the same time think it's not out of the ordinary.' Anyway, it seems I was not as surprised as the first time I saw *gentō*."[65] The critic Maeda Ai cites this passage as evidence that "the desire and anticipation for moving images was subconsciously prepared for in the experience of *gentō* itself."[66] Immensely popular at the time the motion pictures arrived in Japan, *gentō*, then, can be posited as one of the possible discursive structures through which the cinema was first discussed. As Ōkubo Ryō argues, other forms from around the turn of the century, such as *rensageki* and *kineorama*—which complexly combined the cinema with existing modes such as theatrical drama and the diorama, mixing older forms of viewing with new ones—also make it difficult to cleanly narrate a history of perception in which the motion pictures figure as rupture or as even as continuity.[67]

Such examples provide us with a reason for questioning how much Japanese early cinema is, as Cazdyn argues, following Rey Chow's framework, defined by "the spectator [gaining] self-consciousness at the strangeness of seeing images projected on the screen,"[68] an experience constitutive of one form of modernity. Chow herself narrates the famous story of the

Chinese writer Lu Xun and his traumatic encounter with "modernity" via visual representations of China that he saw in a film in Japan around 1905. Chow saw this shock as resulting from Lu's recognition of the inequality of modern perspective—how modern spectators were viewing a "backward" China—combined with a seeming realization that the violent power of Westernized modernity is grounded in visuality, here represented by the cinema.[69] While such a shock may have happened at some point for some spectators in Japan as well, it is important to interrogate the presumptions behind these narratives. First, the shock of modernity may not have occurred when the cinematic apparatus arrived in Japan—in fact, it may have happened well before or well after that point—and did not necessarily involve that spectacle of Otherness (here the West) that prompts self-consciousness and even nationalism. Given the domestic development of projected visuality, the Otherness could equally stem from divisions from within, such as class, and thus be open to struggle. Second, the cinema may not have represented the shock of visualized modernity precisely because it was not yet defined as visual. As we shall see, definitions of cinema as a verbal or bodily medium were present as well, and it took the conscious activities of film reformers in the 1910s to define it as purely visual. This underlines the point that the modernity that cinema may have represented in fact had several potential historical trajectories, a point that the narrative of shock, based on a naturalized, physical, and psychic reaction, tends to obfuscate. The shock of the medium could be a constructed and not a natural experience and, thus, part of a sociopolitical action that developed over time and through concrete operations of power and struggle. That is one reason why it could have occurred long after the cinema came to Japan.

So one could argue that the discourse on cinema began after the apparatus arrived in Japan. The traditional way of arguing this is to claim that early productions are not true cinema, and that a realization of this, in both theory and practice, took time to develop. Another way to assert this— one that I adapt in this book—is to strip that argument of its essentialism (the teleological narrative of filmmaking finally achieving a cinematicity that was always already there) and to concentrate on the history of the discursive invention of cinema after the invention of the machine. Such a move not only avoids the pitfalls of technological determinism—which lashes the discourse on a medium to its material process, as if the latter determines the former—but also thus focuses, similar to the way British cultural studies do, on the processes by which technologies are interpreted, adapted, contested, and reinvented through their uses, which can include which meanings are attached to them and which uses are recommended.

Certainly it is important to investigate the preexisting discursive formations that shaped the creation of the medium, but it would be problematic to assume those frameworks are unalterably chiseled into the machine. That would fix the medium both temporally and spatially.

The same historicism should be adopted in considering the question of modernity in early Japanese film history. The common paradigm was to connect Japanese cinema to aspects of traditional culture, as Paul Schrader did by linking Ozu Yasujirō to Zen, and Stephen Prince did by linking Kurosawa to *bushidō*.[70] But those who narrated histories that went further back in time, like Iijima Tadashi or Satō Tadao, often provided a tale of cinematic evolution that described the Pure Film Movement as a good form of modernization, and the films before it as backward and premodern.[71] This was the cinematic equivalent to the modernization theory that dominated especially American studies of Japan after World War II, one that sought to explain Japan's economic and industrial advances by applying a universal narrative of development (though one based in the Western experience), which at the same time accounted for Japan's quick modernization among non-Western nations by citing its cultural essences.[72] Utilizing a similar story, film critics like Satō could claim first-rung status for Japanese film in a global history of cinematic advancement while also asserting a cultural uniqueness that was ahistorical. The argument that Japanese cinema was just as cinematic as European or American film often depended on accepting Western film history's own long-held evolutionary narrative, and thus on denigrating early Japanese cinema. It was Noël Burch who made an important, though ultimately flawed, intervention in these stories of Japanese cinematic modernity by effectively reversing modernization theory and claiming the superiority of early cinema because of its links to traditional Heian aesthetics. This was not a case of traditionalism, but rather of a European postmodernism attempting to critique the universalist pretensions of Western modernism by finding an effectively a-, or antimodern, culture in the age of modernity.

Burch has been criticized for assuming an essentially orientalist stance, for projecting a dream Japan that answers less to the reality of Japan than to his needs in the conjuncture of 1970s Western cinema theory.[73] While his claims about the historical continuity of Heian aesthetics are suspect, ironically they prove that his attempts—and those by other scholars—to directly link Japanese cinema to traditional culture are problematic: they illustrate how much the use and definition of tradition is mediated by the historical situation of the user. Recalling Eric Hobsbawm's dictum about "the invention of tradition,"[74] one could argue that traditions, or at least the constitutive difference between tradition and the modern that often defines the two, are always modern in the sense of being new, contingent, and contemporary. This is not to deny the importance of long-lasting historical determinants like the *longue durée* or Anthony Smith's *ethnie*,[75] but to emphasize the always mediated nature of their effects. A discursive history, as precisely a history of a media—discourse—is particularly appropriate for apprehending the transitory nature of the new, since it is a historical methodology that emphasizes the fluid struggles over shaping history on the ground at a particular moment.

This method must be applied not only to tradition but also to the modern. There is of course a venerable lineage of conceptualizations of modernity in the West offered by such luminaries as Baudelaire, Weber, Benjamin, Kracauer, Simmel, and many others. There is also a long history of Japanese thinkers, including prewar Marxists debating Japanese capitalism, wartime romanticists considering "overcoming the modern," and even postwar filmmakers seeking a more modern subjectivity, all contemplating the significance of the modern in Japan. There is still need to further analyze and build on the work of these theorists, but my aim in this book is to expand the field of discourse on modernity beyond such prominent figures to include others just as involved, or perhaps even more directly involved, in the battle over modernity and one of its representatives, cinema, such as film critics, filmmakers, fans, censors, police officers, educators, politicians, and journalists. My focus is less on what their statements tell us about an existing modernity or some universal condition than on how they attempted to articulate it. It is less on what was really new than on what people *thought* was new and how their definitions were subject to real skirmishes over shaping and interpreting modernity, ones that involved issues of class and power. This is a history not of modernity's appearance in Japan but of conflicts over what kind of modernity should appear, and of the actual processes involved in those attempts to mold the modern experience. In this study, modernity is not a condition but a locus of conflict; my concern is less with the modernity that shaped people's perceptions than with the concrete practices, from writing to speaking, from filmmaking to filmgoing, that shaped the modernity people perceived, as well as the power dynamics that made the resulting modernity important. Simply put, I examine modernity as a discursive object in the same way that I examine cinema, although the latter remains the dominant focus of this book. In some ways, I am simply doing to a history of Japanese cinematic modernity what film scholars have tried to do the history of early cinema since the 1978 Brighton conference. Such historians rejected a teleological history in which early films were merely a primitive stage on the way to a singular form of advanced cinema, and instead argued that they represented equal if not alternative forms of cinema, multiple possibilities that were not all pursued—not because they did not adequately manifest the essence of cinema, but because concrete historical and ideological operations forced selection and elimination. Similarly, I want to see modernity not as an essence that Japanese early film either came to manifest or did not, but as a range of real, multiple, and sometimes conflicting possibilities, none more "truly modern" than the others, that were narrowed down through struggles, particularly in the discursive sphere.

Because I stress the struggle over defining the new, the articulations of modernity are necessarily plural and embody conflicts based in class, gender, town/country, and other social divides. This method offers a shift in perspective from that of previous scholarship critical of modernization theory, especially in relation to Japan. There already exists an incisive postcolonial argument about the unequal global power relations between Japan and the West in terms of modernity. In it, the West is seen as defining itself as modern precisely through its difference from (and in some cases colonization of) the nonmodern, the East; modernity, then, is that state of being non-East, not-colonized, a fact that renders non-Western nations into what, by definition, cannot modernize. In practical terms, they can at best achieve technological modernization but not the actual subject position of modernity. Naoki Sakai, in elaborating on the theories of Takeuchi Yoshimi, states:

> As is amply shown by the fact that the Orient had to modernize and
> adopt things from the West in order to resist it, the modernization of
> the Orient attests to an advance or success for the West, and, there-
> fore, it is always Westernization or Europeanization. So it necessarily
> appears that, even in its resistance, the Orient is subjugated to the
> mode of representation dominated by the West. Its attempt to resist
> the West is doomed to fail; the Orient cannot occupy the position of a
> subject. Is it possible, then, to define the Orient as that which can never
> be a subject?[76]

Establishing how the West has defined modernity through itself, and thereby set an impossible agenda for non-Western nations attempting to achieve modernity, has given scholars a powerful tool for understanding, for instance, the dilemmas of Japanese artists faced with the inequalities of global cultural power. The contradictory need to both catch up with the West by emulating it, and establish a nation-state based on difference, has created fundamental aporia in the modern Japanese experience. Dennis

Washburn, for one, has noted that, "while many Japanese recognized the predicament of their self-identity—that they could never be wholly modern in the Western sense nor wholly Japanese in the traditional sense—the process of Westernization marginalized Japanese culture and created [an] extreme self-consciousness and sense of belatedness."[77] Mitsuhiro Yoshimoto has used a similar contradiction to describe how film melodrama has functioned at crucial historical moments as an ideologeme attempting to alleviate the fundamental contradiction of Japan modernizing while being excluded from modernity.[78]

Such discussions have produced powerful accounts of the transnational conflicts experienced by Japanese especially in the twentieth century, but there is always the danger that, in emphasizing the walls the West has created, these studies reify them rather than focus on cracks in the wall, on the contradictions in the system or on alternative constructions. Even modernity in the West can be contradictory: "a paradoxical unity, a unity of disunity," says Marshall Berman, who argues that the tradition of modernism has always contained a complex mixture of advocacy and critique of modernity.[79] Even if Japan may not fit the definition of modernity created in the West, there are benefits to questioning the West's conceit that it alone can achieve modernity, to asking whether there are ways of constructing the new that are not wholly dependent on or defined in relation to Western modernity. Tom LaMarre has pointed out that questions like "Does cinema 'westernize' Japan, or does Japan 'japanify' cinema?" are problematic because "they suppose an insurmountable contradiction or incommensurable difference between Westernization and 'Japanization.' Yet the two processes can and usually do proceed apace."[80] The East and the West, the modern and the "nonmodern," are not as mutually exclusive and impenetrable as they seem.

Especially given the rise of the Asian tigers, the accelerating and more decentralized flows of global capital, and the increased interest in local inflections in the global/local nexus, there has been recent emphasis on conceptualizing Asian economies as something more than substandard examples of Western modernization, and thus as different approaches to a modernity that is no longer seen as the exclusive property of the West. Social scientists, for instance, have been talking about "multiple modernities,"[81] a term that tends to spotlight those different forms and not the relations of power or opposition between them. And cultural theorists have been discussing "alternative modernities,"[82] a concept that concentrates on modes more directly opposed to the Western center. López's work and Hansen's notion of vernacular modernism are examples of the latter in film studies. Harry Harootunian has warned us, however, that the "problem raised by the formulation of an 'alternative' modernity is the unstated presumption of exceptionalism and uniqueness. The appeal to the adjectival 'alternative' implies not just difference but one that constitutes a better choice." This privileging, in effect, is only a reverse of, and not a solution to, the previous privileging of Western modernity, one that produced the "scandal of imagining modernities that are not quite modern," of modernities that are late compared to the West. Harootunian instead proposes the concept of "co-eval modernity," which decenters the narrative of modernity by seeing Japan as sharing "the same historical temporality of modernity . . . found elsewhere in Europe and the United States." His concept thus suggests "contemporaneity yet the possibility of difference." It brings him closer to the proponents of multiple modernities but does not ignore the complex global dynamics of power.[83]

Drawing on the notion of "co-eval modernity," I focus on the complicated history of struggle over the meaning of modernity in the film world as parallel and linked to, but not necessarily dependent on, cinematic modernities in other countries. Although the bulk of my research concentrates on the Pure Film Movement, which was deeply indebted to the example of Hollywood cinema, I do not privilege it here as a "vernacular" appropriation of the then burgeoning classical mode—first, because I have already discussed elsewhere its complicated relation to foreign examples, and second, because I am more interested in how it opposed, appropriated, defined, and sometimes silenced other modes within Japan. I am thus less concerned with the development of a Japanese cinematic modernity against Hollywood than with the conflicts between various potential modernisms within the Japanese sphere, ones that sometimes, but not always, looked to Hollywood for support. The Pure Film Movement is not the only vernacular modernism; another is the film culture that supported Onoe Matsunosuke, for instance, the star of Kabuki-based movies that pure film critics despised and labeled uncinematic because the style of these movies did not resemble Hollywood's nascent classical style. Not only the speed and visual tricks of Matsunosuke's films, but also their combination of the theatrical (such as acting styles and narratives from known plays) with a medium that is flat and black-and-white (unlike the colorful Kabuki, where actors can go into the audience), can be said to provide an inscription of culture in the modern age that was as new and as unique as later Japanese films influenced by the classical style. Focusing on the popular level, I agree with Cazdyn that there were "a whole new pack of possible modern subjects and modern nations that were realizable in Meiji Japan" and after.[84] It

is important to understand the Pure Film Movement as a process of enforcing one option and suppressing others on the local level, rather than to
focus on it solely as an adaptation or appropriation of Western modes. This
is because, without knowing the former, one cannot discern the full context
of the latter. The two histories are linked, especially when pure film critics aligned their gaze with that of the West and looked on Matsunosuke's
films as a national shame, or when they relied on export and the prospect of
foreign viewers to promote their version of cinema. But these links do not
tell the whole story. This book focuses on these other histories.

First some terminological clarification is necessary. The confusion
between and various definitions of such key terms as *modern, modernization, modernity,* and *modernism* are among the central burdens of research
on modernity. Research is further complicated by the possible equivalent
terms in Japanese, such as *kindai, gendai, modan, kindaishugi, kindaika,*
and *modanizumu.* One of the hallmarks of the 1910s, the primary decade
I discuss, is the amorphousness of this terminology, which makes this a
period when articulating concepts about cinema as well as about modernity, in language as well as in practice, was a central issue in the cultural
struggle over modernity.[85] The terms did not become completely settled
in Japan or in the West, a fact that underlines how much the modern is
still a site of conflict. To some, *modernity* refers to the modern experience
itself—it is "a mode of vital experience."[86] To others, it is "the modes of
experiencing that which is 'new',"[87] and yet others see it as a particular set
of "values, beliefs and dispositions concerning the theoretical foundation,
practices, and aims of society" in the modern era.[88] These different views
mean that *modernism* can designate a range of phenomena, from simply "a
bundle of cultural practices, some of them adversarial," to the "values and
ideas that aim to make men and women the subjects as well as the objects
of modernization," to "an ideologization of the process of capitalist modernization and transformation," or to "the suppositions of an aesthetic-
artistic movement clarified toward the end of the nineteenth century."[89]

It is not my intention to rectify these definitional differences, in part
because they actually do well to illustrate that perceptions of modernity are multiple. But to clarify the framework of the terms I use, I have
adopted the following definitions because of their appropriateness for narrating this discursive history. I define *modernism* as a set of tenets, values,
and practices that interpret and attempt to define "modernity," which I
consider to be a potential social, cultural, economic, and political form, on
the material level, of the modern, the state of being new. While the "modern" here is simply the frame or the question of the new, "modernities" are

the contingent material manifestations of what is new, and "modernism" is the set of discourses attempting to shape a particular version of modernity, though not always in a positive, consistent and noncontradictory manner. Each "modernism," then, attempts to enact (or prevent) a certain modernity, in a process called "modernization," in a field of struggle where there are not only other competing modernisms (and thus formations of modernity) but also complex traversing forces of power and historical contingencies. These prevent any modernism from either monopolizing the field or even commanding its own discourse to the extent that it can enact all that each modernism desires. A discursive history of modernity thus focuses on the articulations of modernity by various modernisms within a field of power where what is not said—and what is not allowed to be said—can be just as important as what is.

The history I narrate features roughly two competing strands of modernism. One is dedicated to purity, unity, and homogeneity, to clearly and rationally distinguishing things and practices according to their essences, which are by definition universal. Distinction here is aligned with knowledge (shaped by both neo-Confucianism and the Western scientific enlightenment), which operates in tandem with authority: knowledge determines and validates purity and authority, while authority enforces—and legitimizes itself through—the enforcement of the purity determined by knowledge. Inspired by new technologies of social and industrial management, this can translate into hierarchical forms of rational organization in the spheres of aesthetics, society, nation, and global culture that depend on the formation of subjects who internalize these hierarchies.

The other strand of modernism, aligned with the anonymous urban crowd, the new flows of goods and services, and the acceleration of daily life, celebrates instances of mixture, heterogeneity, the chance, the local, the specific. Central to it is the pleasure of experiencing combinations that come together at particular moments or locations, but which still reference and play with widely known forms, codes, and meanings. Taking advantage of transformations in technology, the flow of information, and urban space, it can still seek alternatives to rationalizing or universalizing tendencies in some forms of modernity. It does not reject power or hierarchies, but allows for play and reversals precisely because the social or cultural map— if not also the subject of signification—is less distinct and in motion. If the former historically was found in bourgeois intellectual or bureaucratic classes, the latter was more evident in the urban working class. These two trends may have parallels elsewhere. The former may seem more like the rational or efficient modernity of Weber and Habermas or of Fordism and

Taylorism; the latter "the transitory, the fugitive, the contingent" modernity of Baudelaire.[90] One could also find similarities to the two modernities Matei Calinescu outlines, one bourgeois the other antibourgeois, one professing "a stage in the history of Western civilization," the other an "aesthetic concept."[91]

But just as Dilip Gaonkar has warned us that "the tale of two modernities, however compelling it is for mapping the Western experience of modernity and its dilemmas, cannot be extended, without important modifications, to cover other theaters of modernity,"[92] so we must note the differences in this case. The modernism of purism, for instance, was actually more an aesthetic than a model of efficient social organization, yet one in an uneasy alliance with capitalism and state power, both of which sometimes opted more for aesthetic than rational solutions. Purism was one way of dealing with the change introduced by industrial and urban capitalism, and was an attempt to control its transformative excesses. The modernism of mixture, on the other hand, was tied less to antibourgeois intellectual avant-gardes than to popular forms of cultural appropriation that few intellectuals could keep up with. It could thus celebrate the flow and flamboyance of money and capital, even as it resisted corporate attempts to mold and manage desire. The former, which in the realm of film is closely tied to appropriations of the classical style by pure film reformers, is centered on the visual, but in a way that revolves around the realm of what Hansen calls the "optical conscious." If classical cinema does not merely show a new world (the optical conscious) but also enables or accommodates new or hitherto undeveloped forms of perceiving and understanding the world (the optical unconscious),[93] then the modernism of purity attempts to render the latter more conscious, because here the consciousness of both purity and the nation is supposed to serve as the engine and the framework regulating proper perception. The modernity of mixture, however, inhabits the realm of what one could call the bodily unconscious, or at least of modes of perception that, as Gonda argues, are less tied to higher intellectual faculties of reason than previous cultural forms. Whereas one tried to discipline the senses proliferating through these transformations—while taking advantage of new forms of perception such as surveillance—the other celebrated these new sensations.

Both modernities also lacked complete unity, a fact that could become apparent over time. The aesthetic purists in the Pure Film Movement, for instance, advocating a visuality that undermined language, could by the end of the 1920s, as was evident in the debates over Kinugasa Teinosuke's *Kurutta ichipeiji* (A Page of Madness, 1927), split with other reformers who envisioned cinematic visuality as an efficient tool for universal communication.[94] Those on the political left who advocated a cinema of the masses could be seen on both sides of the issue, some proposing a strong and pure textuality that could influence lower-class spectators, and others, like Gonda in the 1910s or Nakai Masakazu in the 1930s, describing a film culture in which spectators could make the film from the bottom up because of inherent gaps and fissures in the cinematic text. It possible to argue that even more strands of modernism exist in prewar Japan.

The particular nature of these two threads and their relation can be traced to the historical conditions of Japan, especially its rapid economic development at the end of the nineteenth century. As Harootunian explains, this led to severely uneven development, with modern urban centers sporting technological advances and a bright cosmopolitan consumer culture existing not far from sectors operating in agricultural or more craft-based modes.[95] It was the effort on the part of both the urban left and the rural right to hide this gap that led to various kinds of warped modern fantasies regarding the masses and the nation. Thus we should not mistake the above two modernist strands as the conflict between the modern and the traditional, since both responded to uniquely new phenomena that they neither entirely rejected nor accepted.

One could argue, as Karatani Kōjin has done, that there are in fact two nineteenth centuries in Japan, one defined by the lightning-fast adoption of Westernized forms of cultural modernity around the turn of the century, the other by what could almost be thought of as a pre-postmodern critique of rationalization found in late Edo culture.[96] The two complicate any simple narrative of the premodern followed by the modern followed by postmodernism and thus force us to look at the particular conditions of modernity in Japan. When naturalism and romanticism, opposed in Europe, could proceed in concert in turn-of-the-century Japan, or when Yokomitsu Riichi, one of the most important literary modernists in the 1920s, could declare, "I recognize Futurism, Cubism, Expressionism, Dadaism, Symbolism, Constructivism, and some of the realists as all belonging to [his "New Impressionist"] Shinkankaku school,"[97] one was witnessing less the shallowness of Japanese modernism than the complex interweaving of its multiple modernities.

In relating these two strands of modernism, it is possible to emphasize various factors. For instance, I stress the opposition between a form of universalism, which grounds knowledge claims in a perceived universal essence, and a practice celebrating the particular. This is not the opposition between universalism and particularism, because, as Naoki Sakai notes, those two are often in league, as universalism is usually just a particularism claiming universality for itself.[98] Nationalism, then, which may seem to be a form of particularism, is actually fundamentally universalist to the degree that it claims its values are the standard for all or asserts the nation itself as the basic unit of humankind. The form of the particular I describe here is not an "ism" (since that would render it universal) but rather the experience of concrete and unreproducible moments of combination, ones in line with the culture of montage and code-switching that Miriam Silverberg locates in 1920s and 1930s Japanese culture.[99] It is here that we can speak of the practice of making only one print of a film, a practice common in the Japanese industry in the 1910s that appears to violate Benjamin's description of "art in the age of mechanical reproduction,"[100] not as a recalcitrant traditional format, but as a modernism itself. But this also behooves us to refrain from easily describing this other modernism as a kind of resistance to the first, given that such socially significant forms of resistance can also be claims to universality. If this is a resistance, it is of a different kind, one also resisting the universalization of resistance. If vernacular modernism, as Hansen argues, functions as a "sensory-reflex horizon for the experience of modernization and modernity,"[101] then the modernism of mixture and particularity may be thought of as a means of rethinking the homogenization, the rationalization, and the routinization of everyday life in the modern capitalist era.[102]

This book primarily narrates a history of struggles to discursively define the cinema within these two conflicting modernisms. Given that the discourses I analyze do not merely work to shape and create the object cinema, but also shape those subjects who create and receive this medium, the process of articulating the cinema is not just one manifestation of these modernisms. It is also one of the central means by which these modernisms defined themselves and modernity, since the motion pictures served as one of the privileged loci for articulating modernity, its benefits, and its dangers.

Chapter 1 begins the history by complicating the notion of beginning, showing how cinema arrived in discourse long after the apparatus itself arrived in Japan, and how it emerged as a medium distinct from existing discourses about fairground entertainments only because it, and the modernity it was seen to represent, were conceived as dangerous. The media and police furor over banning the French film *Zigomar* marked a point not only where cinema was "discovered" but also where it became defined as a long-standing object of correction. Chapter 2 introduces early efforts to deal with the problem of cinema through the process of study, to regulate this new phenomenon by corralling it in knowledge. Here I spotlight the film study of Gonda Yasunosuke, who presents a fascinating, but still contradictory, effort to both celebrate cinema's newness, originating from below in mass society, and correct its deviations from a true cinematic essence. In chapter 3, I introduce the Pure Film Movement as a different effort to celebrate cinema in film study, one that involved a conscious effort to suppress one form of film—one more aligned with a modernism of mixture—in favor of another modernism, one grounded in a class-based, authoritative vision of modernity. Next, in chapter 4, I focus in particular on how the Pure Film Movement attempted to define the proper subjects for speaking about and receiving the cinematic text, primarily by criticizing and ultimately redefining the role of such figures as the benshi, the author, and the producer along Fordist lines. Finally, chapter 5 explores how state authorities were often aligned with the pure film project, but in a way that involved articulating a new modern subject with an internality that became the object of not only regulation but also manipulation by film authors. This book is ultimately the history of the establishment of the dominant form of cinema—and cinematic modernity—in twentieth-century Japan, and it concludes with a discussion of this cinema's implications and complications.

1 The Motion Pictures as a Problem

THE ARRIVAL OF CINEMA

Moving Pictures, X-Rays, and Other Entertainments

Japan is one case where it is hard to align the history of discourse on film with the arrival of the apparatus from the West. First, long before the cinema's arrival in Japan, books described in rather sensationalistic terms the marvels of Western knowledge, including such protocinematic devices as the zoetrope.[1] Then, entering the 1890s, Japanese newspapers, which were always interested in news of the latest trends in Western culture and science, began running articles announcing Thomas Edison's initial work. The film historian and collector Tsukada Yoshinobu painstakingly accumulated over his lifetime most of the newspaper and magazine articles printed in Japan about the motion pictures before and in the first year after the medium was imported into Japan, and he published them in his lifework, *Nihon eigashi no kenkyū* ("A Study of Japanese Film History"). Devoted to determining the exact facts and chronology relating to the first year of cinema in Japan (who imported what machine when and how), the book is also a treasure trove of examples of how the Japanese media first approached the motion pictures. According to Tsukada's research, the first article on Edison's new invention was published in the *Fukuoka nichi nichi shinbun* on April 12, 1890, more than a year before Edison even applied for a patent. Several other articles followed over the years, but since one that appeared in the English language *Japan Weekly Mail* (on July 18, 1891) was reprinted from the *London Times*, it is likely that most of them were translations of pieces that had run in foreign papers. As such, they exemplify the degree to which even the very first discussions of cinema in Japanese crisscrossed whatever boundaries existed between Japan and the West.

As one would expect, the focus of these articles is on the reproduction of movement, emphasizing the new apparatus's ability to represent even the most fleeting and precise transformations, preserving past events so that they could be shown again in the present just as they once were. Underlying these discussions was a conception of realism that praised the machine's ability to present a vision "that is no different than looking at the real thing."[2] The Japanese articles were seemingly not content with describing a new machine that humans could use in their quest to control the natural world. The headline of the first article in the *Fukuoka nichi nichi shinbun* on the Kinetograph (Edison's early attempt to combine motion pictures and the phonograph) is most telling: "Pictures Give a Speech" (Shashin, ensetsu o nasu). The article goes on to explain that "the pictures can seem as if they are truly moving and giving a speech."[3] Without mentioning that it is the people in the pictures who presumably move and speak, the article focuses attention on technology itself becoming an enunciative subject, spectacularizing the technology by underlining its marvelous qualities. It is this fascination with the apparatus that would dominate discussions of the Kinetoscope, the Cinématographe, and the Vitascope in the year after they were imported to Japan.[4] Yet in attempting to describe the marvels of these new inventions, writers would avail themselves of a variety of existing discourses to connect cinema to known phenomena, discussing it in relation to such discursive categories as *gentō*, *misemono*, Westernization, realism, and the wonders of science.

In approaching the technology itself, many availed themselves of *gentō* as a protocinematic reference point. The *Yomiuri shinbun* likened the process of projecting the image onto a white screen to that of the *gentō* (in many pieces, the term *gentō* itself was used to signify the process of projection),[5] and then went on to describe the motion pictures as "the most evolved version of *utsushi-e*,"[6] thereby creating a history in which the imported cinema was an outgrowth of the Japanese version of the magic lantern. A writer with the pen name Dōjin Shiin wrote in 1903 of a friend who still argued that *gentō*, in addition to being able to show the same "transformations" as the moving pictures, did not suffer from flicker and was certainly more rich in entertainment value than the new technology. While Dōjin himself agreed with his colleague on the emotional impact created by a skilled *gentō* performance, he went on to insist that "one cannot show the state of living moving beings without the moving pictures."[7] Although highly praised as an early means of moving image entertainment, the *gentō* in the end was used in most discussions as a difference against which cinema would be defined. The *Fusō shinbun* in Nagoya declared the Vitascope to be "completely different in content from the existing *gentō* in that it looks as if it truly moves."[8] Komada Kōyō, arguably the most prominent of the early motion picture showmen, reproduced a newspaper article in his early pamphlet explaining the Vitascope which declared that the device was "not something like the *gentō* which is made of slipshod imaginary pictures, but directly projects photographs. . . . Since these do not immediately differ from the real thing, . . . they do not move outside of natural laws."[9] The motion pictures were thus valorized over *gentō* on the scale of realism, but only in a field of knowledge in which film was depicted as an extension of the magic lantern. Such is evident in one of the many names given to the cinema in its first few years in Japan: *jidō gentō*, or self-moving magic lantern.[10]

In further explaining the technology, much early discourse on cinema would avail itself of the interest or even faith in scientific knowledge and progress prominent in the Meiji quest to catch up with the West. The motion pictures were sold to Japanese audiences as a great scientific discovery, which Komada declared was "brought back to our country to develop the scientific thought of our colleagues."[11] Komada then went on in his pamphlet to offer a hagiography of the "great inventor" of the Vitascope, Thomas Edison.[12] Another early publication on the new medium began by citing an 1830s French science fiction novel to show how the future dreamed of in the past was being outdone today with the invention of motion pictures.[13] Attaching the cinema to the centerpiece of Meiji enlightenment, scientific thought, was clearly a sales pitch by the motion pictures' first promoters in Japan, but it was also a means of inserting the medium into a narrative of progress that contemporary Japanese society was eagerly trying to write.

In fact, much of the tone of early accounts of the cinema in Japan depicted the apparatus as both a symbol of Western society and a fount of knowledge useful for Japanese anxious to approach the West. The *Osaka asahi shinbun* reported that the promoters of the March 1897 screening of the Cinématographe at Kyoto's Kyōgokuza, claiming that the invention was "sufficient for knowing at a glance the customs of Western Europe," were planning to distribute free tickets to all those over the age of sixty in Kyoto so that they could "fully understand the situation in Western Europe." Such elderly Japanese, their explanation went, "by still thinking that Americans and Europeans are beasts . . . are harming the education of the young."[14] Thus advertised as a means of "showing the customs, manners, and famous places and cities in Europe and America,"[15] the motion pictures were often presented within a Western frame, with the lecturer who explained the apparatus wearing in the early days a frock coat as he expounded on the wonders of Western science. For the showing at Kyoto's Shinkyōgoku Mototōkō Engekijō, the theater was reportedly decorated in Western trappings, and Western music was occasionally performed "so that the audience would not get bored."[16] Early film exhibition, then, was constructed as a means by which Japanese could vicariously enter a Western space and overcome the divisions in time and geography to achieve, if only in mind, Fukuzawa's call to "leave Asia and join Europe." The fruits of Western science promised an amazing (and amazingly easy) means of catching up with the Enlightenment, of consuming the West without having to leave local boundaries.

Yet if reference to existing discourses on Western science and civilization, or use of Western music, was a central means of understanding the cinematic apparatus, one could hardly say the tactic made film more "familiar." Although Western music had by the 1890s made headway in Japan in the form of military music and school songs, as a popular form of entertainment, more traditional forms of Japanese music were far more recognizable to early film audiences. If Western music prevented Kyoto audiences from being bored, it was less because it was comfortably entertaining than because it was an exciting curiosity, one which did not so much explain the motion pictures as mark them by association as a marvelous new spectacle from abroad. Western trappings and the vicarious trip to Europe were more often an attraction, in Tom Gunning's sense of the term—a spectacle to be enjoyed more for its shock value and curiousness[17]—than a means of knowing either the medium or the West.

Labeling the cinema a new scientific discovery did not necessarily contain it within a field of knowledge in which its wonders were attributable to human mastery of natural laws. It is interesting to note that, while the article in English in the *Japan Weekly Mail* from April 1891 took pains to explain in detail the process by which film was moved and then stopped before the shutter in the Kinetograph—one of the central technical means by which the illusion of motion is produced—practically none of the Japanese articles reprinted in Tsukada's book made any endeavor to explain the process of intermittent motion.[18] In the early explanations of film technology in Japan, the catchphrases were *electricity* and *speed*. Given that much was made in advertisements of the power source used by the new invention, it was not surprising to see the *Yomiuri shinbun* "mistaking" (and thus mystifying) the cinematic signifier by explaining that "people and things shot in these photographs move through the use of electric power."[19] Many other papers resorted to reciting colossal numbers, emphasizing how many thousands of pictures were taken each minute and how precisely a second of time was divided, as if the speed and numbers involved were sufficient to explain how people in the film moved. If the *Mainichi shinbun* could call the Kinetoscope "one great step for science" in one sentence, there was little keeping it from adding in the next that the invention "borrowed power from the miraculous mysteries of creation and destruction."[20] The laws of science themselves, in some ways, were merely some of the inexplicable powers to which the cinema owed its fascinating talents, a field of mystery and wonder that, by association, paradoxically made the cinema understandable in its marvelousness, fitting easily into the discourse of the fairground entertainments, or *misemono*.

This fascination with the technology of cinema ultimately revolved around the apparatus's capacity to reproduce reality. The primary focus of newspaper reports would continue to be on the realism of the motion pictures, as they declared that viewing the new spectacle was "no different from seeing the true thing,"[21] that it gave "the feeling of touching the real thing."[22] In praising cinema's talent for presenting the real as it truly is, the first book written on the motion pictures, published soon after the first screenings, went so far as to claim, like Dziga Vertov would decades later, that the new invention was "in practice more clear than looking at the true conditions."[23] Contemporary newspaper articles lauded the machine's ability to capture everything under the sun. Many papers echoed the *Yomiuri shinbun*'s claim that it could "copy down the situation of people's movements without letting anything escape, large or small," and proceeded to offer examples from the films being screened in Japan.[24] In the early discourse on cinema, there was a distinct interest, mixed with a wishful desire, in the motion pictures as a means of revealing all the hidden aspects of reality. The *Osaka asahi shinbun* speculated that, if Edison succeeded in his efforts to add color to this "self-moving means of photography," then "there will not be a single thing under heaven not exposed in front of our eyes."[25] Another paper, already lamenting that the current film technology could only show us limited aspects of things, was hoping that the addition of the newly discovered x-ray photography would allow the apparatus to see everything move.[26]

On a more general level, Akira Mizuta Lippit has written about the connections between cinema, x-ray technology, and visuality in later Japanese cinema,[27] but it is interesting to note that this connection was actually realized—in an odd fashion—in early motion picture exhibition in Japan. In August 1897, Arai Kazuichi, one of the first importers and promoters of Edison's Vitascope in Japan, hit upon x-rays as a means of reviving flagging interest in the "new invention" that had been shown in Japan for nearly a year, and inserted demonstrations of x-ray technology into the bill with film screenings. The film historian Komatsu Hiroshi, in pointing out how such a mode of exhibition was not uncommon in America and Europe as well, has argued that cinema in general in its early days was received by audiences as "an apparatus that shows what cannot be seen even though it is close at hand."[28] Komatsu has presented this desire to see the unseen, or view the visible anew, as an unconscious "way of seeing"—and as the sole influence of Western ideologies on Japanese audiences and film—that was produced by the importation of cinema.[29] The dynamics of power in vision, especially when coupled with a quest for realism, are important issues in early Japanese cinema, but beyond doubting Komatsu's claim about the limited influence of foreign cinema on Japan, I think it is important in this discussion to qualify his contention about cinema and sight in Japan. First, as we have seen with discourse emphasizing the tactile and physical proximity generated by the movies ("the feeling of touching the real thing")— and as we will later see with complaints about the "obscenity" of the film experience in such movie districts as Asakusa—the cinema from the start was also a medium of the body, not just of sight. The benshi, who was present from the first showings, also made it strongly verbal. Second, Komatsu presupposes that a Japanese spectator watching a Lumière film is largely assuming the ideological position inscribed in the work's regime of sight, a presumption that potentially idealizes the spectator and erases the processes of (mis)reading linked to cultural or historical differences in modes of reception. It is possible to argue, for instance, following the art historian Kinoshita Naoyuki, who has discussed the issue of the gaze with regard to the Lumière Company's activities in Japan, that the Western exoticism and ethnographic viewpoint embodied in many of the Lumière *actualités* were not sufficiently understood by contemporary Japanese spectators.[30]

In the same way, one can take issue with Komatsu's attempt to connect the desire to see the unseen with the importation of cinema. While it is essential to locate the motion pictures within the issue of vision in the late 1800s, it is equally important to note that cinema was not alone in cultivating this desire. Kinoshita, in his provocative analysis of the role of the *misemono* in modern Japanese art history, *Bijutsu to iu misemono* (The *Misemono* Called Art), repeatedly stresses that a discourse of realism intersected with the *misemono* from the early 1800s, even before the arrival of Commodore Matthew Perry and forms of Western art. As Kinoshita sees it, these ways of speaking not only help define the *misemono* but also elucidate how Western art was introduced into Japan. Kinoshita focuses some attention on *ikiningyō,* the papier-mâché "living dolls" that, when arranged to re-create scenes from history or literature or introduce views of foreign lands, were a popular variety of *misemono* in entertainment districts like Edo's (or Tokyo's) Asakusa in the mid-1800s. When writing of these superbly crafted dolls, especially those molded by the most celebrated master of the art, Matsumoto Kisaburō, contemporary observers noted that viewing them "was like facing living people."[31] Arguing that the *misemono* satisfied desires for realism ignored by other art forms, Kinoshita traces the quest for realism in *misemono* back centuries earlier, but stresses that *ikiningyō* marked a significant shift. Previous *misemono* modes of representation, such as *kago saikō* (baskets woven in the form of people and animals), were enjoyable to the degree that there was a gap between the materials used and the image represented; never forgetting they were viewing baskets, people marveled at how skillfully the materials were made to resemble real people. But everything was done to *ikiningyō* to eliminate the difference between the materials used and real persons, to make viewers forget they were looking at papier-mâché dolls.[32] It is unlikely, of course, that anyone really failed to remember that these were made of paper, and so amid a general shift from stressing the physicality of the object to hiding that, the tension between knowledge of the object and the wonders of technique/technology became a core aspect of the pleasure of *misemono.* Early cinema in Japan would carry on this enjoyable tension.

Ikiningyō were intricately tied to this discourse of realism, the name of the craft itself often being termed *shōutsushi ikiningyō,* with a term meaning "accurate reflection" added at the front. It is interesting to note, as Kinoshita does, that the word *shōutsushi* was central to early artistic debates on realism that would eventually give birth to the modern meaning of the term *shashin,* or photography (the ideographic characters *sha* [also read "utsushi"] and *shin* literally meaning "reflecting the truth").[33] As an early mode of "photography," then, *ikiningyō* can be taken as another form of protocinema in Japan along with the *gentō,* satisfying desires to see the unseen (the foreign) or the fantastic (pictures move, dolls "live"). More important for this discussion, the forms for describing *ikiningyō* and later kinds of *misemono* strongly resemble those subsequently used for cinema. The Western looking glass *(Seiyō megane),* an early Meiji apparatus with numerous lenses through which spectators could see skillfully produced views of the West (usually with a well-lit, three-dimensional effect), was described as "the truly mysterious art of traveling through foreign lands without going to the West"; looking through it was "just like living in the various European countries."[34] The discourse of seeing the unseen was less a property of the cinema, as Komatsu contends, than an established way of speaking about visual entertainments in the field of the *misemono*. The term *misemono* literally does mean, after all, "showing something."

The discourses of realism, the West, and the power of sight outlined above are less a unique discursive pattern—a reflection or discovery of the essence of the new medium—than a continuation of a mode of speaking common to the *misemono*. As was the case with other *misemono*, the first film showings in Japan were often described as performances, complete with music and a lecture, in which the presentation of the apparatus was more important than what was represented (thus carrying on *misemono*'s pleasurable tension over the knowledge of technique).[35] Even tying early film exhibition to the West or to x-ray technology was less a matter of reinforcing a unique ideology of sight inherent to the cinema and more a manifestation of the logic of the *misemono*, rendering both equally spectacular attractions. Discursively aligned with the power of the gods, science itself, as well as many things Western, was tied into this logic, such that cinema and x-rays were to a certain degree simply interchangeable blocks within the misemono structure. The demands of spectacle, performance, and visual and sometimes bodily fascination common to all *misemono* thereby overrode the necessity to explain why and how the cinematic apparatus worked. Imbricated with existing discourses on the *gentō*, science, Westernization, and realism, cinema may have occupied a particular space shaped by the intersections of these discourses, but such a space was not unique and therefore could not define the motion pictures as significantly different from other forms of *misemono* entertainment. As long as x-rays could be added to the bill, even the discourse of exhibition was not enough to set cinema apart. In their first years in Japan, the motion pictures were talked about mostly as just the latest attraction, one in a series of similar forms of entertainment that, exchangeable in the space of exhibition, could be discussed using the same terms and concepts.[36]

A Medium Not Yet Arrived

Although, in the years following the importation of the motion pictures, *katsudō shashin* (or, literally, "moving photographs") would become the name of the new medium, discourse on cinema would, for some time, continue to center on the field of the *misemono*, never fully distinguishing cinema from other forms of entertainment. It was only after the cinema was defined as a specific problem that demanded particular discursive solutions that film would begin to be discussed as a unique and separate medium. That, however, would take some time.

Dōjin Shiin's book, *Katsudō shashinjutsu jizai* (All about Moving Picture Craft), is a good example of the continued prevalence of *misemono* discourse on cinema. Printed in 1903, it came out the year the first permanent movie theater in Japan, the Denkikan, was established in Tokyo's Asakusa. Cloaked as a technical introduction, the work is basically a fantastic rendition of the wonders of cinema. Dōjin begins by claiming that the cinema was invented by the "anatomist" Lumière in order to show his students the workings of the human heart that could not be sufficiently explained in words or regular pictures. He echoes the first descriptions of cinema offered in Japan, praising it for being able to "continually copy down a state of infinite change without leaving anything out" and for picturing "not the slightest difference from the real thing."[37] Dōjin further pursues the potential of film to capture the motions inside the human body and devotes pages to speculating on whether film can be made to capture the motions of the mind. Citing a report that an Englishman had acquired such a machine from the king of Siam, he even ponders the ethical dilemma of being able to read other people's thoughts. While still focusing attention on the body, Dōjin takes the desire to see the unseen, stressed by Komatsu, to the extreme, but in a way that again draws on the founding traditions of the *misemono*, where the presentation of deformed creatures, mostly taking place on the grounds of temples and shrines, was used as a means of educating people about the punishments they would receive if they committed sins and accumulated bad karma.[38] That Dōjin's moral lesson, woven in a fantastic and excessive language, was unproblematically combined with both technical explanations of film and photography and a resolute belief in human progress is itself a sign of how inextricably the discourses of science and the motion pictures were still connected with the *misemono* imaginary even in 1903.[39]

The Russo-Japanese War in 1904–1905 provided a boost to the motion pictures, as films treating the war proved box office hits, composing 80 percent of the films shown. Fervently patriotic audiences were eager to see visual evidence that Japan was the first Asian country to defeat a European power. But this did not necessarily single the cinema out: as Ueda Manabu has shown, such visual evidence could in some cases, such as Komada Kōyō's *shinematekku* attraction, be a mixture of moving dioramas and motion pictures, in which the latter was actually the less important feature.[40] The discourse of realism did come to the fore again as exhibitors boasted of showing actual scenes from the latest battles and film producers sent cameramen to the front to acquire images that could sell. Yet as Komatsu Hiroshi argues, this version of realism was in no way based on a firm cinematic division between fiction and nonfiction. Fake documentaries, featuring miniature ships and cigar smoke, were just as likely to be classified as "war subjects" as works actually filmed at the front.[41] According to Komatsu, audiences themselves did not seem to mind: "Authenticity on the level of film reception was not that important; all these works were part of a homogenous filmic representation. When spectators got angry that the war images unfolding before their eyes were false, their anger was in no way based on a conceptual opposition of nonfiction to fiction, but was simply directed against the fact the representation was inaccurate."[42]

Whether the representation was seen as real had little to do with a Bazinian perception of the ontological relation of the image to reality; it was merely based on a comparison of known facts with what was presented on the screen. In this logic, panoramas and *ikiningyō*, as long as they were accurate, were equally as real as—and thus interchangeable with—the cinema. According to Komatsu, the modes of film categorization that made fake and real documentaries equal under the rubric "war subjects" were borrowed from nineteenth-century magic lantern catalogs.[43] Abé Mark Nornes takes issue with Komatsu's general claim about a "homogeneous cinema," as well as with his tendency to narrate early film history from the position of fiction film. He notes some early actualities, such as *Kankoku Kōtaishi Denka, Itō Daishi Kankoku omiya nyūkyō no kōkei* (Scene of His Imperial Highness the Prince of Korea and Ito Hirobumi Entering the Imperial Palace, 1907), that could not have performed their intended functions (such as proving to Koreans that their prince, rumored to be dead, was still alive) had cinema not been recognized as providing truthful evidence.[44] Such films link up with the initial claims about the realism of the new medium, and they point to one way it would be distinguished in the coming years, but it would take time before such distinctions were made across the discursive field.

By the end of the first decade of the twentieth century, Japanese intellectuals began recording their observations about the new medium in writing, but it would be several years before they asserted such distinctions. A special collection of such essays, penned by illustrious figures such as the novelists Shimazaki Tōson and Nagai Kafū and the theater director Osanai Kaoru (whose interest in film would later lead him to serve as an advisor to Shōchiku in its early years), appeared in the journal *Shumi* (Taste) in August 1909, one of the first such collections to appear at a time when film magazines did not yet exist. I discuss essays by Osanai and Ogawa Mimei in chapter 3; for now, it is important to note that many of the other articles, while focused on the motion pictures as a specific topic, still did not offer a unique definition of the medium. Kafū, like the aficionado of traditional *shitamachi* (downtown Tokyo) culture that he was, merely used the motion pictures as an excuse to grumble about the lack of purity in literature and art in a modernizing age, commenting how, since "the modern is a terrible age," it was "more truly an honor to fail and be buried by the modern."[45] With Kafū helping to establish a pattern of inventing tradition by lamenting the arrival of the modern, cinema served as only one of many unspecified signs of the new that facilitated the creation of the boundaries of old Japan.

Other authors, while more favorable to the motion pictures, mostly treated them as merely a new object of interest. Shimazaki, in a short piece, remarked that viewing films reminded him of the ever-present difference between East and West.[46] Yoshie Kogan, a scholar of French literature, was still using the language the first newspaper articles about film in Japan had used, commenting on how the device allowed one to preserve the past and witness everyday life in the West. The cinema's interest, to him, remained on the level of the reproduction of simple motion.[47] Finally, the account by the poet and literary critic Kubota Utsubo was largely a skeptical record of his first trip to see the motion pictures earlier that year. Expecting the movies to be of interest only to children, he had been surprised not only because the audience had been mostly adults, but also because the pictures had been worthy of being shown to adults. Given that he saw cinema's role as limited only to the introduction of rare sights, however, he ultimately restricts the motion pictures to the discourse of the *misemono* by claiming they "were the most interesting of the *misemono* of that kind."[48]

In the first years of twentieth century, there was another major field of discourse that made little attempt to define a difference between cinema and other *misemono* entertainments: the law. Starting with Yoshiyama Kyokkō, one of the first film critics in Japan, many have cited the Copyright Law as the first law to recognize the existence of film: one section declares that reproducing or exhibiting the copyrighted work of another person as a motion picture was to be considered a copyright violation.[49] Such statutes, however, did little to define cinema as a unique object under the law. In fact, Japanese law was very late compared to other nations in clarifying cinema's status as intellectual property. As is well known, early American films, without any clear statutory guidelines, were initially copyrighted as series of photographs until court decisions in 1903 allowed films to be submitted as single entities; even then, it took until 1912 for the law to be amended to treat the motion pictures as a distinct medium. Richard Abel has described how French law was initially reluctant to accord cinema status as a unique form of intellectual property, refusing it any protection on the grounds that it was the product of a machine. Later, in conjunction with revisions of the Berne Convention in Berlin in 1908, which recognized some of the international property rights of films, French law gave cinema only limited protection as an extension of authorial rights or as a work related to a literary text.[50]

While Japan, as a signatory to the Berne Convention, technically consented to the provisions in the treaty protecting film, it did nothing to clarify this protection in Japanese law other than establish cinema as a threat to literary copyright. As late as 1929, Yanai Yoshio, legal scholar and former head of film censorship at the Home Ministry, had to devote a major section of his monumental *Katsudō shashin no hogo to torishimari* (Protection and Regulation of the Moving Pictures) to arguing copyright law. He proposed that, while Japanese copyright law did not specifically state that film was subject to protection, the motion pictures were included under the rubric of "other products in the realm of literature, academics, and art," found in Article 1 of the law, and that Japan, by ratifying revisions of the Berne treaty, was obligated to treat domestic films as protected even if this was not specified in its own law.[51] Despite this tacit protection, the film industry would continue asking for some years for more specific provisions in the law. It seems typical of the ironies of early discourse on cinema in Japan that the medium was singled out, first, only as a threat to an established art like literature, and offered positive legal protection solely as part of an undistinguished, unnamed mass of "other arts."

As a larger potential threat, films were subject to censorship from the very beginning. There is the oft-related anecdote about Edison's film *The Kiss*, in which the police attempted to stop the famous filmed kiss between May Irvin and John C. Rice from being shown in Osaka in 1897, complaining that it harmed public morals. The story goes that the quick-witted benshi Ueda Hoteiken apparently convinced the overly prudish police that a kiss was similar to a handshake in America and prevented the film from being banned.[52] According to Yoshiyama, the first film to actually be refused permission for exhibition in Japan was one produced by the French company Pathé Frères, *Le Inquisition* (1905), which was cited for excessive cruelty in 1906.[53] Such cases of police intervention, however, did not take place on the basis of any law that specifically named the motion pictures. Cinema was treated as a *misemono* as much in law as in popular discourse and, thus, initially regulated by the laws that covered those entertainments.[54] In Tokyo during the very first years, this meant either the Regulations for Viewing Establishments—the 1891 statute that covered sports or sideshow entertainments performed in front of public audiences, such as sumō, acrobatics, and panoramas—or, for films shown in regular theaters, possibly also the Theater Regulations from 1890 (overhauled as the Theater Exhibition Regulations of 1900, the first attempt to systematize theater censorship). Such statutes required that exhibitors acquire police permission before presenting entertainments and stipulated that applications deemed to be potentially injurious of public peace and morals would not be approved.

Neither of these regulations, nor the corresponding ones in other localities, specifically cited the motion pictures or contained statutes that called for particular systems of control for film. Cinema certainly existed to the degree that authorities recognized it as an entertainment capable of harming public peace, manners, and morals, but in both the procedures to which it was submitted and the way it was articulated in law, film did not exist independently from other *misemono*. Subject to laws written before the apparatus even appeared on Japanese shores, the motion pictures were merely inserted into a series of long-standing censorship procedures and traditions and treated no differently from Edo-era entertainments. According to legal discourse, as well as to many other discourses dealing with film, it was as if cinema either had not yet appeared in Japan or, since it was treated like any other *misemono*, had always already been in Japan and was only assuming a shape not yet its own.

ZIGOMAR AND THE PROBLEM OF CINEMA

Cinema would make its appearance in Japan—almost with a vengeance—partly through the incident surrounding the French serial *Zigomar*, directed by Victorin Jasset for the Société Française des Films Eclair, which was imported to Japan by Fukuhōdō, a relatively new film company, and opened at their Asakusa theater, the Kinryūkan, on November 11, 1911. The fast-paced detective film, featuring repeated clashes between the debonair criminal mastermind and master of disguise Zigomar and a series of detectives (including one named Nick Carter), proved immensely popular with Japanese fans. The phenomenal success it enjoyed, and the authorities' reaction to it, had a major impact on Japanese film culture and created a series of shock waves that would alter the ways in which cinema was discussed and defined. While I do not intend to argue that the Zigomar incident was the sole cause of these changes in the way film was defined (there were pointed criticisms of cinema before the series' appearance), it is in many ways a condensation of these transformations.

The Japanese film industry had been enjoying its own small boom starting in about 1909, before the *Zigomar* sensation. With the industry earning

Figure 2. The debonair criminal mastermind and master of disguise, Zigomar. (Courtesy of the Kawakita Memorial Film Institute)

vital capital from the success of Russo-Japanese War films—another indication of the important role war has played in the formation of Japanese cinema—the number of permanent motion picture theaters increased, and several companies were formed to regularize production within Japan. Yoshizawa Shōten constructed the first film studio in Tokyo's Meguro district in January 1908, as well as a theme park in Asakusa named after Coney Island's Luna Park; Makino Shōzō began producing immensely popular *kyūgeki* (old style) films starring Onoe Matsunosuke for Yokota Shōkai in 1909; and M. Pathé's Umeya Shōkichi sent cameramen off to the South Pole to record the exploits of a Japanese expedition in one of the industry's first feature documentaries. With Fukuhōdō entering the picture in 1909 with a string of well-built theaters, the number of Tokyo movie houses rose to a total of forty-four by 1912.[55] Film had finally come into its own as a domestic industry, and the papers were replete with comments on how vigorous business was.[56] In July of the same year, the four existing film companies, partly in a belated effort to emulate the monopoly trust formed by the Motion Picture Patents Company in the United States, but also to consolidate the business as a legitimate industry, merged to form the Nihon Katsudō Shashin Kabushiki Kaisha (Japan Moving Picture Company), or Nikkatsu for short. After the Meiji emperor died at the end of July, the Japanese film industry set out on a new path as Japan entered the Taishō era (1912–1926).

At this time, any detective stories featuring chase scenes and criminal masterminds seemed to be a hit with Japanese movie audiences. The first *Zigomar* was followed by a sequel, and other foreign productions were brought in to cash in on the craze. Even Japanese producers began filming their own *Zigomar* imitations, with such works as *Nihon Jigoma* (Japanese Zigomar; Yoshizawa, 1912), *Shin Jigoma daitantei* (New Great Detective Zigomar; M. Pathé, 1912), and *Jigoma kaishinroku* (The Record of Zigomar's Reformation; Yoshizawa, 1912) doing much to introduce European techniques such as faster editing into Japanese cinema. The *Tokyo asahi shinbun* reported that four of the major movie theaters in Asakusa were showing *Zigomar* imitations on the night of October 4, 1912.[57] The craze even spread to the publishing industry, which began printing novelizations of these films (or stories based on them), a successful trend that had a definite effect on the development of the Japanese mystery novel.[58] *Zigomar* had become a nationwide sensation and came to represent the success of the motion pictures, if not the existence of cinema itself.[59] Newspapers reported that the name had become part of Japanese slang ("He's a Zigomar!" referred to a dapper, though somewhat suspicious, man), and that children in empty lots all over were enjoying themselves by creating their own versions of the detective Nick Carter chasing the elusive evildoer.

The popularity of *Zigomar*, arguably the first example of a truly mass, modern entertainment fad in Japanese history—if not also, as Nagamine Shigetoshi has argued, of a complex multimedia phenomenon[60]—was not always greeted with favor in public discourse. Education officials began worrying aloud about the potential harmful effects movies were having on children, prompting a Tokyo school board committee to issue a report in July 1911 warning of the dangers of the medium and its places of exhibition and recommending that the lower schools in the area bar filmgoing by their pupils.[61] As if to verify those worries, rumors spread of minors committing crimes based on what they had learned watching films like *Zigomar*. There arose what Hase Masato has called a kind of "cinemaphobia."[62] Without mentioning the French production, the powerful *Tokyo asahi shinbun* newspaper first ran a ten-part series of articles in February 1912 warning of the dangers of motion pictures to children, and then, on October 4, 1912, began an eight-part series of reports on the *Zigomar* phenomena that characterized these films as "inspiring crime" and roundly criticized the Tokyo Metropolitan Police for not banning the movies before their release. Almost as if directly reacting to these criticisms (the *Asahi* actually took credit in print), the police announced on the 9th that they were banning *Zigomar* and other similar films from Tokyo screens (films that had already started their runs, however, were allowed to be shown until the 20th; new films of a similar vein would not be given permission to screen after the 10th). Other localities soon followed Tokyo's lead; in this way, Japan's first experience with film as a mass cultural phenomenon was deemed injurious to public morals and effectively stamped out.[63] In this action, and in the discussions surrounding the *Zigomar* craze, one can sense a shift in the way cinema was defined in discourse in Japan.

The *Tokyo asahi* took considerable effort to introduce the *Zigomar* phenomenon to its readership, starting the first article in its series with the inquiring title "Just What Is *Zigomar*?" The subsequent articles attempted to answer this question, explaining that this was "the last phenomenon of the Meiji era"[64] and offering a detailed summary of the plots of the first two French *Zigomar* productions. But this was an *Asahi* that in February had railed, "There are a hundred evils [to the motion pictures] and not one benefit."[65] The series did not stop at objectively describing the craze: in a mixture of reportage and editorializing common to Japanese journalism at the time, it unequivocally stated, "Once you see *Zigomar*, you cannot call it a detective film, but rather a film promoting crime or a film glorifying criminals."[66] Declaring that "the fact that [the *Zigomar* films] have a bad influence on or corrupt audiences is a fact that none can deny,"[67] the *Asahi* proceeded to claim the existence of two or three cases of such corruption. No specifics were given, and the assertion itself seems suspicious when looked at from our point in time. There were virtually no accounts detailing such "corruption" (e.g., examples of crimes being committed because of something the perpetrator had witnessed in a Zigomar film), except, ironically, ones *after* the banning of the film.[68] One may wonder if the claimed ill effect was more a result of the media coverage and police reaction than of the film itself (where cinema was not evil until named so officially), and this problem again prompts us to focus on the role that discourse played in defining cinema in Japan in the early 1910s.

The *Tokyo asahi shinbun* was quick to offer various objects of blame for the *Zigomar* phenomenon. Part of the problem, it said, lay with the film and its producers. In a world of cutthroat competition, companies spared no cost in topping both their competition and previous successes. As a result, works like *Zigomar* were "born of the ferocious competition based in commercialism," exposing the fact that the profit motive was not always consistent with the quest to foster a positive influence on society.[69] Thus, the *Asahi* was introducing a theme that would shape many discussions on film up until World War II: that the problem of cinema lay in part in its nature as an industrial art based on capitalistic practices that did not always support the Neo-Confucian national and social goals central to national ideology from the Meiji on.

At the center of the *Asahi* analysis was a detailed consideration of the uniqueness of cinema as a medium, which began with the fact that films like *Zigomar* were fictional products. Reflecting a Neo-Confucian mistrust of fabrication, the *Asahi* began its series by openly wondering why a fictional creation could have so much power over people. Answering its own question, and thereby underlining its own worries about cinema, the newspaper declared, "Even if one can say that every villain is the product of a serials author's imagination, one cannot neglect the fact that once he appears in a work of the moving pictures, the sense that he is the real thing is more prominent than one's feeling in watching theater. Accordingly, the degree to which film itself exerts a lasting influence on audiences is a problem that cannot be neglected."[70] The fact that cinema could make the fictional seem real was both part of its appeal and a major problem, because "simply and ingeniously flavoring the work with fantasy and fact is itself sufficient to strengthen and spread the film's lasting influence."[71] In emphasizing cinema's unique capacity to turn the imaginary into reality, the *Asahi* was constructing a narrative in which audience influence depended on a difference represented by the cinema. Film was finally beginning to peek out from the shadows of the *misemono,* but ironically, in the *Tokyo asahi's* view, only to the extent that it was a social problem.

At the time, it was felt that not only the realism of the films themselves but also the entire space surrounding cinema distinguished it as a dangerous medium and created a plethora of strong stimuli that left a lasting mark on spectators. In the eighth part of the Zigomar series, the *Asahi* offered a vivid account of the sensory experience of going to the movies in 1912 in the movie theater district of Tokyo's Asakusa:

> Beyond the electric lights that dazzle the eyes and the noise from the bands that tend to stray off-key—both of which lead the minds of passersby astray—the first set of stimuli offered by the moving picture district are the placards painted in strong colors of red, blue, yellow, and purple which incite curious hearts. Men and women who set foot in this area quickly become the prisoners of the moving pictures even before they watch a film, already losing their mental balance.

Figure 3. Asakusa's moving picture district in 1910, showing the garish banners and ornate facades of the Taishōkan and the Sekaikan. (Courtesy of the National Diet Library, www.ndl.go.jp)

> Audiences stimulated and led on in this way first taste an unpleasant feeling as they enter the darkness from the light. Their state of mind, having lost its balance, eventually falls into an uneasy mood. Here the air inside the theater, inadequately ventilated, assaults people with a kind of unclean humidity and attacks the sense of smell with tobacco smoke, the fragrance of face powder, and the odor of sweat.
>
> In an insecure and unpleasant theater, what is projected into the eyes of people having lost mental tranquility is *Zigomar*. . . . The conditions for extending an evil influence and for causing corruption have all been prepared in these elements.[72]

There were of course other entertainments in Asakusa that contributed to this cacophony, but here cinema was being blamed for an entire environment; it was starting to figure in discourse as the core of a new, but threatening, modern life. Not only the films themselves but also cinema as a modern spatial experience assaulting the senses seemed to contribute to the motion pictures' influence. As the paper had previously stressed, the movie hall represented a dangerous, crass, and almost obscene form of physicality, harming not only the spirits of spectators but also their very bodies (as such, cinema eventually became the object of legal and educational, as well as medical, forms of correction).[73] Carrying on but rendering negative such earlier discourses, cinema was demonized not just for its visuality but also for its physicality. Another example of such medical discourse was the recurring emphasis on film as a form of "stimulation" *(shigeki)*, according to which the cinema's influence seemed to bypass the filtering effects of reason and judgment to affect people's character bodily and directly. Unique not only as a technology, film was identified as a central facet of a new but disorientating culture in which both the boundaries between mind and body and the divisions between social groups were undermined and confused, creating a kind of "heterotopia" in Foucault's sense of the term.[74] Such boundary transgressions were a source of fear to the *Asahi* and cited as the basis of the kind of demolition of normal modes of thought that distinguished the moviegoing experience.

In the *Tokyo asahi*'s vision, conditions of reception were not completely to blame for undermining spectators' processes of reason: moving picture audiences were somehow different from the start. Why, after all, would any normal human being tolerate time and time again the inherently "insecure and unpleasant," the physically damaging conditions of the theater as movie fans did? Implied in the paper's account was a cinema audience almost abnormal in character, made up of fans who possessed addictive personalities that forced them to become "prisoners" of the unpleasant as a perverse necessity. As a whole, the paper characterized movie audiences in less than complementary terms, stating that those "sucked into this *Zigomar*" were "like ants swarming around a piece of sweet sugar."[75] With the *Asahi* claiming that "sensible-minded people would undoubtedly frown upon this fashion for crime films within the moving picture theaters,"[76] the paper was distancing itself from regular filmgoers, placing them on a lower rung in a hierarchy of right-mindedness and siding itself (and its readers) with the "sensible," who refrained from the moblike behavior of the movie masses. Reflecting a fear of the modern crowd common in later Japanese intellectual descriptions of mass culture, the discourse established an "us" versus "them" division that defined the medium in class-based terms and placed cinema spectatorship outside the boundaries of right-minded behavior. It was cinema's influence on this other set of people that was of central concern.

A description of the composition of the film audience served in part to justify this hierarchy. According to the *Tokyo asahi*, "the grand majority of the audience is young boys and girls of lower or middle school age,"[77] and such future leaders of society were seemingly vulnerable to the motion pictures' authority.

With these scenes and props, the film first leads the audience into a field of realistic impression and there shows, putting into motion, various evil deeds. Even adult audiences with good sense and judgment are so impressed they call it "an interesting novelty that works well." The film naturally offers even more intense excitement in the minds of the young who like both adventure and strong individuals, and who idealize the winner in any situation.

For instance, even if the conclusion results in the death of the villain, just how much does the moral point of view indicated by the death of the villain transmit an authoritative impression in the minds of the young living in today's society? Most of them will only see the success of the elusive on-screen hero, and think in the end how they would like to become a figure on screen themselves, to act and appear as if on film.[78]

On the one hand, it was believed that children (and other lesser spectators, like women) did not possess the discernment necessary to both properly read the film's ending and ward off the pernicious stimulations of cinema, especially since the motion pictures offered them modes of identification that were previously unheard of. Given that it is debatable whether the audience was dominated by children as the *Asahi* believed,[79] the problem concerning the film audience was less one of age than of modes of understanding and knowledge.

On the other hand, contemporary discourse was describing a potentially ineluctable historical difference that posed a distinct threat. An editorial in the *Yomiuri shinbun* cited the motion pictures (along with the phonograph) as one of the great modern inventions that had truly penetrated the everyday lives of normal people.[80] But to the *Tokyo asahi shinbun*, this modernity served as the background for a new breed of young Japanese who increasingly expressed desires that approved modes of moral discourse could not accommodate. The problem concerned not just a minority of children who were visibly cruel and mischievous by nature, but a majority born with such instincts.[81] The cinema, then, did not simply produce but "conform[ed] to these instincts and tastes," representing a new age that threatened to overturn established orders.[82] Film spectators were not simply undereducated but also fundamentally different in their way of perceiving the world and acting on their desires.

As a problem of knowledge, cinema was considered by many officials an educational issue from the 1910s on.[83] To them, film viewers both young and old required instruction, a mental preparedness that would protect them from the disorienting assault of the cinematic experience and enable them to produce approved meanings from specific film works. But what surfaced in the *Zigomar* incident, and what presented an obstacle not encountered earlier, was the problem of alterity, this time as represented by the question of the image. The *Tokyo asahi* noted, "As expected, the style of explanation of the benshi charged with lecturing did not neglect the lesson that good is rewarded and evil punished, . . . but in the minds of audiences who were watching the changes appear before their eyes on screen, no sense arose of good being rewarded and evil being punished."[84] It was thus felt that spoken language was unable to direct the interpretive processes of cinema audiences; there was something in the image that exceeded or even worked against the word. An official from the Tokyo Metropolitan Police, in explaining their difficulties with the film, also noted the difference between the film summary submitted as part of the censorship procedure and the film itself: "At police headquarters, it was thought, looking at the original story of the French *Zigomar*, that there was nothing much to it. Among works of this kind, you would think they were only a kind of child's play when you inspect the moving picture license. That's why we approved it up until today, thinking it had no effect on public morals. However, looking at the actual film, there is a world of difference from the explanation in both the scenery and the characters."[85]

This was not simply a problem of the accuracy of the plot summary: there was increasing concern that the motion pictures were a medium fundamentally different from existing linguistic arts, one that posed unique problems. The *Tokyo asahi* defined this difference: "Compared to *jōruri* and *naniwa-bushi*,[86] which specialize in the aural, and compared to theater, which attacks using both the visual and the aural, the impression received from the moving pictures is stronger and the influence caused is greater."[87] Cinema was defined as visual, not because of its essence, but because of the problems it supposedly posed. With the image seemingly resistant to the restrictions of the word, there was no guarantee that the minds of audiences were producing even the desired meanings. It was the alterity of the image, coupled with spectator desires associated with it, that helped define the cinema and mass cultural modernity as a threat to a Meiji order that had just seen its leader pass away.

It is important to emphasize that the problem of the image was not one exclusive to *Zigomar*; in the end, cinema itself was the issue. *Zigomar* was thought to merely represent a dangerous trend in motion picture culture that necessitated banning not just this French production but also all others similar to it. *Zigomar* had become a problem in other nations as well (it was eventually banned in France, for instance), often because of its supposed elevation of criminality through the figure of an upper-class criminal. While class would become a central problem in later discussions of film censorship in Japan, *Zigomar*'s social portrayals were barely mentioned in the discourse surrounding the film. Many did voice concern that the film was teaching minors the methods of crime, but it is significant that, despite the recommendations of several newspapers,[88] police never pulled any of the *Zigomar*-influenced novels from the bookstore shelves. It was *Zigomar*'s new and unique depiction of crime through the image that was the issue.

The *Asahi* in particular was already citing a driving force behind this evolution in the image: "When people get used to the moving pictures and will no longer be satisfied with most products, it will be necessary to provide something unprecedented and strongly stimulating so as to shock the visual senses."[89] This, the *Asahi shinbun* felt, was what *Zigomar* and its ilk were doing at an accelerating rate: offering a thrilling and singular mode of visual sensation, a new phenomenon that the paper would call "motion-picture-like" *(katsudō shashinteki)*.[90] This emerging uniqueness of cinematic narration was itself cited as a problem. Earlier, the newspaper had complained in general about the "unnaturalness" and incomprehensibility of new film techniques such as ellipses and cutting within the scene, arguing that jumping from scene to scene or cutting out (what, in the classical narrative economy, are considered unimportant) actions confused and fatigued spectators, especially younger ones.[91] The transformation of time and space enabled by editing was itself seen as a threat. In *Zigomar*, this was coupled with the villain's ability to appear and disappear, to change costumes in an instant and mysteriously jump from one place to another while eluding his pursuers, but in a way that, the *Asahi* acknowledged, proved absolutely fascinating to new Japanese youth.

This fluidity of space and identity, analogous to the circulatory anonymity of the modern crowd, was, according to Tom Gunning, a central concern of not only early trick films but also nineteenth-century phenomena like photography (which both undermined established forms of identity through mechanical reproduction and instituted new ones by documenting the individual body) and detective fiction (which tried to assert the certainty of an individual's guilt against an ever-changing urban environment).[92] We can speculate that it was this transcendence of space and time and Zigomar's ability to disguise himself and change identities (aided by Jasset's skillful use of trick photography)—elements similar to the "motionless voyage" Noël Burch cites as central to the classical film experience—that both fascinated and disturbed contemporary observers. That is perhaps why so much of the discourse on these films worried about the audience's ability to recognize and identify who was the villain and who was the hero. If, as Gunning says, *Zigomar* "envisioned a new cinema of narrative integration, moving towards the paradigm of classical film-making,"[93] the discourse on film in Japan marked it as the point at which the moving pictures broke with previous paradigms and stepped into the unknown—the simultaneously alluring and threatening modern realm of spatiotemporal dis- and reconnection—and thereby posed the problem of what cinema is. Here we can say that cinema became foreign after it was familiar. Here the incipient classical mode was being less vernacularized than made alien, and so the Pure Film Movement's task later on would be to reinvent the familiarity of classical forms, in part by rendering other modes of filmmaking alien to cinema if not also Japan.

Nagamine Shigetoshi has offered the interesting hypothesis that *Zigomar* and related films were banned only after the Japanese film versions and novels began appearing. Citing the *Asahi* as evidence, he argues that authorities became worried because the stories were becoming domesticated, or Japanized, taking place with Japanese actors in familiar Japanese settings, and thus better able to influence unsuspecting homegrown audiences.[94] That certainly was a fear, and in the following decades censors would come down harder on Japanese films for portraying certain actions such as kissing (which was banned in cinema until after World War II) than on foreign films for portraying the same actions (where an innocent kiss was allowed on occasion). Authorities could sometimes accept images of certain behaviors if these were comfortably framed as "foreign," but not if they crossed the border and entered Japanese everyday life. *Zigomar* was probably one such case, but I emphasize that the majority of discourse on the film focused less on such border crossings in content—and the fear that foreign behavior was becoming familiar—and more on the realization that the cinema, the means by which these actions were shown and which had until then appeared just to be another *misemono*, was itself alien. The parallel anxiety was less that Japanese would become foreign, and more that they were already new and different and that cinema both represented and exacerbated this fact.

It was against these anxieties surrounding new media and the idea of identity changing from both within and without, that many discourses on film tried to operate. Just as Gunning emphasizes the important role of regimes of knowledge in processing photographic information so as to refix and reestablish identity within a modern social context, so we can investigate how discourses after the *Zigomar* incident attempted to name and classify this particular visual experience. On the one hand, such discourses, represented by the efforts of educational authorities and newspapers to describe and categorize cinema and its individual texts, laid the foundations for film study in Japan. On the other, in the hands of film reformers like those in the Jun'eigageki Undō (Pure Film Movement) in the 1910s, these discussions would work to merge the cinema with the culture of the new Japanese middle class and transform the status of Japanese film and its audiences.

The *Zigomar* incident in this way helped define a central problem with the motion pictures that authorities and social leaders would confront for some time: how to control an alluring but elusive visual (and sometimes physical) mode of signification—one that resisted the regulation of the written or spoken word—and its spectatorship. Recognition of this unique problem was reflected in the police's reaction to the incident. A few days after banning the film, the Tokyo police issued a set of internal procedural guidelines detailing what to guard against when evaluating applications for film exhibition:

1. Works constructed from a framework that suggests adultery.
2. Works liable to invite or support methods of crime.
3. Works bordering on cruelty.
4. Works constructed from a pattern that covers love relations or that descend into obscenity, especially ones capable of exciting base emotions.
5. Works contrary to morality, that induce mischief by children, or that cause corruption.[95]

The sections covering adultery, cruelty, obscenity, and morality differed little from the theater regulations in force at the time.[96] What had changed in confronting the problem of film was the perception that cinematic works could not only offend established sensibilities or directly harm public morals but also strongly induce objectionable behavior in spectators, especially in certain sectors of the audience. Theater regulations at the time never posited a narrative of behavioral influence, or specified audiences that should be the object of regulative concern. This was a problem thought specific to cinema, which was posited as influencing a newly defined object of correction and control: thought and behavior; I expand on this in chapter 5.

Cinema was a unique problem that demanded particular modes of correction. It was as cinema that *Zigomar* was banned, not as literature. The special attention—or fear—focused on cinema is evident in reports that authorities even tried to prevent producers from making films on the life of General Nogi Maresuke, the military leader who committed *junshi* (ritual suicide on the occasion of one's lord's death) on the night of the Meiji emperor's funeral, only one month before *Zigomar* was banned.[97] Despite the fact Nogi was already being praised by many as the epitome of *bushidō,* the perfect example of citizenship for Japanese children, cinema and its form of spectatorship were apparently too dangerous to trust them to spread even this important message.

As a Tokyo police official said, there was "a necessity to more strictly watch [the moving pictures] than the theater."[98] The procedure for censoring films started to change. The Tokyo Metropolitan Police attributed their mistake in approving *Zigomar* for exhibition in part to the fact that they had not seen the film beforehand;[99] given the *misemono* regulations that covered cinema at the time, an application required only a written summary of the film or of the benshi's narration.[100] The police did send out officers to investigate the films while they were being screened in the theaters, but this procedure was no different from dispatching foot patrols to the sideshow tents.[101] The *Zigomar* incident made it clear that censoring the content of a film required more than a review of a written summary. The Tokyo police acknowledged that they now needed to base their decisions on preview screenings.[102] The definition of the filmic text itself began to change as censorship procedures started to place importance on the text as a visual object, not just as a written story, as well as on the text as viewed, not just as read. New censorship technologies were deemed necessary (and later proposed in, for instance, the groundbreaking 1917 Tokyo Moving Picture Regulations), ones that molded modern models of subjectivity centered on promoting the internal mental faculties capable of accommodating this visual "stimulation," and ones that regulated the physical side of cinema and created a homology between the structure of the individual subject and the social hierarchy, where the mental (the upper class and the state) would rule over the body (the lower class, the people).

Thus, it is important to stress that reactions against cinema were not simply a manifestation of an existing Japan confronting or domesticating a new or foreign object. Certainly cinema became a mark of the modern, a modern to be feared and regulated, but it was seen as alien only after it was treated as familiar (as a *misemono*). The Japan that encountered it was also assuredly not a traditional entity, given and complete, but one that authorities recognized was already new, different, and changing. And what they proposed against cinema was not the reinforcement of old-time values (although that rhetoric would become more common two decades later, long after these cultural transformations had already begun), but rather a set of new techniques that, as I argue in chapter 5, were conducive to constructing a modern subject within a modern nation. Cinema helped prompt these changes, but only insofar as it became subject to a transformative struggle over its form and meaning. What was emerging here was not a battle between old and new but one between different forces or conceptions of modernity. One site of this battle was the rising field of discourse on cinema, which itself was being shaped by the circumstances of film's "discovery" as a problem.

The history of discourse on the moving pictures in Japan as a specific object began only with the realization that discourse was inadequate to define or accommodate its object. Such a realization itself was not sufficient to generate a discourse on the motion pictures: it had to be linked to a description of the medium as a social problem in need of solution. Only with such a perception did the fact that existing discourses, such as those on the *misemono*, failed to treat the cinema as a differentiated sign become an issue. Discourse on cinema developed by first negating existing discourses, establishing the basis of a semiotics of difference within which the cinema would be defined. Such a semiotic negation was doubled in the social realm, because the motion pictures had to be, in a sense, rejected or posited as objectionable in order to gain a positive definition. Cinema did not become a problem because it was modern and visual; it became modern and visual through the process of being defined as a problem, one dialectically intertwined with many other facets of what was seen as modern. Cinema was defined by being a problem, just as the problem was defined by cinema and its modernity. The question remained, however, how to solve the problems posed by cinema. The very fact that the motion pictures posed a problem that sparked objections meant that film was being durably established in discourse in a way that other, ephemeral *misemono*, like the panorama and the Western looking glass, never did. Again an existing object cinema was not being "discovered"; rather, *cinema* was appearing in discourse as a term considered crucial in identifying central problems of modernity, discourse, visuality, the body, perception, class, and society. Cinema became distinguished in discourse precisely as a medium that exceeded current discourse (if not the word itself), one that utilized a new mode of signification that could not be accommodated in existing forms of speech and writing. It was this contradictory task of delineating in discourse what by definition could not be described—and thus of finding novel forms of discourse to shape and accommodate it—that became the central dynamic of 1910s discourse on cinema in Japan.

2 Gonda Yasunosuke and the Promise of Film Study

Katsudō shashinkai (Moving Picture World), one of the first Japanese film magazines, begun in June 1909 and published by Yoshizawa Shōten, the leading film company at the time, featured in its first issues the results of a survey of prominent writers and painters who were asked their impressions of the motion pictures. While there were those like the novelist Masamune Hakuchō, who confessed to having never seen a movie, most of those surveyed were more or less aware of the phenomenon and responded favorably to the cinema's ability to present rarely seen images of Western society and customs. Some even went on to posit unique qualities in cinema, such as motion and the representation of natural surroundings, that distinguished it from other entertainments. The painter Ishii Tenpū succinctly argued: "The moving pictures can be seen as a complete picture scroll [emaki]. They have merits all their own not sought after in theater or novels and which cannot possibly be obtained in painting. They are true to people and true to scenery. However, many of the contemporary pictures, which are like repetitions of theater, are uninteresting."[1]

Many of Ishii's colleagues echoed his complaints about theater-like films, specifically pointing the finger at Japanese works, described as static reproductions of stage plays, which showed none of the speed or location shooting visible in films from the United States and Europe. The painter Ishikawa Enji confessed that, while he truly liked the moving pictures, "I have a strong objection to Japanese-made theater films. I think they have no value as moving pictures because scenes that are cinematically meaningless continue forever, there is little transformation, and the actions of people are bereft of rhythm."[2] To such discontent about the state of

Figure 4. The cover of the fifth issue (January 1910) of *Katsudō shashinkai,* a high-class magazine that spoke in defense of the motion pictures, featuring a benshi engaged in *maesetsu,* the discourse before the movie began.

Japanese cinema was added a number of complaints about conditions inside movie houses. The painter Kosugi Misei claimed, "One is forced to breathe dreadfully unhealthy air since they do not take care of facilities in the theater";[3] and the religion critic Matsubara Shibun bluntly stated that the theaters were so "narrow and smelly, I refuse to go inside."[4] In the months leading up to the release of *Zigomar,* as the movies were gaining in popularity, praise of the medium by Japanese intellectuals was doubled with criticism of both the results of production and the conditions of exhibition.

The editors of *Katsudō shashinkai* were painfully aware of these and other criticisms leveled at the popular medium. In their early feature "Henshūkyoku yori" (From the Editorial Board), they repeatedly and vigorously tried to defend the cinema against claims that it degraded taste or that dark theaters were injurious to public morals.[5] In responding to the writers and artists who cooperated with their survey, the magazine—the organ of a film company—objected to calls to ban Japanese films but was, at the same time, conciliatory:

> Of course it is very difficult to consider the present situation perfect as it stands. There is plenty of room for study, and we believe this includes research into the methods of improvement.
> As we have said before, in Japan the era of mere fascination in the motion pictures has passed and now, to a certain degree, we are progressing into the realm of study.[6]

Research or study (in Japanese, *kenkyū*) was what the magazine's editors proposed both as a response to critics of cinema and as a means of improving the medium. Study of film, in fact, was to be the next stage for the motion pictures, which were emerging from an era in which cinema audiences had been interested in mere spectacle and fascinated with the apparatus.

The term *study* began peppering discourse on cinema in the early 1910s, just as the medium was being singled out as either a social problem or an object in need of reform. The connection between the study and censure of film is logical given how the issue was defined at the time. Because cinema was accorded particular attention as a social problem, the issue for many became how to solve the difficulties uniquely presented by the motion pictures. Especially after the *Zigomar* incident, the main problem was how to explain the unique processes by which the cinema produced its effects on audiences. Once these were known, it was conceivable to enact policies or strategies that could alleviate or nullify the medium's harmful influences. Knowledge of film became a central facet in the quest to solve cinema as a social problem, thus establishing "study" as one of the primary modes of approaching the medium. The term was picked up not only by representatives of industry discourse like *Katsudō shashinkai*, which hoped to improve the status of cinema, but also by academic or governmental researchers who sought to delineate the social or educational effects of film. In this sense, film study began early in Japan, concurrent with—if not also facilitating—the discovery, if not also the invention, of the medium as distinct. Yet from the start, since cinema was distinguished partly because it was seen as a problem, research was aligned with correction and control of that problem.

Studies of cinema began appearing just at the time when motion pictures' popularity was sparking alarm. Yoshiyama Kyokkō reports that as early as 1909 the welfare activist Tomeoka Kōsuke was studying the harmful influences of film on children in the Kansai region.[7] In November 1911, the Tsūzoku Kyōiku Kenkyūkai (Popular Education Research Group) included in its published study *Tsūzoku kyōiku ni kansuru jigyō to sono shisetsu hōhō* (Activities Relating to Popular Education and Methods of Their Establishment) a chapter on cinema and "popular education," the latter a subject of much debate in educational circles at the time. Makino Mamoru details how one investigative subcommittee formulated proposals not only for inspecting and recommending films for educational use but also for regulating the perceived harmful effects of the medium. While affirming that "moving pictures will become a perfect combination of popular taste and public good as well as an enormous benefit in aiding popular education," the report cited numerous problems at regular theaters:

1. The need for regulation of "health-related conditions" and "public morals" in theaters.
2. The existence of "films showing Western customs [that] go against the morés of our own nation."
3. The exhibition of "films that are harmful to human feelings and public decency and which destroy whatever benefits motion pictures have" in presenting geography, history or industry.
4. The occasional benshi who is "unfit in language and attitude."
5. The presentation of "indecent" songs, dances and music accompanying film screenings.

Thus while also pointing to the potential educational benefits of cinema, this study called for strict regulation by authorities and even gave the following advice to primary schools: "Encourage all to as best possible not show moving pictures to children." If educators were to let children see movies, it should be only after "carefully investigating and selecting the sorts of films and the benshi."[8] Research and study, then, made possible not only regulation of but also preparation for film viewing.

In the same year, the critic Nakagawa Shigeaki presented one of the first aesthetic accounts of the cinema in his *Shokuhai bigaku* (An Aesthetics of Detached Contact).[9] Working from Konrad Lange's definition of art (and presumably that of Kant),[10] Nakagawa argued that art is ruled by such principles as *furifusoku* or *shokuhai*, which express the idea that art should be detached from reality, but not completely divorced from it. Art should not copy reality, since the illusion it shapes must be artistic and conscious. Nakagawa faulted both photography and film for creating an overly realistic illusion that was unmediated by the individual presence of the artist, as well as unconscious, in that it comes directly from reality and can fool the spectator. He found use for the motion pictures in science and recording history, but he echoed many contemporary observers in conceiving of cinematic entertainment as vulgar and low class.[11]

This philosophical rejection of film as art by Lange and Nakagawa would remain influential in Japan,[12] but there were other examples of film study that attempted to legitimize the medium's artistic potentials. One method was to utilize existing notions of art and merely insist on the role of the creative individual in film. This essentially was the tack taken by *Film Record*, the first intellectual film journal founded in 1913 (it changed its name to *Kinema Record* in December) by young film fans like Shigeno Yukiyoshi and Kaeriyama Norimasa, who had begun writing articles on cinema for *Katsudō shashinkai*. Their efforts to reform Japanese cinema by comparing it with what the motion pictures artistically should be (often represented by American and European films) laid the basis for the Jun'eigageki Undō, or Pure Film Movement, a crusade for reform that by the end of the decade would mark a profound shift in the way films were made and talked about in Japan. Another method of proclaiming film art was that of the young sociologist Gonda Yasunosuke, who in 1914 penned the first full-length study of the cinema in Japan, *Katsudō shashin no genri oyobi ōyō* (The Principles and Applications of the Moving Pictures), a colossal 454-page tome that covered virtually every aspect of cinema, from technological minutiae to film's role in shaping modern society. There he tried less to apply existing notions of art to cinema than to argue that film transformed the existence of art itself. Parallel to these aesthetic speculations, Gonda also attempted to illuminate the sociological dimensions of new arts like film. In the spring of 1917, he undertook the first major statistical survey of Tokyo motion picture audiences, with the help of the Ministry of Education's Akiyama Teruji, at the behest of the Imperial Education Association, a survey that eventually had a profound impact on film censorship regulations in Japan.

These various forms of film study, in examining cinema's social effects, considered both the content of the film text and the ways audiences appropriated meaning from it. They asked how cinema was used, and they asked about its essence, attempting to discern what established it as a unique art.

Several of these approaches were united in an early figure like Gonda, who both praised the motion pictures as a singular art form and did sociological research on their effects on children on behalf of governmental and educational institutions. The articles published in *Kinema Record* leaned more toward defining what constituted a pure cinema than considering cinema's social influence, but even then, knowledge of the medium was thought to provide the keys necessary to solve particular film-related problems.

Tied to the quest to address cinema as a social issue, film study in the 1910s presented a range of options for defining the medium, ones that, as solutions to a problem, could alter the course of the motion pictures. How would the relationship between the audience and the text be defined? Where did the source of effect (both social and semiotic) lie? What was the cinema's place in modernity and a changing Japanese society? How was the cinema different from other arts? Just what constituted an acceptable cinematic text? These may appear to be the standard questions of academic film study, but being addressed in Japan by figures ranging from filmmakers to government officials, they were intimately related to Japan's need to regulate and reform the medium. Cinema stood at a crossroads in the 1910s, and film study had a leading role in selecting which road to take.

This posed a dilemma for film study, as the *Zigomar* incident indicates. In attempting to acquire knowledge about film as a means of correcting certain problems, early film researchers found that cinema had secured a unique definition precisely as an image medium that exceeded the bounds of discourse. What was written about film was somehow insufficient to contain the medium, in part because the motion picture experience itself was labeled disorienting and inconsistent with the actions of rational thinking. Against this background, positing cinema as a static, unchanging object of knowledge was potentially futile if it remained outside the range of discourse.

This dilemma shaped much discourse on film in the 1910s. Many wondered to what degree film study could discursively grasp its object and discern the situation of cinema: how much could it involve itself in establishing the authority of knowledge over cinema and directing how the problem of the motion pictures would be solved. The cases of Gonda and the critics in the Pure Film Movement present two examples of how film study approached this dilemma. Gonda expressed a fundamental ambivalence about cinema and film study, both celebrating the joyful excess of motion picture entertainment as enacted by 1910s audiences and seeking to correct spectator misbehavior by establishing an understandable norm for the cinema. Film study in the Pure Film Movement was stricter and more confident, dictating what cinema and audiences should and should not do. But in both cases, the issue was how film study would define itself in relation to the need to control cinema as a problem.

GONDA YASUNOSUKE AND THE SURVEILLANCE OF PLAY

Gonda was born in Tokyo's Kanda area and expressed early on an interest in the Japanese socialism of Abe Isoo and the anarchism of Ōsugi Sakae. It was in fact Abe's translation of Marx's *Capital* that introduced Gonda to historical materialism and sparked his study of German. His own political activities, manifested in the publication of a small revolutionary pamphlet, soon led to his expulsion from Waseda High School. He proceeded on to the Tokyo University of Foreign Languages, majoring in German, and then to Tokyo Imperial University to study aesthetics. There he was strongly influenced by both German statistical sociology and the motion picture medium. Before he graduated, he wrote *The Principles and Applications of the Moving Pictures*, the first book-length study of the cinema in Japan, which predates Vachel Lindsay's *The Art of the Moving Picture* by one year and Hugo Munsterberg's *The Photoplay: A Psychological Study* by two.

This volume certainly earned him a reputation as an expert on film, but it was his work with Takano Iwasaburō that made him a qualified statistical researcher of social phenomena. Takano, along with Toda Teizō, was one of the forefathers of statistical research in Japan, but while Toda trained in American sociology and devoted his efforts to studying Japanese villages, Takano was a leftist economist who focused on the new urban Japan. His 1916 survey of the household finances of Tokyo working-class families was the first survey of its kind in Japan, and his 1919 survey of all aspects of working-class life in a laborers' district in Tokyo, the "Tsukishima Survey," proved to be a milestone in Japanese statistical social research. Gonda was a central member of the research team and took charge of the section on communications and entertainment, learning from Takano the value of thorough fieldwork and participant observation (the researchers lived in Tsukishima while conducting part of their survey). Takano helped Gonda get a position as an assistant and lecturer in the Department of Economics at Tokyo Imperial University, but the two left in protest in 1921 over the Morito Incident, in which two university professors were suspended for writing an article on Peter Kropotkin. In the meantime, Gonda had firmly established himself as an expert on popular entertainment, gaining appointments to research committees run by the Imperial Education Association and the Ministry of Education. After leaving Tokyo University, he joined the leftist Ohara Institute, where he remained until his death in 1951.[13]

Gonda's contradictory relationship with the prewar Japanese state complicates any assessment of his work. As a leftist defendant of the popular, he openly opposed any attempts by intellectuals and bureaucrats to manage forms of amusement he considered fundamentally democratic, yet he served on government committees that regulated film and other media forms. This contradiction bears serious consideration, given that Gonda later produced works during the war celebrating less "popular play" (entertainment emerging from the masses) than "national play" (entertainment expressing the nation), a shift symbolized by his newfound appreciation for Nazi social policy. Miriam Silverberg, in her study of Gonda, admits that his approval of Weimar social policy "prevented him from taking a critical stance toward the intrusion of the state into the realm of cultural policy," but she nevertheless argues that Gonda's stance throughout his career represented a consistent effort to undertake an "ethnography of modernity" in which Japanese culture was not studied as an ahistorical essence but as a modern construction of traditional Japanese and contemporary Western practices.[14] Harry Harootunian has emphasized how Gonda's notion that "national life was always plural and the product of distinct historical formations" countered the essentialist culturalism of the time by focusing on how everyday life and pleasure formulates culture, not the other way around.[15]

What is fascinating about Gonda's early works on cinema and entertainment, particularly *The Principles and Applications of the Moving Pictures*, is that in them he not only uses cinema to conceive of culture as a construction of the new modern masses but also attempts to present in practice a form of film study that embodies his notion of productive play. Yet, as is evident in his Asakusa audience study, Gonda was not immune to existing definitions of cinema as a problem, and so his conception of film study remains in the end crucially ambivalent, one that, in a transitional era on the cusp of pure film reform, envisions possible alternative cinemas while also helping justify discursive regimes to control the problem of cinema.

Cinema as the Art of Social Subjectivity

Gonda's *Principles and Applications of the Moving Pictures* was not the first attempt to study the cinema in Japan, but it does present itself as a new way of talking about cinema that was earnest yet playful, academic yet opposed to existing intellectual approaches that lambasted the medium. Countering criticism by contemporary Japanese educators who voiced their fear that cinema was ruining the nation's youth, Gonda declares in his introduction, "I will not be the only one happy . . . if I can make moving pictures the object of earnest research by scholars, the aim of serious speculation by intellectuals, and a new target of interest that people do not find embarrassing."[16] From the beginning, Gonda saw film study not simply as a solid approach to describing the synchronic state of cinema but also as an intervention in film's current discursive articulation that would offer a diachronic plan for the transformation of its meaning. Film study would make cinema the object of respect by society.[17] Underlining the importance of discourse in the definition of the medium itself, Gonda's work, from the beginning, was intended to create an "unembarrassing" cinema by proposing reforms in the object itself and altering the sum of statements in society about the motion pictures. Film study, then, was a tool for reform.

This was true partly because film study was essentially an issue of language, of naming and discursively articulating the motion pictures. Gonda admits in the introduction to *Principles* that, at the time of his writing, "there are no set technical terms for the moving pictures. Words have not yet been created that even have the attractive tone of being technical terms" (*Principles,* 16). Being the first Japanese to discuss in detail the technological, economic, and social functions of the cinema, Gonda stresses that he does not have at his disposal an established terminology for his discussion. He makes his terms up, doing his best throughout the book to invent Japanese words with available Chinese ideographs to express the ideas that molded his conception of cinema. This did not merely fill a gap, however. Since film reform did not simply involve altering the way films were made but also how they were described, Gonda was taking advantage of the amorphousness of early film discourse by attempting to create a cinema by crafting words to articulate it.

The discourses that already existed, as we have seen, labeled the moving pictures as a social problem requiring regulation, reform, or even, ironically, eradication if they were to conform with the existing set of domestic social values. Gonda announced at the beginning his opposition to this position, but he never declared there was nothing wrong with the medium. In defining his project as one aimed at rendering cinema respectable, he accepted conceptions of the motion pictures' lack of respectability. But instead of calling for censorship or top-down regulation as many of his contemporaries did, he attempted to solve the social problem of the motion pictures by offering a clear articulation of a new kind of cinema through film study.

What is particularly interesting about Gonda's approach is that he located the problem of cinema in the inappropriate words others were using to describe the cinema, as much as he located it in the medium's internal difficulties. He acknowledged on almost every page the criticisms of cinema that he knew surrounded him, devoting much energy to sometimes arguing with, and other times wittily ridiculing, these opinions. Often as playful as the entertainment to which he devoted himself, Gonda was at other times defiant, tossing barbs at those who vilified the motion pictures without taking the time to study it. Toward the end of the book, he describes his motives: "The reason I decided to take up this study of the vulgar-smelling 'moving pictures' was . . . out of a spirit of rebellion; given how there seem to be many who throw to the dogs much better topics, in contrast I wanted at least to take up a base subject and make it the object of serious study" (*Principles*, 441). Working within a context that separated high from low, serious from frivolous, Gonda had to adopt some of the generally used meanings of these oppositions in order to justify to others his research as earnest. At the same time, his strategy, visible throughout the entire work, was to attempt to rework those linguistic oppositions, to alter their pragmatic semiotic valences, and argue, for instance, that the "vulgar" motion pictures are to be celebrated precisely because they are vulgar, or that a playful, colloquial style can be truer to cinema than more "serious" discourse.[18]

Gonda's film study sought to redefine existing discourse primarily by reconsidering the meanings of two important terms: *entertainment (kyōraku)* and *civilization (bunmei)*.[19] At a time when industrialization in Japan was shaping a more culturally and politically active urban lower class, the concepts of "popular entertainment" *(minshū goraku)* and "popular art" *(minshū geijutsu)* became central topics of debate among intellectuals in the mid- to late 1910s. The media historian Yoshimi Shun'ya has categorized the positions in this debate as they relate to Gonda's work. He emphasizes that the disagreement centered on whom the term *minshū* ("masses" or "populace") refers to, and whether entertainment is something "for" the masses or "by" them. Figures like the literary critic Honma Hisao saw the masses as composed of the urban proletariat who, being uncultured and underprivileged, should be given entertainment directed by intellectuals as a means of educating them. The liberal critic Katō Kazuo countered with a vision of popular entertainment as a modern citizenry's free mode of expressing their humanity or national character. As Yoshimi argues, however, both writers "made ambiguous the qualitative difference between popular art and modern bourgeois art, and called 'popular art' the process by which a bourgeois and popular artistic mentality was born among the few people 'awakened to their humanity' and then spread among the larger masses."[20] It was not hard for this top-down model of art and entertainment, where what is general has to emerge from the elite (ultimately the representatives of the "populace"), to align with the kind of view of popular entertainment offered by the Ministry of Education's Tanaka Shunzō. In that view, as Yoshimi describes it, "of course entertainment is neither by nor for the masses, but by the state for the state."[21] One of the main figures opposing this tendency was the anarchist thinker Ōsugi Sakae, who tenaciously argued that true popular entertainment was a product of the new urban proletariat and was composed of a set of social and artistic values qualitatively different from that of bourgeois art.

As Yoshimi stresses, Gonda's position can be aligned with Ōsugi's. Against the view that entertainment was a frivolity that must be subjugated to a serious purpose, such as education, Gonda posits a definition of the term founded on a historical conception of the development of new technology. To him, the motion pictures and other inventions were initially objects of luxurious consumption like the bicycle and the automobile—too expensive for most people to buy, and used only on Sunday outings. It was only at this stage, Gonda implies, that one could truly label cinema and other such inventions objects of mere frivolity: they had "not at all become things [*mono*] from the standpoint of human civilization and human society" (*Principles*, 282). All new technologies, however, pass into a subsequent stage of practical use. Cheaper and more readily available, they truly enter into society and become part of the everyday lives of the majority of people. According to Gonda, at this point such innovations become "things," achieving substance and reality in the social field. The meaning of the object depends on its practical accommodation within a lived historical social formation. Cinema, he asserts, was entering this stage in his time, moving from being a toy of the few to becoming an essential part of the life of many (*Principles*, 281–284).

The motion pictures could not yet be called "entertainment," however. For that to happen, film, in the end, Gonda insists, would have to pass through an intricate teleology until it reached the final stage of entertainment: "The moving pictures must first enter the 'age of practical use' from the 'age of luxury,' after which they must progress into the 'age of entertainment.' When the energy of practical use is collected and purified, a new 'entertainment' in the true sense of the term is born and for the first time a new civilization [*bunmei*] is completed—a civilization called the 'moving pictures' appears. The moving pictures finally reach a conclusion" (*Principles*, 344). Gonda reverses the usual hierarchy of play and practicality and argues that entertainment is the historical transcendence of practical use. As entertainment, cinema ceases to be for something else, and is enjoyed in and of itself; only at this stage does film "conclude" its historical development and become what it essentially is. In Gonda's conception, entertainment is not a tool for bringing civilization to the masses but "an extremely important element within the civilization of human society" (*Principles*, 344). Gonda employs the term *civilization* to denote a particular stage of culture in which technological forms assume an organic continuity with lived experience, and in doing so, he ignores the term's use at the time to designate a state of Westernized technological modernity—the "civilization and enlightenment" proclaimed in the Meiji slogan *bunmei kaika*. Not simply objects for practical use, these technological forms exist in everyday life as they are, enjoyed in and of themselves as essential aspects of social life. "Gonda," says Harootunian, "wanted to strip popular pleasures of any hint of utility or instrumentality";[22] in Silverberg's mind, entertainment to Gonda is not frivolous but valuable as a central aspect of human existence. As expressed in Gonda's later dictum about "play as the creation of everyday practice,"[23] it is not a mere period of rest after productive activity but a central means by which people produce their social existence.[24] In this way, Gonda distances himself from those proffering an elitist, top-down model of popular entertainment and argues for play that is more than a tool of educational policy.

To Gonda, cinema is the medium that best represents the profound transformations of modern life. Viewing history as both materialist and rigidly teleological, he counters his opponents by frequently labeling them as "antiques" who have not recognized that history demands attention to the modern problem of the motion pictures. Gonda does not simply attempt to trump his enemies by siding with the new; he ties his cinema to fundamentally different structures of art and perception. Recall that Konrad Lange held considerable sway over Japanese film theory even up until World War II. While many defending cinema as art did not agree with his early rejection of film, they nonetheless concurred that cinema's mechanical nature posed a problem for artistic creation. Even an advocate of mechanical art like Shimizu Hikaru, for instance, basically accepts that photography was in its essence not art, and argues that film artistically detached itself from reality only through montage.[25] Sugiyama Heiichi, who in 1941 marvelously prefigures André Bazin in his rejection of montage and his valorization of the long take, basically accepts Lange's definition of art but opines that the frame and the rhythms of the long take are sufficient to detach cinema from a slavish reproduction of reality.[26]

Gonda, however, reworks this by shifting the focus away from the problem of technological mimesis and toward the fundamental transformation of perception in modernity. Central in this is the emergence of a different way of looking at art, one that no longer desires the "aura" of unique works. Gonda learned from Marxism the importance of economic factors in accounting for cultural change, particularly in the historical stage of the capitalist mode of production. Capitalism, he argues, has turned every-thing—including art—into an industry, creating the conditions for the production of art that is inexpensive and easy to consume. The motion pictures are to him the epitome of this industrial art, mass-producing—on big budgets—spectacular images that are distributed widely at a low price (*Principles*, 447–448). This new mode of cultural production is accompanied by a uniquely capitalist pattern of consumption. Overworked and lacking the leisure time to become like the *tsū*, the cultural aficionados who domi-nated Edo culture, the capitalist working classes require entertainment that is immediate, requires no training, and is consumable in a short period of time (*Principles*, 409–410). By fulfilling these needs, cinema becomes the medium best suited to the lower classes. Unlike most of his contempo-raries, Gonda does not interpret this negatively, and shows little remorse for the disappearance of the Edo culture of refined and diligently acquired taste that he considered—pointing to the example of the restricted plea-sure quarters—elitist and alienated from everyday lived experience.[27]

A product of industrial capitalism, cinema can be consumed more freely by poorer Japanese. Because of its appearance, Gonda says, "the general, nonintellectual social classes have become the subject of entertainment" for the first time (*Principles*, 410). As Silverberg stresses, Gonda's definition of the "popular" was, like Ōsugi's, class-based well into the 1930s, reject-ing the homogenized and essentialized view of "Japanese culture" in favor of one that conceived of cultural consumption as marked by differences within Japan.[28] Gonda presents popular play and the civilization it repre-sents as properties of working-class culture, but he does so without echoing Theodor Adorno's fears about the culture industry: although disturbed by commercialism, Gonda also emphasizes that capitalism, by creating a truly mass class, has also created the opportunity for overcoming bourgeois art and creating a nonelitist, universal form of popular entertainment. The cinema would do just that, he says: "The moving pictures will eliminate horizontal and vertical divisions within culture," such as those between the upper and lower classes and between East and West (*Principles*, 452).

Gonda repeatedly underlines the radical difference of motion picture entertainment and the working-class culture with which it is aligned: To those who say it degrades cultural taste, he remarks that, through motion pictures, "old, moldy tastes have been smashed and a new, living taste cre-ated" (*Principles*, 9). To those who declare that film is not an art because of its relation to everyday life, he replies that it has transformed the notion of art itself.[29] Gonda ends *The Principles and Applications of the Moving Pictures* with a panegyric for the utopia promised by cinema:

> The present is a time when the notion of "beauty" is unsettled. Beauty related to the quiet, excellent, calm, rare, unique, or the nonpractical is finally losing its importance and meaning, and a new beauty concerned with what is mobile, stupendous, majestic, homogenous, and practical has, step-by-step, begun to move in our minds. An ax has been placed at the trunk of this old concept of beauty, and the time when the moving pictures are established as a brand new art founded in a universal culture is the moment when that ax will fell the old tree. (*Principles*, 453–454)

Modernity is different, Gonda contends, and cinema is the medium that best represents this new zeitgeist. Citing philosophers like Henri Bergson, as well as trends in contemporary life, he defines modernity through such key words as *intuition, pragmatism, the affirmation of ordinary life, movement,* and *apperception,* all of which, he argues, are embodied in the nature of the moving pictures (*Principles*, 443–444). His modernism is centered on the material, the body, the momentary, the experience of play in a flow of change.

Most crucial is Gonda's notion that the spectator's encounter with the silver screen is fundamentally productive: he emphasizes the ability of audiences to construct their own culture by reconfiguring the cheap amusements capitalism provides into meaningful parts of their class-based, lived experience. In his analysis of film as a social phenomenon, Gonda underlines the important role practical appropriation plays in defining the cinematic medium. How people see, talk about, and in general relate film to their everyday lives is central to how they experience cinema and how the motion pictures themselves fulfill their essential role. For this reason, Gonda emphasizes the crucial function of exhibition in film culture: "'Moving picture exhibition' is really where the moving pictures appear with the dignity of true moving pictures, where the way of life and feelings of modern people are strongly woven into the film" (*Principles*, 356). Cinema was thus in part defined through social practice, through presenting films in front of audiences who appropriated them for use in their own lives.

This does not mean that Gonda was uninterested in film aesthetics: a full section of *The Principles and Applications of the Moving Pictures* is in fact devoted to describing the unique art of cinema. Some of his conceptualizations are similar to those later found in Western classical film theory, such as the effort to define film through its binary opposition to theater, and the focus, similar to that found in Rudolf Arnheim, on the limitations of cinema as a source of its unique artistic potential. Yet much of his film aesthetics is aligned with his film sociology, especially where he stresses the economic and technological basis of motion picture art. "If moving picture drama possesses a unique art," he argues, "it must have been born from the mechanical characteristics that accompany the apparatus intended for projecting this art" (*Principles,* 393). Its technological limitations, particularly its lack of sound and color and the use of the frame, he notes, direct the cinema toward emphasizing only some of the aspects of things. What is present on the theatrical stage, in contrast, is visible in all its aspects. This central difference leads Gonda to conclude that cinema is an art of content (*naiyō*), and that theater is an art of form *(keishiki).*

Iwamoto Kenji correctly warns us that Gonda's usage of the loaded terms *form* and *content* differs from their usage in Western art theory, but his own interpretation that Gonda's ambiguous conception of "the art of content" is, in the end, only the art of surface, is insufficient.[30] If Gonda's "content" is in fact just "surface," then cinema's opposite, the stage, must logically be the art of depth and the internal. Gonda says the opposite, however: "The [world of] drama on the stage and the world in which the stage and the audience live are completely different worlds" (*Principles,* 405). Therein lies the reason, he claims, that theater spectators all cry at once, while moviegoers cry at different times according to gender and other differences:

> The stage is a unique world, and the tragedy occurs in the relations of cause and effect that penetrate that world. The people watching sympathize with this tragedy of the world of the stage, which is separated from their own lives. That is why they all become gloomy in the sad sections and cry when they should cry. In the photoplay, however, the self [*jiko*] is active. It dives into the drama amid the cause-and-effect relationships of a subjective world. But subjective content differs from person to person; the experiences of the self are individual. Accordingly, the results are individual and the way people cry differs in type. (*Principles,* 415)

Theater appreciation, then, is detached and performed at a distance; it is, in a sense, centered on the reading of form and symbols. Motion picture spectators, by contrast, consider the filmic space as contiguous to their own real world and, thus, instead of sympathizing with the characters, actually "cooperate" with them (*Principles,* 412). Gonda stresses that technological limitations such as the lack of depth, which prompt the viewer to actively make up for those restrictions to the filmic world, enable a profound form of spectator involvement: "Because of their work with the photoplay to turn the flat into the three-dimensional—an unconscious but difficult task—the viewers' selves are projected out. Then the emotional beauty and the beauty of content [*naiyōbi*] that people in the film drama express become nothing but the beauty of the subjective content and emotions of the spectators" (*Principles* 401). He argues that we cry at a film tragedy because of the experiences undergone by "characters who possess the same emotions as we do, whom we make act in the world we live in now" (*Principles,* 401). Film is essentially a subjective experience for Gonda, one in which each spectator inserts him or herself into the text in a unique way that depends on his or her real life experiences. Cinema is an art of "content" because of the important role of the content of subjective experience, and because of the literal meaning of the two ideographs that compose the Japanese term for "content," which translates literally as "put inside." It is an art that is direct and subjective, and that fundamentally involves the spectators putting themselves inside the film. Gonda's film aesthetics thus reiterates that the subjectivity of the motion pictures is defined by the projection of—the unification with—the subjectivity of real, individual spectators. As such, his conception of cinema as mass culture allows for far more heterogeneity or individual difference than is evident in what he sees as uniformly reacting theater audiences. Despite its massified form, cinema's ability to accommodate subjective participation epitomizes the vitality of mass culture.

This individuation of the film experience may be one way the aura of art sneaks back into Gonda's cinema. This distinguishes him from Walter Benjamin and from Nakai Masakazu, who, immediately after World War II, also saw audiences filling in the gaps in film (specifically, the lack of the copula [*be* as a connecting word or, in Japanese, *de aru*] or the spaces between shots), but on a mass, world-historical scale.[31] This may be a function of Gonda's inadequate digestion of Marxism, but it is also a reflection of his historical context and his stance on theory and civilization. For while Gonda may valorize individual experience, he does not celebrate the individual artist: his notion of modern subjectivity is based less on a vision of the singular creator investing unique works with intended meanings, and more on the conception of new consumers producing identity by incorporating mass-produced items into their everyday lives.

Some have had the impression that Gonda's film aesthetics lack the attention to the essence of cinema that subsequent film theorists would give. Nakamura Yōichi complains that Gonda did very little film analysis for someone who so valued the motion pictures as a mode of popular entertainment, and that he mostly treats cinema as an object of numerical research.[32] Iwamoto echoes this critique by arguing that, to Gonda, film in the end is not a problem of art but of entertainment.[33] In Gonda's defense, it is clear that his film aesthetics stress that cinema is less an aesthetically disinterested text (in the Kantian sense) meant for objective analysis than a means of enjoying meaning production by subjectively participating in the process. Gonda argues that cinema is a social phenomenon, not simply because masses of people can now enjoy it, but also because the social constitution of the spectators and, through them, of cinema in the real world are central factors in understanding film. This is one reason Gonda defines his form of film study as sociological.

Gonda, in the end, most likely refrained from film analysis because he refused to theorize the film text as the holder of meaning. In doing so he reflects a historical situation in which the concept of the auteur/director/screenwriter was not yet established, and cinematic meaning was still largely constructed in the space of exhibition, especially through the narration of the benshi. Yet given that Gonda was well aware of the criticisms leveled at the cinema, some by the neophyte critics in the Pure Film Movement, it is interesting that he did not fully seek their solution, which was to import the model of foreign cinema alongside aesthetic definitions borrowed from existing arts. Being a modernist who resisted the lure of the classical system, he resembles Inagaki Taruho, who in the late 1920s valorized early cinema against the manipulations of continuity editing.[34]

Gonda's focus on reception may embody his sociological perspective, but again, it is interesting that he refused to reduce spectator perception to a uniform phenomenon, despite the fact that he became famous for his statistical surveys of entertainment districts. This was a factor in his conception of cinema, which he contrasted with what he saw as the more homogeneous reception of theater. For Gonda, the lure of film civilization was that it was rooted in everyday life yet also transcended social instrumentality—because it was, quite simply, playful in a myriad of ways.

If his discourse was to help create this cinema, it too had to be rooted in the everyday while also being entertainment. *The Principles and Applications of the Moving Pictures* is written in a witty, colloquial style often structured as a conversation with the reader. The fact that he wrote "about popular matters in a popular mode" (*Principles*, 441) was a crucial element in his stance toward cinema and film study, not only because he wanted to avoid the elitism that cinema itself, he felt, was working against, but also because he wanted his theory to assume a homologous relation with its subject and become rooted in the everyday, a playful part of civilization.

This is a significant difference between *The Principles and Applications of the Moving Pictures* and the central book of the Pure Film Movement: Kaeriyama Norimasa's *Katsudō shashingeki no sōsaku to satsueihō* (The Production and Photography of Moving Picture Drama), which not only elevates the term *serious (majime)* to a mantra for reformers but is itself composed in deadly serious and frankly dull prose. Compared to Kaeriyama's lofty perspective, Gonda's is down to earth. Just as spectators appropriate the cinema for use in their own realities, Gonda inserts himself into debates on cinema, appropriates them, and becomes an interpreter of film. In fact, at one point he even likens himself to a benshi (see *Principles*, 15), as if the work of the theorist is similar to that of this narrator, intervening in the matrix between text and viewer, enabling a detached perspective while also playing with and creating the movie.

In narrating the cinema, Gonda even suggests it can escape his own discourse. As he explains film as an art suited for the working masses, he stresses that, in selecting topics to film, filmmakers must keep in mind that cinema, as an art of content, is emotional and intuitive: "It is inappropriate for the selected topics to spur the powers of association; they must be quickly understandable. Things that are symbolic or that require prior preparation are unsuitable; they must be intuitive. Topics that appeal to the intellect or powers of deduction are wrong; they must be expressed directly. To put it differently, the beauty that the moving picture play expresses must be intuitive and not symbolic" (*Principles*, 410). Cinema may have presented early Japanese film scholars with the problem of the image that exceeded discourse, but Gonda makes use of that to celebrate the motion pictures. It is precisely because film is the medium of the non-intellectual masses, and it is open to the bodily processes of emotion and intuition, that it resists definition by intellectual discourse. Escaping the restrictions of linguistic and symbolic description, cinema becomes an open field for the production of new kinds of meanings, ones fundamentally different from those prescribed by the dominant intellectual discursive field. Gonda's work reflects a unique moment in the 1910s when cinema, established as an object worthy of definition, was open to multiple readings and appropriations, and when audiences and exhibitors held considerable sway over what film would mean in Japanese society. Gonda respects this potential polyphony as a manifestation of both working-class culture and a nascent Japanese democracy. The cinema that he advocates would never really be pursued by pure film reformers, or even by Japanese film history, even though one could argue whether the continued presence of the benshi into the 1930s, or of popular, working-class film genres, such as popular *chanbara,* or swordplay films, might have represented aspects of Gonda's film civilization.

Tanizaki and the Alternative Cinematic

Gonda's approach represents a fascinating alternative to the burgeoning calls in film study for a pure cinema, an alternative that tried to find new forms of scholarship paralleling a modernity of the masses that challenged established modes of social and cultural control. But he was not alone in conceptualizing different cinemas—and different modernities—that went against the tide. I have already noted some affinity between Gonda and Inagaki Taruho, but later there were others on the left, such as Nakai Masakazu, who saw in film a great potential for the masses to become the subject of entertainment. Noting a lack in the enunciative structure of film—the absence of the copula—Nakai proposed that it was the viewing masses who filled this gap, in effect completing films that cinema could not itself complete.[35] I have noted elsewhere that novelists such as Akutagawa Ryūnosuke, in fictional works featuring cinema, also speculated on ambiguous aspects of cinematic enunciation, ones that allowed spectators to project, if not create, the film while also enveloping them in an uncontrollable and sometimes disturbing experience resembling the fantastic.[36]

Tom LaMarre has pursued a similar line with Tanizaki Jun'ichirō's writings on film, both fictional and nonfictional. Trying to find a middle road between my questioning of the historic formation of cinematic essentialism and Joanne Bernardi's assumptions about the Pure Film Movement's role in the evolutionary progression of cinema, he asks whether it is "possible to write a history based on cinematic apparatus or medium that does not turn into a teleological narrative about the gradual attainment of the true nature of essence of cinema." He does so by arguing that Tanizaki "draws attention to the cinematic rather than to cinema. If cinema has an essence, it is a vague material essence, hardly like essence in the usual sense. . . . In sum, if the materiality of cinema somehow determines film form, it is an underdetermination, as it were." At issue in Tanizaki's interest in pure film "is not just cinema but the cinematic, not just what is optically conscious, but what is optically unconscious."[37] The notion of the cinematic, then, allows LaMarre to foreground cinema's unique materiality without falling into essentialism and its necessary historical teleology.

As in his earlier formulations of the anime-ic,[38] LaMarre is attempting to map out different positions within historical conflicts over the moving image. It is a difficult task, and I don't think LaMarre always succeeds,[39] but

I do believe his attempts open productive avenues for reappraising theorists like Gonda or Nagae Michitarō, who, in the late 1930s, also attempted to formulate a different film theory by walking a perilous line while avoiding essentialism and still contemplating the essence of cinema.[40] But there are problems with Tanizaki's approach that are also apparent in Gonda's. LaMarre takes great care to note how Tanizaki's important essay "The Present and the Future of the Moving Pictures"[41] can be read as privileging the cinema over the cinematic, or vice versa. The end of his chapter on the essay, however, describes it as a choice, even though this might not have always been the case. The fact that many of the points Tanizaki argues—he criticizes Japanese film for using *onnagata* and imitating theater, and thus for not giving cinema its own proper place in the arts; advocates the use of natural landscapes; calls for a ban on benshi; and supports efforts to export Japanese cinema—are fully in line with the pure film discourse of the day. Thus the vast majority of his readers, recognizing the genre of his text, would have read it accordingly.[42] We should remember that Tanizaki, just like anyone else we encounter in this book, was not in full command of how his writings were read. The Pure Film Movement was not merely an aesthetic advocacy group but a force within the cinematic social field that, even if not always consciously, took advantage of existing institutions (such as the police) and values (of bourgeois or national society) to press its case and achieve a critical mass that influenced how films were made and thought about. This also influenced how discourse on film would be written and read. Tanizaki was inevitably imbricated in these discursive matrices, especially with nonfictional works like "The Present and the Future of the Moving Pictures." (I believe fictional works like "The Tumor with a Human Face" are actually more complex articulations of cinema, perhaps because generically they are better able to escape these matrices.)

This is particularly evident when Tanizaki uses words like *abolish* and *prohibit* with regard to the existence or actions of the benshi. While this may be an issue separate from LaMarre's notion of underdetermination, in the realm of real world articulation of cinema Tanizaki was like many pure film reformers in calling for the exercise of power to determine the form of cinema according to its essence. This could easily invade the realm of the optical unconscious precisely because, as we shall see in the coming chapters, such uses of force ultimately also entailed conscious efforts to regulate how spectators perceived cinema, entertainment, and even the world of sight and sound (for instance, how they might have defined the cinematic as an aural experience by patronizing verbose narrators) not only in the theater but also in their everyday lives. I believe Gonda, who was generally critical of top-down impositions of aesthetic values, was much more sensitive to these issues than Tanizaki, but even he could be seduced by the promise of realizing the cinematic he loved through the exercise of power. That is how difficult it was to avoid the authoritative matrices of the Pure Film Movement.

Film Study as the Dominant Mode

Gonda thus offers a form of film study in which he not only attempts to approximate the playful entertainment he is researching—hoping film study would become down-to-earth and as much a part of everyday life as the movies—but also strategically takes on prevailing forms of discourse and scholarship from within. The question remains, however, whether Gonda's scholarly play is fully able to critique and avoid the contemporary pitfalls of the dominant modes of film thinking, or whether he, perhaps unwittingly, ends up only reinforcing the very structures of discursive power constraining popular culture that he criticizes. If Gonda is a liminal figure in a diachronic sense, embodying possibilities both old and new during a crucial transitional stage in Japanese film history, perhaps he is also that synchronically too, traversing multiple and sometimes contradictory contemporary positions in defining cinema, modernity, and the intellectual approach to those subjects.

Gonda brazenly announces his "hope to oppose and correct society's mistaken attitude toward moving picture entertainment" (*Principles*, 13), but he nevertheless worked from the assumption that film is a problem that requires study to be resolved. Nowhere does he deny that cinema creates trouble, and thus from the start he worked within the framework of an agenda that defined film negatively, even if he would occasionally downplay the severity of this problem or lay the blame on others outside the medium. This was in part how he justified his investigation, if not film study itself: as a means to solve the problem of film. *The Principles and Applications of the Moving Pictures*, then, is a defensive work, an apologia for cinema aimed at legitimizing its presence in the cultural field, but one framed by an initial negation of cinema. Throughout the work, Gonda attempts to locate what is responsible for these cinematic social ills.

While he focuses on the audience's ability to appropriate cinema and use it in their lives as one of the medium's positive aspects, he also cites particular forms of appropriation as its negative side. For instance, he blames the developmental stagnation of cinematic civilization on both "the audience's crime of assuming a mistaken attitude toward entertainment and the misdeeds of moviemakers with wrong ideas" (*Principles*, 345). The "discreet source of these mistakes," he goes on to say, "is in intending to make and see motion picture dramas as substitutes for dramas on the stage. . . . They have not noticed that the moving pictures possess a unique art" (*Principles*, 346). In this way, Gonda distinguishes between proper and improper appropriations of film, laying the blame for cinema's status as a social ill on its incorrect usage more than on the medium.

Gonda also focuses on mistaken modes of appropriation in his 1917 survey of the effects of motion pictures on Tokyo children. In his survey as a whole, he takes pains to present both the positive and negative aspects of the motion pictures. For instance, while lauding film's ability to educate minors about foreign cultures or Japanese history, he also warns that it could spread values like equality or individualism that could undercut Japanese social mores. Similarly, the complex scene changes found in cinema could on the one hand spur children's ability to concentrate by demanding their constant attention, but on the other these scene changes could have the opposite effect if the editing proved too difficult to follow.[43] As a whole, Gonda takes great efforts to discount many of the prevalent fears about the cinema, primarily by drawing attention away from the medium and focusing it on the conditions of reception. In surveying juvenile delinquents *(furyō shōnen)* here and in other surveys, he casts significant doubt on the prevailing opinion that cinema, not the social and economic factors in the child's environment, led to crime by minors.[44] Because he pictures film as a social phenomenon, Gonda argues that, if the motion pictures are harmful, this is due to the "atmosphere" of the theater itself: "Children receive a more pernicious influence from the moving pictures in the act of going to the movie theater and having contact with the atmosphere inside than from the film itself" (*GYC*, 1:89). While he fears that kids could become habitual moviegoers, forsaking school and family for the lure of the silver screen, Gonda is less concerned about the children who avidly watch the film from the front row than about the youngsters who "do not pay much attention to the picture, but eat something, occasionally and very coolly looking at developments in the film while talking with friends about something, or, as if enjoying the atmosphere inside the theater, taking an attitude completely unrelated to the picture and playing in the dark with their friends" (*GYC*, 1:87). Again refusing to place the source of these kinds of behavior in the text, Gonda asserts that cinema becomes a social problem more in the way it is appropriated in reception than because of its essence. Film could be transformed into a social good by regulating the methods and environment of spectatorial textual appropriation more than by simply censoring the text.

The question then becomes, which methods and contexts are appropriate, who determines this, what means of correction are proposed, and what are the sociopolitical implications of the answers? First, Gonda urges film viewers to cease watching films as if they were theater performances; cinema, he says, requires a mode of viewing proper to it. In its complaints, Gonda's 1917 study implies that spectators should watch films in silence, forget the space of the theater, and immerse themselves in the text (becoming one, as noted earlier, with the characters). That means, logically, that audiences should refrain from behavior that would block the effect of the film, thus allowing what was inherent in the text to work on them. One can argue that this dictum was just Gonda's effort to prod spectators to experience what was uniquely marvelous about the medium, and to curb more detached modes of viewing so as to "put themselves" into the film and perceive it directly and intuitively. Yet in this effort, he places greater emphasis on the essential workings of cinema than on its social or contextual definition. While celebrating the subjective freedom of audiences to create their own text, Gonda is simultaneously placing limits on that liberty, establishing norms by which spectators must corral their subjectivity if the motion pictures are to evolve. Thus, he does not envision audiences reading against the grain, especially in a collective fashion. His conception of subjective appropriations of films presumes that audiences, even with their individual differences, would remain a silent, noninteracting mass, one that respects the homogeneous, universal nature of cinema. The subjectivity he assumes, is closer to that of the modern consumer in the age of mass production than to the subjectivity of the members of the spectatorial public sphere that Miriam Hansen has described in such cases of silent-film reception as the cult surrounding Rudolph Valentino.[45]

Gonda sees film study as a corrective to these mistaken forms of appropriation, providing standards for determining what is proper and how mistakes can be corrected. Those who remain oblivious to the unique character of cinema and insist on producing canned theater are guilty of insufficient study: "Although they unconsciously use these special qualities [of cinema], there is not one who fully studies this unique art and endeavors to use it satisfactorily. This is an utterly lamentable situation. In order for the moving pictures to break away from the age of luxury and dilettantes and truly enter the age of entertainment, there must be a stage of study" (*Principles*, 346).

In Gonda's case, film study is itself a form of reception, of cinematic appropriation, helping the motion pictures become a more essential part of everyday existence. Yet as a means of aiding the evolution of film, it is an inherently different form of film use. First, film study, unlike many appropriations of cinema, is a mode of correction, aiming to alter both audiences and cinema; it chastises mistaken filmmakers, but it also betters film by improving how texts are viewed. This conception of film study presupposes a hierarchy of knowledge in which those who have performed this mode of appropriation earn the authority to comment on or correct other modes of living with cinema. Despite Gonda's efforts to the contrary, hierarchies begin to enter into his analysis.

Gonda was certainly aware of the dangers of hierarchies for the future of entertainment. Especially in the 1920s, he repeatedly opposed efforts by the state and intellectuals to manage entertainment, calling them "authoritarian" strategies to force their "personal tastes onto the general populace" and to "apply unity to the thoughts of the people that have recently been given to disorder" (*GYC*, 1:65). Rejecting definitions of popular entertainment that made bourgeois art the art for all, Gonda asserts that entertainment is not given from above, but grows from below as a fundamentally democratic phenomenon.[46] Yet by stressing the central role of knowledge in the future of entertainment, he opens the door to the control of popular play by those who claim special access to knowledge—by those with the power to speak and articulate cinema. At times he does argue that those educators who, picturing cinema as a vulgar entertainment, deem it unworthy of their involvement are largely to blame for the problem of cinema (*Principles*, 12–13), but this charge still assumes that their intervention is then necessary for the motion pictures to advance. He seems to admit as much when, in advocating cinema as a tool of moral improvement, he advises intellectuals to identify which films are morally uplifting (*Principles*, 289). It should be noted that Gonda later took on this role himself as a member of the Ministry of Education's film recommendation board.

Here we see reflected in thought the contradictions evident in Gonda's own life: a rejection of state management of entertainment paired with his participation in that very endeavor. Part of the problem is Gonda's inability to fully politicize the concepts of the popular and the masses, but it also stems from his failure to sufficiently interrogate the concept of study. At best, his stance is deeply ambivalent: although seeking to redefine the terms used to describe cinema through his own, possibly alternative practice of film study, he neither delves into the implications of his own use of the concept of "serious study" nor repeats the kind of study as play that he postulates in his first book. Power is defined mostly as a property of institutions, not of knowledge itself; as a result, he describes research as an issue of power primarily when it is directly attached to bureaucratic efforts to manage popular play. While Gonda distances himself from other statistical studies of entertainment performed by government agencies, he remains oblivious to the problems inherent in his own statistical research on Japanese culture.

Kakimoto Akihito's analysis of one of Gonda's contemporary "ethnographers of modernity," Kon Wajirō, can help us elaborate on this point.[47] If the role of early Japanese journalistic reports on lower-class culture was to bring what was foreign or "outside" normal society into language, albeit as the "Other," Kakimoto argues that the function of later, more scientific studies of modern urban life was to return that Other to the realm of the normal. Borrowing from Foucault, he argues that Kon assumes the modern role of the "priest" *(bokujin)*. Instead of preaching religion, the "priest" uses science to preach public health, welfare, and state administration of culture and life. The role of knowledge, particularly statistical research, is central to this new function. Kon's meticulous surveys of what people wore on the streets of Ginza may have sought to describe cultural differences in scientific terms, but they also go beyond that to establish averages and norms by which those differences are to be understood. The effect of stating which hat most laborers from Fukugawa wore is in part the implication that such workers *should* wear that kind of hat if they are workers. People's group, sex, and class are neatly defined by their tastes and apparel, allowing the priest-researcher to establish order in contemporary fashion, which, as Kon complains, is too often disorderly. In Kakimoto's analysis, the priest-researcher then functions to ensure the efficient and rational organization of society by rendering evident its structure in statistics. In the end, Kon hoped to restructure modern society on the model he most admired: the Fordian assembly line—ever moving (with the changing fashions) yet eminently rational.

It is true that Gonda differs from Kon and other researchers of modernity. Rejecting their distanced, objective form of observation, he emphasizes his role as a participant; as evidenced by his witty and enjoyable writing in *Principles and Applications of the Moving Pictures,* there was a side to Gonda's character that enjoyed the delightful chaos of the modern entertainment forms he studied. This is partly represented in his conception of the "masses" *(minshū)*. As Nakamura Yōichi perceptively observes, Gonda recognizes the differences reflected in class-based appropriations of entertainment, but he often reduces his democratic "popular play" to the pleasure of the mob, the free-wheeling so-called *eejanaika* spirit of no distinctions, no purpose, and no meaning.[48] This puts him at a distance from the Fordist vision of an ordered modernity—which was pursued by Kon in writing about the Ginza—and thus closer to the "obscene" modernity of Asakusa.[49] One could possibly see Gonda's focus on subjective spectatorial appropriation in cinematic experience as not just the figuring of a new consumer subject who projects herself though her tastes, placing herself in what she is consuming, but also the imagining of a mass that is unruly because it is playful and composed of individuals never completely reacting according to plan. This distinguishes him from later theorists like Itagaki Takao, Shimizu Hikaru, and even Nakai Masakazu, whose attraction to cinema as machine art stems from the hope that the machine could level cultural inequalities, could take artistic agency away from the privileged elite and place it in the hands of a mass that acts with mechanical rationality. Gonda believed working-class spectators could enforce such leveling by themselves by taking advantage of the inherent amorphousness of cinema, the holes and imprecision that allow all spectators to fill in gaps in the film individually and make it part of the everyday.

Yet just as Gonda was uninterested in individual critiques of films, he cared less for these particular subjective appropriations of films than for the experience of participating in a moving, often chaotic unity, one not dissimilar to becoming part of the ever-changing world on screen. This captivated Gonda and prompted him to sometimes lose, in a utopian vision of a universal equality, the real social distinctions evident in how different sectors of the "masses" mobilize films in different ways, depending on class, gender, or region. The subjectivity of culture shifted from particular spectators to the amorphous "masses" with no in-between, a subjectivity enabled by a definition of cinema that ignored its particular manifestations (films) or its genres. Undoubtedly, it was Gonda's enchantment with the phenomenon of the masses that prompted his interest in both Marxism and fascism. Perhaps his film study and statistical research were a means of finding a medium between pure atomism and the Fordist mass, but one still senses in his work the persistent desire to make things clear and knowable. Gonda was decidedly part of a larger "survey boom" centered on the first national census in 1920, in which, as the *Tokyo asahi shinbun* notes, for the first time "the emperor and the four classes are recorded as equals on paper."[50] If Gonda did not look to the machine to level cultural hierarchies, and if he found fault with spectators (who seemed stuck in pursuing mistaken forms of appropriation), then study presented itself as an effective tool of postulating cultural equality in the form of norms of cinema and film viewing. The problem, however, was that the subjectivity of culture then shifted to the "priests" (here, the film scholars), who could guide film and its audiences to civilization. Thus while Gonda attempted to resist the

Fordist modernity of the rationalized mass by celebrating a mass of individual players—an alternative modernity of motion that escapes top-down control—he could not conceive of or even possibly accept play mobilizing itself in a historically significant fashion, either en masse or in different sociologically based spheres. Authoritative figures who could tell the masses what to be were not necessary; what was needed were scholars who led them to be what they were—according to the rationality of study.

Silverberg rightly emphasizes that modern ethnographers like Kon and Gonda, by conceiving culture as construction, refused to analyze mass consumer culture through essentialist dichotomies like "Japan" and "the West." Yet in emphasizing the content of their thought in relation to the problem of the nation, she sometimes loses sight of the ideological functions of ethnographic research in relation to society and culture that Kakimoto details. Missing is a larger appreciation of the discursive field of research in which the two scholars operated. It is unfortunate that she does not consider *The Principles and Applications of the Moving Pictures* in her work on Gonda, because it is in this book that Gonda's contradictory relationship to the audience/consumers he studies and the academic field/research field he inhabits (especially the Pure Film Movement) best comes to light.

Film study assumed such importance in Gonda's outline of cinema history because it delineated the norms around which the masses would mobilize, providing some trajectory for the modern mob of individual spectators reading themselves in cinema, and leading them toward civilization. But the process of collating their behavior, and subjecting it to the strictures of knowledge, threatened to undermine what Gonda valued in the motion picture experience. In order to combat conceptions of popular culture that proposed a top-down imposition of knowledge and ideology on the masses, he described a new medium—the cinema—that uniquely enabled the masses to insert themselves in culture, to build it according to their everyday lives. But that very privileging of the inside of cinema, its essential acceptance of the masses' subjectivity within itself, led Gonda to reject other modes of appropriation on the surface or borders of film (or in the theaters) that did not take advantage of this internality, perhaps because they were not that new (since they may not have involved new forms of perception) or were more disturbingly public forms of personal politics. When he did that, Gonda not only subjected audiences to his appropriation of cinema, but he also postulated a cinema that should restrict the receptive freedom of spectators, a move that ultimately made his film theory the first step away from a cinema defined in the sphere of reception, toward one defined by an essence, one that pure film critics would eventually locate in the realm of production. This, then, signaled the increasing focus on defining both the inside, or essence, of cinema, and the modern subjects who could enter into that new world and be shaped by it internally.

Gonda's conception of film study was fundamentally ambiguous. On the one hand, it presented itself as a mode of rewriting that might reconfigure the language that damned the cinema so as to create a discourse promoting the motion pictures' role in a new civilization. On the other, the definition of film as a social problem necessitated structuring film studies as a mode of correction, establishing hierarchies of knowledge on the basis of the essence of the medium. This threatened to regulate the very kinds of subjective creation of film that Gonda celebrated. He attempted to formulate a definition of film that, emphasizing the ways in which the motion pictures are emotionally and intuitively read, celebrated the image's playfulness and resistance to discourse; yet in responding to attacks on the medium through discourse, he was forced to establish a linguistically based film study as the authority over the image's reception and cinematic evolution. Given the structure of the intellectual field at the time, the dilemma was that the definition of cinema as a social problem—one that exceeded the range of discourse—demanded a response in discourse that unhesitatingly established such linguistically based studies as the keepers of cinematic knowledge. Gonda's film study attempted to halt this trend, but ended up becoming part of it, as his work made way for the critics of the Pure Film Movement.

3　Studying the Pure Film

Despite his unique approach to the question of cinema as a sociohistoric phenomenon, Gonda Yasunosuke was confined to the discourse of the intellectual field in 1910s Japan because his audience was already discussing the moving pictures in ways that laid the foundation for the Pure Film Movement. Although there are crucial distinctions between Gonda and many of his contemporaries, when he expounded on "the unique art of the moving pictures" (*Principles,* 347) it was not difficult to consider him, as the historian Chiba Nobuo has, as the first one "to light the signal fire for pure film dramas."[1] Like many other Japanese intellectuals, Gonda was highly dissatisfied with the Japanese film product, commenting, "Be it the photography, or the dramatic construction, or the use of props, Japanese films are still utterly incapable of being equal to foreign pictures" (*Principles,* 386). Gonda was also a strong influence, Chiba argues, on the main organ for the Pure Film Movement, *Kinema Record.*[2]

Arguments that fundamentally supported the position of the Pure Film Movement were being presented in public even before Gonda's book or *Kinema Record* appeared. A special issue of *Shumi,* for example, mentioned in chapter 1, also featured articles by the theater director Osanai Kaoru and the children's novelist Ogawa Mimei, both of which hint at a growing desire for a pure cinema. Osanai, who later helped found the Bungei Katsudō Shashinkai (Literary Moving Pictures Society) in 1912,[3] confesses in the magazine in 1909 that, whereas watching foreign films gave him the sense "there is a more natural, freer, and brighter world than the one I live in, . . . Japanese works I bump into make me sick before long."[4] In the piece after Osanai's, Ogawa argues, perhaps in the spirit of Georges Meliès, "For theater, there is the field of theater. For dance, the field of dance. Of course, the moving pictures must also have their own territory. I believe that the field of the moving pictures is what theater or dance cannot do, namely what human bodies cannot do, but what a machine for the first time can, such as [what is evident] in those comedies, magic, or adventure films. It is fascinating when it takes something quite fantastic and presents it as real."[5] Ogawa, however, was not ready to call film an independent art: "It is only a *misemono* using the machines of civilization. It is not a work of art. From the standpoint of taste, it is the same as the acrobats in Asakusa: you just look and enjoy."[6] Still, film was being accredited with the ability to do what other arts could not.

Many of the articles in *Katsudō shashinkai,* too, were harbingers of the Pure Film Movement, although the number of different opinions reveals both how eclectic the magazine was and how divisions in intellectual discourse about film still existed at the start of the 1910s. While *Katsudō shashinkai* was technically the publicity organ of Yoshizawa Shōten (and there were plenty of articles praising the company and its output), it also featured submissions by the founders of *Kinema Record,* Kaeriyama Nori-masa and Shigeno Yukiyoshi, as well as many commentaries on cinema by leading writers and artists, who did not hesitate to criticize contemporary Japanese motion pictures. Sōma Gyofū, a poet and literary critic, pointedly explains his preferences: "I go to the moving pictures to see Western pictures. But since the recent trend has gradually gone against my tastes, and Japanese pictures are gaining vitality [at the box office], I cannot help but be bored. It would be all right if Japanese films were made with the moving pictures in mind, but I am stunned that all of them without exception are useless copies of *kyūha* and *shinpa.* This way may go down well with the vulgar crowd, but we cannot help but get tired of it."[7]

Sōma explains his repugnance for Japanese films, foreshadowing the comments of some of the most vociferous pure film reformers, with his claim that they were not "moving pictures," that they were canned theater and not cinema. His was a siege mentality, in which the "vulgar crowd" was not only ignoring the cinema but also forcing its tastes on Sōma and his colleagues by economically promoting the production of such films. The novelist Inaoka Nunosuke echoes Sōma's use of the pronoun "we" with his use of "us," declaring, "I think it would be best to give up on Japanese theater films. Movies imitating theater are of absolutely no interest to us, and it is not good to show them to children either. . . . In general, those who try to see theater through the moving pictures are mistaken."[8] Although there were a few defenders of Japanese filmed theater,[9] most intellectual movie fans throughout the 1910s professed bewilderment over why anyone would even like such works. They were, after all, as a writer who called himself Yanagi dryly comments, "vastly inferior to foreign-made films in three points: one, imperfect focus; two, lack of a difference between light and dark; and three, the scarcity of energy."[10] In offering a goal for Japanese cinema to advance toward, Yanagi later proposes, "It will only be when Japanese-made films can be exported abroad as commodities that we can say that they have reached a stage of completion."[11] The standard by which Japanese motion pictures could be recognized as cinema, as repeatedly stressed by *Kinema Record* a few years later, would be their ability to stand shoulder to shoulder with American and European films on the international marketplace.

Beyond being poorly photographed imitations of third-rate theater, Japanese films presumably could not sell abroad because of their dependency on the benshi, who in those days had begun adopting a style for Japanese pictures that involved mimicking in synchronization the voices of the actors in a style called *kowairo* (benshi for foreign films, however, often used a different, more descriptive style). A writer of family novels, Yanagawa Shun'yō, adds his opinion: "Using tactics such as *kowairo* in the shadows is actually indescribably hideous. By nature, the moving pictures are something that can surely be understood by viewers without *kowairo*, and sometimes without even narrated explanation: with just expressions and actions. . . . The reason that [Japanese films] cannot be understood without explanation or *kowairo* is, in the end, because the actors are bad."[12] To poor acting was added the charge that benshi were ill educated. In launching an attack on the benshi—even ones for foreign films—the sort of thing that would become de rigueur for reformist film critics for decades—the artist Tokunaga Ryūshū charges: "Most of the benshi narrators are uneducated. It is unfortunate that, since they often commit errors in explaining the facts and incidents of foreign lands, they are teaching lies to children."[13] Already, a vision was being formulated of a cinema that did not need benshi to be understood. Echoing this, the actor Fujii Rokusuke comments, "I think pictures are good without dialogue. If at all possible, I'd like to do one that could be completely understood without dialogue or any explanation."[14]

Many of the above points would be taken up by the critics in the Pure Film Movement: the assertion of an essence unique to the cinema, the use of foreign film as the standard for condemning Japanese output, the hierarchy of taste, the criticism of the benshi, and the call for films that could be understood without the benshi. Among Japanese intellectuals, a discursive consensus was forming which a scholar like Gonda could not ignore, one that recognized major problems in the motion pictures. As a discursive picture of the cinema, however, it was still incomplete: little mention was made in the early years about issues such as film authorship, proper spectatorship (other than by Gonda, of course), the nature of the cinematic text, and the role of criticism. Film reformers associated with the Pure Film Movement would develop these as the decade progressed. Their definition of film study provided the basis for a new class-based conception of the audience, cinema, and modernity, one that tied into visions of social power and hierarchy. First let us look at what these Japanese films that upset reformers so much were like.

Japanese Cinema before Reform

A certain image of a film style may come to mind when reading these critiques of Japanese film production: that of the oft-mentioned "canned theater," in which the camera is placed at a distance and films the actors at length in a long shot, the resulting work resembling a series of tableaux typical of theatrical films such as those by the French organization Film d'Art. It is hard to fully verify this impression, however, because almost none of the films to which the writers in *Katsudō shashinkai* or *Kinema Record* refer still exist. Some of the few films or fragments that remain, such as M. Pathé's *Kyūgeki Taikōki jūdanme: Amagasaki no dan* (The Tenth Act of Taikōki, 1908) or M. Kashii's *Sendai hagi: Goten no ba* (Troubles of the Date Clan, the Palace Scene, 1915), both period films, seem to confirm this impression, being largely one-scene works of actors performing famous theatrical scenes in long shot. But it is hard to generalize from such a small corpus. It is, however, helpful to examine an outline of this sort of work in order to better understand the background of the Pure Film Movement.

We can begin by piecing together contemporary accounts with recollections offered by critics and filmmakers, but we must be wary of how much the perspective of the Pure Film Movement, which decidedly shaped much of subsequent discourse on film, colored the image of early Japanese film found even in film histories written decades later. For instance, the director Kinugasa Teinosuke's memoirs of his days performing as an *onnagata* in *shinpa* productions at Nikkatsu's Mukōjima studio in the late 1910s are often quoted in histories of the era.[15] Films made there (probably four to five reels in length), he said, were shot in only five or so days with no rehearsals or retakes. Production consisted of continually photographing the actors in a long shot until the scene ended; if the scene lasted longer than the two-hundred-foot film magazine, actors were asked to freeze until the film was reloaded. No effort was made to vary camera angle or distance, so the performers had to face the camera as if facing an audience. Such anecdotes are intriguing, but they're also suspicious given that they present 1910s cinema only as an aberrant curiosity. Their rhetoric ultimately works to anticipate the film style that will "improve" on these practices and does not describe early Japanese cinema in its particular historical conjuncture.

Komatsu Hiroshi's historical accounts of early Japanese film style provide a much clearer picture of the era. He estimates that the average number of scenes per reel was six or seven in the years around 1910, just when film length was increasing to two to three reels per film. Since experiments in scenes with multiple shots had already been reported in 1909, this did not necessarily indicate the number of *shots* per reel. The popularity of *Zigomar* and the introduction of the chase film prompted an increase in the number of scenes per reel, but such changes were not always permanent, and the number varied depending on the genre. Komatsu claims that in Kabuki-influenced *kyūha* productions between 1908 and 1915, "almost no change or progress was seen in the mode of representation, except in terms of length."[16]

With his research, Komatsu has aimed to formulate a stylistic model of early Japanese film, relating it on most occasions to the patterns or forms of traditional performing arts. This "Kabuki cinema" was based on a rigid representational code that structured formal choices in filmmaking. He sees the use of *oyama* or *onnagata* (terms describing male actors playing female roles), for instance, as not just a holdover from Kabuki but also a practice that prevented the development of close-ups or other devices that could undermine *oyama* by emphasizing physical realism over the abstract femininity that the practice had traditionally signified.[17] The traditional code also shaped the relationship of image, word, and narrativity in this period: "The traditional form of Japanese film did not aim for a cinema narrated only by images. The linguistic aspect of the image was borne by the dialogue of the benshi such that the images themselves were merely the illustration of an independently existing story. Films were articulated into scenes that were largely equivalent to chapters, with the intertitles signifying the titles of those chapters."[18] Such a description seems verified by our experience today: when one tries to watch the few films that exist from the 1910s, one rarely has a clear idea of what is going on narratively. The images do not narrate on their own, depending instead on either the benshi or prior knowledge by spectators (or both) for the transmission of narrative information.

Komatsu's emphasis on a traditional code aligns him somewhat with Noël Burch. While he does not go so far as to, like Burch, claim for films of the 1910s an unbroken lineage with Heian-era aesthetics or a political status of the sort bolstered by Burch's mixture of Roland Barthes and Marxism, he nonetheless reads these traditional film practices as operating in opposition to Western cinema. While I believe it is important to explore the ways 1910s cinema was described by its proponents and opponents, we should take care in labeling all examples of older Japanese performance modes in cinema as "traditional." The term is in danger of reducing the variety of cultural practices at the time to a "modern/traditional" split, when, as we have seen, both aspects of this popular film culture were already being termed disturbingly "new" from the beginning of the decade. Komatsu refreshingly avoids the polemicization of history evident in writings published in the wake of the Pure Film Movement, but, ironically, he allows pure film critics and their followers to lay claim to modernization, even though, as we shall see, other modes of cinema were proposing different experiences of modernity.

It is important to see how even this "traditional" cinema was itself a form of modernity. That it was, is evident first in the fact that its dominant form was an "invented tradition," in Eric Hobsbawm's sense of the term.[19] The majority of Japanese movies in the 1910s were presented with *kagezerifu* (literally, "shadow dialogue") or *kowairo* (voice imitation) benshi narration, where usually multiple benshi used different imitated voices to practically dub the dialogue of the characters on-screen. Given that many—but not all—of the stories used in films came from either the Kabuki or the *shinpa* theater, this dialogue functioned to enhance the impression of seeing a live performance, an experience further augmented in some cases by other theatrical trappings, such as Kabuki curtains, clappers *(hyōshigi)*, or music *(hayashi)*. In this way, the motion pictures, with their lower ticket prices, could have functioned as a poor man's theater starting around 1908, when, as the story goes, Hanai Hideo began presenting Nakamura Kasen's Kabuki films, performed by a female troupe, with *kagezerifu*.[20]

We have seen that cinema was discussed at first as merely another of a myriad of *misemono* that preexisted its arrival, so it was not immediately inserted into traditional theatrical frameworks. Elements of existing theater, from actors to stories, entered into film, and even *Momijigari* (1899)—one of Japan's earliest existing films recording the illustrious actors Ichikawa Danjūrō IX and Onoe Kikugorō V, and which was not originally made for public presentation—was once screened as a substitute for a theatrical performance when Danjūrō fell ill, but utilization of theatrical practices became systematic only after 1908. It was an invented system, one that attracted audiences not just because it was known but also because

Figure 5.   Cinema as Kabuki: a postcard still of Kabuki actors Ichikawa Danjūrō IX and Onoe Kikugorō V performing *Momijigari* (photographed by Shibata Tsunekichi in 1899). (Iwamoto Kenji, ed., *Shashin, kaiga shūsei: Nihon eiga no rekishi* [Tokyo: Nihon Tosho Sentā, 1998])

it was new—the spectacle of shadows speaking, of the movies imitating theater. If it carried on an established tradition, it was initially less that of Kabuki than of the *misemono:* the thrill of experiencing what was known not to be theater become *like* theater was categorically similar to the pleasure of seeing a papier-mâché doll seemingly come to life. Remember that *kowairo* Kabuki theater had its origins in Asakusa, that "obscene" realm of noise and mixture.

This experience generally reinforced Kabuki cinema's relations with theater in the 1910s; it became, like other invented traditions, naturalized and seemingly always already there. To its critics especially, it became the sign of the old that must be supplanted by the truly new. Kabuki cinema had established itself enough in the entertainment world that, by 1911, it became a threat, and the Tokyo theatrical actors' guild banned its members from appearing in this rival form.[21] Kabuki cinema had likely codified its existence, as audiences became used to reading this spectacle as theatrical, but the codes were probably not as strict as Komatsu contends, and did not prevent other elements from entering the set cinematic experience, because mixture was part and parcel of the contemporary filmgoing experience. Not only did the consciousness that these were movies masquerading as theater never disappear, but also, with the average film bill in the 1910s consisting of a mixture of Japanese and foreign fare (the latter of which was often not presented with *kowairo* benshi), even fans of *kyūha* movies had to switch codes of reception to watch *shinpa*, a Max Linder movie, or the live performance that may have also been on the program. Most spectators were accustomed to the various signifying practices of these films. Even the theatrical world in the 1910s was a hodgepodge of different possibilities, with Noh and different levels of Kabuki (from the high to the low class) coexisting with Shingeki (a European-influenced form of realist theater championed by Shimamura Hōgetsu, Osanai Kaoru, and others) and other new forms like Asakusa Opera (a form of operetta that greatly influenced the musical stage), Takarazuka (an all-woman musical theatrical troupe) and Shinkokugeki (a more realistic form of sword drama established by Sawada Shōjirō).

One can see these mixtures in the films of the time. We are fortunate that at least two feature-length films exist from the 1910s: Yokota Shōkai's *Chūshingura* (Tale of the Loyal Forty-seven Retainers) and Tenkatsu's *Gorō Masamune kōshiden* (The Story of the Filial Child Gorō Masamune). Burch discusses the former film, based on the famous story of the Akō vassals who faithfully and patiently revenged their wronged lord. He points to its occasional use of reverse-field editing and concertinas as evidence that Japanese directors knew Hollywood techniques and used them as dramatic effects, but never "as a system," the work ultimately remaining in the realm of the primitive.[22] Nowhere in his analysis, however, does he relate the fact that the existing prints are in fact compilations of several versions of *Chūshingura* from the 1910s, all probably directed by Makino Shōzō and starring Onoe Matsunosuke, which were reedited after the coming of sound and released with a *kowairo* benshi soundtrack.[23] Given that shots within some scenes (such as Asano's attack on Kira, which includes an apparent match cut to a medium close-up of Kira and a medium close-up shot of another official) are clearly from different films (we can see that even costumes have changed between shots), it is difficult to determine if these stylistic elements were present in any of the original films that make up the current version. Within the shot, much of the framing does tend to maintain the theatrical proscenium: the actors are filmed in what is close to an extreme long shot that keeps the top half of the frame empty and makes it very difficult to read their faces. Yet there clearly was, at least in some of the films that make up the current text, a certain variation in framing and camera distance that renders it difficult to claim the film was merely an effort to approximate theater. In addition, the transformations in film style evident between the different versions do not seem to uphold Komatsu's contention that *kyūha* film form experienced few changes at the time.

The 1915 *Gorō Masamune kōshiden*, based on a well-known story of a boy's filial piety, better supports Burch's argument. Directed by Yoshino Jirō, photographed by Edamasa Yoshirō (known at the time as a relatively progressive cameraman), and starring Onoe Matsunosuke's main rival, Sawamura Shirōgorō, *Gorō Masamune* combines one-shot, one-scene, theatrical staging (as when Gorō presents the sword to Kusunoki) with chase scenes, trick editing (in Gorō's climactic fight with the demon), and some fairly complex analytical editing. An example of the latter is when Gorō first happens upon Yukimitsu's smithy: the scene is mainly composed of reverse-field editing centered on long shots of the window where Gorō is spying, and includes a match on action to a medium shot when Gorō is captured. Another is the insertion of a flashback framed by dissolves in the scene when Gorō tells Yukimitsu of his past.

In his discussion of the film, Komatsu acknowledges the presence of such examples of breaking down space and narrating through images, but treats them as aberrations that were "avoided if possible" according to the traditional code.[24] He does not explain, however, why they were included in *Gorō Masamune* in the first place if the code demanded their elimination. While the use of aspects of classical editing may, in some cases, have added dramatic effect, as Burch contends, there is no apparent reason why such techniques could not have been used in other dramatic sequences in the film (for instance, in the scenes where Oaki beats Gorō). One could speculate whether or not this fairly eclectic style is a forerunner of the "cinema of flourishes" that David Bordwell describes in 1930s Japanese cinema,[25] but it is unclear here what constitutes the norm that is being embellished (according to Bordwell, the norm in the 1930s was the classical style). Perhaps it is Komatsu's traditional code, but if these elements of the classical style do not seem to form a "system," it is possibly because the traditional code itself is not that systematic: it arbitrarily allows such elements at some moments and not at others.

Movie fans may have been attached to aspects of this cinema, such as to their favorite *onnagata*, rendered meaningful through a particular system of codification, some of it borrowed from the theater. But their allegiance to a single cinematic code was never strong enough that they could not accept the actresses in foreign films (which continued to dominate the Japanese market until the mid-1920s) or even in *rensageki*, the "chain drama," which combined scenes on stage with scenes on film and was extremely popular in the mid-1910s and often featured actresses.[26]

Figure 6.   The smithy in *Gorō Masamune kōshiden* (The Story of the Filial Child Gorō Masamune, 1915). (Courtesy of the National Museum of Modern Art, Tokyo, the National Film Center)

It was not as if they were devotees of Noh suddenly confronted for the first time with Ibsen. The code of reception for Kabuki cinema was never the only one, and it always coexisted, in the same spectator, with other codes. Some spectators may have been more adept at some codes than others; and some may have tried to keep them strictly apart. But for most it was inevitable that the codes would intersect, overlap, blend, and even interact, if only because each induced in spectators the consciousness that this was not the only form of cinema (just as the spectator of each was conscious that it was also not theater). There were attempts to keep these codes separate, just as "Western painting" *(yōga)* and "Japanese painting" *(nihonga)* still exist today as different styles in the Japanese art world, bolstered by distinct institutional supports (such as different school curricula, exhibition spaces, and art criticism). Benshi styles in part served to create boundaries, as *kowairo* became the chosen style for Japanese films and foreign-film benshi avoided it. But as Jeffery Dym has argued, the 1910s was a period of experimentation in benshi practice, so it was not unusual to hear elements of foreign film narration in a Japanese film and vice versa.[27] There may have been tendencies in film production, exhibition, and reception to divide some practices, but not necessarily strict rules governing these.

That was because Japanese film culture in the 1910s, especially in the first half of the decade, was not as much concerned with creating institutions to distinguish film practices as with celebrating their mixtures. As I have written before, spectators who went to see early film stars like Onoe Matsunosuke or Tachibana Teijirō probably did enjoy the pseudotheatricality of their *kyūha* and *shinpa* films, but they also were attracted to the mixtures of films, people, spaces, and, to some extent, temporalities of which these works were only a part.[28] In this "culture of combination," mixing different experiences and temporalities constituted a particular form of enjoying modernity. Miriam Silverberg has echoed this concept when describing the modes of code-switching and montage she found in her studies of prewar Japanese popular culture.[29] The pleasure of early film viewing came not merely from what could be garnered from a single coded experience but also crucially involved the enjoyment of switching between codes, of juxtaposing different modes (such as film and theater), or of mixing them together. This could often be the experience of the moment, of the particular, unreproducible juxtaposition of different elements (including the live benshi) in a specific location, one quite different from the enjoyment of a universal, coded text that was the same anywhere it was shown. To some, this could itself constitute a traditional form: for instance the "commingled" arts that J. L. Anderson stresses in his analysis of the benshi's cultural valences.[30] Such connections should not be ignored, but neither should the fact that contemporaries saw these mixtures as "new"— often disturbingly so—which is why Silverberg and I, for instance, focus on the relation of this culture to modernity, or to multiple modernities.

On the stylistic level, if spectators were accustomed to shifting between various codes and film styles, the Japanese films they and the filmmakers constructed reveal a similar flexibility textually; audiences and the sphere of exhibition also revealed their flexibility in their reception of these films. What we see here is a more irregular style, one neither "cinematic" nor wholly "theatrical," but one that actually complicates codified divisions between the filmic and the theatrical, between the modern and the traditional, and between self-sufficient narration and storytelling dependent on the benshi. This is one reason that Komatsu's code cannot be as strict as he argues: immersed in this modernism of mixture, codes had to be flexible in order to allow for this other crucial pleasure—of combination and collage. We can postulate that this flexibility in the moment, this avoidance of or play with rigid universal codes, is another kind of vernacular modernism that dealt with both the accelerated flow and changes of modern existence and the increased regulation of everyday life by industry and the state by

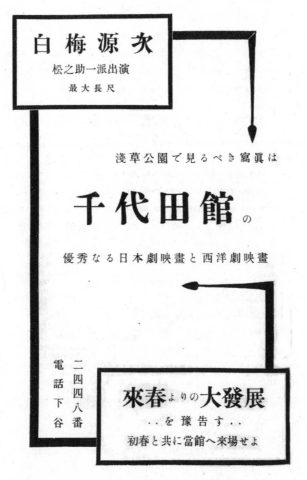

Figure 7.   Onoe Matsunosuke as vernacular "mixed" modernism: an ad for the Chiyodakan theater proclaiming a combination of Kabuki cinema (the theatrical term "the Matsunosuke Troupe" is in the upper left), the foreign pictures "one should see in Asakusa Park" (in celebrating the theater in the middle), and sleek, modern culture (the sparse but mobile ad design). (*Kinema Record* 18 [December 1914]: n.p.)

finding thrills and excitement in particular combinations, in what cannot be rigidly managed or universalized.

While much more work needs to be done to theorize early Japanese film style (if such research is possible, given the loss of so many films), this indeterminacy helps us understand why reformist critics insisted on

founding a universal *pure* cinema. One of the crucial facets of the Pure
Film Movement, and of attempts by authorities to regulate the cinema,
is that reformers cited these combinations and mixtures as one of the
main problems of cinema. As we have already seen with the depictions of
the "obscene" space of Asakusa and in the complaints against theatrical
Japanese films, it was the perception of a lack of strict, regulated codes of
meaning and experience that led many to promote cinema reform. Their
perception may have been exaggerated—the culture of combination did not
completely lack rules and customary practices. But it reflected intellectuals'
and authorities' general fear of mass culture—of an exponential proliferation of these chance, unregulated moments of meaning production—that
would continue for decades. In fact, it was reformist critics and intellectual
film fans who encouraged greater institutional separation between the foreign cinema they admired and the Japanese films they disliked, urging,
for instance, an increase in the number of theaters showing only foreign
films. Such theaters had already appeared because of the growing division
in exhibition by social class (the Pure Film Movement, too, as I will show,
reflected class distinctions).

It should be stressed, however, that the aim of pure film critics was ultimately not to create a set of strictly regulated codes dividing, for instance,
Japanese Kabuki cinema from European film, and thus preventing mixture
by respecting the territory of each. It was to create a single, overreaching,
universal code that would subsume all modes of movie experience into one.
A pure cinema, it was thought, would function more efficiently, better reflect
modern society (this was their vision of modernity), and be easier to manage. Divisions could exist, but they would be more vertical than horizontal,
more of quality (degree of purity) than of kind. This was a modernism of
differentiation, but precisely for the purpose of universalizing the management of difference through notions of purity and efficiency. This modernism of purity can ultimately be linked to class and state authority, and so it
is important to keep in mind the context in which the Pure Film Movement
emerged: it did not propose cinema in a space where it did not exist, but
rather reacted against a different conception of cinema (and modernity) by
labeling it a problem, one their vision of pure film would help solve.

THE PURE FILM MOVEMENT

Given that many of the arguments proffered by the Pure Film Movement
were becoming general parlance even before publications such as *Kinema
Record* began, it is difficult, as I mentioned in the introduction, to periodize

the phenomenon. Certainly we can trace the chronology of figures like Kaeriyama Norimasa or institutions such as *Kinema Record* up until the practical application of their beliefs in such films as *Sei no kagayaki* (The Glow of Life, 1918). But I see the Pure Film Movement less as a specific set of historical events than as the formation of a field of discourse, a group of "natural" assumptions both tacit and explicit about the cinema, that became central to Japanese film culture for long after the 1910s. In this sense, the fact that some of the writers in *Katsudō shashinkai* were already finding it "obvious" that Japanese films were not "cinema" meant that the discursive field was already beginning to take shape at that point. The Pure Film Movement's task was to clarify this still-amorphous notion of what cinema is and put it into practice.

The link with *Katsudō shashinkai* begins with Kaeriyama and Shigeno Yukiyoshi. It is helpful to review Kaeriyama's biography, given how typical it is of many early Japanese film critics. Born in 1893, Kaeriyama was still only a movie-crazed middle school student when he began submitting essays to *Katsudō shashinkai* after seeing the name of a classmate appear in print. Along with Shigeno, Nakano Keiichi, and others, Kaeriyama regularly sent in opinion pieces about various subjects, such as his article "The Moving Pictures and Children," until the magazine went under after Yoshizawa Shōten was swallowed up by Nikkatsu. For a time, there was not a single film magazine in Japan, until Kaeriyama, Shigeno, and Nakano started *Katsudō no tomo* (The Moving Picture Friend)[31] in June 1913. For unknown reasons, however, this magazine stopped publication after only five issues, and many of the same members formed the Japan Cinematographist Association (JCA—the original is English) to publish *Film Record* beginning the following October, with Shigeno as editor. The magazine changed its name to *Kinema Record* in December. It is important to remember that *Kinema Record*, at first only a mimeographed publication—a coterie magazine published monthly by a group of intellectual students (Kaeriyama was enrolled in the Tokyo Higher School of Engineering until 1914)—was the only substantial film periodical in Japan up until *Katsudō shashin zasshi* appeared in June 1915. Later supported by advertising, the journal had rather long legs for a publication of its type and lasted until at least issue number 51, which appeared in December 1917.[32]

Trained as a technician with proficiency in English, Kaeriyama found employment just after graduation at Nihon Kinetophone, a short-lived company that tried in vain to sell Edison's combination of film and the phonograph in Japan. When it went under, Kaeriyama changed companies,[33] getting work in 1917 in the import division of the Tennenshoku

KINEMA - RECORD

Our Editorial Staffs at The Kinetophone Studio.

Left to Right. T. Sudzuki, N. Kaeriyama, Y. Shigeno, T. Hanabusa, Y. Yoshitomi, S. Sakai.

鈴木　歸山　滋野　花房　吉富　酒井

キネマ・レコード社同人の集り

Figure 8.   The young reformers at *Kinema Record*. Kaeriyama Norimasa is second from the left, Shigeno Yuki-yoshi is third. (*Kinema Record* 36 [June 1916]: 279)

Katsudō Shashin Kabushiki Kaisha (Natural Color Moving Picture Company), or Tenkatsu for short, a company formed by Kobayashi Kisaburō, formerly of Fukuhōdō and then Nikkatsu, to exploit Charles Urban and Albert Smith's Kinemacolor system in Japan.[34] When Kinemacolor proved too expensive, the company reverted to regular film production, becoming Nikkatsu's main rival throughout the 1910s. It was Tenkatsu that eventually gave Kaeriyama the opportunity to put his ideas into practice and direct some of the first Japanese "pure films," *Sei no kagayaki* and *Miyama no otome* (Maid of the Deep Mountains) in 1918. In the meantime, Kaeriyama published *Katsudō shashingeki no sōsaku to satsueihō* (The Production and Photography of Moving Picture Drama) in July 1917, the first full-length book on cinema since Gonda's *Principles and Applications of the Moving Pictures*. As a largely technical how-to book, *Production and Photography* was more Kaeriyama's summary of American and European technical manuals than the kind of original exploration of cinema's social role that Gonda performed. Still, the book proved both immensely popular and influential, and it went through ten printings between 1917 and 1924.

In the late 1910s, other reformist magazines sympathetic to Kaeriyama and *Kinema Record* began appearing. *Katsudō no sekai* (Movie World), begun in January 1916 as an opinion magazine with only a slight emphasis on film, was soon transformed into a film specialty journal with strong support for the principles of the Pure Film Movement. *Katsudō gahō* (Film Graphic), started one year later, in January 1917, and was published by Hikōsha, the same company that put out Kaeriyama's book. *Katsudō hyōron* (Movie Review), begun in December 1918 but later renamed *Katsudō kurabu* (Movie Club) in September 1919, was also sympathetic to the Pure Film Movement; it was where Shigeno found work after *Kinema Record* folded. The main magazine to take on the spirit and principles of *Kinema Record*, however, was without a doubt *Kinema junpō* (Moving Picture Times), another coterie magazine started by students, in July 1919, which went on to become Japan's leading film journal, one that maintains its importance even today. One can argue with little difficulty that, by 1920, all the leading film magazines in Japan shared the basic positions of the Pure Film Movement.

The Japanese film industry was also experiencing changes, most of which were unrelated to Kaeriyama's directorial efforts. The industry itself was in a state of transformation as the number of theaters increased and new companies entered the business. The outbreak of World War I dealt a blow to European companies and brought a stop to the dominance of French and Italian films in Japan; in their place, American films, especially serials, comedies, and, later, Universal's Bluebird films, came to monopolize the import market. Japanese consumers, bolstered by the wartime economy, were spending more money than ever before. Movie houses found a new competitor for those spectators in the shape of legitimate theaters running *rensageki*. While originating much earlier, these productions (many of which were produced by Kobayashi's new company, Kobayashi Shōkai, after he broke away from Tenkatsu in 1916) enjoyed significant popularity, until the 1917 Tokyo motion picture regulations dealt them a fatal blow. Motion picture companies were also severely hit by the regulations, which, as I argue in chapter 5, gave significant impetus to reform.

The influence of Shingeki on film reform is important to note, since it was Shingeki directors like Tanaka Eizō, who joined Nikkatsu in 1917 to produce groundbreaking work like *Ikeru shikabane* (The Living Corpse, 1918), and Shingeki actors like Murata Minoru and Kondō Iyokichi, both of whom worked with Kaeriyama, who gave significant impetus to the "pure films." The industry's increased commitment to a new kind of cinema was best represented by the appearance of two new companies in 1920: Shōchiku Kinema (owned by a theatrical producer) and Taikatsu (short for Taishō Katsuei), both of which established schools to train new film personnel. Shingeki director Osanai Kaoru was placed in charge of the Shōchiku training school, where he helped nurture directors like Murata and Itō Daisuke and actors like Suzuki Denmei. Taikatsu's academy produced the director Uchida Tomu and the film star Okada Tokihiko, among others, and the company hired as its advisor the great novelist and proponent of pure films Tanizaki Jun'ichirō. By the mid-1920s, many of the improvements proposed by the Pure Film Movement were in place: *oyama* had disappeared in favor of actresses; forms of visual narration that did not rely on the benshi had become common; and *jidaigeki* (period films) and *gendaigeki* (contemporary films) influenced by American cinema had replaced the old *shinpa* and *kyūha* productions.[35]

Again, the reforms of the Pure Film Movement extended well beyond the actions of any single group of individuals centered on *Kinema Record*.[36] Even if one credits Kaeriyama with filming the first "cinematic" films in Japan, the fact that, as Yoshida Chieo argues, other reformist films like Tanaka's appeared in the full year it took for both *Sei no kagayaki* and *Miyama no otome* to finally be released means it would be hard to say they were influenced by his works.[37] Focusing only on individual biography could lead one to mistakenly believe that, since filmmakers like Kaeriyama, Henry Kotani, and Thomas Kurihara, who were central to reformist filmmaking, did not last long as directors, this is evidence that

Figure 9. Film reform at Nikkatsu and the influence of *shingeki:* a still from Tanaka Eizō's *Ikeru shikabane* (The Living Corpse, 1918). (Courtesy of the National Museum of Modern Art, Tokyo, the National Film Center)

the "Westernized" Pure Film Movement failed in the face of different Japanese tastes.[38] Their fates should not be ignored, but a close look at the construction of discourse on film in the late 1910s, especially starting with *Kinema Record,* demonstrates that a very different picture can be drawn.

PURE CINEMA AND THE HIERARCHY OF STUDY

Studying Japanese Cinema

More than in the case of Gonda or any other contemporary commentators, the discourse of *Kinema Record* centered on the word *study (kenkyū).* It must be stressed that, whereas the Pure Film Movement was a statement on the preferred state of cinema, and an attempt in practice to reform Japanese film, it was first and foremost a form of film study, of attempting to discover the proper way of describing cinema in words. One editorial announced that the magazine's "motto and life force" was "Study and Progress,"[39] and both of these words—its keystones to the discourse of reform—pepper its pages. In an early piece, the editor Shigeno Yukiyoshi outlined the task *Kinema Record* had undertaken: "Our duties and official

responsibility are in fact great. As our film world becomes more complicated, our assignments will also become more numerous. Our direction, we
believe, is completely different from that of an entertainment magazine.
Just how can this magazine fulfill its duty as the organ of our film world?
By what means can we realize the JCA's future aims, and toward what goal
should we passionately progress? I think we should only hope never to
forget serious study."[40] As with Gonda's version of study, but in a less playful and self-critical fashion, the results of *Kinema Record*'s research were
to serve as the guidelines for ordering a chaotic and often errant industry.
Being "serious" and "studious" was often presented as sufficient to change
the world. Soon, the magazine was even boasting, "Our serious study has
directly fostered the desire for improvement in a certain group."[41]

The range of topics for study pursued in the magazine was bewilder-
ingly broad-based, ranging from scriptwriting to film music, from advertising to theater architecture. Kaeriyama and Hanabusa Taneta also added
a series of very technical pieces on such topics as film emulsion and screen
reflectivity that remind one more of pieces in the *Journal of the Society
of Motion Picture Engineers* than *Moving Picture World*. Much of this
research was based on the young students' readings of foreign movie how-
to books or film magazines that could be obtained at select Tokyo bookstores.[42] Study also involved the avid viewing of motion pictures in current
release. When *Kinema Record*'s editors spoke of the standards of cinema,
they most often referred to the foreign films that had made their way to
Japan. Until the outbreak of World War 1, this mostly meant European
cinema, since, as Komatsu emphasizes, very few American films and almost
none of Griffith's work had been imported.[43] The first few years of *Kinema
Record* thus were laced with comments on how excellent the Austrian *Student of Prague* (Stellan Rye and Paul Wegener, 1913) and the Italian *Quo
Vadis?* (Enrico Guazzoni, 1912) were. Not until about 1916 did examples
from Hollywood begin to take a prominent place in reformist literature.

Japanese cinema bore the brunt of *Kinema Record*'s studied criticism.
The faults cited were multiple, and different writers pointed out different problems, but together they sketch the outline of the vision of cinema
that *Kinema Record* was constructing. Shigeno, in a piece in August 1914,
declares, "The first averse reaction we get upon viewing Japanese films is to
the inept photography; the second, to the lifeless and slow-moving drama;
the third, to the actors who are all sloppy and dull-witted; and the fourth,
to the use of *onnagata*."[44] Producers were accused of not understanding
the unique qualities of film: as one editorial argues, they "apparently con-
fuse the moving pictures with regular drama, [when] the moving pictures

[actually] present their value through pantomime."[45] Cinema was seen as an inherently silent medium that communicated through gesture, which meant Japanese companies could be faulted for making films that could not be understood without a benshi.[46] Yet early on, at a time when most Japanese films lacked intertitles (except to announce each scene), the editors called for the greater use of titles, especially ones that were poetic and artistically designed.[47] As part of this, much emphasis was placed on the importance of producing good screenplays and developing writers with knowledge of cinema.[48]

According to *Kinema Record*'s conception of film history, Japanese film was still in its infancy.[49] Its stunted growth was blamed on a number of technical failures. One commentator pointed to slow cranking, poor film developing, and bad lighting as reasons Japanese films had "degenerated," registering shock that a Nikkatsu official actually recommended filming at eight frames per second instead of the usual sixteen.[50] Japanese filmmakers were accused of failing to use the techniques particular to cinema, especially close-ups.[51] As was repeatedly argued, reforming these aspects of Japanese cinema could secure the motion pictures a better social standing in Japanese society, and Japanese productions in particular could be sold in Europe and the United States. In Shigeno's words: "If [producers] pay attention to the reduction of footage we have noticed as a great fault of Japanese films, and rewrite the stories, I think it will be easy to get audiences abroad."[52] The ability to be understood in America and Europe became one standard of judging cinematic quality.

As I have written before, a sort of "dream of export" has served as a structuring myth at significant points in Japanese film history. This includes the time of the Pure Film Movement, when in fact few films were exported other than to the colonies or to Japanese immigrant communities in Hawaii and North and South America. It also happened during World War II and the 1950s, when Japanese movies were actually being shown to non-Japanese audiences abroad.[53] In this dream, not only would the industry expand its markets and profits, but sending films abroad would also spark reform in domestic filmmaking in terms of both industry structure and film style. In the 1910s, export was considered a realistic possibility because both American and European studios were at the time successfully marketing a series of films featuring stories set in Japan, the most famous of which were the Hollywood movies produced by Thomas Ince and starring Sessue Hayakawa. *Kinema Record* notes, "If we can just make films even foreigners can understand, then we should be able to export our works abroad for a long time."[54]

I have argued elsewhere that these foreign-made films set in Japan, which were reviled in Japan for their stereotypes and orientalism and, according to Kaeriyama, for "stealing" the images of Japan,[55] but also revered for their more cinematic use of film form, functioned both as a call to arms, prompting Japanese studios to make more accurate films for export, and as a model for the new Japanese cinema. In an illustration of the transnational, if not also ironic, nature of Japanese film history, it was as if true Japanese cinema (which many historians, like Iijima Tadashi, marked as originating with the Pure Film Movement)[56] began with Ince, since Japanese filmmakers had to internalize foreign definitions of cinema—and assume the foreign gaze—in order to create films that were both cinematic and Japanese.[57] Daisuke Miyao has expanded on my argument in his book on Hayakawa,[58] but I stress here that the engine for this change was the dream of export. For Japanese films to travel abroad and not only appeal to foreigners while offering a "correct" vision of Japan but also enter their markets, they had to exhibit a style recognizable to foreign spectators. What seemed "Japanese" to American and European audiences were not the *kyūha* or *shinpa* films, which were demonstrably different or even incomprehensible in style—which Burch believes embodied Japaneseness in their form—but those works that presented Japanese "difference" in the familiar language of Hollywood. Japanese cinema, in effect, had to be more American to be recognized as more Japanese.

It is important to note that the dream of export made foreign cinematic tastes the measure of cinema, which then fueled the program of pure film reform at home. As one writer argues, "Only when Japanese-made films are exported abroad as commodities can we say that they have for the first time reached the stage of completion."[59] For a film to be successful as an export, it had to be comprehensible to foreign spectators. To reformers this meant the film had to present a text that could communicate on its own. Japanese filmmakers could rely on the benshi to transmit their meaning, but they could not do that with films sent to countries where benshi did not exist. A film, it was argued, had to be a closed text, containing meaning that was inserted in the realm of production by the film's author; one could not rely on the space of exhibition, particularly the benshi and spectators, to complete the film. Filmmakers had to create works that took over the role of narration by means of techniques such as close-ups and analytical editing, ones that led the spectator through the film, explaining the story. To promote this, benshi had to be eliminated so they could no longer serve as a crutch. Other peculiarities of Japanese film culture, such as the *onnagata*, were also to be eradicated because they would seem foreign if not ridiculous to viewers abroad. In fact, the dream of export also linked up with ideas of reforming acting and the Japanese body itself. Complaints that "Japanese actors have no expression" led to proposals to change performance in line with the universal rules of the photoplay,[60] which led to what Deguchi Takehito calls the "Caucasian complex" with regard to Japanese cinema of the 1920s and 1930s, a standard of beauty especially manifested in star discourse that remade Japanese idols into the image of their Hollywood counterparts.[61]

Such trends remind us how much even domestic attempts to define Japanese cinema developed internationally under an unequal distribution of global cultural power, but we should not picture the film reformers as simple victims of the world system. The dream of export functioned not merely to bring Japan in line with Western capitalism and culture but also to justify a universalist modernism at home, providing an excuse to eliminate the particular or unique mixtures found in local film culture and establish ranks of authority in the domestic sphere. Film study was a central tool in this process, first because it was the means by which the tastes and practices of foreign filmmakers and audiences—the universal standard in cinema—could be determined, and second, because the findings could then be rendered general and essential as knowledge and authority. It became a method for making one form the form for all, and then excluding what did not fit.

The discourse of study was a means of determining cinematic specificity, but the young reformers also expanded the notion of study so that it became the prerequisite mode for approaching cinema for anyone involved in the industry. Japanese films were failures as cinema precisely because of a lack of serious study: "In general, what reason is there for the fact that we cannot praise Japanese pictures on any of these points? Simply put, the reason lies in production that is 'not serious' and 'lacking study.' Perhaps we should call the people in the business who are ignorant of the imperfections and tremendous faults of Japanese pictures the idiots of the moving pictures."[62] This is the reason *Kinema Record* repeatedly called on Japanese film producers to study the medium as a solution to its ills. Not just directors but also actors, writers, benshi, and exhibitors were asked to research and understand the unique qualities of cinema as a condition for improving it.[63] Joining this celebration of study, readers often submitted letters proudly terming themselves "researchers" and announcing the results of their own studies.[64]

Having "studied" became a standard for judging various individuals' involvement in the cinema, one reflected in the language the reformers used. Writers in *Kinema Record* often used the adjectival clause *atama no aru* ("intelligent" or "smart") to designate those who could distinguish what the cinema was and was not.[65] A transformation in the taste of the audience was also described in terms of knowledge: "The attitude of spectators has completely changed from olden days: namely, they approach the moving pictures as one studied [*kenkyūteki*] entertainment."[66] The spectators who approached the cinema with serious intelligence were often described as having *ganshiki,* or "discernment" (literally, "knowledgeable eyes").[67] A reader was even kind enough to provide a definition of *discernment* with regard to the cinema, stating, "We can say a person has a discerning eye for cinema when he can understand a certain refined pleasure that cannot be produced in theater."[68]

Having everyone connected to cinema acquire a certain level of knowledge of the medium through study was an essential precondition for the improvement of film. At this level, the discourse of *Kinema Record* differs little from that of Gonda, who also tied the evolution of cinema to the accumulation of knowledge. But the Pure Film Movement reformers refined the practice of study to produce a significantly different social vision of the cinema. They revered knowledge of cinema to the point that they believed film production should, in a sense, be left in the hands of technicians. Kaeriyama emphasizes the fact that "technology is one facet of a creator, and a creator must be one facet of technology."[69] Technicians were to be artists, but in the discourse of study, all artists were to be scholars of the apparatus.

There was a meritocratic, utopian quality to the young reformers' vision of a studied cinema. In an essay later included in his *Production and Photography of Moving Picture Drama,* Kaeriyama laments about the current state of the industry: "The common evil of those in the moving picture business is that they only pursue immediate profit and do not prepare any long-term plans. They set their own sights low and debase themselves, making the moving pictures simply a means for tempting and deceiving people and coveting their money." Against this, Kaeriyama offers his own goals, albeit ones he confesses are probably not immediately realizable: "To strive for progress in the science of the moving pictures, to profit in foreign trade with picture productions as well as materials and chemicals. To introduce our national character to foreign nations through the moving pictures and make foreigners understand our nation and people. Finally, in every field the moving pictures touch, to lend a hand in the social education of Japan, to hope for the mental and intellectual progress of every single citizen, and to contribute to individual improvement and the people's awareness of their national ideals."[70]

Partly as a means to counter its bad reputation, the motion picture business was to operate under a kind of Neo-Confucian ideal mixed with Meiji nationalism and the capitalist business spirit, in which benevolent technocrats raised the level of cinema for the benefit of all. The quest for profit was acceptable, but in the end Kaeriyama's film world was modeled on public-minded academia, where competition was eased in favor of cooperation in studying and improving the cinema and the nation.[71] Especially given the potential social position of the cinema as the medium for a modern age, producers were asked to be serious and responsible, to "hold long-term goals and take a self-sacrificing attitude."[72]

A prerequisite for involvement in the movie business, then, was love for cinema: the willingness to devote oneself to it and not to profit. In Kaeriyama's words: "It must be the lover you love most." If producers did this, it would be only natural for them "to use all honest means to strive for the improvement of the industry."[73] In *Kinema Record* and other journals supporting the principles of the Pure Film Movement, writers often used the term *aikatsuka*, or literally "movie lovers," to refer to those discerning fans, early versions of cinephiles, who enthusiastically studied the cinema as a basis of its improvement. There was an image of group consciousness among these *aikatsuka*, one that both supported the reformist journals and was promoted by these periodicals in turn (many, like *Katsudō no sekai*, held special film events for their readers). In one aspect, *Kinema Record* is a manifestation of this love for the cinema, a magazine created by film fans as a means of communicating their voices to the industry. The editorial policy encouraged participation: letters from readers were promoted, and those with more energy could easily get longer pieces published in the magazine. (Such policies, carried on by *Kinema junpō* and other journals, were in fact how many film critics got their start.) With its modern design, *Kinema Record* represented the beginnings of a Westernized Taishō modernism: clean, intelligent, and high class.

'Aikatsuka' and the Vulgar

These views of cinema and its study reveal much about the class dynamics of film reform in the 1910s, for there was another side to *aikatsuka*. Words like *aikatsuka* were on one level meritocratic, implying that anyone with sufficient love for—and thus the energy to study—cinema could make a difference in the film world. Yet on another they were also hierarchical and exclusive, defining love precisely according to the ideals of the Pure Film Movement, and thus either expelling those who did not share those principles (on the grounds that they must not love the cinema) or requiring

Figure 10.   Movie fans at a film event put on by the reformist cinema journal
Katsudō no sekai for its readers. (*Katsudō no sekai* 1.5 [May 1916]: n.p.)

them to be led by true *aikatsuka*. Unlike Gonda's rejection of the *tsū*, the
celebration of *aikatsuka* valorized those who could be superior to others
in culture. This politics of language was fundamental to the discourse of
Kinema Record. Words were used to distinguish and signal discernment:
the magazine's prose was as dry and serious as the study—or sometimes
the cinema—the reformers propounded, and as a result it never had the
popular, entertaining flavor of Gonda's writing. English was often visible
in *Kinema Record* (both in the roman letters and katakana script), from the
magazine's title to entire articles that appeared in English. Many of these
articles were part of the editors' quixotic effort to convince foreign buyers
to purchase Japanese films, but English also gave the publication an elitist
flavor. Starting with the August 1914 issue, the Japanese was printed hori-
zontally, left to right, and the publication opened from left to right—an
imitation of English writing, rare in Japan at the time. Moreover, words
were not accompanied with the *hiragana rubi* next to the characters that
gave the pronunciation of ideographs. This went counter to a custom prac-
ticed not only by most newspapers but also by magazines aiming for a

general audience (many of the other film magazines—significantly except-ing *Kinema junpō*—used them into the 1920s): Without *rubi*, the many lesser-educated Japanese who could read the phonetic *hiragana* but not the thousands of ideographs were left out in the cold. They presumably could not participate in the community of *aikatsuka* that *Kinema Record* was attempting to form.

Even the use of Japanese words was restrictive. As I mentioned in the introduction, language use was very important to the Pure Film Move-ment, especially the distinction between *eiga* and *katsudō shashin* as terms to name the medium. *Eiga* as a word had been used for a long time to name, in particular, the slides used in magic lanterns, the images projected, or the projection process itself. When cinema was first imported, the film prints were often called *eiga*.[74] This usage continued for some time, and one often saw the combination *katsudō shashin no eiga*, or literally, "moving picture film," which distinguished the term for the specific text from that naming the medium as a whole. As if to emphasize that *eiga* referred to the cel-luloid and not the entire apparatus, newspapers would often add the *rubi* "*firumu*," or, "film," next to the ideographs for *eiga*.[75]

According to an often-told historical anecdote, Kaeriyama himself originated the usage of *eiga* to name the medium and not just its specific manifestations.[76] The film historian Okada Susumu relates: "Kaeriyama Norimasa liked to say the word 'eiga.' It had the same kind of attractively modern nuance as when Germans said 'Kino.' In addition, Kaeriyama repeatedly wrote the word *eiga* in order to emphasize the complete differ-ence between existing theatrical and old-fashioned 'katsudō shashin' and his own ideal—that this was a new art of the camera."[77] The anecdote is not really true.[78] Kaeriyama, as is evident in his famous book, continued for some time to use *katsudō shashin* to name even the form of cinema he favored; he and many of the other writers at *Kinema Record* often used the words *eiga* and *katsudō shashin* interchangeably, though they sometimes experimented with terms such as *katsudō shashingeki* to approximate popular foreign terms such as *photoplay*. Still, as indicated by Tenkatsu's Yamamoto Yoshitarō's reported use of the two terms at the preview screen-ing of *Sei no kagayaki*, their respective connotations were not neutral. As the period progressed and the effects of the Pure Film Movement were felt in film production, the term *katsudō shashin* was largely replaced by *eiga* in journalistic discourse (there were, for instance, no major film magazines with *katsudō shashin* in the title after 1924). *Eiga*, as Okada notes, signaled the new and *katsudō shashin* the old and out-of-style; apart from some use in the industry and in law, the latter term died out for anything but

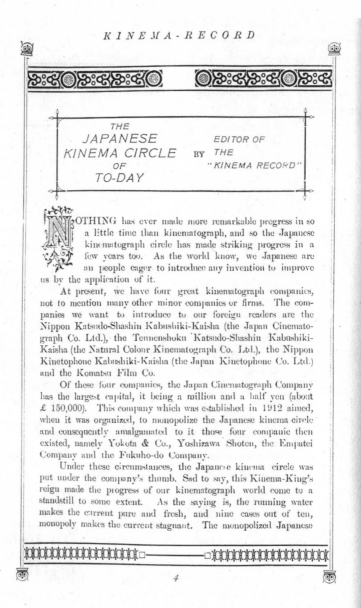

THE JAPANESE KINEMA CIRCLE OF TO-DAY

BY THE EDITOR OF "KINEMA RECORD"

OTHING has ever made more remarkable progress in so a little time than kinematograph, and so the Japanese kinematograph circle has made striking progress in a few years too. As the world know, we Japanese are an people eager to introduce any invention to improve us by the application of it.

At present, we have four great kinematograph companies, not to mention many other minor companies or firms. The companies we want to introduce to our foreign readers are the Nippon Katsudo-Shashin Kabushiki-Kaisha (the Japan Cinematograph Co. Ltd.), the Tennenshoku Katsudo-Shashin Kabushiki-Kaisha (the Natural Colour Kinematograph Co. Ltd.), the Nippon Kinetophone Kabushiki-Kaisha (the Japan Kinetophone Co. Ltd.) and the Komatsu Film Co.

Of these four companies, the Japan Cinematograph Company has the largest capital, it being a million and a half yen (about £ 150,000). This company which was established in 1912 aimed, when it was organized, to monopolize the Japanese kinema circle and consequently amalgamated to it those four companie then existed, namely Yokota & Co., Yoshizawa Shoten, the Empatei Company and the Fukuho-do Company.

Under these circumstances, the Japanese kinema circle was put under the company's thumb. Sad to say, this Kinema-King's reign made the progress of our kinematograph world come to a standstill to some extent. As the saying is, the running water makes the current pure and fresh, and nine cases out of ten, monopoly makes the current stagnant. The monopolized Japanese

Figure 11.   An article in English printed in issue number 22 of *Kinema Record* (April 1915).

kinema circle was not to be excluded from this rule. This was our great regret to point out.

Peace, however, which the King enjoied was soon broken, as in March of the next year the Japan Natural Colour Kinematograph Company was established to be a powerful rival. The company is the sole agent in Japan of the Natural Colour Kinematograph Company in England and the only one in Japan having the right of making kinemacolour film . Another rival rose up soon after. It was the Japan Kinetophone Company established in August of 1913, and it has the exclusive right in Japan to produce the kinetophone films and import and export them.

Thus, to our joy, our kinema circle has become more and more active month after month. Of course, the above mentioned two companies produce the plain films and now the former's production is gradually increasing, the average at present being fifteen reels a month while the Japan Cinematograph Company is now producing only fourteen reels a month on an average. Such being the present state, most of the films exhibited in our picture theatres are imported from foreign countries.

The Komatsu Film Co. is not to be overlooked. This firm was established in 1903, so is the oldest kinematograph company. It is owned by Mr. Kōtarō Saito and its monthly production is only six reels, yet it imports many foreign films and has a great influence over the local kinema circle in Japan more than in Tokyo. It is indeed praiseworthy to have kept, till the present, fighting with the Kinema-King and established its situation very firmly in the kinema circle.

The point we hope to call your attention is this, our companies are Producers, Renters and Exhibitors at the same time so they themselves import or export films and have many picture-theatres under their management. As for foreign films, some of them have their agents in foreign lands but in some cases they import through the London market, except those made in Italy and Germany all of which are imported directly.

(To be Continued.)

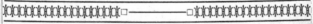

nostalgic purposes.[79] The writers for *Kinema Record* were painfully aware that, in their time, the evils attributed to the cinema had affixed themselves to the word *katsudō shashin:* they often cited *katsudōya* (or "movie man") as a particularly insulting term.[80] In order to lift the cinema out of its origins in the *misemono,* a new term was necessary.

The *Kinema Record* reformers thus were as concerned with reworking language as Gonda was, but there exists a crucial difference between them. Gonda, while forced to create much new terminology, was mostly intent on giving existing words new meaning, partly as a strategy to undermine existing structures of power in culture. By rearticulating language, he hoped to save what was denigrated as the plaything of the masses, not by withdrawing it from lower-class moviegoers, but by valorizing the tastes of the masses themselves. The discourse of Kaeriyama and his colleagues functioned less ambiguously: the reworking of *eiga* and other Japanese terms was a means of establishing a modern, separate language to found an altogether different cinema. Given its importation of English words like *photoplay, audience,* and *cinema,* this new language also functioned as a kind of exclusive vocabulary that restricted admittance to those capable of acquiring this form of symbolic capital.

There was an elite pride among the *aikatsuka,* as if they were the chosen few in a crusade of film reform. A late *Kinema Record* editorial underlines the responsibilities of the *aikatsuka:* "Those who are true *aikatsuka,* who understand the real essence of cinema and are striving for the national improvement of our country's film, . . . possess the single duty to faithfully guide Japanese films, soundly protect them, make them bear glistening fruit, and nurture them into maturing even one day early as adults that can majestically overwhelm foreign cinema."

On the one hand, this is a bold declaration that the new Japanese cinema will be produced not by the film industry but by devoted fans and amateur film scholars. But on the other, it is also the assertion of social authority on behalf of the nation. In chastising some intellectual fans for detesting Japanese cinema so much that they refuse to even associate themselves with it, the same editorial goes on to explain: "Our films take advantage of the weaknesses of innocent people and seem to exist primarily for the nonintellectual. . . . If people of the intellectual classes could advance and become familiar with Japanese films as a means of improving them, the resulting essential demand will produce works that have enough significance to truly satisfy the upper classes."[81] This was a central plank in the platform of the Pure Film Movement. Gonda had also complained of intellectuals refusing to see—and thus to care for or nurture—Japanese films, but even if he expected some authority to enforce the development of the essence of cinema, he also hoped that intellectuals would be transformed by contact with cinema. It was this bottom-up cultural vector that shaped the writing style of *The Principles and Applications of the Moving Pictures*. *Kinema Record*, however, from its language to its philosophy, was bottom-up only within the restricted field of *aikatsuka;* otherwise it maintained a resolutely top-down conception of culture. Article after article argued that the moving pictures—especially Japanese films—suffered a poor reputation among the middle and upper classes—that is, those with intelligence and discernment. The fault in part lay with an industry that was accused of catering to low-brow tastes: "All that is shown now are pictures that simply match vulgar tastes: they have no dignity, no taste—they are like a crude painting in gar-ish red and blue. It is impossible a person with discernment would try to see them."[82] The logic was that cinema required the involvement of the higher classes to improve its social position. The responsibility of *aikatsuka*—by definition, "people of the intellectual classes"—was to serve as the advanced guard, insisting on their tastes as filmgoers and thus promoting a film prod-uct that would attract better audiences to the movie theater.

At this level, the plan differs little from the attitudes of the Motion Picture Patents Company producers, whom Eileen Bowser describes in her history of early American cinema: "To uplift, ennoble, and purify was good business too. Progressive idealism did not conflict with their ideas of how to expand the market. To broaden the base of the audience, to bring in the middle class, to make the movies a respectable place of entertainment for women and children, . . . it would be useful to uplift and educate the immigrant masses and the urban poor."[83] *Kinema Record* often tried to convince those in the industry that they could reap more profits if they reformed the product with the tastes of intellectuals and the middle class in mind. An editorial penned by Kaeriyama argues, "From the standpoint of profit . . . it is quite unwise to produce only low-class works ignoring the fact there are many people of discernment who desire respectable films."[84] Another pointed to the success of more modern theaters specializing in better Western films as proof that middle-class audiences would go to the movies if conditions were right.[85] Producers in general were faulted for not trying to "improve lower-class audiences but instead catering to them."[86] It was claimed that cinema, once reformed, could become "one large organ for the education of society in general."[87]

In the end, the young reformers maintained an ambiguous and often contradictory stance toward a profit-oriented industry. This is best exem-plified by advice they once offered to exhibitors: "First, pour all your energy into satisfying your audiences; making profit is only incidental to that. Exhibitors who make profit their primary principle will inevitably suffer horrible failure afterward."[88] Even if fulfilling viewer pleasure should presumably lead to greater attendance and thus to more profit, the assumption here is that such calculations should never be paramount; what comes first are audience demands, which are themselves presumably disinterested (because "audiences" here probably does not refer to all viewers, but only to the privileged *aikatsuka*). If everyone acts for film and for nation, and not for profit, money will supposedly flow in as a secondary effect.

While arguing that making pure films is good for business, *Kinema Record* often tacked on principles of social mindedness and "self-sacrifice" in demanding that the industry also lay profit aside. The feverish quest for profit was frequently characterized as a remnant of the *misemono* days, when showing films was just part of temple festivals *(ennichi):* thus it was contrary to the cultures of both the cinema and the nation. The language of these arguments, however, appears to belie an awareness that profit was insufficient to lure Japanese motion picture producers into the reform camp: existing Japanese films were successful, if one judges from the laments in *Kinema Record* articles.[89] Anxious that there were audiences whose tastes ran contrary to the tastes of those who demanded a pure cinema, and thus ones who could render impure films profitable, supporters of the Pure Film Movement had to appeal to the social responsibility of motion picture producers to induce reform from the top down, or had to call on the audience to "progress," as one writer did,[90] or, as a more desperate measure, had to force spectators to change.

The mismatch between ideals and reality fostered this tendency to seek out more coercive measures, such as calling for censorship of films of low taste. I expand on this issue in the chapter on censorship, but it is useful to analyze here one of two *Kinema Record* editorials on censorship that ran in the October 1917 issue, because of the typical way it constructs both audiences and the reformers' position toward them. The piece—the second of the two editorials—is a commentary on the 1917 Tokyo Moving Picture Regulations, which, as one of their central planks, established a grading system for films: grade A films were restricted to adults only, and grade B films were available to general audiences, including children. Since the logic of the editorial is important, I summarize it here in detail.

The editorial begins by repeating the charge that film production companies lack "seriousness" and are deficient in cinematic skill and social direction. At the root of the problem is the fact that "the organizational basis of present-day Japanese movie companies is exhibition; production

is in no way the center."[91] The companies take "the easy road" of producing works on the "minimum level" in terms of exhibition potential, ones
made as cheaply as possible but which are still popular among the crowds
in Asakusa or Osaka's Sennichimae. "But when you ask regular people
in society, they will in no way recognize moving picture entertainment
. . . as something refined and respectable." There are many reasons, the
editorial continues, why the regulations are necessary. Even if some theaters are respectable, so long as there are houses that put on shows like at
a "temple festival," "society will focus only on that and intuitively view
the motion pictures as entertainment verging on vulgarity." So while one
could find middle-class spectators and students at Western movie houses
in Asakusa, one would see in theaters showing Japanese fare, such as ghost
stories and tragedies, "customers [who] are almost entirely craftsmen, the
kind of utterly vulgar people carrying clothes in their hands, wearing only
one shirt, or even sitting half-naked as if for the heat." The editorial admits
that "ghost stories and tragedies are probably good for people like craftsmen and women factory workers," but complains that the Japanese exhibition system is unlike that of foreign countries, where "the classes are
separated so that they do not bother each other." Japan instead runs a kind
of "movie-man style" system, where as many people are gathered together
as are willing to pay. *Kinema Record* asserts that it is because the classes
are not "naturally separated" in the Japanese film world that the police
were forced to issue their regulations. Unlike the legitimate stage, motion
pictures must be controlled in this way because they have been "unable to
make clear their own position in society."

Reading this first part, one would imagine *Kinema Record* is about to
propose a system of segregation, which it hinted at in the first editorial in
this issue,[92] or at least echo the call of some intellectual film fans for houses
specializing in Western films that cater exclusively to the middle class. In
that way, film genres and their exhibition could be given a strict social or
even semiotic definition: either for the vulgar or for the cultured, but not
for both. This could conceivably eliminate those hybrid indeterminacies
that colored Japanese film culture. However, the film reformers, with their
contradictory logic, do not ask for this. As they see it, the problem lies in
how the cinema audience is defined. In calling for film producers to "wake
up," the second editorial asserts: "If censorship can be carried out respect-
ably and with principle, exhibition of B grade films will certainly not be
unsuccessful and their production will not be unprofitable. But if the films
remain at the level of ghost stories or *shinpa* tragedy, they will not interest
an adult, whether grade A or even grade B films. One must think that the

audience generally has a better eye than producers." But who is this "audience" the editorial is referring to? It certainly cannot be lower-class workers, who, the editorial has already said, seem to like these genres. The next line states that it is because there are many works that "even we" could not allow as grade A films that "regular people in society" think of the cinema as vulgar and the police issue their regulations. Here as elsewhere, *Kinema Record* shifts its definition of the audience so that viewers who do not share its standards of taste are not included within the categories "we," "audience," or even "regular people."

The editorial also contorts the definition of A and B grade films distinguishing them not by their appropriateness for certain audiences but by level of quality, defined as what would "interest an adult." In the next section, taking a particularly poorly shot newsreel as representative of the faults of Japanese cinema, *Kinema Record* declares: "If one permits us to say so, these kinds of bizarre products cannot fairly be seen as commercially viable or certifiable as either A or B grade films." They were thought so horrible that they could not be rated at any level, nor could they possibly make money (this despite the editorial's previous admission that producers make money off such films).

Yet the writer does not then ask producers to make films of either A or B grade quality, but goes on to conclude that "producers have no need to make a division between A and B grade films; what is important is making works of quality." After expending such effort arguing that the film industry deserves strict censorship because it makes films indiscriminately without attention to social class, the editorial ends by asserting that producers need make no distinctions in film production. The logic is contradictory, but in the end the writer settles on a central difference: what is quality cinema and what is not. Despite the discussion of naturally dividing the audience by class and taste, it is clear *Kinema Record* is not in favor of letting lower-class viewers have their own theaters and films even if the educated are given separate, high-class venues. The image of cinema presumably will be harmed as long as lowbrow houses exist. Eliminating them is a necessity: to the reformers, they are not cinema and their viewers are neither real spectators nor part of "society."[93] For the sake of cinema and public morals—now intimately tied—the films of the lower classes should be eliminated. The solution to hybridity was not strict segregation but homogenization from the top down.

The definition of class at work here and elsewhere is based mostly on education, but also on employment and economic status. The privileging of education tied into Neo-Confucian ideologies carried over from the Meiji era, and to contemporary concerns about being "cultured" *(kyōyō)*, which H.D. Harootunian has described. In the Taishō era, "middle-class intellectuals, on whom the idea of *bunka* and *kyōyō* conferred aristocratic values and elite status, pitted culture and refinement against the threatening claims of mass culture—consumption and consumerism, and the feared 'secularization' and democratization of cultural life which the emergence of the new classes in the Taishō period had promised to promote."[94] The different determinants of economy and education often overlapped as the reformers placed themselves on the same side as the middle and upper classes, claiming a distinction between the reformers and the middle and upper classes only to the extent that *aikatsuka* were supposedly more knowledgeable about cinema than their economically privileged brethren. Their overall unity was often achieved through mutual fear of or repugnance for the new urban, working-class culture and its crass, hybrid tastes.

Also visible in reformist discourse is the language of place, age, and gender. The Pure Film Movement frequently claimed that women and children dominated the audience for Japanese films. This is statistically suspect, but what is more important to emphasize here is the impressions contemporaries had and how they potentially functioned. For instance, it is clear that labeling something the favorite of women and children was one means of denigrating it in this discursive context.[95] Another way of defining class was through geography: one *Kinema Record* editorial distinguished between the tastes of those from Yamanote (the affluent residential part of western Tokyo), who had developed a preference for mood and color influenced by Western films, and those from Asakusa (the *shitamachi* populated by workers and craftsmen), who were "ignorant and vulgar." Echoing the editorial on censorship, this piece remarks, "Asakusa showmanship may be fine for the tastes of Asakusa, . . . but it's truly upsetting when this is done around commonly good families,"[96] as if the lower classes of Asakusa did not belong to the definition of "good families." The aversion to Asakusa of many intellectuals is understandable if one accepts Yoshimi Shun'ya's description of that area's culture: there, all classes, from rich to poor, from intellectual to ignorant, were easily accommodated in a space that, in the *Tokyo asahi*'s description (in chapter 1), was heterotopic to the degree that it undermined social divisions. Of the boundaries that were crossed, a crucial one was that between exhibitor and viewer, between artist and audience, Asakusa being the center of a communal performance of entertainment that Yoshimi stresses was mostly a product of lower-class Tokyo culture.[97] The hybridity of Asakusa showmanship, like that evident in the films shown, disturbed the editors of *Kinema Record*.

Some reformers took pains in other essays to present a vision of Japanese cinema that encompassed viewers both high and low.[98] That ideal, however, was not the mélange of Asakusa's cultural geography but a more rational construction of culture, as these writers often advocated the construction of a film industry essentially no different from a mass-culture industry. I return to this point later, but for the time being, it is important to stress that, in the reformers' reiterations of terms like *audience* and *society*, the mass audience was defined much like the "popular" in contemporary debates on popular art and entertainment, as an entity that encompassed all essential social divisions, but one whose tastes were molded by the bourgeoisie. Gonda also attempted to construct a mass audience, but his was, as I have argued, a vain attempt to do so in terms of working-class tastes. The discourse of the Pure Film Movement made no such attempt.

Reformers were confronted with the economic fact that cinema functioned as low-cost entertainment for the lower classes. With ticket prices ranging on average from ten to thirty sen in 1916 (in contrast, in a legitimate theater like the Teikoku Gekijō—which the *Kinema Record* editorial cites as blissfully lacking the unwashed masses—a ticket could cost as much as five *yen*),[99] cinema was a cheap alternative to the regular stage for the less affluent. Gonda celebrated this fact as the material basis for a new form of culture, a modern one founded in new modes of perception and understanding. Pure film reformers, however, attempted to resist this in their own conception of cinema and culture. The low cost of cinema may have enabled some companies to construct it as a form of cheap theater, but it was the working classes' acceptance of this—the cultural more than the economic issue—that infuriated reformers: it represented not only ignorance of cinema but also the vulgarity of taste in general. In this way, the Pure Film Movement was not just an effort to purify cinema but equally a social movement resisting the modernity represented by lower-class culture and countering it with a different modernity embodied in homogenized bourgeois taste.

Cinema, as a consequence of being located wholly on the side of intellectual taste, was inscribed with the language of class. Although Burch cites Japan as an exception to the embourgeoisement of cinema represented in early cinema in the West by the transition from the primitive to the institutional mode of production, it is clear from an examination of pure film discourse that early cinema in Japan, too, was structured by a shift in the class definition of the cinema. Janet Staiger's thesis about early American cinema is thus inapplicable to Japan. It is possible to argue, as she does, that the shift to classical Hollywood film practices around 1909 in the United States was more a result of the expansion of the cinema audience to include lower-class viewers and immigrants than an attempt to claim a more Anglo-Saxon bourgeois clientele.[100] But the transformation in Japanese cinema was not noticeably spurred by any significant change in audience composition and was clearly coded in class terms, with the importation of Hollywood style constituting an effort to reclaim the medium for the middle class. In this sense, some of the social conditions of early cinema in Japan resemble those of early cinema in Germany described by Heidi Schlüpmann.[101] Finally, the changes in 1910s Japanese film culture were not wholly necessitated by the demands of film narrative. As Charles Musser and Komatsu Hiroshi have argued, the crisis in film narration defined by a movement from stories all spectators knew to original, longer, more complex narratives—a turn that, in the American case, spurred the development of modes of narration less dependent on audience knowledge and thus more self-sufficient—occurred in Japan around 1912 and was successfully solved by increasing the role of the benshi instead of internalizing narration within the text.[102] Any subsequent attempt at such internalization must have involved determinants more contextual (i.e., issues of class and censorship) than textual (the demands of narrative per se).

It is important to detail this shift by again examining the role of film study. Clearly, the definition of cinema as a social problem was central to the discourse of the Pure Film Movement. But while Gonda took this as an attack on the whole of cinema that had to be corrected through film study, *Kinema Record*, in a process of displacement, redirected criticism of the motion pictures away from the medium itself and toward Japanese film. Cinema, the editors claimed, was not the problem; rather, the problem was the lower classes and their tastes. The motion pictures were saved, but at the cost of a double erasure: first, of existing Japanese cinema, and then, of a large portion of the contemporary film audience.

Such a move was justified through the operations of film study and the notion of a cinematic essence. If we follow Gonda's definition, film study was one of the modes for appropriating and molding cinema, albeit a privileged one. Some of the aspects nascent in Gonda's notion of film study— the hierarchy and authority of the norm—would become fully developed in the Pure Film Movement. Gonda, however, insisted on the importance of reception in the space of exhibition, if only because that remained a space of struggle and indeterminacy for film study, as bottom-up definitions of cinema in the theater clashed with top-down efforts to regulate reception. But among *aikatsuka*, the issue of reception was effaced in favor of a film study that lovingly accepted, respected, and preserved the filmic

text and the essence of the medium, thus eliminating reception as a significant factor in cinematic production. Film study was a mark of distinction
for the few who could wield it; others were asked to study the motion pictures only so that they, too, could become *aikatsuka*. This distinction, this
exclusivity, went hand in hand with the exclusivity of cinematic essence,
one that made irrelevant the issue of how meaning was produced in the
space of reception. Film study appropriated the power to authoritatively
speak on cinema, only to transfer it to the cinematic medium in the form
of a "nature" that reformers would then use to criticize other modes of
meaning production.

These other forms of viewing were seen as violating the medium, by
defining films as theater, by laying more importance on the benshi than on
the text, or by valorizing the experience in the theater over absorption in
the film. Study was also a technology of power, a metanarrative that had the
authority to judge, criticize, and correct other modes of understanding film
on the basis of a conception of the essence of cinema. The logic of essence
was central to the Pure Film Movement, as its name implies. An example
of this train of reasoning was apparent in a 1915 *Kinema Record* editorial:
"*How can we construct respectable moving picture plays?* Of course, by
putting into play their essence. Everything displays its essence: for instance,
person A has the essence of a soldier, and person B has the essence of a novelist. But even if A tries out B's literature and B imitates A's soldiery, both
will end in failure: only when A plays out A's essence and B plays out B's
essence can A and B each succeed. Moving pictures are the same."[103]

The declaration that things or people should follow or fulfill their
essence or idea is common in both Western and Eastern philosophy, from
Plato to Confucius, but my concern here is with the phrase "of course"
(mochiron), with the discursive construction of a logic held as "natural,"
in which attention to the need to consummate an essence obfuscates the
operations of and ideological implications behind the process of molding
that identity. Operating as a discipline of knowledge, film study helped
define the field of what is expressible in discourse, silencing other voices for
being not only "wrong" but also incomprehensible and "unnatural." In so
doing, it attempted to shape—not, as it pretended, "reveal"—the medium,
as well as define who was watching and how they and the cinema would fit
within the nation and modern culture.

In the case of 1910s Japanese discourse on film, the reliance on essence
was an attempt to eliminate the multiple possibilities for film culture that
Gonda had recognized, in which different audiences appropriated the cinema in their own ways according to their own horizons of experience. In

their place was constructed a univocal concept of cinema effected in part through the construction of an audience that could only be middle class (all other viewers not being proper cinematic spectators). Cinema's resistance to discourse, which Gonda utilized to valorize the potential for the space of reception to create multiple meanings from the image, was redefined through the authority of film study. Ideal film viewing was no longer the nonintellectual, intuitive, playful, and subjective appropriation of the image Gonda perceived, but the serious intellectual approach represented by a film study that devoted itself to pursuing a single cinematic essence.

The case of 1910s Japanese film culture offers an important intervention in debates on textuality and readership. The writings of Gonda and the Pure Film Movement show that the issue is not whether texts construct readers or vice versa, but how the text-reader relationship is defined through discourse and other means in various historical conjunctures. The problem in the 1910s concerns not only the degree to which the Pure Film Movement redefined the medium, cinematic textuality, and modes of readership in light of middle-class norms—though I later address each of these important issues in turn—but also how the very possibility of appropriating filmic texts was historically constructed and became a locus of struggle. In the shift from Gonda to the Pure Film Movement, the embourgeoisement of Japanese film culture also crucially involved the suppression of film cultures that enabled flexible viewer interpretation, allowing lower-class audiences to make cinema a part of their lives and thus an aspect of their class culture. The Pure Film Movement's appropriation of the Hollywood style could be termed a form of vernacular modernism, which molded the classical style to its needs in dealing with the problems of Japanese modernity. We must not forget, however, that such a vernacular modernism, at least in this case, used its supposed universality (its ties to America and the West) to suppress other forms of film viewing and production and to reinforce its claim to monopolize the ability to appropriate style—cinematic forms that to reformers represented some of the problems of modernity. Such a modernism is less Japan's creolization of modernist style than a particular class definition of modernity, one more Fordist, that attempted to dominate a more hybrid conception of modernity—another, *competing* form of vernacular modernism in Japan. The operations of power and attempts to monopolize the means to define and appropriate cinema should never be left out of the analysis of vernacular modernism.

It is important to recognize how much film study was a creation of the problem of cinema. Proponents of film study, confronting the definition of cinema as a social problem, had to reject other modes of reading film (especially ones that denigrated the medium) in order to resurrect and reform the status of cinema. They could do so, however, only by asserting their own authority as the legitimate spokespersons for the medium and negating other ways of speaking about the cinema. It was probably under these conditions that other options for defining film study itself—evident in Gonda's contradictory but playful stance or even in the (limited) populism of *Kinema Record*—were reduced to the formation of a unified front to defend the medium. Study's proponents displaced the tensions of this defensive position onto their own enemy, onto another set of filmic practices deemed uncinematic, which they took as their task to eliminate. Given that what was to be negated was Japanese cinema and lower-class taste, it should be clear the degree to which film study and even the concept of cinema itself were deeply inscribed with the dynamics of class in the Japanese social sphere. Yet a negation of a negation (rejecting a bad cinema in order to defend the medium from those who wished to eliminate it) proved a weak solution: as a process of negation, film study in prewar Japan would continue to be haunted by the social problem of cinema, if only because it still needed both social critics of the cinema and an uncinematic film practice to perpetuate itself—to define itself—as their negation and reinforce film study and its authority in the cultural field. Thus one would find many film critics repeatedly denigrating Japanese film even during the wartime, when Japanese film had finally been given a privileged status by the state.[104] But then, as before in the Taishō era, film study by intellectual reformers had to look to another mode of dealing with cinema as a social problem for strength; in fact, they had to look to another form of discourse on cinema intimately related to film study: censorship.

4 The Subject of the Text

Benshi, Authors, and Industry

The Benshi in Film History

In histories of the cinema, attitudes toward the benshi diverge. Until recently, histories of Japanese cinema written by Japanese scholars have tended to inherit the Pure Film Movement's disdain for the practice. Satō Tadao, for instance, describes the phenomenon of the benshi in these terms:

> Movie theaters made the energetic and exaggerated explanation of these benshi the selling point, and the benshi were in fact more popular than actors. Their education level, however, was generally low, and this was especially the trend among benshi for Japanese films. That's why there were nonsensical explanations that just suavely rattled off flowery words and phrases. Since the benshi would arbitrarily provide psychological description on his own, it was it harder for benshi to continue talking if the director tried cinematic devices such as cutting more precisely. It was easier to talk if the camera was put in one place for a long take.[1]

The presence of the popular benshi was seen as an obstacle to the cinematic evolution of Japanese film, not only because they supposedly protested when given films difficult to explain, but also because they acted as a crutch for directors who did not have to create narratively self-sufficient scenes because the benshi were there to fill the gaps. Only in the last few years has Japanese scholarship, perhaps influenced by foreign interest in the benshi, sought to valorize the institution, either as a successor to the tradition of Japanese oral storytelling or as a manifestation of lower-class culture.[2]

One of Noël Burch's contributions was to defend the role of the benshi against attacks. He saw the existence of the benshi as one factor preventing the colonization of Japanese film by Western definitions of the cinematic, allowing Japanese cinema to develop into a form radically different from the dominant Hollywood mode. In *To the Distant Observer,* he argues that a film shown with a benshi differs from a Hollywood text that functions as a transparent window into a univocal world: the benshi splits the fictional source of enunciation by assuming the role of narration and thereby purges the text of narrative itself. The film, or more specifically the illusory world viewed in the text, no longer speaks for itself, but rather is spoken for by an external figure. Not only is the system of representation fragmented, but also the signs that make up the text cease to transparently transmit a seemingly preexisting world. They are read by the benshi as independently existing signs that must compete with the words the benshi produces. Spectators are unable to enter the world of the diegesis because they remain aware of the film as something to be read, as only a text. Burch contends that Japanese prewar filmgoers did not succumb to the fictional effect of the film but instead treated spectatorship as the simultaneous viewing of both the spectacle of the text and the reading of the film.[3]

Burch's argument is compelling because it does identify some of the features that bothered reformers about the benshi, but it fails to offer evidence that spectators did read the benshi this way. J.L. Anderson's well-researched work on the institution offers a more historically grounded account, emphasizing benshi (he uses the term *katsuben*) narration as a continuation of the tradition of "commingled media" in the Japanese arts, and adding institutional analysis to discern the economic basis for the benshi's survival long into the 1930s. With less of a theoretical underpinning, he still echoes Burch's arguments in claiming: "To most audiences, the film was an open text and one element in a complex, multi-media, live entertainment. A large part of the pleasure for the audience was in the *katsuben*'s creative and critical reading of the film. . . . Indeed, the presence of the *katsuben* attacked the ontological status of the film. Was truth in the photographic images or in what the *katsuben* said?"[4]

Jeffery Dym provides a well-researched account of the artistry of the benshi, having combed through many contemporary writings to gain a sense of historical difference in an institution that most have treated as monolithic, describing not only a historical periodization of benshi practice but also various styles within different eras.[5] His work provides a detailed picture of the world of the benshi, offering factual evidence for arguments that Donald Kirihara and I have made concerning the benshi's ability to actually promote the diegetic effect.[6] Dym, however, does not adequately analyze this evidence from a theoretical standpoint, and instead offers a partisan if not romanticist celebration of the benshi as a neglected art, rather than a critical consideration of the ideological struggles over benshi and what it might have meant to call their work an art at the time.

One of the theoretical issues Dym fails to address sufficiently is the changing relationship between benshi and the film text over time. Both Burch and Anderson argue the benshi were vitally important precisely because they see them as somehow separate from the text, as an independent signifying system that either counters diegetic illusionism (Burch) or reflects unique Japanese performance traditions (Anderson). The framework separating the enunciative subjectivity of the benshi from that of the film can also be seen in work that discusses the lecturer in American and European cinema. Agreeing with a point made by Miriam Hansen, Tom Gunning argues that, around 1908, "the lecturer's new role consisted in aiding spectator comprehension of, and involvement with, the more complex stories." As such, the lecturer provided the basis for what Gunning calls the classical Hollywood "narrator system," which itself could be described as merely the internalization within the text of the lecturer's role. In the end, however, Gunning contends, following Burch: "The lecturer could supply such values only as a supplement, an additional aid, rather than as an inherent organic unity. . . . The narrator system could not afford a discontinuous presentation which might undermine film's illusionism. Such a practice would be totally at odds with the cinema of narrative integration, which maintained the film's illusion through a strong diegetic realism and an empathetic narrative." In the end, Gunning argues, "the film lecturer could only serve as a short-term solution to narrative comprehensibility. The narrator system offered a more viable solution."[7]

In most of these accounts of processes of narration like that of the benshi, the central presumption is that the system of the lecturer/benshi bore a fundamental incompatibility with the concept of a closed, diegetic text. While the lecture definitely aided the project of narrative comprehension by compellingly relating more complex and psychologically profound stories, "paradoxically," says Hansen, "the lecture effectively undermine[d] an emerging sense of diegetic illusion; the presence of a human voice inhibited closure of the fictional world on screen and thus the perceptual segregation from theater space essential to the diegetic effect."[8] To some extent, these are the problems expressed by reformists in the Pure Film Movement about the institution of the benshi, the issues they believed necessitated its abolition. The question, however, is whether it is justifiable to argue conversely that, since reformers did not succeed in ridding Japanese movie houses of the benshi, we must then accept the conclusion of

Burch and others that the filmic text in Japan was not closed and that it did not produce an illusionistic diegetic effect—that is, that Japanese silent film culture was essentially different from that of the classical system. Analyzing the discourse on the benshi in the late 1910s and early 1920s, and considering how reformers attempted to redefine the institution, I argue that, far from subverting it, the benshi became an important aspect of creating a new definition of the cinematic text founded in diegetic illusionism and the univocality of narration. Establishing this new relationship between benshi and text also became a basis, if at times only metaphorically, for reconceiving the production of cinematic meaning and thus concepts of the author, stars, and industry.

The Benshi and the Text

Critiques of the benshi showed up early in *Katsudō shashinkai* but turned especially vigorous in the late 1910s, just when the first examples of a "purer" cinema were reaching the theater screens only to be presented with *kowairo* narration. As we have seen already, film reformers lambasted benshi for their supposed lack of education, ignorance of cinema, and tendency to seek more attention than the film. More specific criticisms were directed at particular kinds of benshi, for in the mid-1910s there existed various modes of benshi explanation and which mode was used depended most often on the genre of the film. Japanese *kyūgeki* were usually accompanied by a group of *kowairo* benshi who imitated the voices of the characters in time with Kabuki *narimono* music, closely approximating the presentation of a theatrical performance. *Shinpa* was often performed by fewer *kowairo* benshi (two normally narrated one film, switching in the middle), who imitated several voices in a sung style. Western films were also sometimes explained with sung *kowairo* narration, but as the decade went on the dominant style turned to a more plain-voiced and descriptive explanation, increasingly set to Western music. In a leftover from the early days, when benshi provided an explanation only before and not during the film, most benshi, up until the late 1910s, offered a *maesetsu,* or "preexplanation," before projection, using it as their main opportunity to present their patented verbal flourishes while standing in a spotlight, before they went on to explain the film in the dark as it was projected.

Using *kowairo* benshi for Japanese *kyūgeki* was, as we have seen, considered a violation of the unique essence of cinema, presenting what should be a silent medium as theater. The practice itself was believed to be a sign that Japanese film producers and exhibitors did not understand what cinema was. *Kowairo* for *shinpa,* while less of a theatrical presentation, was faulted for its self-serving excess: it was these benshi whom directors of the initial reformist films—all of which were contemporary, not period films—blamed for first resisting and then ruining the intention behind their works.[9] The very fact that benshi explained Japanese films was considered a disgrace, which proved either that producers could not create texts that Japanese could understand without explanation, or that spectators were too ignorant to understand movies on their own.[10] Films should be able to explain themselves, reformers argued, which made the existence of the benshi fundamentally at odds with the inherent interest of the motion pictures.[11]

The potentially destructive practices of the benshi also spilled over into the narration of the foreign films much loved by intellectuals. The benshi's worst crime in the eyes of progressive film fans was their proclivity for excess, for orating in a fashion so irrelevant to the needs of the story that they greatly deviated from the text. In the words of one critic, "Benshi explain with so many adjectives that the result is they make a mess of the intent of the film."[12] Reformers recognized that the textual effect could differ for the same film depending on who the benshi was, what mood he was in, and other ephemeral factors, undermining the consistency and unique identity of the text.[13] Some reformers were aware that the discourses of the benshi and the film text were separate, and that the former could block or alter reception of the latter. One of the dangers was that the benshi, if not the theatrical space of exhibition itself, were assuming the position of authorship, a pretension that some theaters seemed to promote in their advertisements.

In criticizing this situation, reformers availed themselves of the conception of the closed cinematic text, one that bore its own meaning independently of the words of the benshi. This ideal, however, depended in part on the benshi for its existence. Noticing the differences produced by screening the same film with different benshi helped spur reformist critics to postulate a sameness residing in the text that transcended time and place. The benshi also served as the other term in a semiotic system of differences through which the cinematic text was defined, a kind of Derridean supplement that sometimes threatened to supplant what it supplemented. If the benshi's craft was based in words, cinema's was centered on the visual register, as many reformers echoed Gotthold Lessing's aesthetics in defining the art of the motion pictures through its central perceptual register(s).[14] Pure film reformers sought to reverse a situation in which, as one observer described it, "the preconception that the explanation is the lord and the film its servant still occupies the minds of Japanese."[15] The cinema was to be complete and self-sufficient, and the benshi a mere figure who "does not exist apart from the film."[16] Simply put, a pure film did not need explanation, and explanation

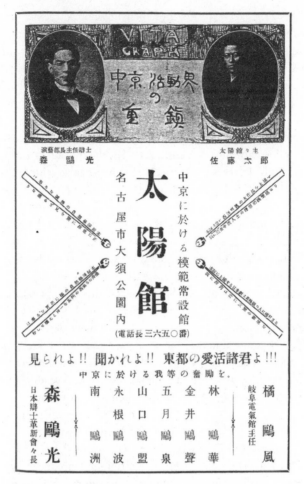

Figure 12.   The men responsible for the film experience at the Taiyōkan theater in Nagoya, according to an ad from 1914: the theater manager Satō Tarō (right) and the lead benshi, Mori Ōkō. (*Kinema Record* 16 [October 1914]: n.p.)

was the crime of the benshi: as one critic asked, "Is there anything except explanation that can fundamentally destroy a pure film?"[17]

There remained a gap between benshi and the essence of the film text, especially with regard to the issue of sound. An early piece in *Katsudō shashinkai* criticized *kowairo* benshi for the fact that they "lack unity with the actions of the characters, lose harmony, and do not further display the expressions of those active in the scene." The benshi's inability to match the text sparked the commentator to propose the use of a phonograph recording of the actor's own voices to facilitate a synchronous sound matching the expressions. Only then would sound seemingly correspond with the ontological realism of the cinematic text. Since *kowairo* imitation fails, the writer concluded, "the explanation of a moving picture should stop, as the word indicates, at explanation."[18]

The problem with the benshi largely centered on his position as mediator between the text and the audience. As Anderson notes, benshi often functioned as representatives of the audience, as exemplars of spectatorship whom individual viewers were asked to follow.[19] It was their position as role models, in fact, that made them central to the project of film censorship. The possibility that these exemplars could commit errors loomed as a serious problem, however. Many analysts of the benshi at that time located the source of their mistakes in an insufficient educational background and in poor working conditions, where benshi were often forced to narrate a film on stage after having seen it only once in a prescreening late the night before a run started. One viewing, it was argued, was insufficient and prompted errors that the audience could readily catch.[20] The moment of error was especially consternating to reformers, given that it, first, reminded spectators that there was a difference between the text and its explanation, and that it, second, brought viewers out of their contemplation of the film's narrative into the space of the theater, reminding them this was a performance, not a complete diegetic world.

More important, error also foregrounded the problem of spectatorship. If benshi were making mistakes after one viewing, what were audiences doing? Weren't all spectators required to understand the film on one viewing? The benshi's "nonserious" approach to film came to symbolize the aberrant reading practices of the mass of spectators with no more, or even less, education than the benshi. Worse yet, benshi misreadings reminded critics of the persistent power that alternative modes of reception had to redefine the text, to read a film differently than it should be. The benshi, then, did not just represent an obstacle to the narrative unity of the text: in the discourse of the Pure Film Movement, they also exposed the persistent problem of difference in both film culture and the social sphere.

Molding Benshi

Reform of the benshi would have to solve such filmic and social problems, but the question was whether both filmic and social problems could be approached in the same way. Here the difference of opinion between authorities and pure film reformers reared its head. If the aim was to perfect a closed diegetic world, perhaps the elimination of the benshi and the internalization of the narrator system would, as Gunning suggests, have offered a more viable alternative. But if the question was how to control film reception by viewers, the continued presence of a reformed benshi had its advantages. This problem would remain inextricable for some reformers, as Kaeriyama and others persisted in trying to create pure films and show them, unsuccessfully, without benshi accompaniment.[21] Even among the most vociferous critics of the benshi, however, there were individuals willing to offer solutions other than abolition of the practice. In these discourses a resolution of the problems posed by the benshi, the text, and the spectator becomes visible.

A well-published critic of the benshi, Katano Akeji, offered his own version of the historical development of the institution. Benshi, he argues, first appeared because the medium itself was foreign and strange and required some form of explanation to satisfy people's curiosity. As audiences became used to the medium, the role of the benshi changed. They remained necessary for foreign films in order to translate titles and explain what might be unknown to Japanese. Benshi were originally necessary for Japanese films, he contends, because such works were copies of theater and needed voices to complete the theatrical illusion. Such films, however, could not truly be called cinema. To Katano, benshi were necessary in Japanese film culture because of a deficiency in the motion pictures; consequently, he insists, "I believe that with the filling of that lack, it becomes possible to accept the idea of eliminating the benshi for Japanese films."[22] Just as Katano could not accept the use of benshi for a Japanese pure film, most reformers would accept the presence of benshi at a Japanese film screening only if the work remained deficient as cinema. Until such deficiencies in film were remedied, however, Katano and others called on the benshi to work for the reform of Japanese cinema by ridding it of its theatrical elements (e.g., by refraining from *kowairo* or otherwise treating the films as theater). For some, the only role left for the benshi was that of interpreter for foreign films.[23]

Reformers devoted much time to delineating the proper function of the benshi, and initially these discussions were often tied to issues of terminology. One critic of the benshi, Takeda Kōkatsu, offers a short history of the words used to name the benshi: "People in society derided them as benshi, or called them *katsuben*, failing to treat them as equal human beings. At the same time, they attacked the moving pictures. Those reverberations have had their effect today, and the word *benshi* has disappeared; and under the name *setsumeisha* [explainer], they have come to explain films. Yet the word *setsumeisha* is definitely not appropriate. . . . Instead of that, it would be better to boldly rename them *hon'yakusha* [translators]."[24] Takeda was not alone in tying the proper role of the benshi to their name. Just as the discourse of the Pure Film Movement tried to free the cinema of its vulgar past by renaming it *eiga*, reformers linked reform of the benshi to changes in language. The old term *benshi* (orator), first prevalent in the early 1910s, reflected a system in which the benshi was truly an orator expected to speak and argue, to enounce his own opinion. While Takeda preferred the term *hon'yakusha*, presumably because the role of explaining gave too much power to the benshi, most of his fellow reformers opted for the term *setsumeisha*, which defined the benshi only as a figure who explains, who simply supplements another text instead of creating his own. The new name became the definition of what the benshi should do. Furukawa Roppa, the film journalist of aristocratic birth who later became one of Japan's great musical-comedy stars, succinctly outlined the function of the benshi: "The answer to the question 'What is the task of the *setsumeisha*?' is extremely simple: 'To explain the film.' That's it. To say it more precisely, it is 'to make the audience understand everything in the film.'"[25] As *setsumeisha*, benshi were defined by a tautology—the explainer who explains—which confined their role to acting *as* a tautology: saying what had already been said, repeating what was already evident in the text so that everyone would clearly understand its meaning. Some cited this redundancy as a reason for eliminating the benshi,[26] but many made this the cornerstone of their advice to practitioners of the craft.

Throughout the 1910s and 1920s, many how-to books and articles on the craft were written for aspiring benshi, and most of these urged the benshi to keep to the text and refrain from excess oration. The *Katsudō shashinkai* essays on film exhibition by Eda Fushiki, himself a benshi, offer a wealth of dos and don'ts for benshi at a time when narration styles and protocols were still shifting, from the presentation of only *maesetsu*, before the film, to the additional presentation of explanation during projection. His comments about the difficulty of explaining everything beforehand are an example of the discursive background behind what Komatsu Hiroshi and Charles Musser identity as the shift in Japanese film history to longer narratives that increasingly relied on the benshi to interpret during projection as well.[27] Eda's further advice to avoid "killing the picture" by disclosing the entire plot before the screening also reveals an increased emphasis on narrative pleasure based on the temporality of the text, not oratorical excess in the theater, which then led him to advise all benshi to narrate "objectively" during projection. Eda's dictum to benshi is that they strive "to bring the picture to life," but he generally warns them to

Figure 13.   Eda Fushiki in 1915, when he was
a benshi at the Denkikan. (*Katsudō shashin
zasshi* 1.2 [July 1915]: n.p.)

remain succinct and refrain from oration irrelevant to the film in both the
maesetsu and the explanation during the screening.[28] His list of mottos
for proper benshi narration includes such advice as: "Refrain from words
of self-praise," "The aim is to clearly and succinctly work toward arousing emotion," "It is impermissible to mention things irrelevant to the
picture," and "Do not tell lies that cause people to err."[29] Foreshadowing
later censorship regulations, he also makes sure to warn benshi to refrain
from drinking and womanizing and, in general, to maintain a good public
character. Already visible in Eda's discourse in 1910 is the effort to dilute
the benshi's presence by confining their narration to transmitting the pleasures of the film, not explaining it.

Over ten years later, in the first book-length work of advice for benshi, a writer using the pseudonym Yume Sōbei developed and codified
Eda's suggestions. Yume comments on what he considered the dominant
style in Eda's era: "The manner of explanation of the benshi in those days

resembled being dragged along by the film. To put it more precisely, it was a feeling less of explaining the film than watching it. This was because the explanation did not try to approach the content of the film but only went along dragged by its surface. . . . Explanation cannot be dragged along by the scene. It must proceed parallel to the scene and cannot take one step out of the emotional and intellectual events expressed in each scene."[30] According to Yume, narration should not work separately from the film, acting like a spectator who merely looks on, trying to follow the progress of an unknown work; explanation had to match the work's content and get behind its surface, becoming one with the narrative process of the film. In this conception, narrational style would not be the property of benshi themselves—that is, a matter of personal style—but would "have to be decided naturally through the content and the type of film."[31]

Yume advises his benshi readers to understand the film they are explaining so as to be able to work with it; ideally, "benshi must to a certain degree penetrate inside the thoughts and emotions of the characters in the drama and explain from there."[32] Required to enter the film, benshi had to refrain from puns to make the audience laugh and overindulgent oration to increase their popularity. In opposition to those benshi who, in order to enhance their prestige among lower-class audiences, tended to overuse highfalutin Chinese-based words, Yume posits a more ideal narrator: "The true attitude benshi must assume is to offer an explanation that will satisfy and make people of all classes understand. Benshi know that reeling off difficult words or phrases will in most cases not bring the film to life but will, on the contrary, mix in other meanings and kill the film. They also are aware that separating themselves from the film when explaining and mixing in their own impressions should be avoided at all costs."[33] In Yume's ideal, the language of the benshi had to be transparent; the narrator had to efface himself in the space of the theater by matching his enunciation to that of the film. Importantly, the requirement that benshi offer explanations that all could understand was also a means of suppressing some spectators' taste for language as spectacle, for filmgoing as the enjoyment of excess. The standard of comprehension, then, presented the transmission of the content of the text as the goal of film viewing, and it constructed a mass audience that was equal to the benshi in its understanding of the same film.

The apparent effect of the advice Eda, Yume, and others gave was visible in changes in actual benshi practice during the 1910s. Prominent benshi related these transformations themselves in articles in the major film journals. One of the main benshi at the Denkikan, Nishimura Rakuten, relates how he had realized the error of his past ways:

Figure 14.   The benshi in transition: Nishimura Rakuten
as both an oratorical star and a man of learning dedicated
to the text. (*Katsudō gahō* 1.3 [March 1917]: n.p.)

I initially used *kōdan*[34] with moving pictures. Most benshi were linking
together flowery words, but I was sadly crying, expressing my feelings
myself [separate from the film]. By chance, I was greatly applauded
and, for the first time, discovered how interesting it was being a benshi.

But thinking about it now, I was a fool. I wasn't faithful to the picture. In other words, I killed the picture. Although in those days, I too
was somewhat satisfied if I pleased the audience, the times don't permit
that anymore. Without knowing it, the time came when we all had to
wake up.[35]

But while Nishimura recognized a change from self-expression to faithfulness to the film, one of the leading benshi, Ikoma Raiyū, describes a transformation in the purpose of explanation itself. According to him, early films were defined only by their stories, such that "the benshi's ability was displayed in how he made a bad story seem interesting, in showing the film in a good light. . . . Sometimes, the explanation would break away from the film and get sidetracked in extraordinary directions. This was explanation not for viewers but for listeners."

Whereas previous filmgoing experience had focused on enjoying the oral presentation of a story, with the film serving only as an occasion for spoken narration, Ikoma argues that present-day cinema, which was now based on mood and not just on the story, demanded a different approach: "The benshi also had to take care not to destroy that mood. This was a revolutionary period among benshi. It was no longer explanation for listening, as with the previous films based on the purpose of the story, but explanation for the convenience of people watching. Naturally, it was not permissible for explanation to leave the boundaries of the film."[36] According to Ikoma, there was a radical shift in the way the cinematic experience was defined: it was no longer a matter of listening to film as simply another form of illustrated storytelling but a matter of viewing it as a cinematic mood that exceeded the story and was unique to the motion pictures. Benshi had to transform their methods because oration was no longer their goal; the point was now to relate a filmic atmosphere, and this meant toning down the spectacle of language and obeying the text. The great benshi Somei Saburō, who first at the Denkikan and then at the Teikokukan pioneered a more objective form of narration for Western films, describes his new style in *Katsudō no sekai:* "When I explain, I first make sure that I completely enter into the picture. If I don't become one with its characters, in the end my explanation will lose energy and seem out of place."[37]

Benshi practice from the 1910s to the 1920s reflects this shift away from the primacy of oral narration to a style that united the benshi's enunciation with that of the film text. Explanation began taking place during projection just before 1910 and then became the only way to narrate a film, as benshi like Tokugawa Musei began to eliminate *maesetsu* around 1917. Now narrating only in the dark, the benshi ceased showing their faces before the audience, losing the spotlight not only literally but also because the explanation was thoroughly conjoined with the film. Explanation during the film could still feature its own excessive independence, such as in *shinpa kowairo*, which had its heyday at the end of the 1910s,

Figure 15. Tokugawa Musei later in life (circa 1930s), when he was a prominent film actor, essayist, and radio raconteur. (Courtesy of the National Museum of Modern Art, Tokyo, the National Film Center)

but that style gradually disappeared at the beginning of the 1920s. In its place, the succinct, objective, and non-*kowairo* style of Tokugawa, the greatest of post–Pure Film Movement benshi and the darling of many intellectual film fans, became the horizon for much of benshi narration, setting the standard against which all the various forms of explanation, whether for Japanese or foreign films, *jidaigeki* or *gendaigeki*, were measured. When most benshi began calling themselves *setsumeisha* at the end of the 1910s (this was how they were referred to in censorship codes too), it was clear that the role of the benshi had been restricted to mere explanation of the film. By 1925, commentators were already proclaiming the end of a golden age in which the benshi were had been more popular than the films they narrated; in the new era, audiences demanded explanation only, and even benshi for Matsunosuke's films abandoned *kagezerifu* for objective narration.[38]

These historical shifts in the role of the benshi are analogous to the changes identified in research on early American film. A benshi more concerned with his oration than with his faithfulness to the film foregrounded the space of the theater and created the kind of "perceptual continuity between the space on the screen and the social space of the theater" that Miriam Hansen cites as an important aspect of early cinema.[39] Although he barely mentions cinema, Yoshimi Shun'ya has described the experience of an entertainment center like Asakusa precisely as "giving birth to what can be called a kind of communal rapport mediated by the intimate communication between audience and stage," a rapport that would forever add new stories and meanings to whatever text appeared in that space.[40] The benshi in the film theater similarly acted as another form of "attraction" in the carnival of cinema, another item in a variety of live entertainments that often created new texts from the ones provided by the film studios. (Remember that many theaters made live acts part of the bill even into the late 1920s.) Restricting the role of the benshi to merely explaining the text would radically alter the filmgoing experience by suppressing the space of the theater and segregating it from the world on-screen, centering pleasure on absorption in a text that was defined as complete before the audience entered the theater.

Tom Gunning emphasizes that the cinema of attractions' "fundamental hold on spectators depends on arousing and satisfying visual curiosity through a direct and acknowledged act of display,"[41] but this is not entirely accurate in the Japanese case. First, as Ikoma stresses, early cinema in Japan was often story oriented, but it was a form of narration centered on the aural, so it would be difficult to describe the experience of Japanese cinema before around 1918 as centered on visual display, given the importance of the benshi. As mentioned before, Komatsu argues that for early Japanese cinema "the linguistic aspect of the images was borne by the dialogue of the benshi, with the images themselves being the illustration of an independently existing storyline."[42] Early "spectators" (the term itself becomes problematic in this case) were more often listeners than viewers,[43] enjoying the intimacy of the theater's space as much as the illusion of the cinematic space.[44]

What they were listening to was, in most cases, stories, narratives in a style similar to that of *kōdan* and other oral storytelling forms. Japanese early cinema, especially after 1910, was very much concerned with narrative, but this does not mean that the motion picture experience at the time was closer to that of classical cinema. It is important to distinguish, as Noël Burch does, between narrative and diegesis: narratives can create a diegetic world to a lesser or greater degree.[45] The problem reformers had with Japanese cinema was less that it was not narrative than that it did not sufficiently produce a diegetic effect; stories were being told, but they were, first, not essentially cinematic, and second, often centered on linguistic or aural forms of display. Early films had the kind of direct address Gunning sees as blocking cinema's diegetic effect, but again, this was mostly a linguistic form of address, not a visual one.

The visual aspect of early cinema in Japan should not be denied, however. As noted in chapter 3, Komatsu has argued that the visuals in a film like *Gorō Masamune kōshiden* could not bear narration because this would conflict with the benshi's subjective expression, undermining the explainer's assumption of the subject of enunciation and "destabiliz[ing] the unity of words and images."[46] This argument, however, presumes univocality in the early cinematic experience, which, we have seen, was not the case; while Komatsu assumes that the visual image remained subordinate to the benshi narration, reformers complained that the two would often conflict. Even if we can accept that the linguistic dominated the visual in the experience of narrative (though not necessarily of the cinema as a whole), some spectators, as is evident from the complaints of Japanese educators, were paying more attention to the images than the narration and, in fact, misunderstanding the gist of the story because the visuals were telling them something different from what they were meant to perceive. The experience of early cinema in Japan, then, should be defined neither as the dominance of visual attractions over narrative nor as the opposite, but as a plethora of equally viable modes of enjoyment, of which the narrative of the benshi was an important aspect but, in the end, only one of many "attractions," which could conflict. Far from being a unified code, it was a sometimes open-ended and contradictory one, permitting less a state of "anything goes" than a form of textual construction in the theater that was often communal but not always unified. It was this kind of cinematic experience of combination and code-switching that transformations in benshi practice undermined.

An Invisible Subjectivity

The effects of these changes both in benshi practice and in the discursive definition of the institution were varied. First, in literary terms, the language of the benshi shifted from a focus on surface play—the foregrounding of verbal technique—to an oral style in which linguistic form was rendered unnoticeable so that the benshi's words could transparently express the inner meaning of the text and of its real author in the space of production. In some ways, this is similar to the transition in Japanese literature from the linguistic playfulness of nineteenth-century *gesaku* comic fiction to the interiority of modern literature, where, after *genbun itchi*, the text was supposed to manifest the inner speech of the writer, not the exteriority and independence of linguistic words. With the benshi's words functioning more to express a given meaning than to provide an opportunity for enjoying linguistic play, the text came to take precedence over processes of reading. The dictum that benshi should be faithful to the text constructed a film work that reflected a transcendental "intent" or original meaning that was already complete once it arrived at the theater. The benshi's job was merely to relate this intent to spectators and ensure that all understood it. The standard of understanding implied that spectators themselves could not produce meaning, but only waited to comprehend what was already complete. Any different reading then became defined as a lack of understanding or simply a mistake. The erasure of the process of reading was most evident in how the model spectator, the benshi, was transformed from someone who "watched" the text (in Yume Sōbei's words), treating the text as a surface against which to produce his own narration, into a servant of the film, one who studied the text in order to enter and become one with it.

The text itself was defined as univocal. Yume Sōbei, for one, stresses that, "in one scene, there cannot possibly be two contrary central ideas at the same time. In other words, there is one meaning to a scene. . . . The benshi must grasp whatever is the main view and thoroughly explain it."[47] Reformist organs like *Kinema Record* asked the benshi to study cinema precisely so that they could always make sure they were relating the one correct meaning, that they were not committing errors and therefore not prompting spectators to read the film incorrectly.[48] Thus, while some called for the total elimination of the benshi, many in the Pure Film Movement tolerated them, first, as agents of reform, improving the cinema and its audience by altering their own mode of practice, and more important, as a means of commanding the majority of spectators. As Takeda Kōkatsu declared to the benshi: "I have no complaint if you yourselves wake up, think things over, and sense your responsibility to lead the masses."[49] By erasing their own role as productive viewers and simply following along with the text's pregiven meaning, benshi helped to divest spectators of the power of interpretation and, further supporting the univocality of the film, to eliminate differences within the audience reflected in divergent reading strategies.

One of the primary ways to ensure this authoritative version of textual meaning was to unite as much as possible the narration of the benshi with the films' own processes of enunciation. Reformist critics offered various ideas on how to ensure that an explanation would not differ from the original intent of a film. Furukawa expanded on the demand of some that benshi should be required never to stray from the intertitle translations provided by the studio, and asked companies to lengthen those scripts to include precise instructions on what the benshi should say in each scene.[50] Interestingly, Furukawa also proposed restructuring the spatial dynamics of the theater to help erase the benshi's subjectivity. Disturbed by the fact that the benshi, by standing next to the screen, often had to look back and forth between the spectators and the screen, he suggested that a small mirror be placed on the benshi's podium to enable him to look at the screen and the audience simultaneously.[51] While there is no evidence Furukawa's proposal caught on, it is nonetheless symbolic of the reformers' vision of the benshi. By turning their heads back and forth between screen and audience, benshi spatially asserted their place as both viewers and textual enunciators, as narrators who could mediate between film and audience because they alternatively took the position of each. Making benshi face only the spectators spatially would have removed them from the audience and placed them in the viewpoint of the film itself. What a benshi would have seen in the mirror, then, would have been not just the screen but also his new face: the film itself. The point of enunciation would have changed. To quote Takeda: "Explanation is not explanation for the audience [that is, a mediation of the text for audience pleasure], but explanation for the film."[52] The benshi forfeited his own subjectivity and became identified with the subjectivity of the film, such that, as Gonda explains at the end of his own short teleological history of the benshi, "there is no explanation outside of the film and no film outside of the explanation." In Gonda's vision, the benshi "must become the film itself."[53]

If Gunning can declare that "the narrator system works as a sort of internalized film lecturer," what is clear in the case of Taishō Japan was that every effort was made by film reformers to place the benshi within the film while allowing the institution to exist. Kaeriyama and his later followers largely succeeded in producing works with "an intervening narrator who comments on the action of the film through the form of the film itself," the kind of situation Gunning describes in which the "narrator was not located off-screen, but was absorbed into the arrangement of the images itself."[54] These were the pure films reformers were aiming for. Yet at the same time, many of them permitted another, newly reformed narrator who, while physically offscreen, was also on-screen in terms of enunciation. Such benshi were invisible, melding their narration with the enunciative subjectivity of the film and eliminating any split between them. It is interesting that some critics, concerned about the disjunction caused when two benshi narrated the same film (which was normal practice at the time), proposed that only one benshi explain each work.[55] That this did in fact become accepted procedure by the end of the 1920s indicates the general trend toward uniting the single explanation of the film with the single narrative subject of the film text.

To many, once the physically present narrator was reformed, there no longer existed a trade-off between the benshi and diegetic illusionism. The ideal form of spectatorship, according to the Pure Film Movement, was, in the end, one immersed in the illusion of film.[56] An article in *Kinema Record* describes an "illusion" (the author uses the katakana form of the English word) in cinema that was different from that of the theater,[57] and a reader of *Katsudō kurabu*, Yamato Tetsurō, argues that the best way to watch motion pictures was in pure silence, without a benshi or music:

> The essential ideal of film drama must lie in silently staring and being absorbed in a titleless film in conditions without sound—not even a benshi or, of course, music. That must be the highest ideal from the standpoint of the essence of cinema. It is by sinking into this atmosphere and contemplating the film (without titles) that one can taste, for the first time, the unique subtleties of film art. With a relaxed feeling, one can enter the film to one's heart's content without anything in the vicinity interfering with one's own contemplative state of mind.[58]

For such reasons, some contended that the presence of benshi ran counter to the ideal of cinematic contemplation. The film journalist Midorikawa Harunosuke, one of the more radical film purists, who would later come to fame as the main screenwriter for Ozu Yasujirō, under the name Noda Kōgo, criticizes the use of a benshi for the titleless film *The Old Swimmin' Hole* (Joseph De Grasse, 1921): "From the standpoint of the audience, there is a fear that the fantasies and associations called forth by illusion are to a certain extent narrowed by the explanation of the benshi."[59]

But many others stressed the power of the benshi to increase the diegetic experience. Yamato, for one, went on to qualify his ideal by explaining that, with some films—particularly, in his words, "Yankee films"—music and the benshi were not a nuisance and could "bring about an even better mood."[60] Several critics argued that being required to read intertitles created a condition of work that upset the entertaining ease and comfort that defined filmgoing.[61] Yume Sōbei comments, "When you consider entertainment psychologically, the fact is that, when our mind demands entertainment, it does not want to be made to simultaneously use other mental functions by that entertainment." If it is made to do so, "the pleasurable stimulation and our absorption in entertainment will definitely be impaired."[62] Another writer claimed that having to read the titles was like reading a novel while simultaneously watching a play:[63] the benshi's presence, far from creating a disjunction in narrative enunciation, actually solved one. To many contemporary critics, the benshi could ensure the effect of cinematic illusionism as long as they narrated properly. Yume, for one, told his benshi readers, "If one can explain in a style that perfectly fits the image, the audience's interest will definitely share in the development of the scene and will undoubtedly cross into the realm of intoxication. If you take this point lightly and treat the film like a second-rate play, even though it is a particularly advanced film drama, blabbering on and on and making a clatter, you'll make the audience feel as if sand has been mixed with their rice, no matter how cinematically blind they are."[64] To Yume, if the benshi subordinated themselves to the film text, they could eliminate any "sandlike" disjunctions and facilitate the narrative enjoyment of the film. At that point, we can say, the benshi would become internalized within the enunciative system of the film, rendering themselves invisible and supporting the illusion that the text spoke itself.[65]

This melding of the subjectivity of the benshi with that of the film's enunciation did not necessarily upset the basic tenets of the Pure Film Movement. As I have argued elsewhere, one of the means of controlling the volatility of the image that the cinema came to represent was the word.[66] Practices such as publishing novelizations in film magazines—a popular practice in many journals in the 1910s—or establishing the screenplay as the blueprint of the film text, functioned not only to secure meaning within the film text as universal (since the film's meaning in the magazine novelizations should not differ from its meaning wherever it was shown) but also to ground an unruly modern image, which could potentially be read in various ways in different spaces, in a more secure and well-known system, the written language. It is crucial to understand that most pure film reformers were not advocating a radically new form of signification that undermined language and challenged conventional processes of creating and receiving meaning. In upholding the silent, titleless film, Midorikawa writes, "Even if silence is meaningless, . . . the silent drama of pantomime is meaningful. At times, it possesses much deeper meaning than a drama with dialogue."[67]

The image in a pure film without titles represented not a return to the narratively voiceless image of early Japanese cinema, which lacked intertitles, but rather the complete internalization of narrative enunciation within the text. Titles were to be eliminated only when the image could equally or better handle the same narrative load. Reformers advocated the divorce of the image and the word only to the degree that the cinematic image had assumed the same certainty of signification as writing or speech. As such, the titleless film would not be allowed to be ambiguous or open to different spectator readings. The metaphor *Katsudō no sekai* used to describe the meaning uniquely expressed by cinema was, in the end, "the words of the moving pictures" *(katsudō shashin no kotoba)*, defined as the "words which substitute for the words of theater."[68] The definition of the cinematic sign was found in an analogy with the word.[69] One would see challenges to this analogy only later, in the 1920s, in explorations of cinematic modernism such as Kinugasa Teinosuke's *Kurutta ichipeiji* (A Page of Madness, 1926), a film that came to represent, as I have argued elsewhere, conflicts in the intellectual film community over the definition and role of the film image.[70] Until then, however, most pure film reformers did not privilege artistic modernism over social modernism; they envisioned not an aesthetic that would overturn dominant modes but rather a form of culture that was more efficient and rational, but which still relied on older, more established signifying practices. This actually brought them closer to the "classical" than the "modernist" side of vernacular modernism.

In this context, we can see that those who viewed cinematic signification as analogous to the word need not necessarily have objected to the presence of the benshi because of their use of the spoken language. In fact, the benshi could be viewed as beneficial to the extent that they not only kept to the text but also performed the role of border keeper. On the one hand, they became a subject of enunciation inside the text that, blending with the enunciation of the film, established the word as the model of cinematic signification, while on the other they regulated the effects of the unruly image outside the text by using the established signifying practice of speech to corral audience reception.

The question remains whether we can speak of the experience of watching a film narrated by this invisible benshi as being equivalent to the experience of primary identification with the camera that Christian Metz theorizes and which Burch locates as central to the diegetic effect.[71] Certainly the other reforms in film style proposed by the Pure Film Movement—close-ups, more "cinematic" editing, and so on—would have helped send spectators, to borrow Burch's words, "on that 'motionless voyage' which is the essence of the institutional experience" of classical cinema, interpellating viewers as "incorporeal individuals."[72] It is also tempting to note the parallel between Furukawa's use of the mirror as a means of having the benshi identify with the film text and the Lacanian mirror stage that Metz cites as the basis of primary identification. Spectators equally become part of the film when their "representative," the benshi, becomes so identified. But it is important to underline slight differences in their pattern of identification. Burch stresses an "iconic hegemony," a particular orchestration of iconic forms of significa-tion (the image, the recorded voice, etc.), as the center of the cinematic form of diegesis, but experiencing a film with a benshi would be less iconically hegemonic. To understand spectator identification with a text produced by a benshi, we should consider forms of noncamera identification as possible alternative means of approximating the diegetic effect. For instance, identifi-cation with a subject of enunciation combining the text and the benshi's nar-ration could serve as the potential basis for a kind of transcendental subject that is not fully reducible to identification with the camera.[73]

Perhaps the elimination of the benshi and the codification of the nar-rator system may have been an equally good, if not a better, option of producing a diegetic effect, but authorities in particular had a stake in the benshi's continued existence, which I discuss in the next chapter. While authorities might have been at odds with some critics' efforts to eliminate the practice, they were definitely aligned with the endeavors of intellectual film fans to reform the benshi. For one, having the benshi stick to the text made censorship easier. As the censor Tachibana Takahiro argues, echoing Yume's dictum: "If film dramas are, as I urge, produced through the prin-ciple of one scene, one meaning, then there will be little fear with regard to the benshi. But in such cases when one scene has two or three meanings, or when the exact opposite explanation is added, one can imagine that the spirit of censorship will be nullified."[74] Univocality both within the text and between the benshi and the film allowed for more efficient regulation, manifesting the "spirit" of censorship by ensuring that meanings appre-hended at the censorship screening were those given to the audience in the theater. The legal requirement in some localities, like Osaka, that the benshi not deviate from the content of the film was then both a means of enabling the exercise of power and a manifestation of the concerns censors had regarding divisions in the audience produced by alternative reading strategies.[75] In this regard, having the benshi present was better than sim-ply internalizing their function within the text. A narrator system borne only by images was not trusted to produce a unified meaning effect on the audience. Since police offered advice to benshi on touchy situations, it is evident they were hoping that the benshi could engage in preventive measures in the theater when it was apparent that audiences were reading the film in socially inappropriate ways. The benshi would act as an adjunct censor in the theater, ensuring that the spirit of censorship was being carried out at the point of reception. Unlike the police officer in the back of the theater, however, he would not appear in the uniform of an agent of the state. Becoming one with the film, melding his enunciative subjectivity with the narrative system of the film, a benshi would bear the kind of "invisibility of power" that Hase Masato stresses was an important development in Taishō film censorship.[76] The benshi could then invest the cinematic text with a power it would not have had otherwise. They might become the film, but they would still have their eyes. With the benshi supplying its new face, film was allowed to look back at the audience and regulate their faithfulness to and understanding of the text.

THE AUTHOR AND INDUSTRY

In debates on the benshi, one would often encounter the statement—this one from a piece by Katano Akeji—"benshi are not artists; they are simply explainers."[77] The word *artists* implied they had the freedom to create their own text, or at least mold the film according to their own vision. But as Takeda Kōkatsu argues, "Explanation is free within an area limited by the titles, but cannot diverge from that space." He asserts, "Benshi are not artists like *rakugo* storytellers, but respectable linguists."[78] Even those who, like Yume Sōbei, argued that the benshi's role went beyond merely linguistically translating the titles did not offer them the commission to be independent artists. As Anderson notes, Yume does claim that explanation is an aspect of production, that a benshi can be counted as one creator of the text, along with the screenwriter and the director,[79] but his creativity is limited to serving the intentions of the other two. As Yume puts it: "There must be an originality that conforms to the scene. In other words, originality is necessary only to appropriately and artistically treat the ideas, feelings, and events expressed by the writer and director on screen." The analogy Yume offers is that of a translator who must be creative in order to preserve the tone of the original: "Translation must be faithful to each word and line of the original work, but a word-for-word translation will just not express the artistic taste permeating the original. The only thing that will bring that to the surface is originality as a translation."[80] Although the standards for distinguishing between benshi recognized the need for oral craft, for skill in presenting a good film in an enjoyable fashion, these standards did not extend into the area of artistic productivity. Textual meaning was produced elsewhere, and it was not the benshi's role to add to it.

Visible in the discourse of the Pure Film Movement, especially that on the benshi, the industry, and film creation, is a restructuring of the process and organization of cinematic production. For reformers, film was no longer a final creation of the conditions of exhibition but a text that arrived complete with a meaning before it was loaded into the projector. The audience's role in meaning production was erased, and when the benshi themselves were redefined as merely skilled translators of an original text, the site of exhibition was transformed into simply a point of reception, of receiving not creating. It was the benshi's final role to ensure that transmitted meaning was taken in. The source of that transmission, the subjects of textual enunciation, began to be those figures who operated in the realm of film production. At this point, heading into the 1920s, the focus of discourses on film shifted away from audiences, theaters, and benshi and toward film companies and motion picture authors.

Authors and Stars

When the benshi ceased to dominate the spotlight, two other enunciators arose to replace them as the main face of the film: directors or writers (the two often conjoined) and film stars. Such figures had existed in the Japanese film world before then, but the ascription of institutional responsibility for the meaning of the text to directors and actors did not occur until about the time the benshi were made objects of reform and redefined as servants of the text. In this sense, an outline of the Japanese star or the director system must at least metaphorically relate their appearance to the decline, first, of the benshi as independent creator and, second, of the site of exhibition as the final determinant of the text, even if these two factors are not the sole determinants of their appearance. Here, I offer a brief sketch of the development of these systems in Japanese cinema.

The first Japanese film star was, in most historical accounts, Onoe Matsunosuke, the third-rate Kabuki actor who, as the ninja or samurai hero of many Yokota and then Nikkatsu *kyūgeki*, became the idol of young film fans in the mid-1910s, many of whom adored him as "Medama no Matchan" (literally, "Matsu of the Eyes"). Tenkatsu put up its star Sawamura Shirōgorō to oppose him, and other stars appeared in Nikkatsu *shinpa*, such as Sekine Tappatsu, Yamamoto Kaichi, and the *onnagata* Tachibana Teijirō. There were stars, but there was no star system per se, especially not one that differed from certain existing theatrical practices. Fujiki Hideaki, too, reports the lack of a cinematic star system in the 1910s.

Figure 16.   The Nikkatsu *kyūgeki* film star Onoe Matsunosuke. (Courtesy of the National Museum of Modern
Art, Tokyo, the National Film Center)

In an industry centered on exhibition, he observes, ads emphasized the
theater and its amenities (including in some cases the benshi) over the
actors, and the films themselves functioned more to contain a theatrical
performance within the shot than to create a unique star image through
such cinematic means as close-ups.[81]

The Hollywood star system was not formed until the first half of the
decade, but in Japan a complete star system was still lacking in the late 1910s,
as is evident from film magazines of the period. All the major film journals
featured glossy frontispiece stills and photos from films already released

Figure 17. Star portraiture for foreign performers only: Edna Mayo on the cover of the April 1916 *Kinema Record*.

or soon to be released. Especially toward the end of the decade, close-up portraits of foreign actresses dominated these publications, serving as one of their main selling points. Nearly three-fourths of the portraits were of women at a time when Japanese films did not feature actresses; articles and readers' letters in fact described ways Japanese film fans could obtain images of their favorite Caucasian movie stars.[82] The star system was making headway in Japan, but primarily with regard to foreign films. The September 1916 issue of *Katsudō no sekai* may have been the "Grace Cunard issue," but that year the same magazine printed no articles on Japanese film stars, except for one on Sawamura Shirōgorō—all the other pieces concerned Japanese *rensageki* actors. The first issues of *Katsudō shashin*

Figure 18. Star portraiture for foreign performers only: Pola Negri on the cover of the August 1, 1924, *Kinema junpō*.

zasshi, a magazine oriented more toward Japanese films, were little different, featuring more articles and photos of benshi than of Matchan and his colleagues. In its entire history, *Kinema Record* did not print a single portrait of a Japanese film performer on its front page. Certainly, some of this discrepancy was the result of the biases against Japanese film held by the journalistic world at the time, but it also was due to the weak star system in the industry. While there was a tradition of photographic portraiture (as evident in portraits of the benshi), photos of Japanese films were almost all long-shot stills featuring scenes from the films. It was uncommon to sell the actors as stars in photos emphasizing their names and personae apart from the film. Moreover, a film style that at the time did not incorporate close-ups was not conducive to producing a star system. Film reviews and posters did not always specify the names of the cast (some reviews did not even mention the company, only the theater), and when they did it was in a style that either approximated that of the stage in the case of *kyūgeki*—"the Onoe Matsunosuke troupe"—or focused on the studio: "Nikkatsu Mukōjima troupe."

Fujiki has described an early star system for the benshi that centered on their bodily performances—the ones enacted in the theater during the *maesetsu* and embellished by publicity photographs that emphasized the benshi's independence from the mundane everydayness, if not also from the film. Fujiki notes that this benshi star system was later institutionalized through efforts to reform explanation and control its excesses. In a seeming trade-off, benshi gained some respectability as stars at the cost of becoming supplements to the text, supplements that, while initially profitable to exhibitors, were easily expendable with the coming of sound.[83] Fujiki emphasizes the influence of foreign cinema in the formation of the Japanese star system, arguing that a truly cinematic concept of the star arose in the realm of distribution before it did in production.[84] This is an important point, but it is coupled with the fact that the downplaying of benshi as independent stars and the rise of actors as cinematic stars became possible largely as a result of two circumstances. First, a reconceptualization of the process of cinematic signification emphasized its universality and location in the sphere of production (privileging that over reception in the space of exhibition); and second, transformations in exhibition practice, often geared to appeal to high-class customers, worked to meld the benshi with the originating, enunciating subject "speaking" in the film.

Photos of Japanese actors began replacing the portraits of benshi when the Pure Film Movement started making headway in changing industry practices. Studios like Shōchiku, which diligently studied American companies, actively publicized its actresses, such as Kurishima Sumiko, who gained fame as Japan's first major female movie star. Shōchiku began selling actress's images in its fan magazine, *Kamata* (begun in July 1922), and other magazines began to print their portraits too starting around 1922. Discourse on stars rose to a point that fan magazines devoted to single stars began appearing around 1925 (e.g., *Tsumasaburō*, dedicated to the *jidaigeki* star Bandō Tsumasaburō, lovingly known as Bantsuma), and the stars became the center of bitter battles as companies started stealing them away from their rival companies. The Japanese star system reached its first peak in the mid- to late 1920s, as many stars, such as Kataoka Chiezō, Ichikawa Utaemon, and Irie Takako, followed Bantsuma's lead in forming (mostly short-lived) production companies bearing their names. In this way, the persona of the star became defined as one of the central subjects behind the production of filmic meaning.[85]

In the same period, the concept of the film author underwent a similar transformation. Early discourse on film rarely broached the subject of who had authored a film. As mentioned in chapter 1, Japanese copyright law did not specifically mention the motion pictures and consequently did not clarify who was considered the author of a film.[86] A more general awareness of the importance of the screenplay led some early journals to equate the author *(sakka)* with the writer of the scenario *(kyakuhon).*[87] *Kinema Record*'s 1914 review of the *shinpa* tragedy *Tanisoko* (Bottom of the Vale), for example, one of the few reviews at the time to list most of the cast, lists the screenwriter Satō Kōroku as the author.[88] In locating a subject responsible for the poverty of Japanese cinema, *Kinema Record* mostly focused its venom on a generic object the editors termed "producers" (in Japanese, *seizōsha*). March and April 1916 editorials also cite the lack of "dramatists" and "stage directors"—the former signifying scenarists and the latter cameramen—as reasons for the mediocrity of Japanese cinema. Their point was that Japanese film production did not yet have a D.W. Griffith,[89] but it is clear that it was still difficult at the time to name this powerful cinematic figure, since most of the terms were simply borrowed from theater. As with the case of stars, foreign examples provided some impetus to the conceptualization of film authorship, with the media celebration of Griffith during the opening of *Intolerance* in Japan in 1919, for instance, helping spur the popular image of the director.[90] There were changes evident earlier, around 1917, when magazines like *Katsudō no sekai* began focusing on the absence of writers or directors *(sakka* or *kantoku)* in Japanese film and printed reviews that mentioned the names of the few who did exist (but in some cases these were cameramen, not directors as we know them today).[91] The lack of a full-fledged conception of the film author is evident in the debates over the 1917 Tokyo Moving Picture Regulations, which I discuss in more detail in the next chapter. During the uproar over the codes, no one to my knowledge ever registered a complaint in print that the regulations might restrict the filmmaker's freedom of expression. Such arguments did appear later on as, for example, *Katsudō shashin zasshi* and later *Kinema junpō* tried to remind censors that they should keep the filmmaker's intentions in mind when approaching a film.[92] The fact that these comments came well after the regulations were imposed lends credence to Hase Masato's argument that the 1917 codes, far from restricting authorial intention, in fact helped create the conditions for filmmaker expression.[93]

The larger project of the Pure Film Movement, then, which sought to downplay the importance of elements in exhibition in the production of cinematic meaning, was one condition for the birth of the author in Japanese cinema. Pure film directors like Kaeriyama were the first to be accredited, in journals, with authorial status at the end of the decade. The increased emphasis on the author after 1920 could also be traced to the importation of "authors" from other media into the film industry, such as Osanai Kaoru from the legitimate stage and Tanizaki Jun'ichirō from literature. As I have argued elsewhere, pure film reformers in fact relied on the notion of the writer, especially the writer of film criticism but also of literature, as a model for the structure of meaning production in cinema.[94] It was thus no coincidence that quite a number of critics went on to become film authors, including Kaeriyama Norimasa, Midorikawa Harunosuke, Furukawa Roppa, Mori Iwao (who later wrote scripts and became vice president of Tōhō), Takada Tamotsu (a *Katsudō kurabu* reporter who supported the Pure Film Movement and later became a prominent film and theater director and essayist), Kishi Matsuo (a long-standing critic and biographer who also later worked at Tōhō as a scriptwriter and director), Murakami Tokusaburō (a *Katsudō kurabu* writer turned scenarist), Oda Takashi (first a reporter for *Katsudō kurabu* and then a scriptwriter for Shōchiku and Nikkatsu), and Kisaragi Bin (one of the more avid amateur critics, who went on write scenarios at Nikkatsu), to name just a few. By 1922, *Kinema junpō* was running a series of feature articles on the new pure film directors like Kaeriyama, Henry Kotani, Thomas Kurihara, and Murata Minoru.[95] With studios like Shōchiku soon organizing the studio structure into teams led by directors, the groundwork was laid for the Japanese director system.

Toward a Pure Film Industry

If the locus of the production of cinematic meaning was to shift from the sphere of exhibition to the site of production, the structure of the industry itself had to be transformed. To this end, the discourse of film reform in the late 1910s was not confined only to questions of motion picture aesthetics but also inquired into what kind of industry was necessary to support the production of pure films. *Katsudō no sekai,* for example, devoted the September 1917 and October 1918 issues to analyzing the industry, and *Kinema Record,* calling itself, in English, "the Illustrated Leading Cinema Trade Journal in Japan," followed the model of United States motion picture trade journals and appointed itself the industry's business advisor. While not all of its proposals became reality, evident in its statements is a new conception of cinema's productive base.

Figure 19.   Japan's leading film company as a poverty row studio? Nikkatsu's Kansai studio in 1915 was little more than a shack. (*Katsudō shashin zasshi* 1.7 [December 1915]: n.p.)

In analyzing the structural reasons for the poverty of existing Japanese cinema, *Kinema Record* laid most of the blame on a system that emphasized exhibition over production. A February 1915 editorial declares that the main reason Japanese films had not improved was the fact that production was based on the "standard of exhibition" *(kōgyō hon'i)*, which itself resulted from a system where "producers are the subordinates of exhibitors."[96] In some ways this structure was only natural, given that the exhibition market at the time was dominated by foreign products: according to *Katsudō no sekai*'s figures, Japanese films made up only 26 percent of the works shown in 1917.[97] The primary business for most companies was in fact importing films and showing them at theaters they owned or had under contract; Japanese film production in those days was practically a market supplement adding variety to the available product. It is a historical fact that the majority of Japanese film companies, from early companies like Yoshizawa and Fukuhōdō to Taishō-era enterprises like Kobayashi Shōkai, originated as exhibitors or were owned by theater owners.[98] The Japanese film industry differed from its American counterpart in formulating at an earlier time a vertically integrated structure, where one company would control or own production, distribution, and exhibition arms, and was supported by block-booking practices. But unlike in Hollywood, the center of power and decision making was located in the exhibition sector, not in production.

Critics focused on the economics of production. Citing a system in which, in many cases, only one positive was made of any produced film negative,[99] reformers argued that producers had no incentive to improve their product. Films would not be treated as mass-produced commodities to be sold, as prints to be offered to bidders competing to show the best films, but as one-time-only, uniquely produced objects that merely supplied an entertainment experience that really originated in a theater managed by the film company itself. A brief look at the industry around 1916–17 supports this view. The number of prints struck from any negative would remain low throughout the decade (and even afterward)[100] and manifested a kind of exploitative film production, in which a print that was first released in Tokyo's Asakusa would then make the rounds of Osaka, Yokohama, and maybe a non-Asakusa Tokyo theater before being sent around the country until it literally fell apart. In a notorious practice, the remaining scraps of film would be cut into single frames and sold at temple fairs (this is one of several reasons few films exist from this period). The structure of exhibition at the time did not support making more prints. Unlike in the United States, which at the time had nearly 20,000 theaters, there were only about 350 in Japan in 1917.[101] Given the industry's concentration in urban centers like Tokyo, producers needed to largely recoup their investments there, which usually meant it made better business sense to milk as much as possible from a few prints showing in the big cities, which then toured the countryside for a year or two to make extra profit, than to make more prints to show sooner in less-populated towns.

The cost factor also supported the low number of prints. According to *Katsudō no sekai*, the average four-thousand-foot Japanese film at the time cost ¥2,270 to make, but with Japan importing all its raw stock at fairly high prices during World War I, the price of one positive print accounted for 16 percent of that cost.[102] This means it would take striking only six prints to double production expenses. Doing so would have been viable had the return been large, but the *Katsudō no sekai* survey reports that rentals were not that considerable at the time: a special contract theater, which made a deal with a film company to obtain a regular supply of films in exchange for not showing others' products, paid the parent company from ¥300 to ¥700 a month depending on its size, a price that was divided over several films.[103] At that rate, it could take months of running at several theaters to get back production costs.

The figures were rosier if the film ran at a company-owned theater, but even those houses did not exactly rake in yen at the box office. Some of the big Asakusa theaters had more than seventy regular employees, and even an average Tokyo city theater employed around twenty-five.[104] The magazine estimated that it cost an average-size theater with a capacity of six

Figure 20. Selling the theater: the Ushigomekan advertised itself as a high-class theater for a new age, featuring a new mode of exhibition for the middle-class Yamanote patrons who ventured into Tokyo's Kagurazaka district. (*Kinema Record* 13 [July 1914]: n.p.)

hundred to seven hundred (that, it added, could fit fifteen hundred when crowded) about ¥1,530 to operate for a month (including rentals). In good years like 1916, theaters could average about ¥2,000 a month in gross revenue, which could be good money when the company owned the theater (and thus took in both the profits and the equivalent of the rentals). But not all years were good years, and the fact is that film companies did not own many theaters. Nikkatsu, which boasted a chain of 177 theaters nationwide

Figure 21. Exhibition at the center: the Konparukan (also known as the Komparukan), in Tokyo's Ginza area, advertised itself as providing the best pictures *first* for the *aikatsuka*. (*Kinema Record* 22 [April 1915]: xi)

in 1917 (or about 50 percent of the total), probably owned or directly operated only a little over twenty of them.[105] The fact that these tended to be in the best locations, such as the Teikokukan in Asakusa, coupled with the poor revenue received from contract theaters, explains why about half of Nikkatsu's gross income still came from these twenty theaters.[106] It was only natural that Nikkatsu's production, as many reformers charged, was largely geared toward what succeeded among the crowds in Asakusa or Osaka's Sennichimae; Nikkatsu was a company dependent on its small number of directly run theaters in those areas. Business was profitable, but certainly not enough to allow for mass expansion of production facilities.

In terms of the power structure of the industry, it is evident that exhibitors were largely in control in those days. *Katsudō no sekai* divided theaters into three types: directly run (but not always directly owned), special contract, and commission theaters. For directly operated theaters, the film company paid all the costs and in turn received all the revenue. The grand majority of theaters in the country, however, were special contract theaters. Although the owners of such houses tied themselves to a single company through a block-booking contract and were obliged to pay the same monthly contract fee even if box office was bad, their position was still strong vis-à-vis the production companies. First, in all cases, the company was made to bear the burden of paying for equipment, technicians, and benshi, costs that were subtracted from the income received through contract fees. Second, the theater could easily buy out of the contract and switch to another company if it felt this was in its best interests. The example *Katsudō no sekai* cites, in which Kobayashi Shōkai increased its number of contract theaters from a mere four or five in 1916 to over fifty in less than a year, indicates how much power these exhibitors had to alter their relationship with producers. Third, it appears contract exhibitors had significant freedom to select films: while there were restrictions on the number of prints available in the pecking order, *Katsudō no sekai* did emphasize that "most theater owners usually get the films they want." The degree to which contract theaters dominated the industry is evident from the fact that the revenue the film companies received from them tended to be less than that obtained from the third, and weakest, kind of movie hall, the commission theaters.[107] In such theaters, exhibitors had to bear all the costs and share a percentage of the box office with the production company. They also tended to be in less profitable areas and play older films.[108] A final indication of the power of exhibitors is represented in the fact that some major theaters, usually the Asakusa ones, could specifically order films from producers to suit their audiences.[109]

In general, the early Japanese movie industry was not an efficiently organized, mass producer of commodified entertainment, a fact Anderson also underlines.[110] Having theaters that were on average larger than their American counterparts allowed the industry to spread the cost of such expenses as the benshi over many patrons, an important factor in why the institution outlasted that of the lecturer in the United States.[111] Yet when such theaters tended to concentrate in only a few locations, like Asakusa, which had eleven big theaters within yards of one another,

臺 舞 の 館 國 帝

THE STAGE OF THE TEIKOKUKAN.

Figure 22.   The industrial emphasis was on a few major theaters
such as the picture palace called the Teikokukan, in Asakusa. The
photo was taken when it was a Yoshizawa Shōten theater, just before
that company merged to form Nikkatsu. (*Katsudō shashinkai* 20
[May 1911]: n.p.)

cutthroat competition kept down admission prices, lengthened programs,
and increased the number of attractions (like benshi, live shows, or pretty
usherettes), conditions that made the cost of running a theater so high that
one could not make money operating small-size theaters.

Film production was then directed at only a small number of theaters, a
factor making those exhibition sites all the more important in the industry structure. This is evident in the problem of subtitling films. It was not
uncommon for reformers to ask distributors to simply translate intertitles
into Japanese and eliminate the need for the benshi. Most Japanese companies, however, since they usually bought only one print from foreign
dealers for a few large theaters, did not have the economic incentive to
make up a new Japanese-titled print.[112] The benshi were a more convenient
alternative. In this case as with others, Japanese film companies were often

forced to cede their authority over their products to the space of exhibition and rely on it to complete the production process.

To correct this situation, reformist organs like *Kinema Record* began suggesting alternative models for the industry. In general, as Kaeriyama argued, they believed that "producers must not be showmen but business-men. If our producers were fortunate enough to be true moving picture businessmen, they would probably pursue their trade more enthusiasti-cally, study the cinema more deeply, and produce respectable products."[113] As mentioned before, the issue was partly moral, as reformers demanded that producers cease acting like rapacious, vulgar showmen and begin work-ing to elevate the social position of the cinema. In Kaeriyama's words: "It is hopeless to ask showmen to work for the spiritual and artistic profit of the nation."[114] Producers needed to separate themselves from the debased world of *misemono* operators and become businessmen, who, it was said, were more respectable and could be trusted to approach the medium seri-ously and with the public good in mind.[115]

The problem was economic, too, since what reformers were urging was also a modernization of the Japanese film industry that would turn it into a form of capitalist and Fordist, commodity-centered culture industry. The essential issue was, first, establishing a clear division of labor between producers and exhibitors,[116] and then reversing the existing hierarchy by pushing producers into a position equal to that of exhibitors or dominant over them. According to Kaeriyama, "If producers strive for improvement and create respectable, authoritative works, this will bring an end to the current situation, in which producers are forced to make products under the direction of exhibitors. Producers will splendidly achieve their own ide-als, and exhibitors, on the other hand, will move to compete and wait for the producers' films."[117] Reforming the existing structure in the industry, in both moral and economic terms, was seen as the means by which pro-ducers could reclaim control over their own products and force exhibitors to listen to their demands with regard to the films.

The scope of reform was broad-based, since other reformist planks, such as the regulation of the benshi, the suppression of the role of exhibition in producing meanings, and the univocality of the text, could also support the goal of bolstering commodity capitalism by centralizing power in pro-duction. In the American case, Miriam Hansen has argued, "the industry's growth and stabilization seemed to mandate a concentration of meaning within the film as a product and commodity, and thus its increased inde-pendence from the sphere of exhibition."[118] That exhibition could alter the meaning of a film was the central sign that exhibitors held sway over suppliers of the text. By essentializing meaning in the text, producers could downplay the importance of exhibition and more efficiently regulate their product. The text could also be redefined as a commodity. The problem with the existing structure, symbolized by the popularity of the benshi, was that audiences were consuming not the film but the performance in the theater. Their purchasing decisions proved difficult for the industry to discern and regulate because spectators did not buy a film based solely on their taste for the content of the film. Studios could not therefore channel audience desires into set patterns corresponding to identifiable textual formulas, because what ultimately defined the product were ephemeral factors occurring in the theater. By reasserting control over the text, producers could remake films into reified commodities with recognizable product identities, ones that spanned local differences and became the objects of consumer desires and purchasing decisions. As in the United States, spectators themselves would be unified under "the commodity form of reception" and their reception standardized "to ensure consumption across class, ethnic, and cultural boundaries."[119] These processes of commodification would also allow the selling of other, related commodities, like stars.

Reformers clearly had in mind a Fordist, mass-production industry when discussing the future of the Japanese film world. The model was, to a great extent, foreign companies like Universal and Pathé, which were objects both of interest and of brand-name appeal. *Kinema Record,* while emphasizing these companies' "tremendous capital" and "enormous organizations," registered amazement that "their film production capacity, despite the surprising numbers, still possesses an ability sufficient to create orderly works under a well-arranged system."[120] In proposing a larger, more orderly industry, Kaeriyama also suggested the model of publishing, in which the industry would encompass everything from production and printing to retail sales while still maintaining a precise division of labor in which exhibitors would be reduced to simply being the equivalent of local bookstores, with little control over the content of the product.[121]

Given the limitations on the industry, like the low number of theaters, the main tactic offered by almost every reformist journal to pressure structural reform in the industry was to sell films abroad.[122] I discussed in chapter 3 the ways the dream of export functioned to crystallize the concept of pure film, but reformers also offered this plan as a means of molding a modern industry. In promoting the strategy, Mori Tomita, the editor of *Katsudō hyōron,* argued that, "since existing Japanese films are not produced for sale but for the purpose of exhibition, it is impossible to spend several tens of thousands of *yen* on one film." Selling numerous prints abroad for profit would first supposedly create the capital necessary for the industry to improve. The focus of producers would then change as they shifted attention from exhibiting films to purveying a mass-produced commodity, the fact of export itself naturally creating clear distinctions between production and exhibition. The industry would be transformed into "one large film production and export company,"[123] accomplishing the dream many reformers had of making the moving pictures a truly national industry. As a product that had to sell itself without the help of benshi or other external factors, films would also become more self-sufficient and, in a word, purely cinematic. The focus of film production would be not the crowds in Asakusa but the spectators in America and Europe; this would support a form of cinema that both mobilized the cinematic forms developed in those countries and bore an international filmic essence that was self-explanatory in any nation.

This may sound like a pipe dream for an industry that could not even produce multiple prints of its own films, but it was taken seriously by both reformist critics and progressive elements in the industry. Everyone was aware of Sessue Hayakawa's success in Hollywood and that companies in the United States and Europe, sparked by a fad for Japonisme, were producing successful films (and would throughout the decade) "based" on Japanese stories and "set" in Japan. If they were making money from them, why couldn't Japanese do the same by making films really set in Japan? It was deeply felt that pure films could best be made if there existed the prospect of exportation. When Kaeriyama was having problems selling his work to exhibitors during his stay at Kokkatsu (short for Kokusai Katsuei Kabushiki Kaisha), the company formed by Kobayashi Kisaburō in 1919, and which bought up Tenkatsu in 1920, he urged Kobayashi to at least sell the new pure films abroad.[124] Even if these more cinematic works had a hard time making money in Japan, it was believed they would always be supported overseas.

Kaeriyama's plea may have fallen on deaf ears at Kokkatsu and older companies like Nikkatsu, but there were new industry players at the end of the decade who took the prospect of export more seriously.[125] With the economic boom following World War I, the film industry was experiencing record profits: after the slump following the 1917 regulations, Nikkatsu, for one, had tripled its profits in 1919 compared to 1916. The business euphoria both gave companies leeway to test the uncertain road of reformist films and made the film industry itself look very attractive to the kind of business investors Kaeriyama and others preferred. Shōchiku Kinema, which was started by a prominent theatrical producer of Kabuki and Shin-geki, decided to jump into the movie business precisely with the intention of producing more cinematic films that it could sell abroad.[126] Its opening declaration stated: "The main purpose of this company will be the production of artistic films resembling the latest and most flourishing styles of the Occidental cinema; it will distribute these both at home and abroad; it will introduce the true state of our national life to foreign countries; and it will assist in international reconciliation both here and abroad."[127]

To learn more about foreign production techniques, the company founders, Ōtani Takejirō and Shirai Matsujirō, sent Shirai's film-loving adopted son, Shirai Shintarō, to America to tour some Hollywood studios with the theater director Matsui Shōyō. There they hired the cameraman Henry Kotani and other Japanese then working in the American industry to assist the company in producing the latest styles that could sell abroad. What they learned was also used in organizing production at the studio. Shōchiku was not alone in this endeavor. Taikatsu, the other major progressive company formed in 1920, was founded by Asahara Ryūzō, a shipping magnate who had made a bundle in the wartime economy. Hiring an American-trained director, Thomas Kurihara, and the modern aesthete Tanizaki Jun'ichirō, Taikatsu was reportedly so focused on producing films for sale abroad that it did not make a significant effort to acquire its own chain of theaters in Japan.[128]

Needless to say, neither company succeeded in its dream of selling Japanese films abroad. Shōchiku did give it a try,[129] but apparently with little success; Taikatsu soon went bankrupt, in 1923, with few theaters to support itself in Japan. Export had failed, but the Japanese industry had still changed. Even if export was a dream, the discourse on export was emblematic of processes of transformation represented on other levels by the Pure Film Movement itself, and it was a kind of structuring fiction that forced the Japanese industry to consider other models in reshaping itself. The shock of the Great Kantō Earthquake in September 1923, which leveled most of the Tokyo studios and theaters, accelerated transformations in the industry, but the change had begun before then. The invasion of foreign distribution companies like Universal was credited with forcing the industry to focus more on producing its own films,[130] a trend that led to an increase in the number of Japanese films, which reached a kind of milestone in 1924, when domestic movies, measured in number of reels, finally topped the American product.[131] With the boom in attendance (monthly attendance in Tokyo doubled between 1918 and 1923), the number of theaters in the nation nearly tripled (to 976 cinemas in December 1924) compared to 1917, rendering such centralities like Asakusa, the thorn in the reformers' backs, less important to the industry.[132] The industry was now more national and more focused on making Japanese films on a greater scale.

Nikkatsu had completely revamped its internal organization early in 1923, and, perhaps as a result, a significant change began to appear in Nikkatsu's earnings charts: starting in 1924, the company's revenue from the vastly larger number of contract and concession theaters finally topped that of the company's directly run theaters.[133] This may be one of the best indications that companies had at last gained some power to demand their share of exhibition profits, that the hierarchy of the film industry had begun to reverse, and that the subjectivity of cinematic creation had decisively shifted from the space of exhibition to the realm of film production.[134]

Complaints about the power of exhibition and the small number of film prints would continue until World War II, just as criticisms of Japanese film in general also did not cease. Changes in industrial structure were not as quick as those in the critical or even filmmaking worlds. The early 1920s saw significant changes in the industry, but other transformations had to wait until the mid-1930s, with the coming of sound and the producer system pioneered by Tōhō,[135] or the wartime, when some of the government-led reforms were actually designed to stamp out these industrial deficiencies.[136] All these changes, however, were fed and justified by a discourse that originated in the 1910s, providing further evidence of how writing about cinema could shape the material basis of the production of motion pictures.

Both writings on cinema and changes in the practices of benshi, producers, and exhibitors combined to formulate a new cinematic experience centered in the authority of the text, in a meaning constructed as originating from expressive subjects such as stars and directors in the sphere of production, not from benshi in the theaters. All this was organized within a conception of modernity in which signification was centralized and corralled through Fordist modes and the unequal appropriation of the power to speak and enunciate the text. Benshi were allowed to speak, one could say, only when they tied their subjectivity to that of the text. This does not mean they completely lost their agency. Shifts in the production and reception of cinema were paralleled, and perhaps even reinforced, by changes in state power, through censorship and regulation and eventually benshi, which were designed to mold the subject of the text and the spectator.

5   Managing the Internal

At the same time that pure film critics were studying ways to cure cinema of the virus of Japanese film, local Japanese police officials were researching how censorship could effectively treat the problems posed by the motion pictures. The *Zigomar* incident had presented censors with a difficulty: a film that had been censored on the basis of a written summary of its contents, just as any other *misemono* would be censored, proved to be somehow "different" upon viewing. A discourse emerged both inside and outside the police that determined the cinema to be distinct from other sideshow entertainments, such as the panorama or *gentō*, first, because the image itself was seen as somehow exceeding the meaning described in writing, and second, because mass numbers of spectators were evincing significant attachment to the medium not found in other cases. In responding to these issues, police and other government officials resorted to tactics like those of Gonda and the pure film reformers: they applied the discourse of study to the problem of cinema. Starting with the application of study, censorship began to share much with the project of the Pure Film Movement. By analyzing the results of these "studies," we can see how film censorship in the 1910s, especially as represented in the 1917 Tokyo Moving Picture Regulations, formed an essential part of the reformist process of redefining the cinema.[1] At the same time, altered technologies of censorship "produced a reality before they repressed it," to paraphrase Deleuze on Foucault;[2] carved out a new internal reality for cinema and the spectator, as objects of regulation; and aimed to shape an emerging modern Japan.

Incidents such as the police banning of *Zigomar* and related films may have prompted different authorities throughout Japan to begin dealing with the problems posed by the motion pictures, but the process was slow and often confused as censors studied the cinema through trial and error. The general pattern was to create licensing procedures for cinema exhibition: some regions only carried over the regulations that applied to *misemono* (which, like theater, required prior permission), but other areas attempted to produce different procedures for the cinema. In either case, the licensing option was the rule, rather than the exception, when governments throughout the world dealt with the motion pictures. Most European nations instituted national censorship laws centered on preexhibition censorship, and even areas like Chicago (in 1907) and New York (in 1921) in the United States produced licensing laws.[3] (In an approach similar to the one adopted in this book [albeit with different results], Richard Abel has skillfully shown how early legal discourses on cinema in France prompted the budding industry to aspire to legitimate the medium precisely as a theatrical enterprise.)[4]

At the beginning, few locales in Japan tried to create specific censorship laws. The Osaka police had written up some internal guidelines in 1911, the year before the *Zigomar* ban, in an attempt to specify censorship procedures for film.[5] These were not official regulations, and cinema continued to be covered in Osaka by the laws governing *misemono* entertainments.[6] An examination of the guidelines reveals that they are as much a set of standards for approaching the benshi and movie houses as for dealing with the films themselves. Section 4 of Article 2, which details forbidden content, was specifically directed at both "the film and the explanation." The guidelines were in fact particularly harsh on benshi: while the narrators were not yet required to carry a license as they would be later, those who violated public morals were, according to Article 6, to be summarily fired and their names publicly posted, and they would then be banned from taking employment in any entertainment business for a year. This tar-and-feather policy reflected a state of mind in which, to censors, the words spoken by the benshi were still of more concern than the film. The guidelines did not require preapproval screenings of the film: according to Article 3, "when the summary of the film or the explanation are under suspicion of violating Section 4 of the previous article, permission will given after projecting and explaining said work at the said place of exhibition or at another convenient site." It was solely when the written summary was thought dubious that screenings were required, and then only with the necessary accompaniment of the benshi.

The object of regulation, then, was the written or spoken word more than the image: censorship was directed more at what was narrated by the benshi in the space of the theater than at what was represented inside the filmic text. In terms of content, Article 2, Section 4, beyond prohibiting stories suggestive of adultery and obscenity, reflected the growing concern over cinema's influence on children by banning "works feared to aid or induce the methods of crime," and "works feared to invite mischief by children." In this way, the guidelines focused attention on the audience in the space of the theater, beginning to trace both a narrative of influence involving young spectators and a picture of the audience, but without resorting to such measures as age limits for admission. Children were not the only subject of worry. The guidelines, in addition to specifying health and safety requirements for the theater, gave police the right to demand that men and women be seated in separate areas when deemed necessary. This regulation, which, according to Yoshiyama Kyokkō, can be traced back to a police order in Matsuyama in 1898,[7] was without precedent in other entertainments and, says legal historian Okudaira Yasuhiro, was unique to the cinema.[8] While moving pictures in 1911 were becoming subject to specific censorship procedures—if only out of the fear that movie houses were dens of sexual vice and a hotbed of crime—this was more in line with Gonda's fears about the theater atmosphere than with the Pure Film Movement's complaints about film quality. One could also wonder about the guidelines' efficacy, since they apparently did nothing to stop Zigomar from harming public morals in Osaka (Osaka police banned it only after Tokyo did).[9]

In the months following the Zigomar ban, police in several other localities introduced their own regulations to cover the motion pictures. Shizuoka Prefecture issued its own Moving Picture Regulations in December 1912, but these proved little different from the Osaka guidelines. They were more specific about procedures for applying for permission to exhibit a film and made it mandatory to seat men and women in separate areas, but did not require a film screening before issuing a permit.[10] According to Article 1, all that was required to receive permission to exhibit a film was to submit the name of the theater, the screening times, the price, the genre of the film and its summary, and the name and address of the benshi. It is clear Shizuoka police still defined cinema as an object that could be sufficiently described by a written summary of its contents. Again focusing attention on the benshi, the law made the one speaking words in the theater the person most responsible for the film.

Aomori Prefecture opted for a different procedure in its Moving Picture Regulations of 1914. While requiring that applications provide the same kind of information required by Shizuoka, Article 2 stipulated that, before approval, "when the police department deems it necessary, it can order the submission of the film or the projection of said work."[11] The Aomori procedure thus was not much different from Osaka's (with the exception that the benshi had started to become a lesser object of concern). During the early and mid-1910s, many localities throughout Japan, like Aomori, increasingly recognized the possible need to view a film before granting approval. The biggest issue for preexhibition censorship, however, was the manpower and facilities needed to prescreen all the films. At the time of the *Zigomar* crisis, the Tokyo police confessed that they could not handle the task. In localities outside the metropolitan center, it was not as hard. In the Hokkaido town of Sapporo, for instance, there were only about three permanent movie houses in 1916, so Chief Patrol Officer Maruyama apparently easily made the rounds of the theaters on the opening day of a new run to check out the films.[12] If he found any offensive, he could ban it on the spot. Viewing all the films was possible in many localities like Sapporo, but screenings had to take place in the movie theater after the work had been released. If the police could view the film before, it was usually at the preview screening for the benshi assigned to explain it, which often took place late the night before opening. Most censor viewings still occurred after films began their runs, which is why almost all censorship regulations gave police summary power to rescind approval after a film opened if it was discovered that the work was offensive. Codes also usually required theaters to set up a special seat or box in the back of the theater for the police officer who would view the film. This requirement was found in regulations for the stage as well[13] and goes back to mid-Meiji censorship of theater entertainments.[14] With added regulations dictating the conditions of film reception, such as those restricting the benshi's speech or separating men and women in the audience, a police officer in the theater was particularly necessary. This officer, even a greenhorn on the lowest rung of the police ladder, had the authority to order cuts in the film or ban it outright. *Kinema Record* in June 1914 related the words of one Percy Wark, a Kinemacolor engineer who gave a report of his time spent in Japan to the *Kinematograph and Lantern Weekly*, expressing great surprise at the ability of regular patrol officers to enter the theater at any time and suddenly demand that the film be cut.[15]

For film companies like Nikkatsu and Tenkatsu, which had a national release circuit, the state of local censorship was a source of constant consternation. Censorship had been centralized in some localities on the prefectural level after the *Zigomar* incident, but there were still forty-six prefectures, including some, like Tokyo, that continued to leave censorship up to the local police station. This could lead to such cases as when the

French serial *Fantomas* (Louis Feuillade, 1913) was banned in Asakusa only to be freely shown elsewhere in Tokyo under a different title.[16] Suffering from both cost and inconvenience, the industry complained to the Tokyo Metropolitan Police at least once, in August 1913, upon which an official promised to consider both centralizing censorship in the city and shifting responsibility from individual patrol officers to detectives with degrees.[17] The matter must have remained under study for some time, however, because in December 1915 the *Tokyo asahi shinbun* was still reporting calls for censorship to be carried out in a central location by experts. The police apparently did not yet have the facilities.[18] *Kinema Record* related in 1916 that, when a reporter accompanied different police on their late-night prescreenings, the officers from one Tokyo station ordered cuts on June 10th that were different from those demanded for the same film by another precinct on the 8th. *Kinema Record* again reiterated the call for centralized censorship.[19]

Police probably were not eager to make matters easier for the film industry. Long after the *Zigomar* incident, police and other officials continued to look on the motion pictures as a social evil that required strict regulation. In June 1913, the head of the Kisakata police station in Tokyo, which had Asakusa in its jurisdiction, called in the theater owners to warn them again about films depicting crime or ones that were sexually provocative. He also felt it necessary to caution them on the use of theater props and costumes in the live entertainments interspersed throughout the film program.[20] Japanese movie houses, like their American and European counterparts, often presented entertainments other than cinema in a variety-style program, acts mostly out of Japanese vaudeville, or *yose*, such as the *naniwa-bushi* storytelling that was popular at the time. This remnant of *misemono* showmanship, in which cinema remained but one of many attractions, may have been central to the "cinema of attractions" Tom Gunning speaks of, but it was apparently unpopular with Japanese police, especially if it involved the presentation of live stage plays. In August 1913, when theater acts were an increasingly popular attraction in motion picture theaters, the Tokyo police officially discouraged such performances (still leaving the way open, for the time being, for regular theaters to show films as part of *rensageki*). The reason was ostensibly public safety, since stage plays were often performed in barracklike movie houses that did not conform to the building codes for theater; as one official said, "For the safety of viewers, it is necessary to create truly tough restrictions in order to make clear the distinction between a theater and a nontheater." It is evident that the police were finding it necessary to ensure that the filmgoing experience differed from that of the theater. This was done partly to protect the legitimate stage: the same officer commented that theater in movie houses was an "injustice to true theater operators," adding how "disgraceful" it was for prominent actors to appear on such a stage.[21] Around the same time, the Tokyo police, worried about a sudden increase in movie house construction, announced they were going to put a halt to approving new movie houses because of "the extremely bad influence this has on spectators, including grade school students."[22] Film as a social phenomenon would be contained; film, even down to the experience it offered in the theater and its uniqueness as a medium, remained an open target of police procedure.

The motion pictures were under attack on a number of fronts in the early to mid-1910s. The fact that an enthusiastic northern censor like Officer Maruyama could ban a total of fifty-two films in 1917 did not make it easy to erase the public image that cinema was a social problem.[23] Newspapers too remained suspicious of the movies, repeatedly running reports of one or another group of juvenile delinquents—often called "Zigomar gangs"—led into a life of crime by the motion pictures. A rash of such reports in December 1915 in Okayama, Nagoya, and Takamatsu sparked a small amount of public hysteria and moved educators to demand greater restrictions governing film viewing by minors.[24] Educators would remain some of film's most prominent enemies throughout the 1910s. Tokyo city officials claimed that, of the 169 juvenile offenders in Kawagoe Jail, "several dozen were moved to commit evil upon seeing a moving picture or committed robbery out of the desire to see moving pictures."[25] Thinking that the fragile minds of minors were particularly susceptible to the effects of the cinema, education authorities in locations like Sapporo actually prohibited all their students from entering movie theaters.[26] More liberal minded educators were aware of the difficulties in banning such a popular entertainment, noting, "If you say no, children will only want to see it more." Yet they still suggested that parents tell children: "It's best not to see [the movies]."[27] At the very least, social reformers demanded the creation of special theaters for children,[28] or, like *Kinema Record*, they proposed creating Children's Days at movie houses.[29] Emulating an idea first realized in 1901 by Sugita Kametarō and his Educational Moving Picture Society,[30] some places, like the city of Moji, also tried putting on educational film shows for local schoolchildren.[31]

During this period, education authorities began studying and instituting the regulation of motion pictures. In one of the first national regulations covering the cinema, the Ministry of Education's Popular Education Investigation Committee created, in 1911, the Provisions for Inspecting

Lantern Slides and Moving Picture Films,[32] rules which required ministry approval for all films and slides used for educational purposes (the guidelines were revised in 1913 in the Provisions for Approving Lantern Slides and Moving Picture Films).[33] The Home Ministry announced, in May 1914, that it would cooperate with the Ministry of Education in carrying out a survey of the motion pictures to determine standards for regulation.[34] As part of this, the Ministry of Education surveyed foreign censorship regulations (particularly those of Germany) and published them in translation in a report titled *Kyōiku to katsudō shashin* (Education and the Moving Pictures).[35]

The Home Ministry did not actually nationalize film censorship until 1925; in the meanwhile, most of the studies of cinema were left up to local organizations. The *Yomiuri shinbun* reported in March 1914 the results of a survey by educators that declared that the motion pictures "not only harmed the health of children due to impure air and the lack of light, [but they also led to] mistaken ideas and fancies becoming diseased and planted an impression in the brain through [film's tendency to beget] mental weakness. Their excessive stimulation of the emotions also causes the illness of dullness of the nerves."[36] Tokyo city officials apparently formed an Alliance on Regulating Children Outside School and began surveying and studying the motion pictures.[37] Perhaps it was as a result of one of these studies that the city's Bureau of Education sent out a notice to parents of schoolchildren delineating cinema's dangers:

> There is a significant health hazard due to insufficient facilities at exhibition sites.
>
> Many films easily teach evil and wicked methods and naturally infect children with the vices of obscenity and cruelty.
>
> Moving pictures induce inferior grades as a result of stimulating the emotions and tiring the mind and eyes.
>
> The entire surroundings are harmful, with the explanation also being questionable.
>
> Actions which should be guarded against take place in the audience.[38]

Possibly involved with these studies was Sandaya Hiraku, a well-known child psychologist and social worker who surveyed juvenile film-viewing habits in major cities in 1915. While not completely rejecting the cinema—he in fact called for educators and the film industry to cooperatively develop educational uses—he argued that films inflict psychological and physical injury and imprint suggestions in the weak minds of minors, and thus he equated parents taking children to the movies to "child abuse."[39]

The language of his survey reveals that film study in this era was as much an effort to shape the facts as to discover them. Although Sandaya offers empirical statistics of children's viewing patterns, he cherry-picks the results and uses vague terms like *many* and *a lot* to warn, despite the fact that most of the theaters he surveyed had more adults in the audience than children, of the danger of children overflowing the movie halls. Given the number of times he claims something is a "remarkable fact" or is a "widely known fact,"[40] his study appears less to unveil what is unknown about the cinema than to confirm the dominant perception of film as a problem. Study, then, functioned to reveal the problem, not the medium, and then to define the cinema—and its correction—though this authoritative revelation.

It was around this time, at the end of 1916, that the issue of the cinema as a social and educational evil began to come to a boil. The Tokyo Metropolitan Police were finally wrapping up their study of film censorship and the Imperial Education Association was preparing its own report on the moving pictures as they related to education. The Association would hire the young Gonda Yasunosuke to survey the relationship between cinema and children in Tokyo, and these three studies would eventually lead to the 1917 Tokyo Moving Picture Regulations, the first comprehensive film censorship code in Japan.

THE 1917 REGULATIONS AND FILM REFORM
Three Studies

The connection between the discursive articulation of film in Japan and structures of power in the social sphere is no better exemplified than in the case of the three studies that led to the 1917 codes. Identifying cinema as a social problem, the Tokyo police, the Imperial Education Association, and finally Gonda Yasunosuke each opted to research the medium before taking action against it. Their statements about cinema intricately linked a definition of the medium with the operation of correcting it; power embodied in discourse was again creating its object at the same time it was controlling it. These regulations ultimately provided a powerful impetus to the effort to create a pure film in Japan.

In late February 1917, the Imperial Education Association, after consulting with the Home and Education ministries as well as with the Tokyo police, passed a resolution calling for greater cooperation between authorities in censoring the motion pictures.[41] The resolution called for the following:

1. Stricter censorship and greater cooperation between the Ministry of Education and the Tokyo police
2. Centralization of censorship around a single standard
3. Licensing each benshi upon investigation of his or her character
4. Censoring the explanation with the film
5. Promoting educational films
6. Prohibiting filmgoing at night by children under sixteen
7. School-based regulation of filmgoing by children
8. Surveys of "the educational effect of moving pictures" and warnings to students' families by "relevant government agencies, offices, schools, and educational associations."

The resolution was almost guaranteed to influence policy, since government officials were already sitting on the committee that approved it.

The Association fulfilled its promise to further study the medium by asking Gonda, then twenty-nine years old, to find statistical evidence on how often children viewed movies and what effect their viewing habits had on their character and learning. Relying on police statistics, but also implementing his own survey of over thirteen thousand Tokyo schoolchildren, Gonda carefully investigated children's likes and dislikes, their favorite stars and benshi, when they went to the movies and with whom, and even how they believed they may have been harmed by film. He then published his report, titled "Katsudō shashin no chōsa" (A Survey of the Moving Pictures), in *Teikoku kyōiku* (Imperial Education) in two parts in May and August of that year.[42]

The first major statistical study of the motion picture medium in Japan proved to be both influential and infamous. According to many at the time, it and the Association's resolution had a significant effect on the regulations police were drawing up.[43] As a result of his involvement, Gonda and his survey were initially subject to ridicule by the film industry after the unpopular regulations were promulgated, with the editor of *Katsudō no sekai* even questioning Gonda's sanity.[44] In his defense, Gonda, as we have seen, did not actually diagnose cinema as being inherently pernicious, and he also expressed in print his misgivings about the new regulations.[45] Still, the report was interpreted by many as condemning the medium: Sawayanagi Masatarō, the head of the Imperial Education Association, in fact declared in print that, "according to the results of this survey, there is in the end harm [in the moving pictures] and no benefits."[46] Ironically, the first commissioned study of the moving pictures was interpreted as condemning the medium itself.

At the same time these studies were released, the Tokyo police were conducting their own research on the problem of film censorship, and they made a point of letting the press know this. Articles on upcoming regulations began appearing in print as early as December 1916, one of which announced: "The Ministry of Education, the Home Ministry, the Tokyo Metropolitan Police, the city of Tokyo and other cities have been conducting various studies on regulating the moving pictures."[47] Interviews with Numata Minoru, the officer in charge of motion picture regulation at headquarters, revealed that the police extensively investigated film censorship regulations both inside and outside Japan. Regulations in Austria, which prohibited filmgoing by children under fourteen except at special children's theaters, had specifically caught his eye. Numata, however, insists that, since "the national character of our country is different, we cannot directly apply such cases here."[48] The police were aiming for a standard of censorship particular to the perceived specificities of Japanese audiences and motion pictures.

Numata's comments reveal many of the issues that faced the police in their study of the cinema. He asserts that "independent regulations separate from the codes governing entertainments are necessary since the moving pictures are a great force in society";[49] cinema had, through its very popularity, earned a specific discourse of its own within the law. Such specificity clearly required special knowledge of cinema. Numata recognizes that there were questions as to "how much knowledge officers had concerning what kind of films harm public morals and customs, or to what degree [the police] had the power to judge and appreciate what was truly an artistic film."[50] In part to solve the problem of knowledge, Numata admitted the necessity to centralize censorship at headquarters under experts, but claimed that the lack of funds and logistical problems made it difficult to require prescreenings there; instead, he proposed sending officers from headquarters to censor films at the local theaters. He confesses some doubts about the idea of centralization, however: "The same film can be permitted in some places and not in others. For example, there is a difference between the audiences around Asakusa and those from Yamanote, so it does not make sense to place emphasis only on standardization and not look at the state of the audience."[51] Numata's concern for the conditions of reception was represented by his emphasis on reforming benshi: he worries not only that they were "all uneducated persons of vulgar character" but also that they could "corrupt an audience even with a good film."[52]

The Tokyo police, in preparing their regulations, were directly confronted with a variety of possibilities on how to approach the cinema. How differently should cinema be treated from other media? Was there something unique about the motion pictures that demanded specific regulations? Was there anything about the cinema that must be eliminated or corrected? What procedures other than cutting and banning were at the police's disposal? How would the audience be defined, and what could be done to regulate it? What was a greater object of concern: the film text or the conditions of reception? There were several viable alternatives for dealing with these and other issues, and it was clear the police were not always unified in their approach. Numata himself, it was reported, quit his position because of differences with his superiors over the new regulations, became a film critic, and left for the United States to study film and censorship there.[53] Again, the motion pictures in Japan were at a crossroads at which a different conception of cinema could have been defined in discourse.

Numata's position, as revealed in his essay in the February 1917 *Katsudō shashin zasshi*, was a somewhat eccentric mix of the ideas of Gonda, the Pure Film Movement, and Christianity.[54] Placing most of the blame for the disgrace of Japanese cinema on audiences who simply watched movies without studying them, he objected to the practice of banning films because it undermined the "spontaneous activity" (he used the English terms) of the audience. Wholly supporting the idea that cinema has a natural essence given to it by God, he believed that it was our responsibility to raise the "orphan" (cinema) until it matured into a fully expressive adult. Numata's articulation of film is visible in parts of the 1917 regulations, but as implied by his disagreements with superiors, the Tokyo regulations attempted to raise a rather different baby cinema.

Censorship, the Industry, and Film Reform

As if to stress that the cinema was an educational problem, the police first announced the regulations at a meeting of the city education board on July 10, 1917. They revealed that, as a result of their studies, they had pared down their original draft of seventy-one articles to a mere fifty-one in six chapters.[55] The regulations were officially distributed on the 14th and took effect on August 1, causing considerable controversy in the press and the industry. While the education board favored regulation, the industry rose up in protest.

Although not all of the new censorship procedures were written into the regulations (for example, an exact specification of prohibited content was nowhere to be found), the codes stipulated the following changes:[56]

1. A shift in the regulative authority over film from local police stations to central police headquarters, where a central censorship screening room would be constructed (Article 15)

2. The classification of films and film exhibition into grade B films, which could be viewed by children under the age of fifteen, and grade A films, which could not (Articles 14 and 27)

3. The division of audience seating into three sections: one for men, another for women, and a mixed section for married couples and families who entered together (Article 35.1)

4. A requirement that each benshi submit a copy of his or her curriculum vitae to the police and receive a license to practice (Article 20). Benshi deemed to have violated public morals would lose that license (Article 26)

5. Codification of the building specifications required of permanent movie theaters (Chapter 2)

6. A requirement that the exhibition of a film program at sites that did not fulfill the specifications of a movie theater could not run for longer than ten days (Article 29)

7. A stipulation that theaters showing A films could operate from sunrise to 11 P.M., with a single program length of less than four hours; and that theaters showing grade B films could be open only from 12 P.M. to 9 PM., with programs limited to three hours (Article 31)

8. A condition for "turning on a light during projection to enable one to recognize the features of the audience" (Article 35.4)

9. A stipulation prohibiting "soliciting the business of passers-by without permission" (Article 35.6)

10. The stipulation that theater billboards would be regulated under the advertisement codes and would be limited in size and number

The film industry could look favorably at some of the sections. A Tenkatsu official welcomed the restrictions on program time, since, in areas of cutthroat competition like Asakusa, increasing program length had been one of the only ways to get ahead of the competition.[57] The centralization of censorship was also the realization of longtime industry demand (and the industry would soon be asking for national censorship). The papers reported that theater managers registered little resistance to licensing their benshi or, in principle, to dividing the audience by sex (other than questioning how they were to determine which couples were married).

For Nikkatsu, Tenkatsu, Kobayashi, and other small producers and exhibitors, it was the other regulations that were the problem. The question publicly voiced by most in the business was why cinema was the only medium suffering such treatment. Even if cinema managers could separate customers by sex, it was unfair that the same regulation was not applied to theater or to film's main rival, *rensageki*.[58] The regulation was partly inspired by fears that innocent young ladies from Yamanote, the higher-class section of Tokyo, would fall prey to Asakusa mashers upon entering the dark moving picture theater. Yet as many contemporary commentators pointed out, it made no sense to ban contact between single members of the opposite sex in movie theaters when they could easily snuggle up in theatrical establishments that were just as dark.[59] Film was singled out as something especially dangerous, and this attitude was reflected in the way police officers enforced the regulations. The industry complained that some patrolmen stood at theater entrances, almost blocking them, and treated customers like criminals, interrogating them about their age and marital status. They feared this took the fun out of entertainment and that audiences would hesitate to come back.[60] Absurd tales abounded of young-looking fifteen-year-olds having to get a copy of their family register in order to see a movie, and of officers complaining to couples that, if they were married, they should act more like it.[61] With cinema defined as a social problem, police were apparently treating the medium just like any other vice.[62]

In the end, the main problem for the industry was that provisions such as the A/B grading system, by making it difficult for children to see movies, had a major effect on their business. It is hard to paint an accurate and objective picture of how important child audiences were to the film industry in 1917. As I mentioned before, it was not uncommon for film reformers to use the terms *women* and *children* as class markers that did not describe actual audiences so much as formulate hierarchies in class and knowledge. In a context where cinema was accused of causing much juvenile crime, hyperbole was often the order of the day. One 1913 newspaper article claimed that 50 percent of film audiences were composed of grade school children and 40 percent of audiences were women. But the tone of this same article generally warned of the increasing danger of film by claiming, for instance, that there were over one hundred theaters in Tokyo at the time (there were in fact only forty-three, according to the police).[63] Characterizing cinema audiences as dominated by children was an efficient means of portraying the medium as a wolf preying on the innocent, thereby justifying state intervention on behalf of the weak. In defending themselves, some exhibitors countered by saying children composed only 1 percent of the audience.[64]

There is enough evidence to confirm that the industry suffered economically from the regulations. If we assume that Gonda's and Sendaya's surveys are accurate, it seems the average size of the child audience greatly varied depending on the place, time, and type of film, numbers which do not always back up the prevailing opinion that the majority of spectators, especially for Japanese films, were children. In Asakusa, for instance, children amounted to about 15 percent of the audience for both Japanese and Western films. The number slightly increased among audiences in theaters in the rest of the city, but still, Gonda's statistics show that children composed on average about 15 to 20 percent of the motion picture audience, reaching 50 percent in some out-of-the-way theaters only on Sundays.[65] Although not a majority, children still composed on average one-fifth of paying customers—and even more on lucrative days like Sunday—and theater operators could not help but be hurt by restrictions on that portion of the audience.[66] Paired with the excessive police crackdown and the bad press, the A/B grading system reportedly left A theaters half empty. Within days of the implementation of the regulations, theaters related reductions in revenue of from 30 to 80 percent. *Katsudō shashin zasshi* printed statistics in its November issue showing how box office for the major Asakusa theaters had dropped on average about 30 percent compared to the same time the previous year.[67] According to Nikkatsu's company history, while the studio did not lose money in the last half of 1917, its profits did go down for the first time in years.[68] Perhaps sensing this, investors at the time sent the price of Nikkatsu stock plummeting 25 percent, from ¥36 to ¥27; the impression among some was that, at this rate, "the entire movie business will go bankrupt."[69] Ōhata, the head of the Public Peace Section in charge of the new regulations, was quoted in the *Tokyo mainichi shinbun* as saying: "Children would not suffer in the least if moving pictures did not exist in this world; they would in fact benefit, not be injured. People such as myself rather [wish] they did not exist."[70] The industry could not help but wonder if the police and education authorities were not really out to crush the medium itself.

It is true that the regulations did not ban filmgoing by minors but only restricted it to a certain grade of films. In practice, however, censorship made it hard for anyone to make a profit out of showing grade B films. Police censors, using standards neither contained in the regulations nor made public,[71] took up what some commentators called a "no-harm policy" and cracked down hard on any film aspiring to a B grade, eliminating any element that could conceivably cause "damage" to what was seen as the malleable mind of a minor.[72] Judging from the complaints of critics, they sometimes even cut the villains out of the story—even if they got their comeuppance at the end—for fear that children would imitate their criminal ways.[73] One 500-foot-long animated film was reportedly chopped down to less than 350 feet as comedic mischief making was also deemed a bad example for minors.[74] The results after censorship were reportedly bland, insipid movies that no one, least of all children, would pay to see. Under such strict censorship, the common complaint was that there were very few B grade films left to show: *Katsudō shashin zasshi* reported that, in the forty-eight days after the start of the regulations, only 138 works had been approved as grade B films, over half of which were nonfiction shorts—not nearly enough to regularly supply the quickly rotating programs of many theaters.[75] Even if an exhibitor could put together a program, its prospects were dim because the furor had reportedly created the public impression that grade B films were not general audience pictures but kiddie flicks. If losing the child audience for grade A films was one blow to exhibitors, being deprived of the full-price paying adult customers for grade B films was another.[76] Film producers also made little from the grade B films they specially created to fit the regulations, because they were salable only in Tokyo and the one other locality that opted for the grading system, Nagasaki.[77]

For these and other reasons, the industry protested the regulations. At the beginning of August, theaters in the city formed an organization, the Friends of the Moving Pictures, to petition the police as well as the Home and Education ministries, first, for the authorization to admit minors to grade A films if accompanied by an adult, and second, for a yearlong extension to allow time for the importation and production of grade B films. When the police authorities refused to back down, the industry even attempted some political pressure, pleading with prominent political party bigwigs,[78] and convincing the Asakusa Ward Council, which was worried about the apparent loss of business in its district, to argue on the industry's behalf.[79] When even this failed to bear fruit, theater owners tried to present a united front by having each company sign a pledge not to present grade B films.[80] Given the importance of children to its business, however, Tenkatsu eventually broke the pledge at the end of the year and the unified action failed.[81] Some success was reported at first with grade B exhibition, but with the lack of entertainment value in such films and the continued shortage in their supply, it was clear the film industry had been forced into dire straits out of which it could escape only by doing something itself.

One could attempt to draw parallels between this crisis and what early U.S. film producers had faced when Mayor George B. McClellan of New York City banned moving picture exhibition at the end of December 1908. That drastic action against the perceived social evil of film may have been cut short by the courts, but it did give impetus to a film industry trying to transform itself into a supplier of entertainment that appealed to the middle classes. The Board of Censorship was formed as a response, and, as Tom Gunning states, "censorship became a factor in film's narra-tive form."[82] The Japanese censorship regulations of 1917 likely prompted Japanese companies to support some of the reforms proffered by the Pure Film Movement. It is important, however, to note the differences between the cases of New York and Tokyo. At that time in the United States, New York was a major film market, but the ban there was short-lived and the industry could rely on other major markets. In contrast, the Tokyo regula-tions were long-lasting: the A/B grading system was repealed on Novem-ber 15th, 1919, but other provisions lasted for years, and schools continued to restrict film attendance by their pupils for decades. Furthermore, Tokyo assumed an importance to the Japanese industry far greater than that of New York to its American cousins. It is true that, outside of Tokyo, the A/B grading system was adopted only by Nagasaki, but it did create a wave of concern over film viewing by minors as other localities took up different procedures with the same aim of limiting such spectators (banning, for instance, evening admittance).[83] Moreover, Tokyo was the center of a film industry still largely focused on exhibition over production, sporting at least 62 moving picture theaters in 1917 out of a national total of 334, or nearly one-fifth of the total.[84] Business structure was such that a single Tokyo theater could be powerful enough to influence the production of a major company like Tenkatsu.[85] A change administered in this metropolis could not help but have a profound effect on the industry. One can postu-late, then, that the 1917 regulations posed a threat to Japanese filmmak-ers, even if only a perceived one, that was greater than any faced by their American counterparts. In this climate the Pure Film Movement began to make its way into the film industry.[86]

Certainly the police portrayed their regulations as a tool for reform. After the order was promulgated, one official declared: "People from strict families in the Yamanote area, who up until now had never even tried to see a moving picture for fear their morals would be corrupted, can now go with peace of mind." In his view, making the cinema safe for the middle class also affected the quality of the films: "Within less than a month of thor-oughly carrying out uniform censorship," he boasts, "we have become able to present only superlative pictures to audiences in our jurisdiction."[87] The head of the Public Peace Section defended the regulations in terms remi-niscent of those used by *Kinema Record*, claiming that they were created out of years of "study" with the "idea of developing the moving pictures," and adding that "no matter how I look at it, I cannot understand how such works as the Japanese *shinpa* love stories have any value as drama or as cinema."[88] Connections between censors and film reformers extended to the level of personnel as well: the police ranks included not only Numata but also his replacement, the journalist Tachibana Takahiro, who, although he later shifted to publications censorship, would remain active as one of the main film critics and theorists of censorship throughout the 1920s and early 1930s. At its base, censorship was interpreted through the narratives of both social and film reform; the police admitted the regulations would hurt the industry at first, but they asserted that such deprivation would prompt the industry to develop as Japanese pharmaceutical companies had when supplies from Germany were cut off during the war.[89] Censorship, then, was intended not merely as a means of ridding cinema of immoral and vulgar content but also as a productive force in encouraging the creation of motion pictures with value "as cinema."

The discourse of reformist journalists reacting to the regulations echoed this logic of censorship.[90] While one journal, *Katsudō shashin zasshi*, initially denounced the regulations vociferously, declaring that they destroyed the glorious and unique imperial Japanese family system by prohibiting children from accompanying their parents to the movies,[91] most of the publications showed a mixed though generally favorable reaction to the code. Ide Tetsujo, the editor of *Katsudō no sekai*, registered typical complaints about the system of separating men and women, about sacrificing the entertainment of many children for the crimes of a few, and about overzealous police enforcement, but in the end, in an argument reminiscent of that of *Kinema Record*, he blames not the police for these difficulties but the film industry: "Although there is little doubt that the regulations themselves were the product of a draft by the metropolitan police authorities, what first unfortunately made it necessary to regulate through censorship? It was not public opinion, not the intellectuals, not educators, but the industry itself."[92]

Another critic, claiming that "society was sick . . . of flat copies of theater with no interest at all as a picture," thought that "these regulations . . . will certainly serve as a motive for the social improvement [of cinema]."[93] The children's novelist Iwaya Sazanami, who was a frequent commentator on the regulations, also linked censorship with the creation of more cinematic works, arguing that in order to make a truly "complete grade B film . . . [producers] must learn that the moving pictures possess their own special art."[94] *Kinema Record* also offered its recommendations for censorship procedures: "A progressive method to positively reform our cinema is to warn our producers, who must be the basis of positive film reform, and encourage them to create good works (good works in the eyes of a respectable censor—that is, a truly good work), and apply the stick to socially frivolous films (for example, those like the degenerate *shinpa* tragedies)."[95] It is interesting that the primary opponent of the regulations, *Katsudō shashin zasshi*, reversed its position the next year to cite how the regulations had forced the industry to concern itself more with film quality. The journal then called for the state and the citizenry to cooperate in creating even more stringent film regulations—including script censorship—in order to take control of the industry and force it to reform. Okamura Shihō, the editor, concluded by stating: "I would like to force the improvement of cinema . . . by borrowing the power of the authorities."[96]

It was against this background that the Pure Film Movement began as a mode of film practice. With censors and film reformers speaking the same language, the film industry had both social and economic incentives to improve the image of its product and get censors off its back. Censorship had already proven that it could severely damage business. It made good economic sense, then, to allow such reformers as Tanaka Eizō and Kaeriyama Norimasa to try their hands at directing, and so it is no coincidence that the first films that could be aligned with the movement were shot not long after the regulations went into effect. Tanaka produced such classics as *Ikeru shikabane* in March of 1918, and Kaeriyama was given the go-ahead for *Sei no kagayaki* less than a year after the codes were put in place. According to Okada Susumu, there was a rush of "reform" films at Nikkatsu in 1918, including *Nogi Shōgun* (General Nogi, 1918), a work by Tanaka's colleague Oguchi Tadashi and one of the few grade B films praised by critics.[97] While it is difficult, given the paucity of internal industry documents from the time, to make a final judgment on the role of the 1917 Tokyo Moving Picture Regulations in prompting a fundamental shift in the way films were made in Japan, it is clear that, in the contemporary context, censorship lent both urgency and authority to the demands for film reform.

CENSORSHIP AND THE DISCOVERY OF INTERIORITY

The Unique Object

Beyond speculating on the impetus censorship gave to reform, it is useful to closely analyze the picture of cinema that censorship constructed, as contained in both the codes and the discussions of them, in order to understand the close relationship between censorship and reform in the context of the 1910s. The discourse of and on censorship can be viewed as a kind of film theory.[98] At this level of articulation, censorship merges, albeit not completely, with the Pure Film Movement as an attempt to locate an internal essence in the cinematic apparatus and to found another mode of study that would mold and correct approved forms of spectatorship, which would themselves involve new kinds of internality. The 1917 codes and the debates surrounding them bring into relief a complex set of contemporary discourses about the motion pictures. Cinema itself was the focus of furious debate as journalists, police, and educators discussed whether it was an entertainment or an educational tool, whether it should be shown for profit or for the good of society, and what place the image had in contemporary education. Conceptions of the modern age came into view as many argued that one or another aspect of the regulations might be behind the times. The codes also raised questions about the constitution of the mind and the image's cause-and-effect relation to it, about what new forms of subjectivity cinema and its censorship implied. Finally, Japan itself became an issue as both sides argued over whether the regulations did or did not accord with their vision of the Japanese empire.

At the very least, the regulations proved to be a means by which the motion pictures assumed a prominent place in the public eye. It was as if film, as the legal historian Okudaira Yasuhiro puts it, "by being regulated, was for better or worse finally being treated as an adult."[99] The police often repeated this logic, pointing to foreign examples to argue how the severity of film censorship indicated the degree to which others—but not yet the Japanese—had recognized the importance of the cinema.[100] Treating the motion pictures as a special object in the eyes of the law, one requiring its own regulations, was seen in a peculiar way as an essential step in molding the cinema into an important and unique object.

Beyond asserting that the cinema was particular enough to deserve its own codes, the 1917 regulations operated in several ways—ones that often aligned them with the positions of the Pure Film Movement—to mark the medium of film as a separate art. This is evident in how the regulations treated *rensageki*, the hybrid performance art that mixed film and theater and was reaching its peak of popularity right around the time the regulations were implemented. Speaking of Tenkatsu's *rensageki*, Komatsu Hiroshi has discussed how the form allowed for certain innovations that the coded world of existing Japanese film could not, particularly the use of actresses and of acting styles more specific to the cinema than to the Kabuki or *shinpa* stage.[101] These "chain dramas," however, more often represented the kind of cultural combinations that reveal the malleability or lack of rigidity in the codes.

Most reformers gave *rensageki* positive press only because of its use of female performers, hoping that these actresses would, in the future, develop into true film players.[102] Otherwise, *rensageki* often suffered the barbs of film reformers' criticism because it countered the effort to produce a purer cinema and was popular among the lower classes. According to one *Kinema Record* editorial, "those who enjoy watching things like *rensageki* are people who do not know true moving pictures—*rensageki* is a horrendous corruption of the cinema."[103] The problem was its hybridity; it mixed elements of film and theater, which the Pure Film Movement was doing all it could to separate. The novelist and playwright Okamoto Kidō, writing about the need for specialist film actors, laments about *rensageki:* "Today's urgent task is to nurture good actors specializing in the cinema. . . . But are the actors themselves endeavoring to comprehend whether they are meant to be stage or film actors? This is the evil of forms like *rensageki*. Except for the rare maestro, those suited for acting on the stage are in most cases failures at cinema, and those appropriate for film are failures at the theater. In the end, theater is theater and cinema is cinema, and there must be a clear distinction between them."[104] *Rensageki* was damned for undermining such clear distinctions.

Rensageki were only partly covered by the 1917 regulations. On the one hand, their film portions had to be submitted for prior censorship, as were all other publicly presented movies; on the other hand, *rensageki* audiences were exempt from sexually segregated seating, because as a whole the performances were still treated as theater. Such exclusions gave rise to complaints from some film exhibitors that the regulations "protected *rensageki* and suppressed the movies."[105] But it is clear that other statutes severely damaged the art form. Efforts to improve the fire safety of cinemas prompted police to define what properly constituted a movie theater and, in theaters that did not meet the code, to restrict the projection of motion pictures to ten-day runs, much shorter than the usual *rensageki* run. This law did not affect *rensageki* performances in properly constructed theaters, but police had already voiced their objection to theater being performed in movie houses. Most observers, including *rensageki* producers like Kobayashi Kisaburō, felt the regulations would damage this hybrid form.[106] Numata declares that this was in fact the police's intention: "The idea is definitely to block this trend in the future and, in certain cases, prohibit the production of *rensageki,* since the current pictures completely lack seriousness."[107] Authorities also presented the measure as a means of protecting movie theaters.[108] While *rensageki* was not eliminated—it could still be freely performed in many other localities—it quickly went into decline, suffering enough of a blow that journalists later pointed to the *rensageki* clause in the regulations as one definitely producing benefits for the film industry.[109] Here, then, was a case where censorship regulations were not only designed to block harmful information from reaching the eyes and ears of viewers but also actively engaged in eliminating a particular medium, not because it was obscene, but because of concerns for quality and the purity of a related medium. Authorities clearly sided with pure cinema reformers to work against a hybrid form and attempt to define a space proper to cinema, divesting it of its attachment to theater. Film reform—and the modernity it propounded—was thus historically tied to the exercise and interests of authority.

Another regulation also worked to separate cinema from other entertainments. Theaters in Asakusa were especially notorious for borrowing the promotion techniques of other popular entertainments, like *misemono*, in attracting customers. These included hanging enormous billboards depicting scenes from the film in garish colors on the sides of the theater, as well as using boisterous and pushy *yobikomi*, the hawkers who stood at the entrance to the theater and used their verbal skills to entice passersby to see the movie. Reformers criticized the public face that cinema presented in these methods, identifying their extremes in color and rhetoric as signs of film's vulgar status and its childishness.[110] As if supporting these largely class-based notions of aesthetic taste, the new regulations limited the number and size of the signboards and made it illegal for theaters to entice passersby, a section that effectively banned *yobikomi* for film exhibition, but not for other entertainments, like *misemono*. Interestingly, film was again singled out as a medium in need of public reform, but in such away that it was deemed more important (or more dangerous) than its show business cousins that did not receive such recognition.[111] The new billboards were both smaller and more literary, using words as well as pictures to lure the customer.[112] One contemporary commentator, praising the changes, claims, "You can now watch with ease since the noisy *yobikomi* have gone away. . . . Every theater had competed through the size and vulgarity of their billboards, but the size specified in the new regulations is probably sufficient to draw the attention of adults."[113] Film exhibition now required promotion techniques unique to the motion pictures; these techniques had to address the need to sell to an audience that was better than the crowds for *misemono*. No longer viable, argues Hase Masato in his excellent analysis of the 1917 regulations, was the kind of bodily or sensual advertising common to the *misemono;* the codes instead promoted "smart advertising that emphasized the visual."[114] Film advertising thus began to change: the design historian Kayano Yatsuka in fact cites the late Taishō era as the point when Japanese film posters shifted from a style that differed little from that of theater posters to a more modern touch that emphasized the new center of cinema, the star.[115] It would not be difficult to connect this change in visual style, especially in the public face of cinema, to the increasing use of Western architecture in theater construction. One sees a shift in the late Meiji from Japanese-style cinema architecture to the overly ornate Western facades of Asakusa theaters and then, after the 1923 earthquake, to the sleeker, modern design epitomized by houses like the Aoikan.[116] Overall, it appears that authorities were acting to support the shift in cinema culture from an obscene, physical modernism to one that was more visual and that appealed to the mind.

Ultimately, the Tokyo regulations did not repress the moving pictures as a public annoyance so much as work to point the cinema in a different direction by offering a definition of the medium itself. In introducing the regulations, the *Yomiuri shinbun* said that they actually "clarify the essence" or "offer a definition of what is called the moving pictures."[117] This essence, it must be recognized, was slowly being drawn away from the sphere of exhibition and into the text as created in the realm of production. To begin with, the film text began to be defined as possessing universal characteristics. Centralization of the regulatory apparatus in prescreenings at police headquarters, as well as the granting of one-year permits to approved films, postulated an essence that transcended the here and now, one that was separate from and resistant to the spatially and temporally specific discursive operations of the benshi and local exhibition practices. The necessities of bureaucratic centralization, as well as the inconvenience to film producers caused by differences in local censorship, spurred a discourse on cinema that defined filmic meaning as something permanent within the work itself. What was seen by censors in the screening room (formerly the police department's English classroom) was then assumed to be what was received by spectators no matter when and where they saw it.[118]

To insure this, as Hase argues, "the regulations against film's 'mode of exhibition' rejected cinema's quality as live performance (its spontaneity) and tried to enable censorship's mode of repression."[119] As examples of the effort to repress the spontaneous creation of meaning in the site of exhibition, Hase cites the suppression of *rensageki* (which made the performance in the theater central to the creation of the text) and the expulsion of children (who, as Gonda notes, sometimes enjoyed the atmosphere of the theater more than the movie itself). Since such localized modes of meaning production made centralized censorship difficult if not impossible (they were one reason officers were stationed in the theaters), the creation of an inside in the text that contained unmalleable meanings was not just an idea forwarded by film reformers but was crucial in enabling censorship itself. Censorship made little sense if the significance of a text could be easily altered when it left the censor's office; posting the prying eyes of officers in every theater was also impractical. With the new regulations, just as Foucault suggests, power produced the conditions of its own existence, attempting to mold a cinema that made censorship itself possible. Creating a modern cinematic text that traversed local divisions and thus became more national (because simultaneous, in Benedict Anderson's notion of the term), in part by more vigorously and efficiently enforcing its meaning, was a crucial facet of establishing a more rationalized, if not Fordist, censorship apparatus. Other forms of conceiving of cinema, even if they represented other kinds of modern modes of perception, were inimical to this new censorship.

Creating a text with a universal content is important for censors of any medium, but provisions such as the A/B grading system, which applied only to film, also clearly indicate a shift in emphasis away from the site of exhibition and toward the cinematic apparatus. A persistent complaint against the grading system was that it was applied only to the motion pictures, whereas other entertainments were left alone. Some observers noted the absurdities of a policy that prohibited children from seeing a film on a topic they could easily walk down the street and see if it were presented as a play.[120] Clearly, as with the *Zigomar* affair (where the novelizations were left untouched), cinema was censored not simply because of its content but because of the way it transmitted it, the very form and essence of the apparatus itself. This was unique in the history of Japanese censorship, where standards of censorship were normally the same for all, aimed at a content that was not deemed specific to the medium; there may have been separate regulations for various media to accommodate their different distribution forms, but ultimately obscenity was obscenity whether found in theater, in *misemono*, or in woodblock prints. Obscenity in film, however, was somehow more threatening to public peace and morals because of the nature of the medium. The creation of regulations directed at film marked not only the perception of cinematic specificity but also the genesis of new procedures of power that, because they deemed the apparatus of representation just as influential as what was represented, manifested a kind of formalism in the realm of censorship. These procedures of power recognized the coming of the machine age, where the importance of the device also made the technology of censorship crucial, formulating modern modes of control in conjunction with the new subjects to be controlled.

In censoring plays, it was sufficient to cut lines, warn actors and playwrights, and stop performances, because it was thought that was all there was to theater. Film, however, was more than the sum of the creators, the intertitles, or the lines of the benshi; it was a machine that could not be sent to jail (even though the exhibitor or the benshi could), a technology that created effects beyond the culpability of human agents. As such, it demanded special attention: censorship, then, regulated cinema itself as much as its individual examples, a task that required it to remold itself into a different technology of power. Attention paid to the cinematic apparatus was conjoined with increased concern for the apparatus of censorship—the ways it could be pursued—as censors changed from simply cutting cinematic content to attempting to mold ways of producing and receiving meaning. Paralleling the ways cinema as an apparatus affected audiences, the technology of censorship began working to mold the insides of spectators themselves.

The New Spectators

In focusing on the cinematic apparatus—not just on meaning but also on how it was formed—the Tokyo regulations also placed special importance on the problem of spectatorship. First, the creation of a cinematic text with universal meaning was accompanied by imagining a similarly transcendent spectator. The police rejected Numata's concerns about local differences to assert a norm—perhaps similar to the "society" *Kinema Record* often spoke of—that could serve as the moral yardstick for judging films for all of Tokyo. In this way they imagined an abstract citizen—a mass of homogenized film consumers—that would now be the object of protection and correction. This did not mean that the regulations were then oblivious to divisions within the film audience. Paradoxically, it was because the codes were so focused on postulating a universal spectator that they also devoted attention to differences between viewers.

First, there was the separation of the audience by gender. This provision, unique to film regulations, was certainly sparked by fears that the medium "provoked carnal desire and caused obscene behavior between men and women."[121] Even the more vulgar carnival entertainments were acquitted of this crime, and thus cinema gained the dubious distinction of being inextricably linked with dangerous sexuality. In the process, not only cinema but also film spectatorship was being distinguished and articulated. The cinema hall, which "to the degree it is accompanied by darkness, inevitably forces some kind of interference with the body,"[122] foregrounded the problem of sexuality and sexual difference. Dividing the audience, inscribing gender difference and marital status into the spatial arrangement of the theater itself, may have made obvious these divisions, but it was done in an attempt to make them irrelevant. Spatially separated or confined to the institution of marriage and the family, differently gendered spectators could no longer express their sexual difference and were posited as sexually neutered, desexed, and abstract audiences. The regulations did name and distinguish the genders of spectators (the body of the female viewer was particularly subject to control), but they did so in order to render sexual difference (especially as manifested in bodily desire) irrelevant to the experience of watching the movies. Once gender ceased to matter, so presumably would the problem of the theater itself: spectators could cease their hanky-panky in the dark movie house and concentrate on the film, shifting from bodily to more visual and mental forms of cinematic experience.

The system of dividing motion pictures according to their appropriateness for children under fifteen elaborated on this vision of the spectator. Police argued that children should not be able to watch certain films because, as the head of the Public Peace Section argues, "Children under fifteen are unable to digest and comprehend the meaning of an entire reel of film, but only perceive it in parts without mediation. Therefore, if there is a scene of a murder in one episode, children adversely perceive this one bit of behavior even if it is a story based on rewarding good and punishing evil."[123] Cinema itself was seen as overwhelming the faculties of children, being too disjointed and complex for them to absorb proper lessons from competing images of good and evil. The educator Dr. Sandaya Hiraku, commenting on Gonda's study, claims:

> There are quite a lot children who have thought of committing robbery after receiving malicious suggestions from the moving pictures. For example, if a person of little resistance sees a skillful robbery in a film where the criminals escape and spend the money on play, this will cause him to unwittingly commit a crime. Not only that, but no matter how long the moving picture is, the ending is shown only after ten to twenty minutes [of the story], and the content quickly moves from one thing to the next, so there is absolutely no time to judge between good and evil. Therefore, the mind is extremely agitated, and any suggestions received fail to fade away, becoming a variety of influences.[124]

It was felt that the minds of children were not equipped with the powers of "resistance" to enable them to escape damaging influence. *Kinema Record* emphasized that "children have a primitive psychology," without the faculties to select the films that were good or bad for them.[125]

Interestingly, this psychology of child spectators resembles the temporality of the "cinema of attractions" that Tom Gunning has theorized. While Gunning tends to place emphasis more on the textual framework of attractions than on the way audiences perceived them, his distinction between the temporality of narrative and of attractions is instructive: "Time in narrative . . . is never just linear progression (one damn thing after another), it is also the gathering of successive moments into a pattern, a trajectory, a sense. Attractions, on the other hand, . . . basically do not build up incidents into the configuration with which a story makes its individual moments cohere. In effect, attractions have one basic temporality, that of the alternation of presence/absence which is embodied in the act of display."[126] The complaints of Japanese educators may not have been specifically directed at film practice that emphasized display over narrative (the "cinema of attractions" as a textual phenomenon), but they were concerned about a mode of spectatorship that took even strongly narrative films and viewed them as only series of attractions, as unconnected sets of presences/absences without proper narrative connections. Such spectator psychology could be likened, following Gunning's citation of Lynn Kirby, to that of a victim of hysteria, subject to "the sudden rupture of stability by the irruption of transformation."[127]

This spectatorship could be connected more closely to the Japanese historical context. One picture of the viewing subject was being drawn in contemporary discourse, of a viewer who received influences directly, without any mediation, in a simple, almost behaviorist relation between sensory input and output. This "primitive" or "child" subject in curious ways is an extension of the subject carved out in earlier Japanese censorship regulations for film and the other arts, although cinema's influence in this case was supposedly stronger and more direct. Unlike the older subject, the new "primitive" subject was also constituted in a complex structural relationship with other possibilities. The technology of previous codes was based on the simple procedure of first determining what was harmful and then regulating its flow. In this form of censorship, subjects were faceless, indistinguishable, and unnamed—in effect irrelevant to the censorship procedures.[128] Certainly, a picture was created of a being that could be injured by one form of image and not by another, but the focus there was on the content of that image. The subject itself was undifferentiated and above all inert; what was crucial to censorship was the presence or lack of obscenity, more than how that obscenity worked on the being perceiving it. There was no theory of how influence operated; it was always assumed to operate directly, unproblematically, and almost bodily. The subject implied in previous censorship techniques, then, was a tabula rasa, a passive, malleable ball of clay that was molded, inscribed, and impelled by external influences that worked only its surface, since it was without depth or significant content. There was nothing *inside* the subject that regulated or redirected how those influences would or would not bear fruit; censorship was necessary because the subject was otherwise defenseless. Fully external, the subject was completely public, it being censorship's responsibility less to regulate the private than to ensure the proper ordering of public behaviors.

The 1917 regulations assumed this vision of the subject, but only in relation to child viewers. They were largely to be treated in the same old way; censorship acted only to allow or disallow certain stimuli, a procedure that explains why grade B films were so brutally cut. What is groundbreaking about the Tokyo codes is that, by separating these primitive spectators into one class of exhibition, censors were positing a radically different subject to occupy the other class, thus formulating in their relationship a more complex architecture of the subject. The difference between the two is visible in a comment by Akashi Takaichirō, the head of the Ministry of Education's Regular Education Bureau and a member of the committee that approved the Imperial Education Association's resolution: "With an object such as the moving pictures that exerts a direct and considerable influence on public morals, its harmful aspects are smaller and duller and its beneficial points greater and keener depending on the preparation of those showing it and the judgment of those viewing it."[129] "Judgment" separated the two spectatorial subjects: children were defined as undereducated and lacking complete faculties of reason, while adults possessed the powers of resistance that allowed them to properly process cinematic stimuli.

To a certain degree, this division was analogous to the Pure Film Movement's distinction between lower-class audiences and *aikatsuka* described previously, so much so that one can speculate whether concern over child film viewers in the 1910s was not in fact the displacement of a much larger fear about a much broader range of spectators, including women and the lower classes. Audiences who were not *aikatsuka* were often described in terms similar to those used to describe children. For example, one series of essays on female cinema audiences in *Kinema Record* made a distinction between women of the "highly intelligent classes" and those from the "less intelligent classes." One writer says of the latter:

> Viewing only a surface beauty ruled by the players, they blindly offer themselves up to an absolute admiration based on an emotion without any kind of reason or understanding, holding an attachment that borders on the extreme and thereby creating, in a sense, a mentally degenerate trend called "going to the movies." . . . Women with insufficient self-control have committed, through an extreme error, the great fault of just watching the moving pictures. Viewed from the perspective of the high-class artistic rapture that this writer is contemplating,

it seems the behavior of such women evident in reality is just too far from the ideal standard.[130]

Like children, certain women viewed films without using the faculties of reason or self-control, instead just "watching" the surface images with an emotional attachment that failed to appreciate the film's deeper artistry, that merely took in the visual display without attention to the narrative the images were relating. The attitude of such spectators, the *Kinema Record* writer continues, "ignores the mission of the motion pictures as a social entertainment. . . . Approaching the moving pictures with the one goal of becoming intoxicated in a moment's pleasure should probably be seen as a sin when investigated in terms of the truly noble moral sense with which human beings are essentially equipped." Such spectatorship itself bordered on the obscene, permitting bodily pleasure to rule over perception and understanding in the reception of what is truly an art, the cinema. In contrast to this degraded form of spectatorship, the article presents a new form of female spectatorship both serious and studied: "A new and wonderful phenomenon is continuing to arise among the middle classes of brightly and seriously appreciating films with a pure and proper idea and expressing the noble thought of appreciating the players."[131] While the piece still limits female spectatorship to the appreciation of actors, downgrading women viewers in general (they are said not to possess cinematic sense), here as elsewhere the advanced forms of spectatorship are considered variations of the mode of study: the suppression of personal desire and bodily pleasure for the mental savoring of higher forms of beauty.

It was this kind of spectatorial subject with a studied mind that the Tokyo regulations began to postulate. Confronted with a new technology that apparently affected the simple subject—the one postulated in previous censorship regulations and discourse on media reception—with even greater force than other entertainments, censorship worked to solve the problem by not just eliminating the harmful stimuli (the old form of regulation) but also using new technologies to postulate both a new spectatorial subject who could better handle these attractions (and this medium) and a new cinema that would rely less on simple stimuli. Instead this new cinema would depend more on new techniques to encourage—and in some cases shape and corral—the faculties of this subject, for the sake of both cinema and the state. The subject was no longer an inert, passive, and blank body or surface but a receptacle with a past and an education; it had a mind that could negotiate its encounter with the text, depending on the subject's contents and filtering apparatus, and construct a narrative that united the moments of visual display. The subject now had an inside, a complicated combination of attitudes, capabilities, and knowledges that censors had to consider when applying modes of correction. Technically, the subjects without complete internal faculties—children, women, the lower classes—were of most concern; the educated and the reasonable were presumably capable of reading films properly.

One of the tasks of censors was to act as the faculty of reason for the former, previewing motion pictures and selecting those images and meanings from both grade A and grade B films that would do no harm. Ultimately, those subjects would develop proper filters themselves, presumably under the direction of benevolent authorities. By definition, censorship became a form of study: to best accomplish its task of selection and filtration, the censor had to know both the cinema and its spectators. As Ide Tetsujo argues, "If one is going to take the lead and engage in the selection of children's films, there is nothing more grievous in terms of children's education than simply using commonsense judgment. The question is about children's film dramas. In the natural order of things, one must first study children, one must first study cinema. It is difficult to select children's film dramas without knowing children."[132] Constantly iterated by both censors and critics of the regulations was the necessity to study the problem. Censors had to be experts. Study was both preliminary to censorship and part of the regulations: Article 37 of the Tokyo codes required exhibitors to report their monthly attendance figures to their local police station. Such statistics, especially in the hands of censors like Tachibana, who were authorities on film, founded more studies of cinema that, like Gonda's, in turn helped improve censorship procedures. Amid this dialectical relationship with censorship, film study was both a tool of regulation, laying the groundwork for the more efficient manipulation of how spectators saw, and an apparatus of power itself: those who studied film exercised power simply by describing, and by offering recommendations about what cinema and its viewers were and should be.

The study of children, women, lower-class, and other less developed spectators was necessary not simply to help fill in for the faculties they lacked but also to understand what it meant to have complete faculties and why those tools were lacking in such spectators. New technologies of knowledge like psychology and sociology could help, but there was awareness in much discourse on censorship that inferior spectators were not simply incapable of viewing films reasonably but were reading them differently. This is a crucial point, because it underlines the fact that the vision of the simple, bodily subject was never a description of a reality, old or new, but a formulation that, in combination with the conception of a more advanced subject, was supposed to function as a means of defining, promoting, and denigrating various modern forms of subjectivity.

As evident in *Kinema Record*'s castigation of errant women spectators, there was a fear of difference contained in descriptions of the misreadings of lesser film viewers, an apprehension that their irrational modes of reception were impervious to study and constituted a threat to the rule of reason. Most commentators recognized that there were many ways of interpreting the same film. In pointing out the difficulties of establishing censorship standards, *Kinema Record* argues: "Even with the same film, person A will see it as a respectable artistic work and not recognize any pernicious elements, while spectator B will simply place importance on the few bad parts. A good example is the nude paintings at the Ministry of Education exhibition. Even if there is nothing wrong to a person with a considerable eye, if you show it to the Joe Blows on the street, they'll probably see nothing but a nude."[133] The editors posed this as a question of education, but it is important to note that the problem here is not just defenseless spectators but ones who mistakenly "place importance" on the wrong things. Different reading strategies were at stake, which meant the problem was not the presence or absence of simple stimuli but what spectators did with stimuli using faculties heretofore ignored in censorship regulations. These bodily modes of viewing were now more complex than previously thought and could no longer be managed by old methods.

The example of nude paintings the piece cites is important because it, like the 1917 regulations, is one of the first cases in the history of Japanese censorship where censorship procedures recognized differences between spectators. In part influenced by European codes of morality, Meiji officials had cracked down hard on obscene imagery (including traditional *shunga* [erotic wood-block prints], although those had already been regulated by Tokugawa shogunate officials), but were at a loss for an approach to new Westernized modes of realist Japanese painting that began appearing in the 1890s and featured the nude figures celebrated in Western codes of beauty. The first big uproar was over Kuroda Kiyoteru's nude paintings on exhibit at the Domestic Industrial Exhibition in Kyoto in 1896. Some newspapers rallied to have them censored, and the police tried to do just that. Although in some respects this was a conflict between the School of Art (at which Kuroda taught), which was sponsored by the Ministry of Education, and the police, who were led by the Home Ministry, a debate soon arose between those who argued that there was a standard of art that distinguished between an obscene painting and an art work, and those who contended that all nude work should be banned for the general public since such a distinction was difficult to make.[134] Faced with vociferous opposition from influential artists in this and later incidents, police often compromised by demanding that nude paintings and statues be placed in a separate room for special viewers.[135] Conflicts arose every time such an exhibition took place, however, including one over Asakura Fumio's nude sculpture at the Ministry of Education Exhibition just at the time the 1917 Moving Picture Regulations were released. In the end, the sculpture was placed in a separate room at the School of Art. This procedure of separating out the object for special viewers, never written down and usually opposed by the police,[136] is similar to the film code in its assumption that viewers would or would not suffer pernicious effects from an art work depending in their constitution, that reading strategies differed between spectators, and that these interpretations and the mental or perceptual faculties behind them, not just the work of art, were a problem. The similarity between the two practices poses the interesting possibility that the invasion of Western technologies (from machines to methods like realist painting) first posited the problem of the internal processes of viewing—the external that makes apparent the internal. The example from the plastic arts, however, differs to the extent that censorship did not concern itself with trying to alter how meaning was produced. The police still focused on the content of the medium, not the nature of the medium itself: obscenity was the problem, regardless of whether it was painting, or sculpture, or *ikiningyō*.

With cinema, however, the medium did make a difference. If censorship procedures constructed a cinema in which it mattered how the film delivered its content—if, that is, the procedures paid attention to the cinematic apparatus itself—then they also necessarily concerned themselves with how any and all film viewers were reading the text. Separating children from adults may have posited two different subjectivities, but as with the gendered seating, externalizing difference was one means of postulating a unified subjectivity. On the one hand, the separation was important, if only figuratively, in constituting interiority. Setting the child subject against the newer, more complex one replicates the kind of "discovery of landscape"—marked here as the discovery of "ordinary people" or "people-as-landscape"—that Karatani Kōjin sees as central in the formation of interiority in late Meiji literature.[137] It may have been the perception of the more brutishly affected—more "childish"—subject with cinema, which helped those "studying" the cinema to imagine the externality central to positing a new subject defined by interiority.

In this schema, the continued existence of this exteriority, this simple, behaviorist subject, was important in maintaining the new, interior subjectivity ultimately claimed by the intellectual classes. That is likely one reason why the specter of the Pavlovian spectator, directly influenced by cinema's power, remained a foil for film reformers for decades to come, providing justification for both the reformers' own higher status and the continued exercise of power. On another level, however, these two models of reception could also be combined. Inferior and superior spectators were divided in a kind of public architectural model of cinematic subjectivity: all spectators, it could be posited, possessed both primitive and advanced faculties of reception, but privileging the adult viewers with better intellectual faculties helped objectivize the proper relationship between these modes of reception, placing reason and thought over the body and irrational processes. Segregation was one means of constructing the proper relationship between the two modes within any spectator. The issue in subsequent years would then be how to internalize this architecture in each spectator. This tiered model described not just the hierarchy of spectators or their psychology, however, but also the authority of censorship itself (censorship serving as the rational faculty that can view all texts without harm and then pass on to lesser spectators the ones considered harmless to any person) and the structure of the imperial state (with the bureaucratic agents of the paternal emperor caring for the childlike citizenry).

In this articulation of psychology, influence could occur not just on the surface of the subject but also on the inside, manifested in outward forms of behavior into which the subject was impelled as well as in changes in attitude, modes of thought, ideas. The problem was not merely that spectators were viewing inappropriate images but that they were taking even potentially good images (the beautiful nude) and misreading them. While there was the fear that the mass of lower-class cinema viewers would, without a proper set of internal faculties, react directly to film's powerful stimuli, there was also the trepidation that such spectators might in fact also possess interiority, one defined not by the rule of reason, authority, and morality but by different operations, ones more irrational, emotional, physical, and subject to chance. Recall that fears aroused around the time of *Zigomar* were not just about how existing spectators, using long-standing modes of reception, would handle the motion pictures, but also about new viewers—those the *Asahi* said swarmed like ants—who were fundamentally different, operating internally in incomprehensible ways. The opposition, then, was not always between the new, modern subject and the spectator of old, but also between two different versions of a modern subject, one defined by the hierarchical rule of universal intellectual standards, the other by the less stratified combinations of thoughts, perceptions, and bodily impulses. The former could be seen as attempting to manage as much this latter subjectivity as any premodern form of externalized subjectivity. In fact, one can speculate that the concept of the surface spectator, who reacted to stimuli in a predictable, almost Pavlovian fashion, was by this stage in time less a remnant of old concepts of reception than an image functioning to corral and regulate other, new forms of spectatorship as childlike and in need of the rule of modern reason. This "old" image denied their complex, even modern interiority, partly to negate them or to place them at the bottom of a proper hierarchy, both internally and socially. The internalization of this primitive subject in the subjective architecture of all spectators functioned not only to keep lower-class spectators in their place but also, ultimately, to identify all audiences as equally in danger of succumbing to problematic modes of reception and, thus, as a modern citizenry uniformly in need of management by the modern imperial state.

The fear of another form of interiority was crucial, because it necessitated new technologies of censorship that focused on the internal, and made the management of internal subjectivities, both alternative and dominant, a positive aim in a rationalized modernity, in effect changing the role of censorship and state power.

In positing a subject with an inside, film regulations established a new technology of power concerned less with corralling behaviorist subjects by turning on and off the transmission of stimuli than with organizing how knowledges took shape within an interiorized subject and how the subject used them to act. On the basis of this new concept of the subject, it was not hard for the aim of censorship to begin gradually shifting from prevention to promotion, from the control of immoral modes of behavior to the creation of subjects who thought like ideal Japanese citizens. What was being constructed here was, in part, a new communication model in which producers and audiences would relate not on a physical level but through their new-found interiorities. Hase Masato has argued that the 1917 codes, far from restricting authorial intention, in fact helped create the conditions for film-maker expression. An effort to control the live aspect of the filmgoing experience by licensing the benshi, restricting child viewing, and segregating the audience by gender ultimately, by subordinating exhibition to the text,

> stole back the final right of film production from the hands of exhibitors and remolded film into [filmmakers'] own directorial *expression*.

However, this itself could be called a condition for the possibility of censorship. This is because it is only when the idea spreads that a motion picture is the expression of the *director* and that it is impermissible to alter this in the space of exhibition does censorship hold meaning. In other words, . . . the power of censorship and the free self-expression of a director are not at all contradictory. Rather, you could even say the free expression of a director is the pre-condition for censorship.

While I believe Hase overemphasizes the creation of the author as a precondition for censorship, we have seen how important the generation of a univocal text, one that was not significantly transformed in the process of reception, was to regulative authorities; the creation of the author was an important step in locating who was responsible for this univocal meaning (up until then, censorship regulations placed most of the responsibility for a film on exhibitors and benshi). As Hase notes, there was something attractive to censors about filmic meaning so created: "The regulation of live aspects of the mode of exhibition constituted a plan for establishing the cinematic work as a director's internal 'expression.' Correspondingly, the regulation of the 'obscene movie mood' in the mode of reception was a plan for placing the internal expression of the director directly inside each of the spectators."[138] Censorship again worked to suppress the external elements of the filmic text precisely in order to construct a version of interiority, here in the person of the director. Such an emphasis on who was producing what paved the road for increased attention by censors and authorities to the space of production, starting first with script censorship and moving on to government supervision of the film industry after 1939. This emphasis would also lay the groundwork for a model of thought transmission where, in what authorities called the "thought war" *(shisōsen)* during World War II, the ideas of the imperial bureaucracy would be expressed in a sphere of state production and communicated into the minds of citizen receivers.

Regulating Reception

Censors now looked at how spectators viewed films, and they considered it to be a problem analogous to how the apparatus worked. They did not stop at regulating film content but went on to tackle the modes of reception that influenced filmic meaning. Recall that Akashi of the Ministry of Education stressed that a film's final effect depended on the "preparation of those showing it and the judgment of those viewing it." The 1917 codes may have focused attention on the way films were presented in the sphere of exhibition in part because censors still defined cinema as a product of exhibition, but it was equally because they were concerned with influencing the internal faculties of audiences and how they produced cinematic meaning.

Inside the movie theater itself, the codes required a level of lighting during projection sufficient for the police officer in the back of the theater to distinguish the faces of patrons. The lighting requirement was related to fire safety considerations, but when you compare it to police regulations for other types of theaters, it is clear that codes for those theaters required light so that the spectators could see, whereas film statutes did it so that viewers could *be seen*.[139] Hase emphasizes that "police probably viewed places like film theaters as dangerous [locations] in which a mass of unspecified people gathered together in a crowded form of communication."[140] Illumination enabled the officer to determine if viewers had settled into the proper seating area, but it also represented a surveillance procedure by which officers could observe the dangerous crowd, watching viewers at a moment when they were feared to be unable to watch themselves. The increased illumination also reminded spectators that they were not alone, that even inside the space of the movie theater they were members of a public and still bound to the social obligations that existed in the world outside. If film viewing was linked by authorities with asocial and physical desires, the fact of being viewed was supposed to channel and redirect that desire, enmeshing the spectator in a web of vision that marked a public invasion of the subject. The codes postulated an audience that was neither the collection of individual, consumerist spectators that Miriam Hansen sees created in early American cinema, nor the kind of alternative public sphere she maintains was a possibility in the same era.[141] Even if film in Japan was intimately tied to a rising consumer society, such "consumers may not be called merely *consumers*," Miriam Silverberg argues, "but must be identified as imperial subjects at the same time."[142] The complicated mix of public and private was a unique facet of the spectatorship molded by censorship codes.

The regulations also placed premium importance on another figure present at the moment of viewing: the benshi. At first glance, it would seem better for censors to have attempted to eliminate them. Beyond scarring the image of cinema with their seedy reputation as ill-educated windbags who piled up debts and seduced female audience members, benshi were often blamed for imparting incorrect information and even for making good films harmful. They were also part of the "live performance" quality of early cinema that Hase mentions as an obstacle to efficient censorship. Even licensing benshi was not enough to guarantee that they would adhere to the summary approved by censors on any given day—again officers in the theater would be necessary.

Yet police did little to eliminate the institution of the benshi—by some reports, they even required their presence.[143] The Ministry of Education was also said to have published a study strongly recommending the benshi's presence at the exhibition of children's films.[144] The playwright Matsui Shōyō (later known as Matsui Shōō) succinctly explains the reasoning behind such support of the benshi: "It was the explanation of the benshi that pointedly impressed Zigomar and other villains on the minds of both children and adults, so the sin of the films themselves has been relatively small. Now conversely, if the benshi can skillfully save a film's suspicious portions, I think the evil influence will be significantly lessened. This is where the idea of reforming the benshi naturally arises."[145] The degree to which the benshi could be a pernicious influence was also the degree to which they held the same potential for "pointedly impressing" beneficial ideas on viewers' minds. Thus authorities attached great importance to the benshi's ability to guide people in how they watched films. One lower-school principal, Hiruta Taiichirō, while blaming corrupt benshi for the pernicious effects of film, hoped for a day when parents could safely send their children off to the movies because they knew that the benshi was good and that their kids would suffer no harm.[146]

Some perceived the need for benshi assistance given the problems experienced with audience readings of film. As mentioned above, many observers were concerned that inferior spectators could not accurately follow film narratives. Scholars of early American film have pointed out how lecturers had served an important narrative function, especially in the transition around 1908 to more complex modes of storytelling. As Miriam Hansen argues, "The live commentary accompanying the projection of a film actually became part of the elaboration of classical narrative, a temporary solution to problems eventually resolved in a more stable and efficient matter by classical codification."[147] As Japanese censors and educators saw it, the benshi functioned to ensure that audiences understood the narrative progression and moral universe of the characters, but this was ultimately less to facilitate narrative comprehension than to correct and promote approved modes of viewing. According to Komatsu Hiroshi and Charles Musser, Japanese film had, by this time, already long availed itself of the benshi's ability to unify longer and more complex narratives.[148] Despite official concern that spectators were losing themselves to disjointed visual displays, the cinematic experience of the mid-1910s was already deeply entwined with narrative. The problem as critics saw it was, first, that some spectators were downplaying the narrative in favor of other forms of pleasure (the visuals, the attractions in the theater space, etc.), and second, that even if they were paying attention to the story, some were not grasping its moral worth or interpreting it properly. The benshi became a central means of correcting these mistaken forms of spectatorship. In such ways censorship became intimately related to centralizing narrative pleasure and structuring interpretation in early Japanese cinema.

Censors were also worried about the social implications of film reception. Tachibana Takahiro cited the case of an Asakusa screening of a film on the French Revolution that was greeted with silence by the first-class seats and cheers from regular spectators. Stating that an unwise statement by the benshi at that point could have triggered a riot, Tachibana hoped for, in general, explanations that, "as much as possible, gently take care of films related to ideology or romance."[149] The explanation that accompanied a film not only had to ensure correct comprehension of the text, but it also had to work to eliminate conflicts among viewers and construct a unified, classless audience. In such cases, the benshi's function was to intervene at the point of reception to rewrite the text and lead viewers to apprehend a socially more appropriate meaning.

Given this function, who the benshi were became an issue of central importance. In 1917, benshi in Tokyo were required to apply for three-year licenses, and then to take a test in 1920 in order to renew them. Interestingly, the licensing exam quizzed the test takers less on general knowledge or skills specific to benshi explanation than on such essay topics as "the influence of the moving pictures on audiences," "public peace and morality," and "the duty of the benshi."[150] It was as if the authorities were more concerned with whether benshi knew their place in the moving picture system than with whether they possessed accurate factual knowledge or could tell a good story. To ensure that benshi were cognizant of their function, the Ministry of Education in 1921 held an educational lecture series for benshi (which was later published), featuring such prominent authorities on cinema as Gonda and Tachibana. In this way, the education of the benshi became of paramount importance, since it was argued that they should have greater educational credentials than their audiences.[151] The benshi's role, then, was not merely to explain the text to the viewers but to teach and lead them to proper understanding. A common metaphor at the time indicated that a benshi was like a teacher. An article in the *Kinema Record* puts it this way: "To all you benshi standing for a moment in front of the screen, think that there is absolutely no difference between you and a schoolteacher standing on the podium in front of a blackboard."[152] The benshi, then, were to be transformed from popular entertainers into teachers, from performers in an entertainment industry into an element of the educational state apparatus.

As with the new spectators, the internal subjectivity of benshi—how they interpreted and processed their explanations—was as crucial to authorities as whether they were mashers. The requirement in the 1917 regulations that each benshi submit a copy of his résumé to the police—a request not made of stage actors—and receive a license to practice made that apparent. Police were described as "undertaking a strict investigation into their background" and approving those "appropriate to be benshi."[153] Appropriateness, however, was judged not according to an individual benshi's oratorical skill or entertainment value but according to a "character standard" as manifested in his curriculum vitae.[154] The benshi was pictured less as a performer who assumed a part using a skill that was irrelevant to his personal character, as an actor would, and more as a figure whose role depended on his true personality. His persona inside the theater was continuous with his character outside, and thus his real person was never supposed to be concealed by his role as purveyor of the film's fiction. Thus, localities like Ehime prohibited ex-convicts and others guilty of "improper conduct" from being given licenses to practice as benshi.[155]

The benshi's mental state had to be different from that of his audience. The psychologist Sugawara Kyōzō, who instructed benshi on their responsibilities to the public at the Ministry of Education lecture series, reminded his charges of what kind of spectators the cinema constructs:

> Inside the moving picture theater it is dim and the multitude of people cannot be seen; there, the mentality of the individual self operates more than that of public feelings. Because it is dark, primitive thoughts will occur more than in a bright location. Uninhibited feelings come to dominate over reason or the strictures of instinct. . . . People may think about a certain issue and say, "We should do this," but in the shadows, feelings appear that refuse to do that. Although saying something is good, people can possess a mentality that wants to defame that good, saying, "The hell with that!" In the end, people have double values. . . . It seems that they desire reasonable things as well as unreasonable things they don't understand. . . . When such people come in contact with the mysteries of the dark theater, what kind of feelings are operating? That is the important issue I would like all of you to think about carefully.[156]

To Sugawara, the original motion picture experience was fundamentally private, one in which people thought and felt things normally subject to public opprobrium. By being associated with a subject featuring interiority, the cinema posited possible conflicts between the internal and the external, the private and the public, and, in the worse case, the private, internal self developed in the dark movie house could spill out on the street.

In asking the benshi to think about such an issue, Sugawara was reminding them that their responsibility was to keep an eye on those who entered the world of the film, to be the public presence who would prevent spectators from giving in to their private selves. The benshi had to present an upright public stature because they were the representatives of the public in the space of entertainment. A benshi's public duty, which related to his moral self, was the same as that of the police officer in the back of the theater: to bring the responsibilities of the outside world into the space of the theater to ensure that spectators watched films in a rational, publicly acceptable fashion. The police officer positioned in the back of the theater, away from the screen, acted as a gaze from without, which guarded the boundary between the inside of the theater and the outside world precisely in order to guarantee that the inner space could not leak out and that the external world would instead always pressure the audience from behind. Coupled with the benshi's gaze from the shadows in front, the officer's stare helped envelop the audience in what could be termed a cinematic approximation of Michel Foucault's panopticon.[157] Engrossed in the diegetic world and urged by censors and film reformers to forget the space of the theater, spectators were subject to the power of surveillance, reminded of a public eye but told to concentrate on the film.

The benshi, however, could operate in ways the police officer could not: he stood in front, next to the screen, spatially the most removed from the threshold to the outside world. His sentry point, in fact, was the window into the space of the film, that fictional diegesis the spectators had paid their money to experience. Yet his role was not so much to perfect that escape into the internal world of film as to provide a constant link between the inside of film and the external, public world, ensuring that the fictional apparatus of cinema was performing its nonfictional, public duty. Similarly, he watched out for the spectators, inserting public meaning into their personal experience of the film and instructing them on how to view the film responsibly. Unlike the police officer, the benshi, then, could enter the world of the film—even that imagined by the spectator in his or her mind—in order to effect the insertion of external, public concerns into the film experience. The benshi came to represent the model of the new censor himself, acting on behalf of underequipped spectators and correcting those making mistakes, utilizing the newfound internality of cinema and the viewing subject to fold the external within that internal and ensure that what was inside was obligated to what was outside.

In other cultural contexts, one form of resistance to the kind of surveillance enacted here by the benshi and the police was for spectators to reject their construction as atomistic individuals and recognize their fellow viewers, emphasizing their power as a collective, as a social entity that produces its own meanings (this, to some extent, is Hansen's argument). Japanese authorities did fear the formation of such public spheres inside the movie house, but their solution was not, as in the American case, to promote the model of the individualistic consumer spectator, since that itself might have released private desires antithetical to public order. Instead, they encouraged the audience's consciousness of its existence as a social entity, but only insofar as it approximated the ordered structures of the public world. The Meiji model of society was precisely that of the family-state, a body politic *(kokutai)* that found its analogy in the form of the family, where the citizens *(kokumin)* acted as children to their father, the emperor. Smaller collectives like the individual family were supposed to replicate this structure, with the father serving as a kind of miniemperor at home.[158] Just as the internal architecture of the modern subject also replicated this hierarchical structure, with reason and public duty overruling hidden irrational desires, clearly the social collective promoted inside the movie theater was supposed to resemble this family, a smaller version of the hierarchical *kokutai*. Within this cinematic social body, the benshi served as the head, the reasonable father-teacher who guided his children through the obstacles of a difficult diegetic world,[159] the emperor in the theater watching over his subjects.[160] But as an element in a panopticon-like apparatus, his presence was not readily apparent. His voice dominated the proceedings, but as disembodied speech,[161] reminding spectators of their duties—by making them hear it as part of their own process of understanding the film. Especially when tied to the narrative apparatus, that voice entered the minds of viewers and to some extent became their own: audiences internalized the emperor system *(tennōsei)* through the process of cinematic understanding.

Kitada Akihiro's work on the voice in Taishō Japan raises important questions about the exercise of power and the possibilities of resistance. Kitada has delineated how struggles over spectatorship in the 1920s laid the groundwork for wartime modes of control. He focuses in particular on a film culture that was centered on the voice of the benshi—which to him represents a mode of perception and subjectivity that takes a bodily form and is participatory and practical (and which resembles the modernism of mixture I describe here). This was superseded by a modern one centered on the visual, which remained dominant even with the coming of sound, and which promoted a subject that is semiotic and divorced from the physical.[162] Kitada, thus, echoes several of my earlier arguments, especially with regard to the Pure Film Movement. But there are problems involving this binary division, since it potentially ignores how complex and possibly contradictory each side could be: how benshi, for instance could be aligned with the police, or pure film reformers like Gonda with participatory spectatorship.

Kitada's division could be seen be seen as bringing him in line with Jeffery Dym's attempt to picture benshi as "countercultural heroes" who "often ignored the rules" given by censors.[163] Kitada, however, in no way repeats Dym's often anecdotal and romantically colored tales of benshi resistance, but instead firmly places them in a history of a progressively pervasive fascistic power structure. The question is whether the benshi continued to represent such an alternative cultural politics. As I argued earlier, the degree to which early benshi were an object of criticism indicates, at least to officials and pure film reformers, the extent to which they could represent more disorderly, combinatory, obscene, perhaps Baudelairian, forms of modernity. Censors tried to regulate this culture, but it was certainly possible—and Dym points to occasional examples—for benshi to fail to behave as the morally superior teachers they were supposed to become. Such examples require more research and theorization than Dym provides to determine whether they truly constitute cultural resistance and not just simple deviation. Authorities no longer considered the benshi a major problem when they nationalized censorship in 1925, since nationalization was logically possible only because the movies had become national or universal texts, no longer significantly influenced by local factors such as the live benshi in the theater. The authorities may not have been fully correct in supposing that, but it is important to reiterate that the strategy of officials, in loose alignment with pure film reformers, was not to suppress the benshi but to transform their practice into one that conformed both to aesthetic and textual principles and to social and moral principles. The benshi, then, was not an oppositional figure but a site of struggle, where the benshi's voice could as much embody a chaotic physical externality—the individual voice resounding in the theatrical space—as it could serve as a model for internal voices meant to rule over asocial thought and desire. Kitada concedes the latter when he describes how modern benshi like Tokugawa Musei could, though narrating styles that subordinated the voice to the visuals, promote a modern visual subjectivity and prefigure the coming of sound cinema.[164]

I described efforts to mold such forms of benshi narration in the previous chapter. But Kitada, in his dualistic account of the struggle, does not fully consider how the voice in this new subjectivity might still straddle the physical and the disembodied just as the benshi himself had to inhabit the line between public and private, between being in the movie and outside it, between being inside the mind of the spectator and surveying it from without. This hybrid situation may suggest that the modern subjectivity Kitada describes never became completely visual but continued to rely on the word, especially as embodied in an authoritative speaker. I have written elsewhere about the continued distrust of the image during the interwar period that led some to still look to the word as the best means of corralling the visual.[165] In general, state authorities were more likely to bear this distrust than were pure film reformers. This is one reason why wartime authorities revived the institution of the benshi when dealing with non-Japanese spectators during World War II, and why the regulative force of the benshi-like voice continued in movie voice-overs as the benshi was absorbed into sound cinema. Many did not entirely trust a visual medium to enforce the transmission of approved meanings, and thus to control aberrant readings and other forms of subjectivity. Pure film advocates put greater faith in the image and thus were more opposed to the institution of the benshi than were police censors.

Such distinctions show us that the problem of the cinematic image, raised by the *Zigomar* incident, had not been completely solved, or, to put it more precisely, that it was still being pursued through various options, which reveals that the rational, efficient, authoritative modernism forwarded by reformers and censors was not completely unified. Disagreements still existed over how much the interiorized individual subject—or text—could rule itself, and whether it required external public assistance; over how much the image could itself be ruled, and whether it required the intervention of the word; and thus over how much an aesthetic modernism focused on the visual could be accommodated within a nationalist modernism. In some ways, the conception of a visual, rational modernity still logically required that specter of an irrational, physical culture necessitating control, in order to justify itself; thus it continued to project that shadow as a means of self-perpetuation, even as those alternative forms of modernity persisted in bubbling up around cinema and other popular cultural forms at the limits of discourse. Even pure film supporters increasingly exhibited disagreements, as some in the 1920s, influenced by European cinematic modernism, particularly German Expressionism and then French Impressionism, broke with the dominant trend of the Pure Film

Movement and began to imagine a cinematic visuality free of the model of language. Debates over the image and the voice/word would then continue throughout the prewar period, not only on the pages of magazines and in censorship decisions but also in a range of films, from Kinugasa Teinosuke's *Kurutta ichipeiji* to Itō Daisuke's *chanbara,* or swordplay movies.

Censorship and Education

Debates would also continue in noncinematic spaces like the school and the family home. In the effort to insert the public into the private and regulate modes of viewing, authorities did not restrict their attention to the space inside the theater: there were other institutions through which proper spectators could also be constructed. The comments of even critics of the 1917 regulations mentioned these. While some contended that children could indeed properly identify the villain as a figure not to imitate,[166] most opponents of the code accepted the dominant description of young people as defective spectators but argued that the best way to correct their defects was through instruction by educators and parents, not by preventing film viewing. *Katsudō shashin zasshi* maintained that the industry's proposal to allow children into grade A films if accompanied by an adult family member was in no way a violation of the spirit of the regulations: "Even if there are some children who do not have the capacity to interpret the meaning of all the reels of a film, [the adults] can instruct and make them understand. If adults recognize something harmful to a child, they should take the lead and warn them."[167] In this way, parents were to act like the benshi, teaching and correcting modes of film viewing. In fact, from this period on, parent and teacher associations across Japan began involving themselves in the problem of cinema as the family system became enrolled in the state project of creating proper spectators.

Given that the motion pictures were often defined as an educational issue, education became another means of managing the internal faculties of spectators. A question often asked was why certain spectators had inadequate faculties or were misreading films. As the editors of *Kinema Record* kept insisting, it was largely an issue of educational difference. One grade school principal argues, "If there are children who see a villain in a movie and immediately imitate him, that is not the fault of the picture but of educators."[168] Spectators needed preparation and instruction even before they paid for their tickets, and that was apparently the responsibility of the educational system. Educators were asked to maintain their role even after children entered the theater: the principal Komagine Shigeji asserts, "Educators should go out to the movies with children and, while watching with the youngsters, study their mental state. If there is a scene that is not very good for children, it would not be harmful if teachers appropriately explain and lead the children in a beneficial direction. Pictures can become anything through explanation."[169]

In a situation where the power of the word was substantial, educators were asked to become benshi as benshi were to become teachers, instructing their charges on how to properly watch films as they viewed them together. When moving pictures started entering the classroom (something urged by *Kinema Record* and other reformers seeking to promote the cinema), schools began to get more and more involved in film. After the A/B grading system was abolished, the regulation of film viewing by children was left to schools, which began instituting rules determining which films their children were allowed to see and when. Many school codes after this date prevented motion picture attendance by students unless accompanied by a teacher or parent (a practice that continues in some places even today).[170] The Ministry of Education, which had already begun authorizing films for classroom use, also stepped into the picture by recommending individual films for society in general, beginning in 1916, a practice that became regularized in 1921 (and still occurs even now). As the ministry's Akashi Takaichirō said in endorsing the system, spectators and exhibitors could always rely on the ministry's recommendations if they did not know which films were good.[171] The historian Nishimoto Hajime, in analyzing the ministry's decision to promote rather than reject the cinema, emphasizes that it was defined as a special tool: "Film, as the process or medium for imprinting the expected policy effects on the 'original administrative object'—the minds (to put it bluntly) of film spectators—was not itself the administrative object. Whether or not these effects were appropriately induced definitely depended on the 'superiority' of the content and the mode of expression of the medium cinema. In that sense, film was a kind of 'god,' a go-between connecting administrative goals with the 'original administrative object.'"[172] In the minds of educational authorities, cinema shifted from being solely an object of regulation to becoming a means of controlling other administrative objects. Now a kind of "divine" means of affecting the internal state of citizens, film was grasped as an important tool, one that had to be promoted and improved, treated with care so that it could dutifully fulfill policy goals.

Soon it was not uncommon, as Komagine proposed, for classes to go on school field trips to the movies and see approved films accompanied by explanations provided by their teachers. Schools became an essential part of the process of defining cinema and film spectatorship, raising spectators who watched movies as good Japanese citizens should. The Ministry of Education's effort to offer film education ultimately extended to the general populace, an endeavor best represented by the ministry-sponsored Moving Picture Exhibition in October 1921, a kind of industrial fair that promoted both the industry and approved films and sought to improve the status of the medium, if only by having the film star Onoe Matsunosuke perform live in front of Crown Prince (and future emperor) Hirohito.

Film Use and the Internalization of Censorship

As the question of how to address the problem of cinema brought more and more institutions into the process of regulation, extending beyond the police to include the family and the schools, the moving pictures began to assume a definition that exceeded mere entertainment. First, given the prevailing value systems, it seemed that, for the industry and film fans, the only way to make cinema respectable was to assert that it was more socially beneficial than entertaining. Second, as public meaning was increasingly inserted into the space of the theater, the benshi's explanations, and the inside of the filmic text, cinema could no longer be conceived as simply a form of private escape or sensual pleasure. *Kinema Record,* for one, featured in its last year many essays foregrounding the positive social uses of the cinema. I have already cited Kaeriyama's essay about his ideals for the cinema, in which he expressed his dreams that it would nurture the spirit and intellect of the citizenry and awaken them to national goals. In a continuation of that essay, he later argues: "Producers must be respectable philosophers, they must be educators, they must be serious scientists." Absent was the dictum that they must be entertainers, for that was somehow not "serious." Kaeriyama goes on to explain: "Although cinemas can be called places of entertainment where people meet, they are different from a theater or a *yose.* Simply, they are schools for society."[173] For him, the measure for cinema was ultimately its moral, intellectual, and social worth; in giving a standard for cinematic value, he contends that "producers with ability must transmit emotions that lead people to true feeling and good conscience."[174] Such a discourse appeared to shift the goal of the Pure Film Movement away from pure cinema and to motion pictures subordinate to social aims. There is little trace here of Gonda's effort to reverse the hierarchy of use and entertainment and establish entertainment as a lived experience in and of itself—as the epitome of human civilization.

The Pure Film Movement did not drop the concept of cinema as entertainment in prewar Japan. But, while supported in part by neo-Confucian social theories, it did help establish social usefulness as a standard for entertainment and a means by which cinema could claim not to be a social problem. Of course not all producers adopted this standard, much to the consternation of many film critics and government officials, but it would become one of the tenets of official culture, inscribed in the discourse of many institutions, educational and governmental. Well after World War II, commentaries on cinema by critics, educators, and PTA groups continued to include complaints about the frivolousness of movie entertainment, as well as calls for more serious and educational film content. It is important to recognize that such standards, first introduced in order to save cinema from threats of prohibition and to define the value of its unique existence, laid the discursive groundwork for the programmatic use of motion pictures in the service of the state up to and during the war years, when entertainment itself was subject to much opprobrium.

At the same time, this official emphasis on usefulness over entertainment reminds us that cinematic pleasure could still have functioned as a site for resistance and alternative forms of desire. If attempts to render cinema utilitarian had aligned with efforts to mold the medium according to a more Fordist version of modernity, the modernism of mixture could have found refuge in forms of entertainment that still emphasized sensual pleasure or cinematic play over social utility. I have elsewhere discussed an alternative tradition in Japanese cinema—from the wild *chanbara* of the 1920s to the action movies of Hayafusa Hideto in the 1930s to the kiddie monster movies of the 1960s—which celebrated the kinetic, the chaotic, the mobile, and the physical, and thus often earned criticism for being "childish" or "frivolous."[175] While it is beyond the scope of this book, it is possible to trace this phenomenon back to the 1910s, especially so as to understand the stakes in labeling entertainment "childish" and the ideological issues such entertainment potentially posed, earning it such criticism.

One of the central problems of film entertainment was that it seemingly promoted a subject not beholden either to the external hierarchies of public consciousness and social surveillance, or to hierarchies internalized in the family-state at home and the self-regulation of desire in the individual. It was the emergence of asocial desires from a new interiorized subject that led to new technologies of censorship, which included locating censorship in the individual. Cinema's usefulness was again founded in a new vision of the subject. Efforts to educate spectators to properly read films did not constitute the construction of independent, critical viewers who could sift any image or information through faculties of judgment. Rather, the hope was for spectators who would dutifully absorb beneficial messages while only critically engaging with the harmful ones. The faculties of reason and discernment to be fostered in spectatorial subjects, then, were not meant to be wielded independently, but rather these subjects were to obey the dictates of those more knowledgeable about the social good, thus remaining "children" within the framework of the family-state. Especially under the instruction of the benshi, the spectators' modes of film interpretation were to be mere extensions of the censorship apparatus as viewers came to internalize the means of censorship in their very thought processes. Just as many authorities asked the industry to censor itself in addition to being censored,[176] so spectators were mobilized to participate in self-regulation. Okudaira characterizes the changes in late 1920s and early 1930s film censorship procedures as reflecting a shift from the regulation of immorality to the imposition of thought control,[177] but I contend that the seeds of this transition were already firmly planted in the 1917 Moving Picture Regulations. Ultimately censorship would lead to the discourses on "training spectators" and "proper spectatorship" that inhabited official film policy during World War II.[178]

The Tokyo codes did not last long: they were first amended in November 1919, when the A/B system was dropped, and then entirely replaced by the Performance and Performance Site Regulations in July 1921. The changes were part of the authorities' continuing efforts to study film and try new modes of censorship if others failed to produce the cinema they had in mind. In fact, the provisions of the 1917 regulations were withdrawn in part because they had served their purpose. The Home Ministry's expert on film censorship in the 1920s, Yanai Yoshio, argued in his remarkable analysis of Japanese censorship that the 1917 codes were repealed in part because they had succeeded in reforming the cinema.[179] In a sense, systems like the A/B grading, which externalized differences so as to map out the internal structure of the new subject, became unnecessary once those structures were seemingly internalized in a homogenized citizenry.

The Tokyo regulations should, in the end, not simply be characterized as a repressive measure that sought to dampen a vibrant cinema culture. Within their discourse was contained a new vision of the cinema that confirmed film's unique place in Japanese society. In regulating the medium by using procedures applied to no other entertainment, censorship singled out the moving pictures as the site for a modern form of subjectivity that transcended gender and class differences, and that bore internal mechanisms which allowed that citizenry not just to sensually enjoy but also to think about and interpret film. Such subjects were to be the basis of a newly emerging modern Japanese society, supportive of consumer capitalism but—perhaps not without tension—ultimately in service to the new Japanese state. They were to be *kokumin,* "citizens" of the Japanese nation who, while expressing individual desires and mental processes, were always firmly tied to public obligations that structured their private interiority so that it, too, could service the state.

Conclusion

Mixture, Hegemony, and Resistance

The first few decades of cinema in Japan witnessed a certain historical thrust, a conjunction, if not at times a collaboration, between different sectors in Japanese society—intellectual film fans, progressive filmmakers, benshi, censors, and even educators—in what is loosely called the Pure Film Movement, that worked to realize and enforce a certain definition of cinema. This effort took place largely in the field of discourse, broadly speaking, as definitive ways of speaking about cinema, as well as modes of enacting such articulations, were formed and established in the first thirty years after the apparatus's importation into Japan. These ways and modes not only created the dominant channels for future discourse on cinema but also agglomerated around the medium itself, shaping how it would be conceived, used, received, and regulated. Central in this process was the notion that the definition of film would be exclusive, that cinema's meaning was singular and other definitions should be barred: other definitions could not exist alongside or meld with film's true definition, which remained constant over time and space. Purity distinguished both the discourse and the object it described, preventing other forms of speaking and other forms of cinema from cluttering up the motion picture field, such as the practice of seeing cinema as a mixture of various cultural forms, experiences, perceptions, and meanings, which could vary from time to time and place to place.

Such hybridity was anathema to film purists, who, in all respects, sought to mold a cinematic body unified in essence and void of handicaps or mixed genetics. But for all their effort to create a pure cinema, reformers and censors did not themselves always form an untainted bloc. My research on the discursive definition of cinema in Japan focused on an influential group of critics and films that, precisely because it aimed for purity, gives the impression of assuming a monolithic position in Japanese cinema history.

But the Pure Film Movement and its conception of cinema suffered from cracks and contradictions that one must understand in order to approach the motion pictures from this time on. It not only failed to be uniform in itself, but it also often depended on a precarious set of alliances with others ranging from intellectuals to censors to educators to industry officials, who did not always see eye-to-eye with them. Conceptions of cinema formulated around the Pure Film Movement dominated in part because they were accepted as natural in the sites that wielded much authority over the film world: the press, the censors, educators, many filmmakers, and, with the coming of such studios as Taikatsu and Tōhō, the corporate offices. Since they were dominant forces, not totalities, they did not exclusively rule over the way cinema operated or was conceived in every spectator, locale, theater, or single film screening. If these conceptions came to dominate film culture, this was more the result of the emergence of a hegemonic set of relations between these forces (in Gramsci's sense) than of the establishment of a monolithic power.

The cracks and conflicts in pure film discourse were not due simply to the fact that the forces in the alliance were occasionally at odds and out of sync with each other. The very concepts they propounded could contain fundamental contradictions and fissures, some of which figured as a sort of return of what the discourse repressed, some as the recoil after the considerable use of force, some as the manifestation of the particular aporia of early Japanese cinematic modernity. The hybridity that pure film critics saw in contemporary Japanese film culture was also a manifestation (if not also sometimes a projection) of central contradictions in the discourse of the Pure Film Movement, incongruities that nonetheless defined its project and often represented the situation of the intellectual in prewar Japan. First, there was the attempt to create a univocal text that spoke on its own while also placing utmost importance on the perfect transmission of cinematic meaning—a position that, in the end, supported the use of censorship and the benshi to ensure that what the text said was actually what was read. Second, there was a supposition of a mass, homogeneous audience that was a standard for cinema devoid of differences (especially in reading strategies) yet beholden to the hierarchical knowledge of *aikatsuka* and censors. Third, pure film advocates who actually entered the industry strove to remodel the business in the form of a culture industry, producing commodities with a universal status while, at the same time, rejecting the capitalist system of profit and self-interest. Fourth, the ideal form of spectatorship was posited as a mode of entrancement, an absorption into the illusory world of the film text, but one based on a serious and studied posture that advocated distance from the text. Fifth, the cinema was praised as an image medium whose ability to signify exceeded the scope of the word, yet the desire to ensure univocality also at times prompted binding and reducing the image to the word. Sixth, the effort to mold a modernity centered on rational efficiency and pure, universal standards, a modernity conjoined with a new subjectivity contradictorily combining imperial subjectivity with consumerist desires needed both to exclude "irrational" spectators when defining purity and to project and internalize them in order to precariously establish the architecture of intellect over body, public over private, father/emperor over woman and child, and the rule of a particular class structure—now defined as national—over other social possibilities. And seventh, the desire to introduce to the world a more accurate Japanese reality depended on constructing a modern Japanese cinematic body that would be Japanese only to the degree that it was recognized—and it resembled—the Western cinematic body.

Such contradictions were echoed in the structure of the Japanese film world after the Pure Film Movement completed its course as a practical movement. Much of what the Movement proposed had become industry practice by the end of the 1920s: the star and director systems were firmly in place with the emergence of figures like Bando Tsumasaburō, Kurishima Sumiko, Itō Daisuke, Abe Yutaka, and Mizoguchi Kenji; the screenplay was an accepted form, and among its prominent practitioners were Susukita Rokuhei and Yamagami Itarō; production forces gained additional power over exhibition; actresses replaced *onnagata;* and intellectuals made significant headway in the industry as the social status of the cinema rose. Most important, many of the aspects of film style that reformers had advocated—the close-up, parallel editing, and so on—were firmly a part of common film practice as first Shōchiku in the 1920s and then Tōhō in the 1930s gained a reputation for having a more Americanized film style. While Burch has argued for the complete alterity of Japanese film style before World War II, which is accurate in relation to the work of a few filmmakers, there is significant evidence to support David Bordwell's more reasonable claim that Japanese cinema as a whole in the 1930s reflects its significant absorption of Hollywood and European modes of filmic narration.[1]

As J.L. Anderson and others stress, however, Japanese film studios in the prewar era failed to create a culture industry like that of the United States. Theater sizes were too large, keeping down the number of theaters in the country and available prints. Never fully becoming a mass production industry, the studios lacked capital and maintained a precarious relationship with theaters, two factors that, for instance, helped delay the introduction of sound. The industry still opted to make more films rather than make more prints of a single film, a course of action that stemmed from the lack of capital and emphasized a quick return on minimal investments over longer-run returns on larger capital outlays. Censors still failed to fully recognize film as an artifact of the sphere of production, largely ignoring the screenplay (until the Film Law of 1939) and still censoring each *print* of the film, not each title.[2] Perhaps it is as an intimate product of such conditions that Japanese cinema of the late 1920s and 1930s, while understandable by Hollywood codes, has nonetheless appeared odd to foreign observers. Bordwell names these cinematic oddities "flourishes" or cinematic "ornamentation." He defines a flourish as a "stylistic device or pattern [that] is seen to exceed its denotative, thematic, or expressive function. This obtains when the stylistic device or pattern can plausibly be treated as an elaboration of a simpler, more norm-based device or pattern that would suffice to achieve these other functions."[3]

However, far from constituting surface excess, such devices were a mark of a more fundamental, yet complicated, hybrid norm of cinematic production—the mixed body of Japanese cinema that authorities were still attempting to correct during the war. The Film Law and subsequent state directives were not a new development in Japanese film policy that suddenly instituted national influence over film production, but a continuation of the effort begun in the 1910s to purify, modernize, and massify ("nation-alize") the motion picture industry by emphasizing the script in the sphere of production, stemming overproduction, and encouraging the production of more prints.[4]

The "failures" in the project of producing a pure cinema are not so much an indication that the Pure Film Movement was unsuccessful, as they are manifestations of the contradictions inherent both in the historical conditions and in the discourse of reformers themselves. The prewar social and economic spheres were rife with conflict and division, as the uneven development that Harootunian has stressed resulted in the production of a mass urban consumer culture that overlapped with ideologies of agrarianism at a time when Japan was still overwhelmingly a rural, agricultural nation. Pure film discourse, if not much of motion picture culture, was significantly urban, and its pronouncements of a rationalized, metropolitan modernity were intimately tied to assertions of authority over improperly modernized spectators, which could mean city audiences with a different experience of urban modernity, as well as rural spectators. Ignoring or denigrating the other half was central in defining this modern cinematic city, and it reflected the divisions that would prevent the creation of a complete national film experience. It would be hard to construct a mass spectator-ship, a culture industry, or even a national cinema so long as many rural communities lacked movie theaters, so long as fundamental differences between city and country, or between classes in the city, still persisted.

On the other hand, the failures of "pure film" were to some degree inherent in the system of cinematic modernism. Purity needed mixture to define itself, and authority required a "problem" in order to justify its hier-archical power. Given that cinema in Japan around the time of *Zigomar* was defined as a unique medium through the process of negation—reformers cited it as a problem and then endeavored to negate that—the discourse of the Pure Film Movement tended to articulate a pure cinema through negative statements, such as "Cinema is not *onnagata*," "Cinema is not the benshi," "Cinema is not theater," and so on. Such negativity had to be reiterated to maintain film's definition, and so critics continued to complain about what was not cinema long after the Pure Film Movement ended as an experiment in film practice, making Japanese film a conspicuous object of censure even up to the 1990s. On a more abstract level, the models of the new film text and the new spectatorial subject—in which a rational, ordered, and publicly minded authority corralled the unruliness of either the image or the impulsive body and its emotions—both relied to a certain degree on internalizing the elements of combination, mixture, and hybrid-ity as that which must be controlled. Those elements were necessary to the system to justify the internalized hierarchies of power that defined the modern text/subject. On the social level, this meant that unruly spectators and film texts remained an important facet of this form of modernism, as there continued to be cases that stayed "uncinematic," "premodern," or "un-Japanese," thus requiring the perpetual exercise of cinematic knowl-edge and institutional authority. If Western modernism needed others (the East, the South) to define itself, so did this modernism of purity, only its others were located as much in Japan as in the colonies, if not also in the Japanese text and the Japanese subject. Modernism, in this case, was not a state to be achieved but a seemingly self-perpetuating process.

It had to be that way because conditions were not stable enough to sup-port a constant sociocultural state. This raises the issue of resistance. What kind of resistance was there to this dominant cinematic hegemony? We have seen the conflicts over what cinema should be, many of which revolve around class divisions in film culture. Research on actual forms of resis-tance, however, has been hampered by the lack of source materials. When it is difficult to find copies of journals like *Katsudō no sekai*, which forwarded the dominant cause of pure film,[5] it is even harder to locate voices speaking of other kinds of cinema, especially those of the nonintellectual classes. I have, like Miriam Hansen, attempted to cull out forces of difference from the complaints about other film cultures in the dominant discourse. The danger there is that such citations of difference (mixture, unruliness), as I suggested earlier, may have reflected as much the needs and projections of the system of purist modernism as any real cultural practice. This view that images of resistance may be linked to the forces of power themselves can become even more problematic if one effectively defines resistance as necessary to, and thus as an effect of, power, as some have said Foucault does.[6] This could mean, in our discussion, that expressions of fear about audiences harboring asocial thoughts inside the dark movie hall—that is, fears about a new modern subject possessing interiority—may simply have been part of a system that, in reverse, used such fears to open up interiority as a new space for exercising other modern technologies of power.

The crucial question, then, is when does resistance escape this system? One instance is when resistance is able to mobilize its own hegemony and secure sufficient power to define the meaning of its own actions. This can occur when sectors of film culture form their own public spheres, in Hansen's sense of the term. It is hard to see this happening in Japan against pure film discourse, however, at least before 1925; the proletarian film league Prokino, in the few years around 1930, may, however, have managed to do it. But one might say that resistance in a different sense occurred before that if one considers the attempts to escape the system by evading processes of universalization. The formula in which pure film advocates needed the impure in order to define their cinema as a pure, universal standard could work only if the impure film culture itself was universalized or systematized within the process of modernization.[7] That was precisely one way that reformers dealt with the problem of cultural mixture, if not the issue of cinema as a whole. One aspect that consternated critics about hybrid spaces like Asakusa, or *rensageki*, or the films of Onoe Matsunosuke was their perceived chaos, noise, and obscenity—their assault on the mind and the senses and, thus, on one's ability to contain them rationally through abstraction or language. Describing them by means of generalizations about class or gender (e.g., labeling them as part of the culture of women and children) was a means of solving the problem. This is one reason why the discursive articulation of cinema was crucial to at least the first thirty years of film history in Japan: naming and labeling was a central aspect of this kind of modernism, both articulating its aims and limiting its opponents.

But naming was not a perfect solution, because what was truly particular about these phenomena, and the pleasure they entailed, could not be completely captured by such discourse. They precisely played with or even resisted the processes of universalization. The struggle could continue, but precisely at the limits of naming. This infuriated reformers, and many of them called for the exercise of both discursive control and state power to manage what was escaping. This was difference at the level of the particular and the everyday, one that could utilize a new interiorized subject as a site, not for the internalization of universal values, but as an additional element in the particular and not always rational combinations that yielded a vital, lived form of entertainment. To some, it seemed this could be combated only through state intervention on the level of the internal and the everyday.

The problem of universalization complicates efforts to label or name resistance. Much research on Japanese film, from Burch on, has been quick to label any difference between Japanese film and classical Hollywood as oppositional or resistant. Not only does this reduce complex cultural interactions to binary oppositions, but it also too easily turns difference into political opposition. Komatsu Hiroshi, Jeffrey Dym, and others have provided valuable evidence showing that some spectators were not happy with the new pure films being produced, and that some benshi were not as compliant with censorship requirements as authorities would have liked.[8] Citing such instances as resistance, however, trivializes the notion. I share Tom Gunning's sense that "'resistant' has become an over-used term,"[9] one in need of more precise usage. It may be productive to find forms of subcultural resistance, keeping in mind Dick Hebdige's conception of sub-cultures,[10] among fans of *shinpa* or Onoe Matsunosuke, but locating such resistance would require charting formations of cultural allegiances and power as well as overlaying these lower-class cinematic positions with maps of contemporary political or class dynamics, which include conflicts between different modernisms and the opposition between universalism and the particular. Those who would map such resistance must therefore recognize that it may be counterproductive to universalize as "resistance" the practices that used the specific or the particular (in mixtures or combi-nations) precisely to escape such universalizing.

My statements about the modernism of mixture in 1910s Japan have sometimes bordered on the vague or imprecise, again largely because of a lack of sources, but also because the very cultural practices celebrating specificity that I am hypothesizing (and at some levels, they unfortunately still remain a series of postulates) are difficult to capture in the universal-izing processes of language—a fact as true then as it is today. They posed a problem for film study in the early twentieth century, and they do again for us. One of the lessons to be learned from approaching the multiple modernities of early cinema in Japan is precisely the problem and the function of film study: we must understand, and at the same time critique, the different tactics pursued by such practitioners of study as Gonda or the pure film reformers, and remain conscious of how our discourse can insert alternative practices in structures of power by defining them, and must also contemplate methodologies that allow the culture of combination to live outside our controlling grasp. While it is politically important to consider how spectator behavior and tastes may have been connected to larger group or to class dynamics, another challenge is to theorize such general phenomena without resorting to the kind of universalizing that reformist critics engaged in. This study has been only a first step in that direction; I look forward to continued research in the future.

The resistance I find in this period is not direct political opposition so much as forms of insusceptibility, the kinds of cinematic culture that, while not necessarily opposing pure film, had a degree of autonomy and pliability that meant they did not immediately fall into the mold of pure film advocates. The frustration evident in much of the reformist discourse against Japanese cinema, while colored by the identity dynamics of self-definition (the need to create a persistent Other), also speaks volumes about the other forms of cinema that failed to be swallowed up in the desired totality. Reformers definitely opposed these other forms, but it is not certain the opposition was always returned in kind, as the multiple players on the field, and the complexity of the field, meant that they were not all fighting each other. What in part distinguishes the modernism of mixture or the particular was its aversion to universalized opposition; it found instead meaning and pleasure in local, particular moments that could not be abstracted or reproduced. On various levels, competition and struggle were what best describes the dynamics of Taishō-era film culture. Prizes included the right to define cinema, modernity, and the nation, but the persistence of the struggle indicates how complex or hybrid this competition was; it was one in which some players bore fundamental contradictions and others did not quite play the game.

Terming any one player on this field as representative of "Japanese cinema" would be inaccurate. It is better to call Japanese cinema the historical specificity of this complex struggle. In countering much of the scholarship that seeks in Japanese film a radical alterity, I have shown how the discourse of the Pure Film Movement presumed a universality, a sameness between Japanese and foreign cinema, as the basis for selling a differentiated Japanese product. In doing so, I do not deny the specificity of Japanese cinema or, by arguing for its sameness, reject the value of studying it. Rather, the particular construction of these hybrid contradictions in a discursive field marked by the hierarchies I have discussed sets Japanese cinema apart as a historical phenomenon. Exploring this specificity as scholars, we must at the same time recognize that a significant portion of the contemporary discursive context has articulated these mixtures and combinations in another way: as the failure to make Japanese film both Japanese and cinema.

The question remains whether the body of Japanese cinema ceased being hybrid and became pure. It did not, but the continually powerful forces involved in the push toward a pure, nonhybrid cinema persisted after the Taishō era, ones that make the discursive definition of cinema offered by the Pure Film Movement even more dominant. Consider what Slavoj Žižek says about the Master. Following Lacan, he states that the Master's role is "to introduce balance, to regulate the excess"—that is, to manage the extreme enjoyment by the Other within the national self and thus alleviate inherent antagonisms. "With the figure of the Master, the antagonism inherent to the social structure is transformed into the relationship of power." Fascism, Žižek argues, is "the return to the figure of the Master—Leader—who guarantees the stability and balance of the social fabric, who again saves us from the society's structural imbalance," but it does so by projecting "the figure of the Jew whose 'excessive' accumulation and greed are deemed the cause of social antagonism."[11] I argue that the recourse to the Master becomes a dominant thrust of prewar Japanese film history, even if we leave open the question of whether wartime Japan was truly fascist. Film reformers repeatedly relied on the authority of censors as a means of eliminating the antagonisms, both within their own system and within the cinematic field, stamping out the signs of the Other in the Japanese sphere so that the state itself could help construct a proper, stable, and pure Japanese cinema. Progressive critics encouraged censorship procedures such as preproduction script censorship as a means of producing a purer, more socially responsible cinema. The state was seen as the ideal means of producing educated spectators who read films the proper way and of punishing those who did not, of eliminating conflicts over cinema in order to produce a univocal definition of the moving pictures.

Such a discourse promoted a subjectivity that meshed with public concerns about power, a private interiority that internalized the public gaze. Difference inside and outside the film was annulled when every text was fully explained beforehand and was received uniformly in a spectatorship that was uncritical and accepting. The subjects so created, already bearing within themselves the operations of the state, were both modern consumers and *kokumin*, members of the indivisible *kokutai*. While it is excessive to blame the cinema, à la Siegfried Kracauer, for causing the march to fascism and war, the discourse on cinema in the late 1910s must be considered in the larger context of the creation of a brutal and oppressive state and whatever popular support it might have had. Scholars such as Abé Mark Nornes, Mitsuyo Wada-Marciano, and Peter B. High have similarly considered in their own research on documentary, Shōchiku Kamata film production, and imperialist cinema, respectively, how cinema, modernism, and nation were intimately intertwined, especially in the 1930s, in establishing dominant styles of filmmaking.[12]

It is important to recall that, while much scholarship has focused on the inequalities of power between Western modernism and non-Western culture—inequalities perhaps central to the formation of that modernism—it is necessary, at least in film history, to consider how inequalities of power within Japan are just as important in the formation of Japanese modernisms. This in part justifies a focus on the local over the transnational. And while other research has looked at the ways local cultures have received or appropriated Western modernity in vernacular forms, it is important to acknowledge that any articulation of Japanese modernity is crucially shaped by imbalances of power within Japan and, at times, its colonies. We must also think about how the local, defined as the singular and particular, may itself have been the fundamental principle in a more pliable form of resistance to a discourse of the Master, which attempted to regulate the excess proliferating from local mixtures through purity, universalization, and the nation. There is a need to map out the local structures of power that attempted to define film, while also considering how other modernisms and other mixtures, coupled with contradictions in the modernism of purity, may have complicated or posed alternatives to the rising tide of authoritarianism in the Shōwa era. Struggles and slippages continued, much to the consternation of authorities.

In pursuing such a study, however, we must note that developments in the late 1930s further tried to put an end to such alternatives and lay the foundations for a more national cinema. In the end, it was the Film Law of 1939 and later acts of state intervention that most forcefully attempted to counter hybridity and help produce a pure cinema.[13] At that time, the number of production companies was reduced to three, and distribution was centralized in one company. Preproduction censorship reinforced the new dominance of production as exhibition itself was rationalized and centralized. All personnel were licensed and organized in associations that ensured the efficient enactment of state policy. Finally, foreign films were banned after the bombing of Pearl Harbor (including many from Japan's ally Germany). As Gregory Kasza puts it, "The Film Law thus gave the state unconditional authority over every person and organization in the film industry." Far from being resisted as authoritarian, however, "the Film Law was not only applauded in the Diet, but also well received by the film industry. Film people had once been considered less than respectable in polite society, and to many the law was long-overdue recognition of their achievements."[14] One could say that the state itself became the gaze of the Other that gave Japanese cinema its needed approval.

We must not ignore the threads, however tenuous, that connect pure film discourse with the conception of cinema put forward by the Film Law. While these measures were intended to protect the industry and ensure the production of meanings acceptable to the state, they also had the ironic result of making the industry more like an American culture industry, one in which hybridity went into decline. Because of the need to produce film propaganda in a situation where producers could no longer rely on the benshi, Japanese films began to lose those flourishes, those hybrid differences from foreign works that had made them the object of fascination to many Japanese film scholars (which is why Burch frowns on most postwar Japanese cinema).[15] Yet at this point, Japanese cinema started to come into its own. The industry structure created by the Film Law survived the war and eventually developed into the dominant culture industry of Japan.[16] Finally fulfilling the dreams of the Pure Film Movement, Japanese cinema began to sell abroad, gaining the attention of film festivals and critics, proving Japan's successful completion of the path of cinematic modernization, and making Godzilla a household name in the United States. Japanese cinema became the object of analysis by foreign critics and scholars, a category that was used to name a particular body of cinema. In an ironic culmination of a series of paradoxes that mark its history, Japanese cinema, finally equal to foreign film, at last seemed pure and full grown.

Even during the war, however, as I have argued elsewhere, the unique and particular reading acts of spectators remained a concern of producers and authorities, so much so that there were calls for training spectators. Concern for what "other" audiences were thinking about Japanese films led to paranoid calls for even greater control.[17] The problems would not be solved in the postwar period, as bodily forms of cinema and spectatorship (e.g., the Sun Tribe films or pink cinema)[18] revived alongside attempts to theorize popular reception as a rejection of intellectual abstraction. Much of 1990s independent cinema could be considered an effort to revive the particular against nationalist forms of universalism.[19] While another book will be necessary to argue how much such trends can be traced back to the

1910s, it is clear that the struggles to define cinema, control spectatorship, and articulate modernity (or postmodernity) continue today, perhaps shifting their form and content in conjunction with historical transformations in culture and economy, but still functioning as a central space for shaping Japanese cinema culture and its relation to local and global spheres.

Notes

GYC	*Gonda Yasunosuke chosakushū* (Selected Works of Gonda Yasunosuke)
MNJ	*Meiji nyūsu jiten* (Directory of Meiji News)
MSGS	Yano Seiichi, ed., *Miyako shinbun geinō shiryō shūsei: Taishō hen* (A Compilation of Materials on Entertainment in the *Miyako shinbun:* Taishō Edition)
NENK	Tsukada Yoshinobu, *Nihon eigashi no kenkyū* (A Study of Japanese Film History)
Principles	Gonda Yasunosuke, *Katsudō shashin no genri oyobi ōyō* (The Principles and Applications of the Moving Pictures)
SST	*Shinbun shūroku Taishō-shi* (A History of Taishō in Collected Newspapers)
TNJ	*Taishō nyūsu jiten* (Directory of Taishō News)

INTRODUCTION

1. Takada Tamotsu, "Eiga kisha no shisha," reprinted in "Shiryō: Kaeriyama Norimasa to Tōmasu Kurihara no gyōseki," ed. Okabe Ryū, *Nihon eiga sōkō* no. 8 (Tokyo: Film Library Council, 1973), 27. Unless otherwise indicated, all translations from the Japanese are my own.

2. For a precise account of the development of film terminology, see Chiba Nobuo, "Eiga yōgo no hassei to rufu no shiteki purosesu," *Eigashi kenkyū* 1 (1973): 40–48.

3. *Jun'eigageki Undō* can be literally translated as "Pure Film Drama Movement" since *geki* means "drama" in Japanese. One must not mistake the

movement, however, as an effort to mold the cinema in the model of stage drama, since one of the reformers' central goals was to cure cinema of its dependence on theater. The word *eigageki* was in fact the chosen translation for the English term *photoplay*, which was considered to be the more cinematic form of film represented by Hollywood production. (In most of my translations, I have rendered *eigageki* as *photoplay* when it appears by itself.)

4. Since around the mid-1990s, when my first research was published in Japan (for example, "Benshi no atarashii kao," trans. Wakao Kayoko, *Eigagaku* 9 [1995]: 55–73, and "Jigoma to eiga no 'hakken'—Nihon eiga gensetsushi josetsu," *Eizōgaku* 58 [1997]: 34–50), a number of scholars, such as Hase Masato, Fujii Jinshi, Fujiki Hideaki, Yamamoto Naoki, and others, have joined my call to pursue a discursive history of Japanese film.

5. Major histories of Japanese film written in Japanese include Tanaka Jun'ichirō, *Nihon eiga hattatsushi*, 5 vols. (Tokyo: Chūō Kōronsha, 1980); Iijima Tadashi, *Nihon eigashi*, 2 vols. (Tokyo: Hakusuisha, 1955); Okada Susumu, *Nihon eiga no rekishi* (Tokyo: Daviddosha, 1967); the collective work *Sekai no eiga sakka 31: Nihon eigashi* (Tokyo: Kinema Junpōsha, 1976); and the most recent, Satō Tadao, *Nihon eigashi*, zōhoban, 4 vols. (Tokyo: Iwanami Shoten, 2006–2007). Joseph L. Anderson and Donald Richie's *The Japanese Film: Art and Industry*, expanded ed. (Princeton, NJ: Princeton University Press, 1982), itself greatly influenced by these histories, very much follows their method.

6. Noël Burch, *To the Distant Observer: Form and Meaning in the Japanese Cinema*, ed. Annette Michelson (Berkeley: University of California Press, 1979): 49, italics in the original. While making this point, Burch does not always provide these contexts himself. Still, he makes us aware of the importance of intertextuality. This important monograph is available through the Michigan Classics Online series at the Center for Japanese Studies at the University of Michigan, www.umich.edu/~iinet/cjs/publications/michclassics/index.html.

7. Ibid., 26.

8. David Bordwell, "A Cinema of Flourishes: Japanese Decorative Classicism of the Prewar Era," in *Reframing Japanese Cinema: Authorship, Genre, History*, ed. Arthur Noletti Jr. and David Desser (Bloomington: University of Indiana Press, 1992), 344.

9. David Bordwell, *Ozu and the Poetics of Cinema* (Princeton, NJ: Princeton University Press, 1988), 146. This book is also available through the Michigan Classics Online series at the University of Michigan's Center for Japanese Studies, www.umich.edu/~iinet/cjs/publications/michclassics/index.html.

10. Michel Foucault, *The Archaeology of Knowledge and the Discourse on Language*, trans. A. M. Sheridan Smith (New York: Pantheon, 1972), 45.

11. Peter B. High, "The *Ancien Régime* of Japanese Film and the Revolt of the Fans: 1911–1918," *Gengo bunka ronshū* 10.2 (1989): 121–148.

12. Joanne Bernardi, *Writing in Light: The Silent Scenario and the Japanese Pure Film Movement* (Detroit: Wayne State University Press, 2001).

13. Foucault, *Archaeology of Knowledge*, 47–48.

14. Ibid., 49.

15. Pierre Bourdieu, "The Field of Cultural Production, or: The Economic World Reversed," *Poetics* 12 (1983): 323.

16. Ibid., 312.

17. See Karatani's *Origins of Modern Japanese Literature*, ed. and trans. Brett de Bary (Durham, NC: Duke University Press, 1993).

18. For a brief summary of the project of recent early cinema scholarship, see Tom Gunning, "'Now You See It, Now You Don't': The Temporality of the Cinema of Attractions," *Velvet Light Trap* 32 (Fall 1993): 3–12.

19. Miriam Hansen, *Babel and Babylon: Spectatorship in American Silent Film* (Cambridge, MA: Harvard University Press, 1991), 24.

20. Burch, in fact, uses this argument in *To the Distant Observer* to propose the alterity of Japanese cinema, in which he claims one can find "the preservation . . . of traits common to the Primitive cinema of the 1890s, and even to some of the most radical Western films of the 1960s and 1970s" (p. 66). See also Noël Burch, "Primitivism and the Avant-Gardes: A Dialectical Approach," in *Narrative, Apparatus, Ideology,* ed. Philip Rosen (New York: Columbia University Press, 1986), 483–506; or Burch, *Life to Those Shadows,* ed. and trans. Ben Brewster (Berkeley: University of California Press, 1990).

21. See Tom Gunning, "The Cinema of Attractions: Early Film, Its Spectators, and the Avant-Garde," in *Early Cinema: Space, Frame, Narrative,* ed. Thomas Elsaesser and Adam Baker (London: British Film Institute, 1990), 56–62.

22. Hansen, *Babel and Babylon,* 62–63.

23. See Lee Grieveson, *Policing Cinema: Movies and Censorship in Early-Twentieth-Century America* (Berkeley: University of California Press, 2004).

24. Burch, *To the Distant Observer,* 90.

25. See, for instance, my "'Nihonjin' Kitano Takeshi: *Hana-Bi* to nashonaru shinema no keisei," *Yuriika* rinji zōkan 30.3 (February 1998): 42–51; "Tatakau kankyaku: Dai Tōa Kyōeiken no Nihon eiga to juyō no mondai," *Gendai shisō* 30.9 (July 2002): 139–149; "Nation, Citizenship, and Cinema," in *A Companion to the Anthropology of Japan,* ed. Jennifer Robertson (Malden, MA: Blackwell Publishers, 2005), 400–414; "Narrating the Nation-ality of a Cinema: The Case of Japanese Prewar Film," in *The Culture of Japanese Fascism,* ed. Alan Tansman (Durham, NC: Duke University Press, 2009), 185–211.

26. One question that has not been asked, for instance, is whether aspects of early Japanese cinema, in all their variety, could serve as alternatives for later *Japanese* cinemas, with an emphasis on the plural.

27. See, for instance, Musser's essay "Rethinking Early Cinema: Cinema of Attractions and Narrativity," *Yale Journal of Criticism* 7.2 (1994): 203–232.

28. See the chapter titled "Rethinking 'Primitive' Cinema: Intertextuality, the Middle-Class Audience, and Reception Studies" in Staiger's book, *Interpreting Films: Studies in the Historical Reception of American Cinema* (Princeton, NJ: Princeton University Press, 1992).

29. Certainly, court decisions like in the 1915 Supreme Court case *Mutual v. Ohio,* which denied cinema protection under the United States Constitution as

a form of free speech, have been an important issue in the study of early American cinema, but censorship in the Japanese case has more in common with Germany, if only because Japanese censors paid close attention to German film censorship standards. The *Mutual* case, after all, only validated censorship by the states; cinema was never censored on the national level in the United States.

30. A set of theories, mostly enunciated by Japan studies scholars in the United States in the postwar era, that attempted to account for Japan's economic and industrial development by applying a norm for "modernization" derived from the United States and Europe while also selectively choosing aspects of Japanese culture and society to explain why it alone among non-Western nations had modernized. See for instance books such as Donald Shively, ed., *Tradition and Modernization in Japanese Culture* (Princeton, NJ: Princeton University Press, 1971). For a critique of modernization theory, see some of the many works by H. D. Harootunian, Tetsuo Najita, Masao Miyoshi, and Naoki Sakai.

31. See his *Taishō bunka* (Tokyo: Kōdansha, 1980), especially 170–192. I also agree with Takemura that the Taishō era exhibits too many changes for the term *Taishō* to be of use in nominating a coherent historical period. (There are also, of course, political problems in using the names of emperors to lend a unity to historical cultures.) Since I myself argue that Japanese film in the Taishō era exhibits a drastic shift, I generally avoid using the concept "Taishō cinema."

32. See his *Shadows on the Screen: Tanizaki Jun'ichirō on Cinema and "Oriental" Aesthetics* (Ann Arbor: Center for Japanese Studies, University of Michigan, 2005).

33. Hansen, *Babel and Babylon*, 91.

34. Research that emphasizes how other early national cinemas differ from the cinema of the United States include Richard Abel, "Booming the Business: The Historical Specificity of Early French Cinema," *Silent Film*, ed. Richard Abel (New Brunswick, NJ: Rutgers University Press, 1996): 109–124; Richard Abel, *The Ciné Goes to Town: French Cinema, 1896–1914* (Berkeley: University of California Press, 1994); Heidi Schlüpmann, "Cinema as Anti-Theater: Actresses and Female Audiences in Wilhelminian Germany," *Iris* 11 (Summer 1990): 77–93; John Fullerton, "Spatial and Temporal Articulation of Pre-classical Swedish Film," in *Early Cinema: Space, Frame, Narrative*, ed. Thomas Elsaesser and Adam Baker (London: British Film Institute, 1990), 375–388; Leon Hunt, "The Student of Prague," *Early Cinema: Space, Frame, Narrative*, ed. Thomas Elsaesser and Adam Baker (London: British Film Institute, 1990), 389–401; Yuri Tsivian, *Early Cinema in Russia and Its Culture Reception* (London: Routledge, 1994); Zhen Zhang, *An Amorous History of the Silver Screen: Shanghai Cinema, 1896–1937* (Chicago: University of Chicago Press, 2005); as well as Noël Burch's *Life to those Shadows*, where he discusses the specificity of French and British early cinema.

35. Fullerton's and Hunt's work tends to fall into the latter category.

36. Ana M. López, "Early Cinema and Modernity in Latin America," *Cinema Journal* 40.1 (Fall 2000): 49.

37. Isolde Standish, in using Jean-Louis Comolli to emphasize the determining role of film technologies, argues that "Japanese . . . were constrained by the ideological motivations that led to the development and use of specific technologies and the rejection of others." She tries to temper this technological determinism by arguing for a dialectic between form (technology) and content, but she neither fully complicates that historically fraught binary, nor considers such later scholars as John Belton, Rick Altman, or Jim Lastra for examples of technological histories critical of Comolli's model. See her *A New History of Japanese Cinema: A Century of Narrative Film* (London: Continuum, 2005): 20.

38. Anderson and Richie, *Japanese Film*, 43.

39. Burch, *To the Distant Observer*, 98.

40. High, "*Ancien Régime* of Japanese Film," 138.

41. Imported from the theater, *shinpa* (new school) and *kyūha* or *kyūgeki* ("old school" or "old drama") were the two major film genres until the early 1920s, the former focusing on modern stories and the latter on period pieces. *Kyūha* largely came from Kabuki and other stories of premodern Japan. *Shinpa* was based on theatrical forms developed at the end of the nineteenth century that attempted to modernize Kabuki by dramatizing stories of contemporary Japan, most famously by such novelists as Ozaki Kōyō, Izumi Kyōka, and Tokutomi Roka, while still remaining formally closer to Kabuki, especially in the initial use of *onnagata*, than to the later realist Shingeki (new theater) movement. Even as *shinpa* theater eventually accepted actresses, it came to be typified by a melodramatic tone that focused on star-crossed lovers and women who fell victim to prejudice and patriarchal structures. The genres of *gendaigeki* and *jidaigeki* repeat this temporal division, but designate a more cinematic rendering of such stories. As with *eiga*, the switch in terminology is historically significant.

42. Yamamoto notes in the introduction how he filled eight notebooks just with comments from 1899 to 1935 on how Japanese cinema had been influenced by foreign films: *Nihon eiga in okeru gaikoku eiga no eikyō—hikaku eigashi kenkyū* (Tokyo: Waseda Daigaku Shuppanbu, 1983), iii.

43. For a collection of some of the contemporary reviews of Kaeriyama's *Sei no kagayaki*, see Okabe Ryū, ed., "Shiryō: Kaeriyama Norimasa to Tōmasu Kurihara no gyōseki," in *Nihon eiga sōkō* no. 8 (Tokyo: Film Library Council, 1973), 21–27. In a rather frank assessment of Kaeriyama's career, *Kinema junpō* later noted, "He is somehow the hero who founded the photoplay in our nation. Yet at the same time, by producing bad films in rapid succession, he is also the man who offered the reasons for why Japanese scorn the photoplay": "Jinbutsu gettan: Kaeriyama Norimasa," *Kinema junpō* 78 (January 1, 1922): 22. The general opinion seems to have been that Kaeriyama, an engineer by training, was no film artist.

44. Karatani Kōjin, "*Senzen*" *no shikō* (Tokyo: Bungei Shunjū, 1994), 27. See also Benedict Anderson, *Imagined Communities: Reflections on the Origin and Spread of Nationalism* (London: Verso, 1983).

45. See the chapter "The Discovery of Landscape" in his *Origins of Modern Japanese Literature*, 11–44.

46. For more on Okakura Tenshin and the role of art history in building the nation, see Stefan Tanaka, "Imaging History: Inscribing Belief in the Nation," *Journal of Asian Studies* 53.1 (February 1994): 24–44.

47. Kang Sang-jung, *Nashonarizumu* (Tokyo: Iwanami Shoten, 2001).

48. Motoori Norinaga was a leading scholar of *kokugaku*, or national studies, during the Edo period. *Kokutai no hongi* was the title of an official publication, first distributed in 1937, attempting to describe the fundamental principles of the nation as it headed toward war.

49. See "'Nihonjin' Kitano Takeshi" and "Narrating the Nation-ality of a Cinema."

50. Okada Susumu, *Nihonjin no imēji kōzō* (Tokyo: Chūō Kōronsha, 1972): 167–173.

51. Koichi Iwabuchi, *Recentering Globalization: Popular Culture and Japanese Transnationalism* (Durham, NC: Duke University Press, 2002): 54.

52. Tanizaki Jun'ichirō, *In Praise of Shadows,* trans. Thomas J. Harper and Edward G. Seidensticker (New Haven, CT: Leete's Island Books, 1977). I should add that Tanizaki's own appropriations of cinema could never be explained as mere fascination with the West or fashionable Westernization. See my "Celluloid Masks: The Cinematic Image and the Image of Japan," *Iris* 16 (1993): 9–22; or Thomas LaMarre's *Shadows on the Screen: Tanizaki Jun'ichirō on Cinema and "Oriental" Aesthetics* (Ann Arbor: Center for Japanese Studies, University of Michigan, 2005).

53. Joseph Tobin, introduction to *Re-Made in Japan: Everyday Life and Consumer Taste in a Changing Society,* edited by Joseph Tobin (New Haven, CT: Yale University Press, 1992).

54. Miriam Hansen, "Fallen Women, Rising Stars, New Horizons: Shanghai Silent Film as Vernacular Modernism," *Film Quarterly* 54.1 (Fall 2000): 10–22; Hansen, "The Mass Production of the Senses: Classical Cinema as Vernacular Modernism," in *Reinventing Film Studies,* ed. Linda Williams and Christine Gledhill (London: Edward Arnold, 2000).

55. Hansen, "Fallen Women, Rising Stars, New Horizons," 19.

56. See also my essay "Nichijō toshite no Hariuddo to sekai kankyaku no shihai," *Gendai shisō* rinji zōkan 31.1 (June 2003): 124–131.

57. Stuart Hall, "Notes on Deconstructing the Popular," in *Cultural Theory and Popular Culture,* ed. John Storey, 2nd ed. (Athens: University of Georgia Press, 1998): 449.

58. Homi Bhabha, "Introduction: Narrating the Nation," in *Nation and Narration,* ed. Homi Bhabha (London: Routledge, 1990), 1–7.

59. Tessa Morris-Suzuki, *Re-inventing Japan: Time, Space, Nation* (Armonk, NY: M.E. Sharpe, 1998).

60. See my "Nation, Citizenship, and Cinema" and "Narrating the Nationality of a Cinema."

61. Eric Cazdyn, *The Flash of Capital: Film and Geopolitics in Japan* (Durham, NC: Duke University Press, 2002).

62. For an excellent history of the *gentō*, see Iwamoto Kenji, *Gentō no seiki: Eiga zen'ya no shikaku bunkashi* (Tokyo: Shinwasha, 2002).

63. See for instance Charles Musser's review of precinematic devices in *The Emergence of Cinema: The American Screen to 1907* (Berkeley: University of California Press, 1990), 14–54. Many of the essays in the anthology edited by Leo Charney and Vanessa R. Schwartz, *Cinema and the Invention of Modern Life* (Berkeley: University of California Press, 1995), explore how such varied nineteenth-century phenomena as photography, window shopping, wax museums, and mail-order catalogs prepared the way for the modernity expressed by cinematic culture.

64. Yamaguchi Masao, "Jo: eiga izen," *Eiga denrai: Shinematogurafu to "Meiji no Nihon,"* ed. Yoshida Yoshishige et al. (Tokyo: Iwanami Shoten, 1995), 12. Yamaguchi's pun on *shadow* and *image* (both pronounced "eizō") supports his effort to draw the history of film back into the era of the *gentō*.

65. See Terada's "Eiga jidai," found in the collection of essays published under his pseudonym, Yoshimura Fuyuhiko: *Zoku Fuyuhiko shū* (Tokyo: Iwanami Shoten, 1932), 284.

66. Maeda Ai, "Sakariba ni eigakan ga dekita," *Kōza Nihon eiga*, ed. Imamura Shōhei et al. (Tokyo: Iwanami Shoten, 1985), 1:348.

67. Ōkubo Ryō, "Kinodorama to kineorama: Ryojun Kaisen to kindaiteki chikaku," *Eizōgaku* 80 (2008): 5–22.

68. Cazdyn, *Flash of Capital*, 21.

69. Rey Chow, *Primitive Passions: Visuality, Sexuality, Ethnography, and Contemporary Chinese Cinema* (New York: Columbia University Press, 1995), 4–11.

70. Paul Schrader, *Transcendental Style in Film: Ozu, Bresson, Dreyer* (Berkeley: University of California Press, 1972); Stephen Prince, *The Warrior's Camera: The Cinema of Akira Kurosawa* (Princeton, NJ: Princeton University Press, 1999).

71. See Iijima Tadashi, *Nihon eigashi* (Tokyo: Hakusuisha, 1955); or the history Satō Tadao serialized in *Kōza Nihon eiga*, ed. Imamura Shōhei et al. (Tokyo: Iwanami Shoten, 1985–1988). Satō shifts his position in his later histories.

72. See note 28.

73. See, for examples, Scott L. Malcomson, "The Pure Land beyond the Seas: Barthes, Burch, and the Uses of Japan," *Screen* 26.3–4 (May–August 1985): 23–33; or Peter Lehman, "The Mysterious Orient, the Crystal Clear Orient, the Non-Existent Orient," *Journal of Film and Video* 39.1 (Winter 1987): 5–15.

74. Eric Hobsbawm, "Introduction: Inventing Traditions," in *The Invention of Tradition*, ed. Eric Hobsbawm and Terence Ranger (Cambridge: Cambridge University Press, 1984), 1–14.

75. Anthony D. Smith, *The Ethnic Origins of Nations* (Oxford: Basil Blackwell, 1986).

76. Naoki Sakai, "Modernity and Its Critique: The Problem of Universalism and Particularism," in *Postmodernism and Japan*, ed. Masao Miyoshi and H.D. Harootunian (Durham, NC: Duke University Press, 1989), 116.

77. Dennis C. Washburn, *The Dilemma of the Modern in Japanese Fiction* (New Haven, CT: Yale University Press, 1995): 4.

78. Mitsuhiro Yoshimoto, "Melodrama, Postmodernism, and Japanese Cinema," in *Melodrama and Asian Cinema*, ed. Wimal Dissanayake (Cambridge: Cambridge University Press, 1993), 101–26.

79. Marshall Berman, *All That Is Solid Melts into Air: The Experience of Modernity* (New York: Simon and Schuster, 1982), 15.

80. LaMarre, *Shadows on the Screen*, 80.

81. See S.N. Eisenstadt, "Multiple Modernities," *Daedalus* 129 (Winter 2000): 1–29; or Dominic Sachsenmaier and Jens Riedel, eds., *Reflections on Multiple Modernities: European, Chinese, and Other Interpretations* (Leiden: Brill, 2002).

82. See, for instance, Dilip Parameshwar Gaonkar, ed., *Alternative Modernities* (Durham, NC: Duke University Press, 2001); or Arjun Appadurai, *Modernity at Large: Cultural Dimensions of Globalization* (Minneapolis: University of Minnesota Press, 1996).

83. Harry Harootunian, *Overcome by Modernity: History, Culture, and Community in Interwar Japan* (Princeton, NJ: Princeton University Press, 2000), xvi–xvii.

84. Cazdyn, *Flash of Capital*, 17.

85. Iwamoto Kenji has discussed the peculiarities of the Japanese terminology, particularly how *modanizumu* came to represent a bright, popular, and consumerist vision of the new. That, however, comes after my period. See Iwamoto Kenji, "Modanizumu to Nihon eiga," in *Nihon eiga to modanizumu, 1920–1930*, ed. Iwamoto Kenji (Tokyo: Riburopōto, 1991), 6–11.

86. Berman, *All That Is Solid Melts into Air*, 15.

87. David Frisby, *Fragments of Modernity: Theories of Modernity in the Work of Simmel, Kracauer, and Benjamin* (Cambridge, U.K.: Polity Press, 1985).

88. Art Berman, *Preface to Modernism* (Urbana: University of Illinois Press, 1994), 3.

89. John Frow, "What Was Post-Modernism?" in *Past the Last Post: Theorizing Post-Colonialism and Post-Modernism*, ed. Ian Adam and Helen Tiffin (New York: Harvester Wheatsheaf, 1991): 139, quoted in Miriam Silverberg, *Erotic Grotesque Nonsense: The Mass Culture of Japanese Modern Times* (Berkeley: University of California Press, 2006): 13; Berman, *All That Is Solid Melts into Air*, 16; Harootunian, *Overcome by Modernity*, xx; Berman, *Preface to Modernism*, 4–5.

90. From Baudelaire's essay "The Painter in Modern Life," quoted in Matei Calinescu, *Five Faces of Modernity* (Durham, NC: Duke University Press, 1987), 48.

91. Calinescu, *Five Faces of Modernity*, 41.

92. Dilip Parameshwar Gaonkar, "On Alternative Modernities," in *Alternative Modernities*, ed. Dilip Parameshwar Gaonkar (Durham, NC: Duke University Press, 2001), 15–16.

93. Hansen, "Mass Production of the Senses," 344.

94. See my book *A Page of Madness: Cinema and Modernity in 1920s Japan* (Ann Arbor: Center for Japanese Studies, the University of Michigan, 2008).

95. Harootunian, *Overcome by Modernity*, 3–33.

96. Karatani Kōjin, "One Spirit, Two Nineteenth Centuries," in *Postmodernism and Japan*, ed. Masao Miyoshi and H.D. Harootunian (Durham, NC: Duke University Press, 1989), 259–272.

97. Yokomitsu Riichi, "Kankaku katsudō," *Bungei jidai* 2.2 (February 1925): 7.

98. Sakai, "Modernity and Its Critique," 93–99.

99. See Silverberg, *Erotic Grotesque Nonsense*.

100. Walter Benjamin, "The Work of Art in the Age of Mechanical Reproduction," in *Illuminations*, trans. Harry Zohn (New York: Schocken Books, 1977), 211–244.

101. Hansen, "Fallen Women, Rising Stars, New Horizons," 10.

102. What intrigues me about focusing on these two modernist strands in terms of the opposition of universalism and the particular is that this framework may be helpful in elucidating other moments in Japanese film history. One sees, for instance, state authorities repeatedly expressing continued concern about particular forms of film reception that cannot be contained through universalities like the nation, concerns that come to a head at moments like wartime. Cinematic radicals in the 1960s looked for alternative realms that were not subsumed under such categories as the Japanese nation-state, the "capitalist world" in the cold war dynamic, or Soviet Stalinism. This was attempted through, for instance, finding a physical or nonintellectual form of theorizing via the *yakuza* film (consider the work of Matsuda Masao or Saitō Ryūhō), or a rural life that was not reducible to the Japanese folk (e.g., Ogawa Shinsuke's documentaries). The framework may also help us think about Japanese cinema of the 1990s, which also saw commercial features made with only one print, as well as filmmakers such as Aoyama Shinji who—through such metaphors as the Polaroid camera (visible in *Helpless* [1996] and *Eureka* [2000])—explored forms of the particular (which to him is a form of otherness or alterity) that were not reproducible or universalizable. This history must wait for another book, but I hope this monograph can begin a discussion of a longer conflict between a universalist modernism and a modernism of the particular in Japanese cultural history. For more on Ogawa Shinsuke, see Abé Mark Nornes's *Forest of Pressure: Ogawa Shinsuke and Postwar Japanese Documentary* (Minneapolis: University of Minnesota Press, 2007). For more on Aoyama, see my "Aoyama Shinji," in *Fifty Contemporary Filmmakers*, ed. Yvonne Tasker (London: Routledge, 2002), 16–25.

1. THE MOTION PICTURES AS A PROBLEM

1. See, for instance, Sakamoto Kitarō's embellished introduction to the scientific oddities of the known world: *Jitchi ōyō butsuri kikan,* 2nd ed. (Tokyo: Hakubunkan, 1891).

2. "Shin hatsumei kendōki," *Jiji shinpō,* July 13, 1894, reproduced in Tsukada Yoshinobu, *Nihon eigashi no kenkyū* (Tokyo: Gendai Shokan, 1980), 15. Tsukada's book is hereafter abbreviated as *NENK.*

3. "Shashin, ensetsu o nasu," *Fukuoka nichi nichi shinbun,* April 12, 1891, in *NENK,* 21–22.

4. Newspaper articles did make distinctions between the three inventions, most emphasizing that the Cinématographe and the Vitascope, by being projected, were an advancement on the Kinetoscope because they presented "all people and things in their natural size" (*Yomiuri shinbun,* February 24, 1897, in *NENK,* 95). Since newspaper articles were also a means of advertising motion picture showings in advance, some would praise Lumière's device over Edison's (or vice versa) if the two were competing in the same market, as they sometimes were. (The two were also differentiated in terms of their Japanese names, a difference stemming from their competing promoters.) For the purposes of my discussion, I have focused only on their points in common.

5. The *Miyako shinbun* distinguished between the Kinetoscope, then showing in Asakusa, and the Vitascope, presented at the Kabukiza, by writing that the latter "took the picture moving machine currently on exhibition at Asakusa Hanayashiki and showed it on a large scale by means of a *gentō.*" "Shashin denki katsudō gentō," *Miyako shinbun,* March 4, 1897, in *NENK,* 197.

6. "Katsudō shashin no kyōsō," *Yomiuri shinbun,* March 4, 1897, in *NENK,* 112.

7. Dōjin Shiin, *Katsudō shashinjutsu jizai* (Tokyo: Daigakukan, 1903), 101–102.

8. "Suehiroza no shashin gentō chikudōki," *Fusō shinbun,* March 2, 1897, in *NENK,* 172.

9. Komada Kōyō, *Katsudō shashin setsumeisho tsuki Ejison-shi shiden* (Tokyo: Katsudō Shashinkai, 1897), reprinted in *NENK,* 222. Komada lists the article as appearing in the *Mainichi shinbun,* but Tsukada reports that, in scouring that newspaper, he was unable to find the original version of the piece. Given Komada's skill as a showman, it is conceivable that he made up this article, which in the end, speaks quite highly of him.

10. This was the name used in ads and articles in the *Kyōto hinode shinbun* on March 3 and 4, 1897, in *NENK,* 106–107.

11. Komada, *Katsudō shashin,* in *NENK,* 289.

12. Such glorification of scientific genius resulted in some of the other names applied to the motion pictures becoming variations on the Japanese name of Edison's other famous invention, the phonograph. The Kinetograph was sometimes called a *chikudōki* (literally, "storing motion machine," *NENK,* 16–17) and a screening of Vitascope films was termed a *chikudō shaeikai* (a

"meeting for projecting shadows of stored motion" (*NENK*, 169), both of which were variations of the word for the phonograph, *chikuonki* (literally, "storing sound machine"). In this way, the names were intended to transmit the authorial mark.

13. Murakami Okaji, *Jitchi ōyō kinsei shinkijutsu*, 2nd ed. (Osaka: Haku-chikan, 1897), 1. The contents of this book exactly duplicate (down to the misprints) the pamphlet *Jidō shashinjutsu* (Osaka: Osaka Shuppan, 1897), written by someone using the pen name Daitōrō Shujin, which is reproduced in Tsukada's work (the section mentioned here is on page 281 in *NENK*). It is still not clear why the two publications have the same contents, despite supposedly being written by two different individuals. The date for the publication of the Murakami version is also in question, given that the second edition refers to some events after its publication. For a discussion of this issue, as well as a history of publications on film in Japan, see Imamura Miyoo, *Nihon eiga bunkenshi* (Tokyo: Kagamiura Shobō, 1967), 11–17. Hereafter, I reference page numbers for both versions.

14. "Inagara meisho," *Osaka asahi shinbun*, March 28, 1897, in *NENK*, 107.

15. See, for example, an advertisement in the *Tokyo asahi shinbun*, April 13, 1897, in *NENK*, 205.

16. "Fukkoku jidō genga," *Kyōto hinode shinbun*, March 4, 1897, in *NENK*, 106.

17. Tom Gunning, "The Cinema of Attractions: Early Film, Its Spectators, and the Avant-Garde," in *Early Cinema: Space, Frame, Narrative*, ed. Thomas Elsaesser and Adam Baker (London: British Film Institute, 1990), 56–62.

18. The only exception is Murakami's book, which, after devoting much attention to the subject of "speed photography" *(sokusha satsueijutsu)* as the main difference between cinema and regular photography, mentions intermittent motion only as an afterthought. Murakami, *Jitchi ōyō kinsei shinkijutsu*, 21; Daitōrō, *Jidō shashinjutsu*, in *NENK*, 287.

19. "Shashin jinbutsu katsudōki," *Yomiuri shinbun*, January 28, 1897, in *NENK*, 49.

20. "Shashin katsudōki o miru," *Mainichi shinbun*, January 30, 1897, in *NENK*, 52.

21. *Osaka asahi shinbun*, February 26, 1897, in *NENK*, 102.

22. "Katsudō shashin," *Jiji shinpō*, January 31, 1897, in *NENK*, 53.

23. Murakami, *Jitchi ōyō kinsei shinkijutsu*, 4; Daitōrō, *Jidō shashinjutsu*, in *NENK*, 282.

24. "Dōtai dōbutsu o ari no mama shashinsu," *Yomiuri shinbun*, February 24, 1897, in *NENK*, 95.

25. *Osaka asahi shinbun*, February 26, 1897, in *NENK*, 103.

26. "Shashin katsudōki o miru," *Mainichi shinbun*, January 30, 1897, in *NENK*, 51.

27. Akira Mizuta Lippit, *Atomic Light (Shadow Optics)* (Minneapolis: University of Minnesota Press, 2005).

28. Komatsu Hiroshi, "Shinematogurafu to wa nan datta no ka—Ideorogī sōchi to shite no eiga," in *Eiga denrai: Shinematogurafu to "Meiji no Nihon,"* ed. Yoshida Yoshishige et al. (Tokyo: Iwanami Shoten, 1995), 108.

29. Ibid., 121–122.

30. Kinoshita Naoyuki, "Egakareta 'Meiji no Nihon': Nihon e no/Nihon kara no manazashi," in *Eiga denrai: Shinematogurafu to "Meiji no Nihon,"* ed. Yoshida Yoshishige et al. (Tokyo: Iwanami Shoten, 1995), 160.

31. So said Saitō Gesshin in his *Bukō nenpyō* when describing Matsumoto's *Chinzei Hachirō shimameguri,* a fantastic rendition of the fictional hero Chinzei Hachirō's travels in foreign lands that was put on in Edo in 1855. Quoted in Kinoshita Naoyuki, *Bijutsu to iu misemono* (Tokyo: Heibonsha, 1993), 42.

32. Kinoshita, *Bijutsu,* 57–62.

33. Ibid., 58.

34. Quoted in ibid., 108. Kinoshita reports that one presentation of the Western looking glass, in a kind of precursor to Hale's Tours (a popular attraction in the United States and Europe, in which the audience would sit in a·replica of a railway car and view films of famous world sights projected outside the windows), was done in a theater shaped like a Western ship, with the looking glasses disguised as portholes.

35. I do not consider the insertion of the motion pictures into *misemono* discourse to be *domestication* in Tobin's sense of the term, first, because *misemono* exhibited a span of vision that rarely was confined to the domestic, and second, because its flexibility as a discourse (its ability to accommodate many different forms from around the world) complicates notions of identity inside and outside that discourse. Simply put, its amorphousness makes it difficult to say that a thing, with identity A, is transformed through a process called *domestication* into another thing, with identity B. At best, it transformed cinema into a similarly amorphous entity. The pure film reformers' task would be to eliminate that amorphousness.

36. See, for instance, an account of seeing the Cinématographe in Kitashiro Kamezō, "Shinematogurafu o miru," *Shōnen kurabu* 1.6 (May 1897), in *NENK,* 108–109.

37. Dōjin, *Katsudō shashinjutsu jizai,* 5, 58.

38. For a short, though somewhat ahistorical, account of the *misemono,* see Katō Hidetoshi, *Misemono kara terebi e* (Tokyo: Iwanami Shoten, 1965), 10–23.

39. One is left with the impression that Dōjin's language resembles that of the sideshow barker introducing a motion picture show or trying to lure customers into his tent. If that is the case, then the writer on film here differs little from the benshi, or "lecturer." And if the latter was one of the attractions of the early cinema experience, then so were such florid depictions of the medium. It is possible that many of Dōjin's readers took less pleasure in the "facts" he conveyed than in the wonderful audacity of his claims and the spectacular visions he offered.

40. Ueda Manabu, "Kankyaku no tomadoi: Eiga sōsōki ni okeru shinematekku no kōgyō o megutte," *Āto risāchi* 7 (2007): 129–139.

41. Examples of such "faked" films produced by the Edison company—*The Battle of Chemulpo Bay* (1904) and *The Battle of the Yalu* (1904)—can be viewed on the Library of Congress website: http://lcweb2.loc.gov/intldl/mtfhtml/mfpercep/igpfilms.html. Both were shot in New York.

42. Komatsu Hiroshi, "Transformations in Film as Reality (Part One): Questions Regarding the Genesis of Nonfiction Film," trans. A.A. Gerow, *Documentary Box* (English ed.) 5 (1994): 3–4. Komatsu here clarifies his position on the issue of fiction and nonfiction in early Japanese cinema found in his earlier "Some Characteristics of Japanese Cinema before World War I," in *Reframing Japanese Cinema: Authorship, Genre, History*, ed. Arthur Noletti Jr. and David Desser (Bloomington: Indiana University Press, 1992), 229–258. Charles Musser makes similar observations about American films on the Spanish-American War, in *The Emergence of Cinema: The American Screen to 1907*, History of the American Cinema, vol. 1 (Berkeley: University of California Press, 1990), 240–261.

43. Komatsu, "Transformations in Film as Reality (Part One)," 3.

44. Abé Mark Nornes, *Japanese Documentary Film: The Meiji Era through Hiroshima* (Minneapolis: University of Minnesota Press, 2003), 10–15.

45. Nagai Kafū, "Asakusa shumi," *Shumi* 4.8 (August 1909): 7.

46. Shimazaki Tōson, "Tōzai no sōi," *Shumi* 4.8 (August 1909): 8.

47. Yoshie Kogan, "Katsudō no omoshiromi," *Shumi* 4.8 (August 1909): 5–6

48. Kubota Utsubo, "Hajimete katsudō shashin o mini itta hi," *Shumi* 4.8 (August 1909): 10.

49. Yoshiyama Kyokkō, *Nihon eigakai jibutsu kigen* (Tokyo: Shinema to Engeisha, 1933), 121. Yoshiyama's citation is ambiguous, but he implies that this section was included in the original Copyright Law was when it was issued in 1899, which is not the case. The section regarding film was added in 1910 to bring Japanese law in line with the 1908 revisions of the Berlin international treaty on copyright. Yoshiyama also quotes the law incorrectly, stating that those who reproduce the work of another "will be considered as producers *[seisakusha]*." The law truly reads: "will be considered as plagiarists *[gisakusha]*." Makino Mamoru, in his history of prewar film censorship, correctly notes the date of the revision but unfortunately reproduces Yoshiyama's misquotation: Makino Mamoru, *Nihon eiga ken'etsushi* (Tokyo: Pandora, 2003), 34. For a copy of the law as it stood in 1928, see Ichikawa Aya, ed., *Nihon eiga hōki ruishū* (Tokyo: Ginza Shobō, 1928), 1–6. Also see Yanai Yoshio, *Katsudō shashin no hogo to torishimari* (Tokyo: Yūhikaku, 1929), for a more accurate account of cinema's place in early copyright law.

50. Abel notes how French courts tended to focus on cinema as a potential threat to literary copyright, issuing decisions that ended up granting films protection as an extension of the copyright of their source (if they were adaptations) or, later, as products of a screenplay (which was all that was allowed

to be submitted to the Bibliothèque nationale): "Booming the Business: The Historical Specificity of Early French Cinema," in *Silent Film,* ed. Abel (New Brunswick, NJ: Rutgers University Press, 1996), 109–124.

51. Yanai cites a 1914 court decision, not related to film, that certified the Berne Convention as equivalent to Japanese law, and a 1925 Tokyo court report (which was not binding) claiming the protection of film as intellectual property, as justification for his argument. Yet Yanai does echo Abel's argument that the revisions of the Berne Convention protected film only in relation to other intellectual property like literature or music. Yanai, *Katsudō shashin no hogo to torishimari,* 33–92.

52. For one account of this tale, see Yoshida Chieo, *Mō hitotsu no eigashi* (Tokyo: Jiji Tsūshinsha, 1978), 25.

53. Yoshiyama, *Nihon eigakai jibutsu kigen,* 120.

54. See Makino, *Nihon eiga ken'etsushi,* 32–76; Makino Mamoru, "On the Conditions of Film Censorship in Japan before Its Systematization," in *In Praise of Film Studies,* ed. Aaron Gerow and Abé Mark Nornes (Yokohama: Kinema Club, 2001), 46–67; and Okudaira Yasuhiro, "Eiga to ken'etsu," in *Kōza Nihon eiga,* ed. Imamura Shōhei et al. (Tokyo: Iwanami Shoten, 1985), 2:303–308.

55. Given that film history has yet to be established as a rigorous discipline in Japan, there is always the problem of how much credence to give to facts and figures describing the state of early cinema. The number of movie theaters in the last years of Meiji is a case in point. Satō Tadao gives the number forty-four (*Nihon eigashi,* 1:113), but Imamura Kanae, in his history of the Japanese film industry, counts over seventy by 1909 (*Eiga sangyō* [Tokyo: Yūhikaku, 1960]: 26), and the *Tokyo asahi shinbun* reported twenty-nine theaters in Asakusa and the rest of the city in early 1912 ("Katsudō shashin to jidō [ichi]: Ichinen happyaku gojū mannin," *Tokyo asahi shinbun,* February 6, 1912, p. 6). Such discrepancies continue to plague even the most recent research. I have opted for Satō's figure mainly because the Tokyo police reportedly counted forty-three theaters in July 1913 ("Katsudō no zōsetsu wa kinshi," *Tokyo nichi nichi shinbun,* July 8, 1913, reprinted in *Taishō nyūsu jiten* [Tokyo: Mainichi Komyunikēshonzu, 1988], 1:87 (hereafter referred to as *TNJ*).

56. The *Tokyo asahi,* for instance, claimed that there were already 8,500,000 movie tickets sold each year in the Tokyo area alone: "Katsudō shashin to jidō (ichi)." But since this is a piece warning readers of the threat of film's popularity, one must take these figures with a grain of salt.

57. "Jigoma (san): Eiga no shushu sentaku," *Tokyo asahi shinbun,* October 7, 1912, p. 5.

58. See Itō Hideo, *Taishō no tantei shōsetsu* (Tokyo: San'ichi Shobō, 1991). The *Yomiuri shinbun* listed twenty such books: "Katsudōkai no kyōkō," *Yomiuri shinbun,* October 12, 1912, p. 3.

59. The *Osaka asahi shinbun* said the film was so popular that it was as if one could say, "If it's not [Zigomar], it's not a moving picture." "Eiga *Jigoma* no kinshi to Osaka," *Ōsaka asahi shinbun,* October 11, 1912, reprinted in

Shinbun shūroku Taishō-shi (Tokyo: Taishō Shuppan, 1978), 1:73 (hereafter referred to as *SST*).

60. Nagamine Shigetoshi, *Kaitō Jigoma to katsudō shashin no jidai* (Tokyo: Shinchōsha, 2006).

61. The report not only voiced concern about unsanitary conditions at theaters, the potential deleterious effects that customs expressed in foreign films had on young Japanese, and the harmful nature of benshi explanation and musical accompaniment, but it also recommended the production of a greater variety of educational films and the establishment of educational film days. See "Katsudō shashin to jidō (jū): Shōgakusei torishimari no mukō," *Tokyo asahi shinbun*, February 20, 1912, p. 6. The *Asahi* commented that the recommendations had little affect on film attendance by minors.

62. Hase Masato, "Cinemaphobia in Taisho Japan: Zigomar, Delinquent Boys, and Somnambulism," *Iconics* 4 (1998): 87–100.

63. Nagamine reports that *Zigomar* did manage to slip into theaters at least once after the Tokyo ban, showing in Asakusa in April 1913 under the title *Tantei kidan* (The Strange Tale of the Detective). *Kaitō Jigoma to katsudō shashin no jidai*, 165.

64. "Jigoma (ichi): Jigoma to wa nan zoya," *Tokyo asahi shinbun*, October 4, 1912, p. 5.

65. "Katsudō shashin to jidō (hachi): Kansetsu ni ukuru heigai," *Tokyo asahi shinbun*, February 18, 1912, p. 6.

66. "Jigoma (san)."

67. "Jigoma (hachi): Akukanka to akueikyō," *Tokyo asahi shinbun*, October 14, 1912, p. 5. The police also reiterated this rhetoric: Chief Detective Tsuzura of the Umamichi Police Station (with Asakusa Park in its jurisdiction) told another paper, "It goes without saying that such films cause corruption." "Jigoma no kanka," *Miyako shinbun*, October 6, 1912, p. 5.

68. The *Asahi* had actually said in February that there were no cases of film content causing crime, though it warned of the potential danger: "Katsudō shashin to jidō (shichi): jidō daraku no jitsurei," *Tokyo asahi shinbun*, February 17, 1912, p. 6. The researcher Fujio Shigeo declared he could not find any articles providing evidence of *Zigomar* triggering crime ("Jigoma genshō to Jigoma enzaisetsu," *Gonda Yasunosuke kenkyū* 3 [Fall 1984]), but Nagamine has found one article from June 15, before the ban, claiming a direct connection between watching *Zigomar* and committing crime. However, we must note that the piece appeared in the *Asahi*, the same paper that declared cinema had no benefits, and which did not fail to editorialize in this article about how frightening the movies are. As is unfortunately often the case in his well-researched book, Nagamine does not analyze such articles critically. He takes this one, clearly biased piece at face value, for instance, as evidence that "the same kind of Zigomar incidents had to a certain degree occurred before" the ban (*Kaitō Jigoma to katsudō shashin no jidai*, 138). Nagamine sees the influx of articles after the ban as only the discovery of an existing problem; he thus ignores the role discourse can play in shaping both reality and impressions of it. The fact

is that the vast majority of claims about the film causing crime appeared after the ban, and they are sufficiently lacking in detail that one can see a cinephobic bias operating in them. For instance, after the *Zigomar* ban was announced, the *Chūgai shōgyō shinbun* reported the existence of a seventeen-year-old criminal from Asakusa, named Fujitani Shin'ichi, who had committed several robberies and called himself "the New Zigomar." The article, however, does not detail how he managed to be corrupted by the film: "Jigoma no shin," *Chūgai shōgyō shinbun*, October 15, 1912 (*TNJ*, 1:258). In the end, most articles only used Zigomar as an attention getter; the actual incidents often just involved youths committing crimes less as a result of viewing a film's content than out of the desire to get into the theater.

69. "*Jigoma* (yon): Shigeki no kyōretsuna mono," *Tokyo asahi shinbun*, October 8, 1912, p. 5. Given the ill effects it felt competition had on the industry, the *Asahi* actually welcomed the formation of the Nikkatsu trust.

70. "*Jigoma* (ni): Katsudō shashin no zaiaku," *Tokyo asahi shinbun*, October 5, 1912, p. 5.

71. "*Jigoma* (shichi): Akunin sūhai no keikō," *Tokyo asahi shinbun*, October 11, 1912, p. 5.

72. "*Jigoma* (hachi)."

73. An earlier article offered detailed statistics proving that the air inside Asakusa theaters contained ten times the normal amount of carbon dioxide. Since even a healthy adult would feel dizzy or even faint after spending two hours in such conditions, theater owners, the piece claimed, had made provisions to have doctors on hand during screenings: "Katsudō shashin to jidō (ichi)."

74. For an analysis of the early film culture as a heterotopia, see Lynn Kirby, "The Urban Spectator and the Crowd in Early American Train Films," *Iris* 11 (1990): 49–62; or Miriam Hansen, *Babel and Babylon: Spectatorship in American Silent Film* (Cambridge, MA: Harvard University Press, 1991), 107–108.

75. "*Jigoma* (ichi)."

76. "*Jigoma* (ni)."

77. "*Jigoma* (san)." Middle school in the prewar Japanese school system approximates the high school level in the present system. The paper is thus referring to minors of about seven to eighteen years of age.

78. "*Jigoma* (san)."

79. Nagamine reports police claims in 1912 that 30–40 percent of Asakusa spectators were children. The survey by Sandaya Hiraku that he cites, however, found children forming the majority only on weekends in some theaters (*Kaitō Jigoma to katsudō shashin no jidai*, 22–24). But Kubota Utsubo, in his account of going to the movies, registered surprise that his fellow spectators were mostly adult. Given how assertions regarding the number of child spectators were often intimately tied to attempts to impose control on the new medium, we have to view these numbers from a critical distance.

80. The paper then went on to complain of the medium's misuse and posed the combination of the cinema with the phonograph—that is, sound film—as

the solution: "Katsudō shashin to chikuonki," *Yomiuri shinbun,* October 20, 1912, p. 1.

81. The *Asahi* claimed that "this [cruelty] is not the nature of only such children but is an instinct borne by the majority of children in this era": "Katsudō shashin to jidō (roku): Jidō shinri to eiga," *Tokyo asahi shinbun,* February 16, 1912, p. 6. The next article emphasized that this character was "inborn": "Katsudō shashin to jidō (shichi)."

82. "Katsudō shashin to jidō (roku)."

83. The author of a letter to the editor in the *Asahi,* Katatani Seizō, claimed that the issue of cinema was one that demanded the attention of education officials. See "Jidō *Jigoma* netsu," *Tokyo asahi shinbun,* October 9, 1912, p. 5.

84. "*Jigoma* (san)."

85. "*Jigoma* no katsudō shashin kinshi to naru," *Tokyo nichi nichi shinbun,* October 10, 1912, p. 7.

86. *Jōruri* is a traditional style of sung narration that often accompanied performing arts like Bunraku (puppet theater) and Kabuki, but which could also be presented alone. *Naniwa-bushi* is a more recent form of sung narration especially popular in the Meiji era.

87. "*Jigoma* (san)."

88. Reflecting the fact that many contemporary Japanese newspapers were generally not opposed to greater publications censorship, the *Asahi* ("*Jigoma* mondai kaiketsu") and the *Yomiuri shinbun* ("Katsudōkai no kyōkō") strongly called for banning the publication of this kind of crime and detective novel.

89. "*Jigoma* (yon)."

90. "*Jigoma* (yon): Shigeki no kyōretsuna mono," *Tokyo asahi shinbun,* October 9, 1912, p. 5. Although this is really the fifth part of the paper's series on *Zigomar,* it is misprinted as number four.

91. "Katsudō shashin to jidō (ni): jidō no ukuru hirō," *Tokyo asahi shinbun,* February 7, 1912, p. 6.

92. See Tom Gunning, "Tracing the Individual Body: Photography, Detectives, and Early Cinema," in *Cinema and the Invention of Modern Life,* ed. Leo Charney and Vanessa R. Schwartz (Berkeley: University of California Press, 1995), 15–45.

93. Tom Gunning, "Attractions, Detection, Disguise: Zigomar, Jasset, and the History of Film Genres," *Griffithiana* 47 (May 1993): 113.

94. Nagamine, *Kaitō Jigoma to katsudō shashin no jidai,* 71–72, 150.

95. Quoted in "*Jigoma* mondai kaiketsu," *Tokyo asahi shinbun,* October 13, 1912, p. 6.

96. For a copy of the 1900 theater regulations, see Takazawa Hatsutarō, *Gendai engeki sōran,* 2nd ed. (Tokyo: Bunseisha, 1919), 211–229, especially Article 23, which regulated the content of theater plays.

97. "Kotogoto," *Miyako shinbun,* October 14, 1912, p. 2. Such a ban did not last long: General Nogi would later become a popular subject in the industry as the government came to recognize cinema's ideological usefulness. Incidentally, Chiba Nobuo has attempted to relate the banning of *Zigomar* to the

mood prevailing after the deaths of the emperor and Nogi: as with most entertainments, film theaters were closed during the mourning period, so it is not inconceivable to think that authorities saw the popularity of *Zigomar*-type films as an affront to the emperor. See Chiba Nobuo, "Engeki eiga no jūnen," *Sekai no eiga sakka 31: Nihon eigashi* (Tokyo: Kinema junpōsha, 1976), 18.

98. "*Jigoma* mondai kaiketsu."

99. One police official was quoted in the *Tokyo nichi nichi shinbun* admitting that the police were "too busy" to have seen the film itself: "*Jigoma* no katsudō shashin kinshi to naru."

100. Article 3 of the regulations in effect in Osaka at the time, for instance, merely stipulated: "When the summary of the film or the explanation are under suspicion of violating Section 4 of the previous article, permission will given after projecting and explaining said work at the said place of exhibition or at another convenient site." Thus screenings were required solely when the written summary was thought dubious, and then only with the necessary accompaniment of the benshi. These codes, which were created in 1911 as only internal guidelines, are reproduced in Terakawa Shin, *Eiga oyobi eigageki* (Osaka: Ōsaka Mainichi Shinbunsha, 1925), 230–233.

101. The *Tokyo asahi shinbun* explained that the normal procedure for the Asakusa area (since censorship was left to local police stations at the time) was to inspect the film and the benshi explanation before it opened; for the rest of the city, the procedure was to check on it after the run had begun: "Katsudō shashin to jidō (kyū): Fujūbunnaru ken'etsu," *Tokyo asahi shinbun*, February 19, 1911, p. 6. But as we have seen, there were films like *Zigomar* that escaped both procedures for some time.

102. So said the head of the Public Peace Section while also admitting that, at that time, it remained very difficult to view every single film before exhibition. See "*Jigoma* mondai kaiketsu."

2. GONDA YASUNOSUKE AND THE PROMISE
OF FILM STUDY

1. See Ishii's comments in "Gaka no mitaru katsudō shashin," *Katsudō shashinkai* 7 (March 1910): 4.

2. See Ishikawa's comments in "Gaka no mitaru katsudō shashin," *Katsudō shashinkai* 6 (February 1910): 4.

3. See Kosugi's comments in "Gaka no mitaru katsudō shashin," *Katsudō shashinkai* 6 (February 1910): 4.

4. See Matsubara's response in "Katsudō shashin to bunshi," *Katsudō shashinkai* 4 (January 1910): 5

5. For one such example, see "Henshūkyoku yori," *Katsudō shashinkai* 8 (April 1910): 3. Beyond asking why such critics fail to complain about theater, the piece pointed to the sheer numbers of moviegoers to argue that cinema's detractors did not understand that the medium's popularity reflected new social trends and tastes.

6. "Henshūkyoku yori," *Katsudō shashinkai* 7 (March 1910): 3.

7. Yoshiyama Kyokkō, *Nihon eigakai jibutsu kigen* (Tokyo: Shinema to Engeisha, 1933), 122.

8. These are quotes from sections of the report presented in Makino Mamoru, "On the Conditions of Film Censorship in Japan before Its Systematization," trans. Aaron Gerow, in *In Praise of Film Studies: Essays in Honor of Makino Mamoru*, ed. Aaron Gerow and Abé Mark Nornes (Yokohama: Kinema Club, 2001), 50–56.

9. Nakagawa Shigeaki, *Shokuhai bigaku: Keiji shin'in* (Tokyo: Hakubunkan, 1911). The title of Nakagawa's book has also been translated as "The Aesthetics of Formal Elegance" (see Kaneda Tomio, "An Aesthetician from Kyoto: Nakagawa Shigeaki," in *A History of Modern Japanese Aesthetics*, trans. and ed. Michael F. Marra [Honolulu: University of Hawai'i Press, 2001], 225–237), but I have used my translation here to emphasize the importance of the literal meaning of the characters in *shokuhai*, a concept which promotes art that both touches *(shoku)* and remains separate (*hai*—literally "turned away") from reality. For more on Nakagawa's book, see Makino Mamoru, "Sōsōki no eiga bigaku ni kansuru shoshiteki kenkyū—Nakagawa Shigeaki-cho *Shokuhai bigaku* ni tsuite," *Eizōgaku* 54 (1995): 65–79. Nakagawa, who was also a poet, was also known by the names Nakagawa Jūrei and Nakagawa Shimei.

10. Konrad Lange, *Das Wesen der Kunst: Grundzüge einer illusionistischen Kunstlehre* (Berlin: G. Grote, 1907).

11. In the motion pictures, says Nakagawa, "the individuality particular to art is not apparent and there is no trace of the creation of a work of art. One only looks and cannot help but be amazed. It is but the entertainment of reason and the invention of a machine." *Keiji shin'in shokuhai bigaku* (Tokyo: Hakubunkan, 1911), 159.

12. The novelist Inagaki Taruho, for instance, who in the 1920s championed cinema through a peculiar futurist stance that combined fascination with mechanical perception with a defense of the aesthetics of early cinema, would utilize Nakagawa's concept of *shokuhai bigaku* in the 1940s to denounce a cinema that he now found ruled by "deception." See his essay "Shokuhai bigaku ni tsuite," in *Taruho eigaron* (Tokyo: Firumu Ātosha, 1995), 114–117.

13. For more on Gonda's life, see Nakamura Yōichi, "Kaisetsu," in *Gonda Yasunosuke chosakushū* (Tokyo: Bunwa Shobō, 1974), 1:405–415 (hereafter referred to in the text and notes as *GYC*), and Tamura Norio, "Kaisetsu," *GYC* 4:71–481.

14. Miriam Silverberg, "Constructing the Japanese Ethnography of Modernity," *Journal of Asian Studies* 51.1 (1992): 46.

15. Harry Harootunian, *Overcome by Modernity: History, Culture, and Community in Interwar Japan* (Princeton, NJ: Princeton University Press, 2000), 149–177.

16. Gonda Yasunosuke, *Katsudō shashin no genri oyobi ōyō* (Tokyo: Uchida Rokakuho, 1914), 16 (hereafter referred to in the text as *Principles*).

17. Although Gonda, at this time, did not have the connections with the industry that Munsterburg had, his work also went a long way toward legitimizing the medium.

18. I explore the potential of Gonda's incompletely "serious" side, especially in contrast to the seriousness of Kaeriyama's discourse, in my introduction to the reprint of his book: "Gonda Yasunosuke ga sōzōshita eiga bunmei gensetsu," in Katsudō shashin no genri oyobi ōyō, by Gonda Yasunosuke, Nihon eigaron gensetsu taikei, vol. 24 (Tokyo: Yumani Shobō, 2006).

19. Gonda would later use the term minshū goraku, which he translated into English as "mob amusements": GYC, 1:16. Given the bad connotations associated with the word mob, however, scholars like Miriam Silverberg have opted for the translation "popular play." While I at times use this translation as well, I believe the translation "popular entertainment" is as good, if not better, because "entertainment" is more likely to connote a business than is simple "play." Given Gonda's emphasis on the economic, specifically capitalistic, determinations on entertainment, this connotation is important.

20. Yoshimi Shun'ya, Toshi no doramaturugi: Tōkyō sakariba no shakaishi (Tokyo: Kōbundō, 1987), 42–44.

21. Ibid., 48.

22. Harootunian, Overcome by Modernity, 153.

23. Quoted in Miriam Silverberg, "Japanese Ethnography of Modernity," 45. This is Silverberg's translation of "seikatsu sōzō to shite no goraku." While in interpreting Gonda she rightly emphasizes everyday life as a form of practice (drawing on Michel de Certeau), the phrase can just as well be translated as "entertainment as the creation of everyday life." Gonda himself rephrases it as "entertainment for creating human living" ("ningen seikatsu no sōzō no tame no goraku") (GYC, 2:211).

24. In this, Gonda is a precursor of the Marxist philosopher Tosaka Jun, who in the 1930s saw the cinema as a means by which the masses could see themselves in everyday life, becoming closer to their own customary existence (fūzoku). See Tosaka Jun, "Eiga no shajitsuteki tokusei to fūzokusei oyobi taishūsei," in Tosaka Jun zenshū, vol. 4 (Tokyo: Keisō Shobō, 1966).

25. Shimizu Hikaru, Eiga to bunka (Kyōiku Tosho, 1941).

26. Sugiyama Heiichi, "Eiga kōseiron," in Eiga bunkaron, ed. Nakatsuka Michihiro (Kyoto: Daiichi Geibunsha, 1941).

27. See the chapter titled "Minshū goraku no hattatsu" in Gonda's Minshū goraku mondai (published in 1921), which can be found in his selected works: GYC, 1:23–30.

28. Silverberg, "Japanese Ethnography of Modernity," 48–49.

29. Gonda does not share Lange's or Rudolf Arnheim's fear that cinema's mechanical reproduction of reality may disqualify it as art. Its technology, to him, explains its unique art (Gonda, Principles, 393).

30. See Iwamoto Kenji, "Senkuteki eiga kenkyūsha Gonda Yasunosuke," Waseda Daigaku Daigakuin Bungaku Kenkyūka kiyō 30 (1984): 191–201.

31. Nakai Masakazu, "Eiga no kūkan" and "Eiga no jikan," in *Ikite iru kūkan* (Tokyo: Tenbinsha, 1964).

32. Nakamura, *GYC*, 1:413.

33. Iwamoto, "Senkuteki eiga kenkyūsha Gonda Yasunosuke," 199.

34. Inagaki Taruho, "Keishiki oyobi naiyō toshite no katsudō shashin," in *Taruho eigaron* (Tokyo: Firumu Ātosha, 1995), 90–97.

35. Although Nakai developed his notion of the lack of the copula in his postwar writings, his prewar film theory already conceives of a central gap in cinema—in effect, a lack in its essence—that the masses can fill as they start performing their collective role as a world historical subject. See such essays as "Kontinyuiti no ronrisei" and "Butsuriteki shūdanteki seikaku" in the compilation *Ikite iru kūkan*. Both were originally published in 1931.

36. See my "The Self Seen as Other: Akutagawa and Film," *Literature/ Film Quarterly* 23.3 (1995): 197–203; or "Celluloid Masks: The Cinematic Image and the Image of Japan," *Iris* 16 (Spring 1993): 23–36.

37. Thomas LaMarre, *Shadows on the Screen: Tanizaki Jun'ichirō on Cinema and "Oriental" Aesthetics* (Ann Arbor: Center for Japanese Studies, University of Michigan, 2005), 82–83.

38. Thomas LaMarre, "From Animation to Anime: Drawing Movements and Moving Drawings," *Japan Forum* 14.2 (2002): 329–367. For more on the anime-ic, see also Thomas Looser, "From Edogawa to Miyazaki: Cinematic and Anime-ic Architectures of Early and Late Twentieth-Century Japan," *Japan Forum* 14.2 (2002): 297–327.

39. Several questions arise from LaMarre's account. The first is whether creating two terms, *cinema* and *cinematic*, really solves the problem of essentialism, especially when the two share the same root (why even call the latter "cinematic" if the former does not determine the latter?). If the "cinema is the apparatus or medium (or mixture thereof) that most thoroughly mobilizes and realizes such cinematic traits and effects, localizing, condensing, and intensifying them" (LaMarre, *Shadows on the Screen*, 60), how does it do this? Doesn't it reintroduce the problem of "seeing the apparatus as determining form" (p. 82)? How does he account for the long history in Japanese thinking about cinema, which starts with the Pure Film Movement and continues through Hasumi Shigehiko, and which fetishes the apparatus and advocates determining the cinematic through cinema? Is Tanizaki merely a brilliant individual who stood against this trend? LaMarre's concept of the cinematic works best when he loosens the ties between cinema and the cinematic (though such concepts as underdetermination), but this threatens to take the latter out of real, everyday lived experience (which Gonda and others would object to). This he already does by calling it "a-modern" (p. 60) in an effort to detach it from the West or a teleological modernity; but for cinema to "realize such cinematic traits and effects," it must be articulated and manipulated in real historical discursive struggles (it would be pure idealism to say the "cinematic" determines

how cinema manifests its traits), struggles that also shape thinking about the cinematic. This only brings us back to where I started, with the need to create a concrete discursive history of material effects. LaMarre's concept of the cinematic functions well in his own project of questioning post-1970s Western film theory, and may even help explain some of the possibilities that Japanese theorists imagined, but it can function as a history only when he shows how it is manifested in material practices. The theorization of the cinematic itself is one such material practice, but then LaMarre's stance and those of Japanese theorists must be historicized.

40. See Nagae Michitarō, *Eiga, hyōgen, keisei* (Kyoto: Kyōiku Tosho, 1942).

41. Tanizaki Jun'ichirō, "Katsudō shashin no genzai to shōrai," *Shinshōsetsu* (September 1917). An English translation appears in LaMarre's *Shadows on the Screen*, 65–74.

42. That Tanizaki's piece appeared not in a film magazine but in a literary journal, *Shinshōsetsu*, did not necessarily mean he was reaching readers unfamiliar with pure film discourse. Many literary and cultural figures outside the film world had been generating similar comments for nearly a decade before this article appeared.

43. *GYC*, 1:69–73. Gonda's survey, titled "Katsudō shashin ni kansuru chōsa oyobi kansatsu," was also included in *Minshū goraku mondai*.

44. See also Gonda Yasunosuke, "Minshū goraku to shite no katsudō shashin," *Katsudō gahō* 5.12 (1921): 36–37.

45. Miriam Hansen, *Babel and Babylon: Spectatorship and American Silent Film* (Cambridge, MA: Harvard University Press, 1991).

46. See especially his essay "Bungei no kan'ei," in *GYC*, 1:60–66.

47. Kakimoto Akihito, "Bokujin = shisai to shite no Kon Wajirō," *Gendai shisō* 21.7 (July 1993): 74–87.

48. Nakamura, *GYC*, 1 415. *Eejanaika* (literally, "Why not?") was one of the popular rebellions at the end of the Edo period that, while tied to religious issues, often manifested an anarchic, end-of-the-world spirit of pleasure and anything-goes. The rebellions are depicted in Imamura Shōhei's 1981 film, *Eejanaika*.

49. Yoshimi also makes this crucial link between Gonda and Asakusa, although within a historical narrative marking the shift in urban dramaturgy from Asakusa to Ginza to Shinjuku and Shibuya.

50. Quoted in Takemura Tamio, *Taishō bunka* (Tokyo: Kōdansha, 1980), 127. According to Takemura, the boom in surveys and commercial sample research, spurred by the development of statistical research, was so prominent it sparked popular songs on the topic.

3. STUDYING THE PURE FILM

1. Chiba Nobuo, "Modanaizēshon jokyoku: eigaron 1914–1918," in *Nihon eiga to modanizumu 1920–1930*, ed. Iwamoto Kenji (Tokyo: Riburopōto, 1991), 32.

2. Ibid., 34. A two-part editorial written in 1917 by someone named Okumura for *Kinema Record* repeats many of Gonda's arguments: "Gendai bunmei no katsudō shashinteki keikō," *Kinema Record* 47 (May 1917): 213; and "Gendai bunmei no katsudō shashinteki keikō: dai-ni," *Kinema Record* 48 (June 1917): 273–274.

3. The society met regularly to view films that were adaptations of famous literary works and to listen to lectures. For more on Osanai's involvement in cinema, see Iwamoto Kenji, "Osanai Kaoru to eiga," *Bungaku Kenkyūka kiyō* 32 (1986): 139–153.

4. Osanai Kaoru, "Mune ga hiroku naru," *Shumi* 4.8 (August 1909): 1–2.

5. Ogawa Mimei, "Akazaru tsuikyū," *Shumi* 4.8 (August 1909): 3.

6. Ibid., 4. In a later piece in *Katsudō shashinkai*, Ogawa reiterated his opinion of the motion pictures, but added that he thought films should always present something new, be it beautiful or ugly. See his "Katsudō shashin zakkan," *Katsudō shashinkai* 10 (June 1910): 8. Presumably, for Ogawa, cinema's interest lay in its ability to ignore art and "let you rest your mind" ("Akazaru," 4).

7. Sōma Gyofū, "Shinkufū ga arisōna mono," *Katsudō shashinkai* 10 (June 1910): 9.

8. Inaoka Nunosuke, "Bunsei rekihōroku: Inaoka Nunosuke-shi," *Katsudō shashinkai* 11 (July 1910): 4.

9. For instance, Yamagami Jōsen, while acknowledging that Japanese cinema was still in its "infancy" and that Western films were best at comedy, wished to make clear that Japanese productions exceeded their overseas competitors at tragedy: "Kansō nyoze," *Katsudō shashinkai* 10 (June 1910): 10. In the same issue, the prominent benshi Somei Tenrai promoted Japanese films as one way of greeting audiences with different tastes: "Shokan no iroiro," *Katsudō shashinkai* 10 (June 1910): 22.

10. Yanagi, "Shokan," *Katsudō shashinkai* 11 (July 1910): 21.

11. Yanagi, "Shokan: zoku," *Katsudō shashinkai* 12 (August 1910): 18.

12. Yanagawa Shun'yō, "Bunsei rekihōroku: Yanagawa Shun'yō-shi," *Katsudō shashinkai* 12 (August 1910): 6.

13. See Tokunaga's comments in "Gaka no mitaru katsudō shashin," *Katsudō shashinkai* 7 (March 1910): 4.

14. See Fujii's comments in "Kotoba no shashin," *Katsudō shashinkai* 12 (August 1910): 5.

15. Kinugasa Teinosuke, *Waga eiga no seishun* (Tokyo: Chūō Kōronsha, 1977).

16. Komatsu Hiroshi, "Some Characteristics of Japanese Cinema before World War I," in *Reframing Japanese Cinema*, ed. Arthur Noletti Jr. and David Desser (Bloomington: Indiana University Press, 1992), 254.

17. Komatsu Hiroshi, "The Fundamental Change: Japanese Cinema before and after the Earthquake of 1923," *Griffithiana* 13.38–39 (October 1990): 186–93.

18. Komatsu Hiroshi, "Tennenshoku kara jun'eigageki e—Nihon eigashi ni okeru Tenkatsu no igi," *Geijutsugaku kenkyū* 5 (1995): 36.

19. Eric Hobsbawm and Terence Ranger, eds., *The Invention of Tradition* (Cambridge: Cambridge University Press, 1983). For an exploration of traditions that were inventions of Japanese modernity, see Stephen Vlastos, ed., *Mirror of Modernity: Invented Traditions of Modern Japan* (Berkeley: University of California Press, 1998).

20. See, for instance, Yoshida Chieo's account: *Mō hitotsu no eigashi: Katsuben no jidai* (Tokyo: Jiji Tsūshinsha, 1978), 45–48. Jeffrey Dym raises doubts about this story, but confesses he has no conclusive proof of an alternative narrative. See his *Benshi, Japanese Silent Film Narrators, and Their Forgotten Narrative Art of Setsumei: A History of Japanese Silent Film Narration* (Lewiston, NY: Edwin Mellen Press, 2003), 65.

21. Ironically, this move hastened the split between film and theater by prompting studios to permanently hire actors, a practice that eventually promoted performers attuned to the specialties of the medium.

22. Noël Burch, *To the Distant Observer: Form and Meaning in the Japanese Cinema*, ed. Annette Michelson (Berkeley: University of California Press, 1979), 81–85.

23. The existing prints seem to differ. The one in the possession of Matsuda Eigasha is fairly long and is composed of films dated from 1910 to 1917. The print in the collection of the National Museum of Modern Art, Tokyo, the National Film Center, has some scenes the other print doesn't have and lacks others (for instance, it includes the scene when Ōishi kills a peasant on the road to Edo, but lacks the crucial meeting of the retainers at an inn before they attack Kira's villa). The National Film Center gives the years 1910 to 1912 as the date of production.

24. Komatsu, "Tennenshoku kara jun'eigageki e," 36.

25. See David Bordwell, "A Cinema of Flourishes: Japanese Decorative Classicism of the Prewar Era," in *Reframing Japanese Cinema*, ed. Arthur Noletti Jr. and David Desser (Bloomington: Indiana University Press, 1992), 328–346.

26. A typical *rensageki* spectacle would present in alternation scenes performed live on stage and others on film. For instance, police would start to chase a criminal on stage, then, after a screen had been lowered, continue the pursuit on film in real locations, and finally return to the stage for the capture.

27. Dym, *Benshi, Japanese Silent Film Narrators*, 61–74.

28. Aaron Gerow, "One Print in the Age of Mechanical Reproduction," *Screening the Past* 11 (2000): www.latrobe.edu.au/screeningthepast/firstrelease/fr1100/agfr11e.htm.

29. See Miriam Silverberg, *Erotic Grotesque Nonsense: The Mass Culture of Japanese Modern Times* (Berkeley: University of California Press, 2006). Silverberg's use of the concept of montage is both intriguing and somewhat justified, given not only its productivity in analyzing prewar mass culture but also the fashion for the term in film and other art circles in the late 1920s and early 1930s. However, this use should be tempered by recognition of the debates over the term in the film world, especially the arguments against it from the mid-1930s on by directors like Itami Mansaku or critics like Sugiyama Heiichi.

Just as the culture of combination was not the uncontested dominant form of experiencing film, so montage was a focus of conflict over the meaning of cinema in modern culture.

30. J.L. Anderson, "Spoken Silents in the Japanese Cinema; or, Talking to Pictures: Essaying the *Katsuben*, Contextualizing the Texts," in *Reframing Japanese Cinema: Authorship, Genre, History* (Bloomington: Indiana University Press, 1992), 259–311.

31. Later issues would sport the English title *Moving Picture Companion*.

32. Given the sketchy history of early Japanese film journalism and inadequate preservation, it is always difficult to determine when an early magazine stopped publication. *Kinema Record* apparently experienced many problems in its last year. Kaeriyama's name stops appearing in the list of editorial board members at the beginning of 1917, even though he continued submitting pieces. Shigeno then stepped down as editor after issue 49 (July 1917) to sell the magazine outright to Kaeriyama. Publication thus shifted from "the Kinema Record Publishing Company" to "the Kinograph Publishing Company," and a notice in issue 50 (which appeared three months later, in October) disclaimed any connection between the magazine and Shigeno. There were apparently financial difficulties, as the next and probably final issue had to wait until December.

33. There is some disagreement over when Kaeriyama joined Tenkatsu. Tanaka Jun'ichirō states that it was in May 1917 ("Kaeriyama Norimasa," in *Nihon eiga kantoku zenshū* [Tokyo: Kinema Junpōsha, 1976], 110), while Yoshida Chieo claims it was in the fall ("Kaeriyama Norimasa to *Sei no kagayaki* no shuppatsu made," in *Kōza Nihon eiga*, ed. Imamura Shōhei et al. [Tokyo: Iwanami Shoten, 1985], 1:242).

34. For more on the history of Tenkatsu, see Komatsu, "Tennenshoku kara jun'eigageki e."

35. Komatsu Hiroshi cites the September 1923 earthquake that devastated much of the Tokyo region as the major impetus in the industry's transformation: Komatsu, "Fundamental Change." Certainly the quake's impact was enormous, both on the film industry (it brought film reform, which was largely based in Tokyo, to Kyoto when studios were forced to shift their Tokyo personnel to their still-standing studios in the Kansai region) and on the culture as a whole (for instance, aiding modernization by almost literally wiping the spatial slate clean), but we should not forget that many of the transformations were already under way long before the quake.

36. The film historian Tajima Ryōichi makes a strong case for giving Kobayashi Kisaburō some credit for the reform of Japanese cinema. As the man responsible for importing *Zigomar*, many American serials, the Bluebird films, and last but not least, *Intolerance*, as well as for supporting reformist journals like *Katsudō no sekai* and *Katsudō hyōron*, Kobayashi can be seen as one figure in the industry who had a great deal of influence, if not always intentional, on transforming Japanese cinema. See Tajima, "Kōgyōshi Kobayashi Kisaburō ron," *Nihon Daigaku Geijutsu Gakubu kiyō* 24 (1994): 27–40.

37. Yoshida, "Kaeriyama Norimasa," 248.

38. Kaeriyama, who never scored many points for his artistry, directed his last feature film in 1924 and returned to what was his original field by working in and writing on film technology. Henry Kotani was one of several Japanese with experience in Hollywood whom new companies like Shōchiku brought in to aid reform. Kotani was a cameraman for the Famous Players–Lasky studio before returning to Japan to direct films like *Gubinjinsō* (Poppy, 1921). He later went on to produce educational films and newsreels. Kurihara worked as an actor in Sessue Hayakawa's troupe before codirecting the U.S.-Japan coproduction *Sanji Goto* in 1918. His work with Tanizaki Jun'ichirō directing films like *Amateur Club* (1920) is well known (see Joanne Bernardi, *Writing in Light: The Silent Scenario and the Japanese Pure Film Movement* [Detroit: Wayne State University Press, 2001]), but he unfortunately died of tuberculosis in 1926.

39. "Honpō katsudō shashinkai to kikanshi no hakkō," *Kinema Record* 28 (October 1915): 2.

40. Shigeno Yukiyoshi, "Tokubetsugō to JCA-sha no shōrai," *Kinema Record* 13 (July 1914): 2.

41. "Shinsōseru hinshi hakkō no aki ni ate," *Kinema Record* 31 (January 1916): 11.

42. In an early issue, a reader gave a list of such works, including *Picture Plays and How to Write Them* and *La Cinématographie pour tous*: Sekizawa Seikō, "Katsudō shashin ni kansuru sankōsho," *Kinema Record* 18 (December 1914): 19. *Kinema Record* printed a list of all the world's film magazines (that it knew of) in its January 1916 issue.

43. Komatsu, "Some Characteristics," 252.

44. Shigeno Yukiyoshi, "Nihon shashin no genjō o hyōsuru koto," *Kinema Record* 14 (August 1914): 2.

45. "Dare ga tsumi zoya?" *Kinema Record* 26 (August 1915): 3.

46. See, for instance, "Nihon eiga yushutsu no kōki ni saishite," *Kinema Record* 40 (October 1916): 428.

47. See "Gūjin no gūgo ka, arui wa Nihon eiga no ketten ka?" *Kinema Record* 40 (October 1916): 427.

48. See the series of essays "Katsudō shashingeki kyakushokujō no kenkyū" found in *Kinema Record* 27 (September 1915): 2–3; and *Kinema Record* 28 (October 1915): 3–5.

49. "Waga sakuhin no kōjōsaku ni tsuite: ni," *Kinema Record* 45 (March 1917): 109.

50. See Mizusawa Takehiko, "Haitaiseru Nikkatsu Kyōto-ha," *Kinema Record* 24 (June 1916): 2–3. Nikkatsu was notorious for pursuing such tactics to save money. Mizusawa Takehiko, by the way, was one of Kaeriyama's several pen names.

51. Toshirō, "Gūjin no gūgo ka, arui wa Nihon eiga no ketten ka?" *Kinema Record* 39 (September 1916): 379.

52. Shigeno Yukiyoshi, "Dōshitara Nihon-sei eiga o gaikoku ni uridasu koto ga dekiru?" *Kinema Record* 21 (March 1915): 10.

53. For more on this "dream of export," see my "'Nihonjin' Kitano Takeshi: *Hana-Bi* to nashonaru shinema no keisei," *Yuriika* rinji zōkan 30.3 (February 1998): 42–51; "Tatakau kankyaku: Dai Tōa Kyōeiken no Nihon eiga to juyō no mondai," *Gendai shisō* 30.9 (July 2002): 139–149; "Nation, Citizenship, and Cinema," in *A Companion to the Anthropology of Japan*, ed. Jennifer Robertson (Malden, MA: Blackwell Publishers, 2005), 400–414; and "Narrating the Nationality of a Cinema: The Case of Japanese Prewar Film," in *The Culture of Japanese Fascism*, ed. Alan Tansman (Durham, NC: Duke University Press, 2009).

54. "Nihon eiga yushutsu no kōki ni saishite," *Kinema Record* 40 (October 1916): 428.

55. Kaeriyama Norimasa, "Jiko o shireri ya?" *Kinema Record* 19 (January 1915): 2.

56. See, for instance, Iijima Tadashi, *Nihon eigashi*, 2 vols. (Tokyo: Hakusuisha, 1955).

57. See especially "Nation, Citizenship, and Cinema" and "Narrating the Nation-ality of a Cinema."

58. Daisuke Miyao, *Sessue Hayakawa: Silent Cinema and Transnational Stardom* (Durham, NC: Duke University Press, 2007).

59. Yanagi, "Shokan: zoku," *Katsudō shashinkai* 12 (August 1910): 18.

60. See Ide Tetsujo, "Eigageki no honshitsu to enshutsuhō no itchi," *Katsudō no sekai* (September 1917): 4–5.

61. See Deguchi Takehito, "Nani ga hakujin konpurekkusu o umidashita ka," in *Nihon eiga to modanizumu: 1920–1930*, ed. Iwamoto Kenji (Tokyo: Riburopōto, 1991), 104–123.

62. "Dare ga tsumi zoya?" 2.

63. For actors, see, for instance, Shigeno Yukiyoshi, "Waga katsuhai no yūki to doryō," *Kinema Record* 20 (February 1915): 4. For writers, see the editorial written by Kizawa Tetsuya, "Nihon eiga ni tsuite," *Kinema Record* 33 (March 1916): 97. For benshi, see Kishirō, "Benshi no shakaiteki kachi," *Kinema Record* 49 (July 1917): 323–324. For exhibitors, see "Kōryo subeki eiga kōgyōhō," *Kinema Record* 51 (December 1917): 1–2.

64. One "M.S." announced, "With the progress in Japanese film, I have recently become interested in viewing in a more investigative manner. This progress is certainly due to the accumulation of study by the actors and photographers." "Nihon eiga no bamen," *Kinema Record* 20 (February 1915): 18.

65. For example: "Moving picture plays that can be understood by intelligent [atama no aru] people are what such people are already demanding." "Nihon eiga ni tsuite," 97.

66. "Katsudō shashin kōgyō hōshin: Jidai no suii to kankyaku no zunō," *Kinema Record* 16 (October 1914): 2.

67. For instance: "All that is shown now are pictures that simply match vulgar tastes. . . . It is impossible a person with discernment would try to see them." "Tashika ni daiheigai nari!" *Kinema Record* 29 (November 1915): 2.

68. So said a reader under the name Gen'ei, in "Shibai to katsudō shashin," *Kinema Record* 23 (May 1915): 17.

69. "Katsudō shashingeki kyakushokujō no kenkyū: dai-ni kai," 5.

70. Kaeriyama Norimasa, "Katsudō shashin no shakaiteki chii oyobi sekimu," *Kinema Record* 41 (November 1916): 479.

71. Kaeriyama called for such cooperation in the industry in "Jiko o shireri ya?" 2–3. The vision of a new industry offered in his book revolved around creating a research center: *Katsudō shashin no sōsaku to satsueihō* (Tokyo: Hikōsha, 1917), appendix 29–30.

72. "Katsudō shashin shakaiteki kyōiku ōyō no tansho," *Kinema Record* 42 (December 1916): 536.

73. Kaeriyama, "Katsudō shashin no shakaiteki chii oyobi sekimu," 479.

74. See, for instance, Komada Kōyō's fictional newspaper article in his *Katsudō shashin setsumeisho tsuki Ejison-shi shiden,* reproduced in Tsukada Yoshinobu, *Nihon eigashi no kenkyū* (Tokyo: Gendai Shokan, 1980).

75. As in the case of the first part of the *Zigomar* series in the *Tokyo asahi shinbun,* October 4, 1912, p. 5.

76. So says Yoshida, "Kaeriyama Norimasa," 243.

77. Okada Susumu, *Nihon eiga no rekishi* (Tokyo: Daviddosha, 1967), 133.

78. Chiba Nobuo has cast doubt on this and many other myths surrounding the development of the term *eiga* in his terminological history: "Eiga yōgo no hassei to rufu no shiteki purosesu," *Eigashi kenkyū* 1 (1973): 40–48. I am indebted to Murayama Kyōichirō for bringing this article to my attention.

79. The changes in terminology seem to have appeared all over the world. Beyond the case of *Kino* in Germany, Eileen Bowser notes how the famed American critic Frank Woods opted for *motion pictures* over *moving pictures* as "a better term for a period of uplift": *The Transformation of Cinema: 1907–1915* (Berkeley: University of California Press, 1990), 136.

80. For instance: "Our film exhibition world has long been detested by people in society as 'katsudōya'": "Kōryo subeki eiga kōgyōhō," 1. The director Yamamoto Kajirō would later proudly display the name in his autobiography, *Katsudōya jitaden* (Tokyo: Shōbunsha, 1972), but by then, *katsudōya* was mostly being used by veterans to distinguish themselves from the young upstarts.

81. "Waga sakuhin no kōjōsaku ni tsuite: ni," 109.

82. "Tashika ni daiheigai nari!" 2.

83. Bowser, *Transformation of Cinema,* 38.

84. Kaeriyama, "Jiko o shireri ya," 2.

85. "Katsudō shashin kōgyō hōshin," 2.

86. "Ikitomaritaru waga eigakai," *Kinema Record* 46 (April 1917): 161.

87. "Katsudō shashin shakaiteki kyōiku ōyō no tansho," 536.

88. "Kōryo subeki eiga kōgyōhō," 1–2.

89. A writer by the name of Kitarō was both amazed and discouraged by the remarkable drawing power of theaters featuring *kowairo* benshi: "Benshi no shigoto," *Kinema Record* 28 (October 1915): 6–7.

90. In trying to counter the popularity of *kowairo* benshi, Kitarō urged, "It is the time for you benshi to wake up and for you spectators to progress a little." Ibid., 6–7.

91. "Seizō kaisha ni atauru sho," *Kinema Record* 50 (October 1917): 4–5. Reformist critics would offer this structural criticism of the industry for years to come.

92. "Shinchōrei tai gyōsha mondai," *Kinema Record* 50 (October 1917): 1–3.

93. The word for society, *shakai*, had a definite modern ring to it at the time and did not always refer to all of the culture, but often only to the more progressive part. *Kinema Record* and the other reformers often used it to write lower-class viewers out of the picture.

94. H.D. Harootunian, "Introduction: A Sense of an Ending and the Problem of Taishō," in *Japan in Crisis: Essays on Taishō Democracy*, ed. Bernard S. Silberman and Harootunian (Princeton, NJ: Princeton University Press, 1974): 16–17. Harootunian emphasizes that *kyōyō shugi*, despite its resistance to the crass vulgarity of consumerism, tended to "dissolve into middle-class apoliticality and mass consumerism" precisely because it advocated withdrawal from the public world into private indifference (p. 15). While the pure film intellectuals could not be accused of promoting private over public considerations, their ideal of the *aikatsuka* was similarly apolitical and not inimical to middle-class consumerism.

95. Nakagawa Shigeaki, for instance, uses the specter of women and children to downplay photographic *misemono*: *Shokuhai bigaku: Keiji shin'in* (Tokyo: Hakubunkan, 1911), 156.

96. "Tashika ni daiheigai nari!" 2.

97. See the section in Yoshimi's book titled "Toposu to shite no 'Asakusa'": *Toshi no doramaturugī: Tōkyō sakariba no shakaishi* (Tokyo: Kōbundō, 1987), 194–219.

98. See, for instance, "Ikitomaritaru waga eigakai," 161.

99. Given the lack of accurate records and the significant differences in pricing, it is hard to state unequivocally what it cost to go to the movies in the mid-1910s. *Kinema Record* mentioned at the time how easy it was for the lower classes to go to the movies at only 10 sen (100 sen = 1 yen). Tanaka Jun'ichirō gives 20 sen as the average theater price in 1918, but notes that theaters outside of Asakusa and the second-run houses could charge as little as half the price of first-run cinemas (and discount tickets were also available): "Eigakan nyūjōryō," *Nedan no Meiji, Taishō, Shōwa fūzokushi* (Tokyo: Asahi Shinbunsha, 1981), 163–167. As a comparison, Tosaka Yasuji lists the prices at the Teigeki in 1916 as ranging from 5 yen to 10 sen: "Gekijō kanranryō," *Zoku nedan no Meiji, Taishō, Shōwa fūzokushi* (Tokyo: Asahi Shinbunsha, 1981), 222–226. Surely there were cheap legit theaters, especially in the provinces, but the general opinion at the time was that the movies were cheaper than the stage. These figures tend to undermine J.L. Anderson's contention that "movies in Japan were not the entertainment of the poor," because of their supposed high price: "Spoken Silents in the Japanese Cinema," 276. The accusations by reform critics that Japanese films catered to lower-class audiences also belie this contention. Given that Takemura Tamio mentions that the average daily wage of a male

worker in 1918 was 92 sen (42 sen for women), one can say it was not hard for many Japanese to go to the movies once or twice a month (*Taishō bunka* [Tokyo: Kōdansha, 1980], 98). But as a comparison, note that *Katsudō no sekai* lists the average daily wage for unskilled movie theater workers such as usherettes and handbill distributors as 28 and 40 sen respectively: "Jōsetsukan o keieisuru to shite sono hiyō to shūnyū," *Katsudō no sekai* 2.9 (September 1917): 69.

100. Janet Staiger, *Interpreting Films: Studies in the Historical Reception of American Cinema* (Princeton, NJ: Princeton University Press, 1992).

101. Heidi Schlüpmann, "Cinema as Anti-Theater: Actresses and Female Audiences in Wilhelminian Germany," *Iris* 11 (Summer 1990): 77–93.

102. Hiroshi Komatsu and Charles Musser, "Benshi Search," *Wide Angle* 9.2 (1987): 85–88.

103. "Katsudō shashingeki kyakushokujō no kenkyū," 3, emphasis in the original.

104. For more on these problems, see my "Narrating the Nation-ality of a Cinema."

4. THE SUBJECT OF THE TEXT

1. Satō Tadao, "Nihon eiga no seiritsushita dodai: Nihon eigashi 1," in *Kōza Nihon eiga*, ed. Imamura Shōhei et al. (Tokyo: Iwanami Shoten, 1985), 1:33–34. This is an argument often cited to explain the resistance certain benshi exhibited against pure film reform, but it is logically suspect. Especially given how benshi of foreign films or even later Japanese films did not experience significant problems narrating films with more involved editing, it is logical to think that what would obstruct long-winded explanations would be quicker narrative progression rather than fast cutting. As long as the scene itself was long enough to accommodate a wordy benshi narration, editing would not affect the basic narrative form of the verbal explanation no matter how it was done. At best, it could only affect the content of that narration in cases when the analytical editing specified particular narrative details that would have been left more ambiguous in a single long shot. Perhaps increases in narrative tempo in foreign and Japanese cinema did prompt a more laconic benshi style—which, in fact, is what Tokugawa Musei championed—but in general, it is difficult to say that a certain film style resisted, specified, or determined a style of benshi narration. Efforts to make such an argument often reflect, as with Satō's piece, biases toward the benshi that tell us little about benshi practice itself.

2. An example of this flip-flop is Satō himself in his later history of Japanese film: see, for instance, his *Nihon eigashi* (Tokyo: Iwanami Shoten, 1995), 1:6–10, 99–106. Satō's defense of the benshi as a representative of traditional lower-class culture confronting the attacks of bourgeois pure-film intellectuals is typical of the binary pattern that shapes his narrative of Japanese cinema.

3. Noël Burch, *To the Distant Observer*, ed. Annette Michelson (Berkeley: University of California Press, 1979), 77–80.

4. J. L. Anderson, "Spoken Silents in the Japanese Cinema; or, Talking to Pictures: Essaying the *Katsuben,* Contextualizing the Texts," in *Reframing Japanese Cinema,* ed. Arthur Noletti Jr. and David Desser (Bloomington: Indiana University Press, 1992), 286–287. Anderson prefers the term *katsuben,* one of many available terms for benshi, to refer to the institution because it is cinema specific; *benshi* can refer equally well to a regular orator. Since his usage has not become the norm in English discussions of the phenomenon, I have opted to use *benshi,* but, as I note later, the name of the institution became an issue of debate. *Katsuben* was often a derisive term.

5. Jeffery A. Dym, *Benshi, Japanese Silent Film Narrators, and Their Forgotten Narrative Art of Setsumei: A History of Japanese Silent Film Narration* (Lewiston, NY: Edwin Mellen Press, 2003).

6. See Donald Kirihara, "A Reconsideration of the Institution of the Benshi," *Film Reader* 6 (1985): 41–53; and Aaron Gerow, "The Benshi's New Face: Defining Cinema in Taishō Japan," *Iconics* 3 (1994): 69–86.

7. Tom Gunning, *D. W. Griffith and the Origins of American Narrative Film* (Urbana: University of Illinois Press, 1991), 92–93.

8. Miriam Hansen, *Babel and Babylon: Spectatorship and American Silent Film* (Cambridge, MA: Harvard University Press, 1991), 97.

9. The stories about *shinpa* benshi like Tsuchiya Shōtō protesting Tanaka Eizō's films are the ones most often related in the historical literature. See, for instance, Satō, "Nihon eiga no seiritsushita dodai: Nihon eigashi 1," 34.

10. Takeda Kōkatsu says, "It is truly embarrassing that audiences cannot understand a film made in their own country without the help of a benshi." "Setsumeisha no shimei," *Katsudō kurabu* 4.12 (December 1921): 97.

11. Ide Tetsujo complains, "True Japanese photoplays would be freely explained by means of close-ups and editing if they were in fact produced. But today's Japanese films make no connections other than through the lines of the benshi and thus often only produce yawns": "Eigageki no honshitsu to enshutsuhō no itchi," *Katsudō no sekai* 2.9 (September 1917): 5.

12. Azuma Yonosuke, "Setsumeisha haishi ronsha ni yosu," *Katsudō kurabu* 4.5 (May 1921): 60.

13. Katano Akeji noted that many argued for the use of titles rather than a benshi based on the fact that the film differed according to the benshi's voice and mood: "Setsumeisha sonpairon no kōsatsu," *Katsudō gahō* 6.2 (February 1922): 38.

14. Murakami Tokusaburō uses this argument to reject both the benshi and the use of intertitles: "Jimaku sonzai no kahi: sono ni," *Katsudō kurabu* 4.7 (July 1921): 46–47.

15. Takeda, "Setsumeisha no shimei," 96.

16. Furukawa Roppa, "Setsumeisha no kenkyū: sono san," *Katsudō gahō* 5.11 (November 1921): 97.

17. Takeda Kōkatsu, "Daben dametsuron: ge," *Katsudō gahō* 6.6 (June 1922): 122.

18. Uchida Shigebumi, "Hyōjō to setsumei," *Katsudō shashinkai* 13 (September 1910): 2.

19. Anderson, "Spoken Silents in the Japanese Cinema," 287–288.

20. Maruyama Kō, "Setsumeisha no gosōdan," *Katsudō kurabu* 3.8 (August 1920): 65.

21. Kaeriyama reportedly could not get *Sei no kagayaki* released for a year because of squabbles with Tenkatsu over his insistence that the film be shown without benshi, or if that was impossible, at least with a benshi who specialized in foreign films and did not use *kowairo*.

22. Katano, "Setsumeisha sonpairon no kōsatsu," 38.

23. This, for instance, was the position of *Kinema junpō*: "Setsumeisha shokun ni chūkokusu: 2," *Kinema junpō* 56 (11 February 1921): 1; and "Setsumeisha shokun ni chūkokusu: 3," *Kinema junpō* 57 (21 February 1921): 1. Even then, the journal suggested that, with the increasing English skills of Japanese and the potential for adding Japanese titles to foreign films, this reason for the benshi's existence, too, was conditional.

24. Takeda, "Setsumeisha no shimei," 96. Regarding Anderson's use of the term *katsuben*, note that here as elsewhere *katsuben* was considered a derogatory term. Kishirō calls it a "term of ridicule": "Benshi no shakaiteki kachi," *Kinema Record* 49 (July 1917): 324.

25. Furukawa, "Setsumeisha no kenkyū: sono san," 97.

26. Midorikawa Harunosuke, for instance, asked benshi if they were not embarrassed explaining a film that already had fully explained itself: "Mondai no mujimaku eiga *Natsukashi no izumi* o miru," *Katsudō gahō* 5.10 (October 1921): 69.

27. Hiroshi Komatsu and Charles Musser, "Benshi Search," *Wide Angle* 9.2 (1987): 72–90.

28. Eda Fushiki, "Katsudō shashin eishahō: zoku," *Katsudō shashinkai* 9 (May 1910): 5–6.

29. Eda Fushiki, "Katsudō shashin eishahō: zoku," *Katsudō shashinkai* 10 (June 1910): 14.

30. Yume Sōbei, *Eiga setsumei no kenkyū* (Tokyo: Chōyōsha, 1923), 58–59. As with most Japanese pseudonyms, it is hard to determine how the characters in "Yume Sōbei" should be read and thus how the name should be transliterated. The Diet Library offers the reading, "Yume Sōbei" (which Joseph Anderson follows), but the Waseda University Library renders it "Musō Hyōe" and the bibliographer Tsuji Kyōhei "Musō Byōe." Other Japanese libraries have rendered it "Musōbei," which I once used in an earlier publication. The pseudonym is likely taken from a character in a Takizawa Bakin story, and that character's name has been read in all these ways except "Yume Sōbei." In the end, I simply decided to follow the Diet Library's reading.

31. Ibid., 83.

32. Ibid., 84–85.

33. Ibid., 94.

34. A traditional form of epic oral storytelling popular in the Meiji era.

35. Nishimura Rakuten, "Benshi setsumeiburi no hensen," *Katsudō gahō* 1.3 (March 1917): 155–156.

36. Ikoma Raiyū, "Eigakai ni tsuite," *Katsudō gahō* 6.2 (February 1922): 42–45.

37. Somei Saburō, "Shashin o ikasu kushin," *Katsudō no sekai* 1.3 (March 1916): 41.

38. See Ishii Meika, "Nihon eigakai no genzai oyobi shōrai ni tsuite," in *Nihon eiga jigyō sōran: 1925-nen han*, ed. Ishii Bunsaku, 2nd ed. (Tokyo: Kokusai Eiga Tsūshinsha, 1926), 21–22.

39. Hansen, *Babel and Babylon*, 36.

40. Yoshimi Shun'ya, *Toshi no doramaturugī: Tōkyō sakariba no shakaishi* (Tokyo: Kōbundō, 1987), 210–211.

41. Tom Gunning, "'Now You See It, Now You Don't': The Temporality of the Cinema of Attractions," *Velvet Light Trap* 32 (Fall 1993): 6.

42. Komatsu Hiroshi, "Tennenshoku kara jun'eigageki e—Nihon eigashi ni okeru Tenkatsu no igi," in *Geijutsugaku kenkyū* 5 (1995), 36.

43. Komatsu and Frances Loden have even argued that the popularity of the benshi experience stemmed from the pleasure of listening, one that recalls the fetus's experience of listening to her mother's voice from inside the womb. See "Mastering the Mute Image: The Role of the Benshi in Japanese Silent Cinema," *Iris* 22 (Autumn 1996): 33–52. Such an account, however, does not provide us with an explanation of the different pleasures that must have accompanied benshi explanations as they shifted over time.

44. In countering attempts to see lecturers as inherently resistant to dominant cinematic modes, Tom Gunning calls on researchers to explore the feelings of comfort and familiarity that contact with human presence on stage must have brought to the film experience. See his "The Scene of Speaking: Two Decades of Discovering the Film Lecturer," *Iris* 27 (Spring 1999): 67–79.

45. See Noël Burch, *Life to Those Shadows*, ed. and trans. Ben Brewster (Berkeley: University of California Press, 1990), 244–247.

46. Komatsu, "Tennenshoku kara jun'eigageki e," 36–37.

47. Yume, *Eiga setsumei no kenkyū*, 66.

48. For instance, in a roundtable talk on the benshi, Hitomi Naoyoshi emphasized that there was only one possible meaning a benshi could relate: "If you cannot grasp the true idea of a film, you cannot correctly explain it. I believe, strictly speaking, that there is only one possible explanation by a benshi for a single film": "Eiga setsumeiburi gappyō," *Katsudō gahō* 7.3 (March 1923): 68.

49. Takeda, "Daben dametsuron: ge," 123. Yume Sōbei also stressed that "the progressive improvement of the film world will be realized only when producers, exhibitors, and benshi assume the attitude of gradually commanding the cinematically blind, who constitute the vast majority of film viewers": *Eiga setsumei no kenkyū*, 47.

50. Furukawa Roppa, "Setsumeisha no kenkyū: sono ni," *Katsudō gahō* 5.10 (October 1921): 93. Gunning notes that, when faced with lecturers diverging

from the film, American companies attempted to reassert control over their discourse by providing detailed scripts: *D. W. Griffith*, 93. In Japan, companies had to compose meticulous scripts to submit for the increasingly comprehensive censorship process, and these, often written in a colloquial style, frequently doubled as a guide to or basis of benshi narration. They could provide invaluable help, since many benshi had little time to prepare their narrations.

51. Furukawa Roppa, "Setsumeisha no kenkyū: sono yon," *Katsudō gahō* 5.12 (December 1921): 95.

52. Takeda, "Daben dametsuron: ge," 122.

53. See Gonda's history of the benshi: "Eiga setsumei no shinka to setsumei geijutsu no tanjō," in *Gonda Yasunosuke chōsakushū* (Tokyo: Bunwa Shobō, 1974), 4:405–415. Gonda traces the various forms of explanation that accompanied the stages of cinematic evolution. In his view, once film "resonate[d] with the real life of humanity," and "tried to grow out of being a toy of women and children and become an art for modern people," the age of explanation outside the film had passed. The art of film explanation was born, and it was not to differ from the text.

54. Gunning, *D. W. Griffith*, 93.

55. See, for instance, the comments by Ōta Kōchō at the roundtable: "Eiga setsumeiburi gappyō," 64.

56. One of the contradictions evident in the discourse of the Pure Film Movement is between the quest for illusion and the desire to study. Spectatorship had to be serious and studied as well as immersed in the film. Perhaps this is another source of hybridity in the Japanese situation.

57. "Katsudō shashingeki kyakushokujō no kenkyū: dai nikai," *Kinema Record* 28 (October 1915): 4.

58. Yamato Tetsurō, "Ongaku, setsumei, jimaku gairon," *Katsudō kurabu* 4.9 (September 1921): 95.

59. Midorikawa, "Mondai no mujimaku eiga," 69. In another essay, Midorikawa argues, "Considering the origin of the photoplay, I feel it is only common sense to completely eliminate everything except for the stillness and movement of illusion and the tone of the image": "Jimaku zakkan," *Katsudō kurabu* 4.7 (July 1921): 40.

60. Yamato, "Ongaku, setsumei, jimaku gairon," 95.

61. Ishii Meika, the editor of *Katsudō gahō*, offers this argument in the roundtable talk: "Eiga setsumeiburi gappyō," 64. Furukawa offers it too: "Setsumeisha no kenkyū: sono yon," 95.

62. Yume, *Eiga setsumei no kenkyū*, 21–22. Yume cites this as a reason why the benshi still existed at the time he was writing.

63. See Arai Saburō, "Setsumei haishi ronsha ni teisu," *Katsudō gahō* 5.5 (May 1921): 98.

64. Yume, *Eiga setsumei no kenkyū*, 49–50.

65. Tom Gunning has commented on my argument by underscoring the parallels between efforts in Japan to align the benshi with the diegetic project and attempts in the United States to make lecturers in the 1908–9 period keep

to the text and avoid the styles of fairground barkers. Personal communication, January 1, 1995.

66. See my "The Word before the Image: Criticism, the Screenplay, and the Regulation of Meaning in Prewar Japanese Film Culture," in *Word and Image in Japanese Cinema*, eds. Carole Cavanaugh and Dennis Washburn (Cambridge: Cambridge University Press, 2000), 3–35.

67. Midorikawa, "Jimaku zakkan," 41.

68. "Kenkyū: Eigageki to butaigeki: Katsudō shashin no kotoba ni tsuite," *Katsudō no sekai* 2.6 (June 1917): 13.

69. This could also be found in later Soviet montage theory, which emphasized an analogy between the shot inserted in a montage sequence and the word in a sentence. Japanese reformers, however, were more concerned with how to contain the threat of polyphony in the image though what was considered a more stable semiotic element, the word.

70. See my book *A Page of Madness: Cinema and Modernity in 1920s Japan* (Ann Arbor: Center for Japanese Studies, University of Michigan, 2008).

71. Christian Metz, *The Imaginary Signifier: Psychoanalysis and the Cinema* (Bloomington: Indiana University Press, 1982).

72. Burch, *Life to Those Shadows*, 250.

73. It would be fruitful to apply studies on sound in the cinema to the experience of watching a film with a benshi, especially in understanding how the benshi's sound in the theater was incorporated into the diegetic process.

74. Tachibana Takahiro, *Minshū goraku no kenkyū* (Tokyo: Keigansha, 1920), 135.

75. Article 10, section 12, clause 1 of the 1921 Osaka Carnival and Amusement Park Regulations, which covered cinema, required that the explanation "not cross into content apart from that of the Film." The regulations are reproduced in Terakawa Shin, *Eiga oyobi eigageki* (Osaka: Osaka Mainichi Shinbunsha, 1925), 234–248. Fukuoka also stipulated in its directions for administrating censorship regulations that the explanation submitted with the application to exhibit a film should not differ significantly from what the benshi actually said: Monbushō Futsū Gakumukyoku, *Zenkoku ni okeru katsudō shashin jōkyō chōsa* (Tokyo: Monbushō, 1921), appendix 23.

76. Hase Masato, "Ken'etsu no tanjō: Taishō-ki no keisatsu to katsudō shashin," *Eizōgaku* 53 (1994): 134–136.

77. Katano, "Setsumeisha sonpairon no kōsatsu," 39.

78. Takeda, "Daben dametsuron: ge," 122.

79. Anderson, "Spoken Silents in the Japanese Cinema," 287.

80. Yume, *Eiga setsumei no kenkyū*, 63–64.

81. Fujiki Hideaki, "The Advent of the Star System in Japanese Cinema Distribution," *Jōhō bunka kenkyū* 15 (2002): 1–22.

82. One of the best ways to possess these images was to buy star photographs, called *buromaido* in Japanese (or "bromides" in English). These portraits were extremely popular even into the 1960s, with many stores specializing

in selling only these images. The young editors of *Kinema junpō* actually scratched together the capital to print their journal by selling bromides.

83. Fujiki Hideaki, "Benshi as Stars: The Irony of the Popularity and Respectability of Voice Performers in Japanese Cinema," *Cinema Journal* 45.2 (Winter 2006): 68–84.

84. Fujiki, "Advent of the Star System."

85. The star persona constituted a problem that would later confront reformist critics, who saw it as a phenomenon that exceeded the diegesis and sometimes upset the illusion of the closed fictional world. While it was not as much of an issue in the 1910s—when the star system was still in its infancy— one can find occasional criticism of the kind of spectatorship (particularly by women) that was devoted more to adoring the stars than to paying attention to the narrative: see, for instance, "Gendai no fujin no mitaru katsudō shashin: dai nikai," *Kinema Record* 48 (June 1917): 178–179.

86. In discussing some of the demands of the film industry in 1929, Yanai Yoshio says that a proper interpretation of Japanese copyright law should make the film's director the holder (the author) of the copyright, except when the director was a contracted employee, in which case (and this was, of course, the case most of the time) the employer (i.e., the production company) would hold the copyright. Yanai Yoshio, *Katsudō shashin no hogo to torishimari* (Tokyo: Yūhikaku, 1929), 292. This would in fact eventually become the way film copyright was codified.

87. See, for instance, a report in *Katsudō shashinkai* on an "exhibition" of films in Tokyo at which the audience was asked to evaluate the author, players, and so on. In the text the terms for *author* and *screenwriter* are often used interchangeably: "At the Great Exhibition of the Hongoza Theatre," *Katsudō shashinkai* 11 (July 1910): 13.

88. In Japanese: "Satō Kōroku saku": "Tanisoko," *Kinema Record* 8 (February 1914): 28.

89. Many scripts were simply taken from theatrical productions, and the directors, if you could call them that, mostly read them aloud as the actors performed. The directors also sometimes doubled as cameramen. Until Tanaka Eizō was hired at Nikkatsu in 1917, there was only one "director" at the Mukō-jima studio, Oguchi Tadashi.

90. For more on the case of *Intolerance* and the director system, see Takinami Yūki, "Masumura Yasuzō kara Jun'eigageki Undō e: *Intoreransu* kōkai," in *Eizō hyōgen no orutanativ*, ed. Nishijima Norio (Tokyo: Shinwasha, 2006), 275–298.

91. See Ide, "Eigageki no honshitsu to enshutsuhō no itchi," 5. The review of Tenkatsu's *Ninjutsu jūyūshi* (Ten Brave Ninjas, 1917) from the same issue notes the rivalry between "Kobayashi Shōkai's Ōta and Tenkatsu's Edamasa" (p. 24). The latter is Edamasa Yoshirō, who worked on *Gorō Masamune kōshiden*. He, however, was officially still a cameraman at the time and did not earn the title of director until 1919.

92. See Okamura, "Ken'etsu kaishi ichinen no kan," *Katsudō shashin zasshi* 4.9 (September 1918): 35–36. *Kinema junpō* echoed this concern later

on when it asked censors "not to harm the dramatic appeal the director or original author tried to give to the audience": "Eiga ken'etsu hōshin ni taisuru kibō: ni," *Kinema junpō* 33 (11 June 11 1920): 1.

93. Hase, "Ken'etsu no tanjō," 133–134.

94. Gerow, "The Word before the Image."

95. The series, first called "Jinbutsu gattan" and later "Honpō eigakai no hitobito," initially focused on directors, but later branched out to include actors such as Onoe Matsunosuke, Iwata Yūkichi, and Sessue Hayakawa. Interestingly, there was one on the benshi Ōtsuji Jirō. The articles were not always favorable to their subjects, the one on Kaeriyama being particularly critical.

96. "Kaku arubeki katsudōkai," *Kinema Record* 20 (February 1915): 2.

97. See "Kakusha ikkagetsukan no eiga seizōdaka oyobi yūnyūdaka," *Katsudō no sekai* 2.9 (September 1917): 56–57. Note that the figures are for footage of film imported and footage of film produced per month, with foreign films accounting for 419,000 feet, and Japanese films 145,800 feet. In terms of the number of films shown at theaters, the magazine estimated there were twenty-four Japanese titles per month compared to ninety-six foreign films.

98. This would continue to be the case even after the 1910s, as new players like Shōchiku and Tōhō ran successful theatrical chains before entering into the filmmaking business.

99. "Ōbei gekidan to Tōyō no geki," *Kinema Record* 9 (March 1914): 3.

100. A 1920 *Miyako shinbun* article reports that seven was the record number of prints made of any Japanese film up until that time: "Shōchiku eiga o gaikoku e yushutsu," *Miyako shinbun*, November 12, 1920, reprinted in *SST*, 8:421. For an analysis of the economics and culture of producing only one print, see my "One Print in the Age of Mechanical Reproduction: Culture and Industry in 1910s Japan," *Screening the Past* 11 (2000), www.latrobe.edu.au/ screeningthepast/firstrelease/fr1100/agfr11e.htm.

101. Japanese theaters were, however, on average larger than their American counterparts. Theater attendance for 1919 was 72,809,000, or about 1.3 trips to the movies per year for every Japanese man, woman, and child (the population then was 55,033,000). Urban residents obviously went to the movies more often. It was also reported that by 1925 an average theater could sell about 40–50,000 tickets a month, or about 1,500 a day. Asakusa theaters could do much better. For these and other statistics, see Ishimaki Yoshio, "Honpō eiga gyōkai gaikan," *Nihon eiga jigyō sōran: 1925-nen han,* ed. Ishii Bunsaku, 2nd ed. (Tokyo: Kokusai Eiga Tsūshinsha, 1926), 32–35.

102. According to the magazine's estimates, the cost of positive film amounted to ¥360, the same as the price for negative stock. The article does not mention that the figures presume that only one print was made, but given that this was an age in which there were no retakes and no rushes, the costs of positive and negative film would be the same if only one print was made. See "Shinkyūha eiga no satsuei nissū to satsuei hiyō," *Katsudō no sekai* 2.9 (September 1917): 55. Note that it was World War I that caused drastic increases in the price of film stock.

103. "Jōsetsukan to kaisha to no kankei," *Katsudō no sekai* 2.9 (September 1917): 66–68.

104. See "Tokyo shinai jōsetsukan jūgyōinsū tōkeihyō," *Katsudō no sekai* 2.9 (September 1917): 64–65.

105. According to Nikkatsu's company history, the studio owned only 19 of its 169 theaters around 1913. This ratio did not change much by 1923, when the company owned only 30 of its 365 chain theaters. See *Nikkatsu shijūnenshi* (Tokyo: Nikkatsu Kabushiki Kaisha, 1952), 41–45.

106. The Nikkatsu history reports ¥903,992.60 as the total revenue for 1917 for directly owned or operated theaters, but only ¥831,499.99 for contract and rental theaters, which meant that the box office of the directly run theaters accounted for 49 percent of total revenue for 1917 (¥1,849,161.94). See the appendixes to *Nikkatsu shijūnenshi*.

107. It is unclear what the exact ratio of commission to contract theaters was, but Nikkatsu's records indicate that the revenue of contract theaters, which were in the majority, was less than that of commission theaters.

108. Information on the distribution system was obtained from "Jōsetsukan to kaisha to no kankei," 66–68.

109. Komatsu discusses the power of Asakusa's Taishōkan theater to order films from Tenkatsu and notes that even some benshi could order films: "Tennenshoku kara jun'eigageki e": 27–28.

110. Anderson, "Spoken Silents in the Japanese Cinema," 277–278.

111. As Charles Musser and Komatsu Hiroshi emphasize, the economic reason that lecturers disappeared from American theaters—such small theaters could not support the expense—were not as much a factor in Japan. See Komatsu and Musser, "Benshi Search," 86.

112. A point Komatsu and Musser stress: "Benshi Search," 86. Dym disagrees with them and me on this point, arguing that "inserting titles into just one print was probably less expensive than it was to employ benshi as verbal intertitle translators for every showing" (p. 158), especially if a film was to be shown all around the country and in the colonies. He does not, however, provide the details that prove his point. The particular structure of the industry has to be figured into calculations. Given that the majority of revenue for a film was obtained in the first few weeks in release in a small number of urban houses, the benefits obtained by spreading the cost of new intertitles among other theaters would be minimal. With celluloid being expensive, even making intertitles (negative and then positive prints) would be costly, and would not produce immediate, perceivable benefits, given that the benshi that mattered were those in that small number of big urban theaters, whose cost was already being spread over many patrons and many films. Especially given that commission theaters, and not the distributor, bore the cost of the benshi, and that these theaters were more prevalent outside urban centers, again the long-term costs of the benshi did not matter much for distributors. There were other costs of translating intertitles, such as time. With some theaters, such as Yokohama's

Odeon-za, priding themselves on showing films right off the boat—and with multiple distributors sometimes importing the same films and thus competing to get them into theaters first—time was money. All this does not mean that benshi were used simply because they were cheaper and faster; they produced benefits as well, by bringing in customers because they provided an extra attraction (like the live music or dance that silent-film houses often provided into the 1920s), as well as by augmenting a moviegoing culture centered on the local and particular movie hall that also reinforced the power of exhibitors.

113. Kaeriyama Norimasa, "Jiko o shireri ya," *Kinema Record* 19 (January 1915): 3.

114. Kaeriyama Norimasa, "Katsudō shashin no shakaiteki chii oyobi sekimu," *Kinema Record* 41 (November 1916): 3.

115. Echoing these hopes, *Kinema junpō*, in a series of editorials in 1920, prayed for the appearance of "practical people" *(jissaika)* in the industry, ones who would produce films both as *aikatsuka* and as "professionals": "Honpō seisaku eigakai no tame ni jissaika no shutsugen o inoru: hachi," *Kinema junpō* 42 (September 21, 1920): 1. Mori Tomita, the editor of *Katsudō hyōron*, also commented that, "as long as film industry people are showmen, there will be no capitalist who will safely invest his money": "Nihon eiga no kaigai hiyaku o teishōsu," *Katsudō hyōron* 2.5 (May 1919): 11.

116. *Kinema Record* called for "making clear the division of labor between production and exhibition": "Kaku arubeki katsudōkai," 2.

117. Kaeriyama, "Katsudō shashin no shakaiteki chii oyobi sekimu," 3.

118. Hansen, *Babel and Babylon*, 98.

119. Ibid., 84.

120. Suikō, "Nihon eiga kōjōsaku ni tsuite: dai ikkai," *Kinema Record* 44 (February 1917): 60.

121. See Kaeriyama, "Katsudō shashin no shakaiteki chii oyobi sekimu," 3.

122. This was suggested in a number of *Kinema Record* editorials, including Kaeriyama, "Jiko o shireri ya," 3; and "Ōbei gekidan to Tōyō no geki," 3. *Katsudō no sekai* offered the same suggestion in "Eigageki to butaigeki," *Katsudō no sekai* 2.9 (September 1917): 36–40; as did Mori Tomita: "Nihon eiga no kaigai hiyaku o teishōsu," 10–11.

123. Mori, "Nihon eiga no kaigai hiyaku o teishōsu," 11.

124. Kaeriyama's letter to Kobayashi is reproduced in Yoshida Chieo, *Mō hitotsu no eigashi* (Tokyo: Jiji Tsūshinsha, 1978), 95.

125. There were earlier cases of Japanese films being exported. *Kinema Record* in 1914 reported some earlier unsuccessful efforts ("Ōbei gekidan to Tōyō no geki," 3), and Bernardi relates other cases of some *shinpa* and an Onoe Matsunosuke film: Joanne Bernardi, *Writing in Light: The Silent Scenario and the Japanese Pure Film Movement* (Detroit: Wayne State University Press, 2001), 138.

126. For more on this and other aspects of Shōchiku's entry into film, see the company's history: *Shōchiku kyūjūnenshi* (Tokyo: Shōchiku Kabushiki Kaisha, 1985), 230–235.

127. Quoted in Joseph L. Anderson and Donald Richie, *The Japanese Film: Art and Industry,* expanded ed. (Princeton, NJ: Princeton University Press, 1982), 41.

128. Reported in *Nikkatsu shijūnenshi,* 44.

129. Shōchiku's efforts to export its second film were reported in the paper: "Shōchiku eiga o gaikoku e yushutsu," *Miyako shinbun,* November 12, 1920.

130. Ishii, "Nihon eigakai no genzai oyobi shōrai ni tsuite," 3.

131. Ishimaki, "Honpō eiga gyōkai gaikan," 46.

132. Ibid., 33–34.

133. The revenue for directly run theaters was ¥2,157,737.20, while that for the rest amounted to ¥2,501,163.33, a gap that would grow bigger in the coming years.

134. An indication of the incompleteness of the transformation is the fact that critics in 1925 were still urging greater separation between exhibitors and producers: see Ishii, "Nihon eigakai no genzai oyobi shōrai ni tsuite," 4.

135. For the central role Tōhō played in the formation of a Fordist industry, see Fujii Jinshi, "Nihon eiga no 1930-nendai," *Eizōgaku* 62 (1999): 21–37.

136. See my "Eigahō to iu eigaron," in *Eigahō kaisetsu/Dai 74-kai Teikoku Gikai eiga hōan giji gaiyō,* Nihon eigaron gensetsu taikei, dai 1-ki: Senjika no eigatōseiki, ed. Makino Mamoru (Tokyo: Yumani Shobō, 2003), 8:589–607.

5. MANAGING THE INTERNAL

1. Makino Mamoru's history of prewar film censorship in Japan offers a fountain of information on the various regulations that existed and their background. I cite the original sources from the time, but I also cite Makino's voluminous work, which includes reprints of many of the regulations as well as a few magazine articles about censorship from the era. See his *Nihon eiga ken'etsushushi* (Tokyo: Pandora, 2003).

2. Gilles Deleuze, *Foucault,* trans. Sean Hand (Minneapolis: University of Minnesota Press, 1986), 29.

3. See Richard S. Randall's review of early censorship law in the United States in his *Censorship of the Movies: The Social and Political Control of a Mass Medium* (Madison: University of Wisconsin Press, 1968).

4. See Richard Abel, "Booming the Business: The Historical Specificity of Early French Cinema," in *Silent Film,* ed. Richard Abel (New Brunswick, NJ: Rutgers University Press, 1996), 116–117.

5. The "Katsudō Shashin Torishimari Naiki" is reproduced in Terakawa Shin, *Eiga oyobi eigageki* (Osaka: Osaka Mainichi Shinbunsha, 1925), 230–233.

6. Terakawa emphasizes that these guidelines, because they were not official regulations, were not as strictly observed as official ones: ibid., 233.

7. Yoshiyama Kyokkō, *Nihon eigakai jibutsu kigen* (Tokyo: Shinema to Engeisha, 1933), 124.

8. Okudaira Yasuhiro, "Eiga to ken'etsu," in *Kōza Nihon eiga,* ed. Imamura Shōhei et al. (Tokyo: Iwanami Shoten, 1985), 2:309.

9. The *Osaka asahi shinbun* reported that the Osaka police were very reluctant to ban *Zigomar* because of the difficulty of establishing standards: if *Zigomar* could be banned for showing criminal methods, by the same logic, so should *Chūshingura*. The paper stated that Osaka could not leave the film alone once Tokyo banned it: "Eiga Zigomar no kinshi to Osaka," *Ōsaka asahi shinbun*, October 12, 1912, reprinted in *SST*, 1:73.

10. The regulations are reprinted in the Ministry of Education's 1921 national survey of the moving pictures: Monbushō Futsū Gakumukyoku, *Zenkoku ni okeru katsudō shashin jōkyō chōsa* (Tokyo: Monbushō, 1921), appendix 6–7.

11. The Aomori regulations are reproduced in *Zenkoku ni okeru katsudō shashin jōkyō chōsa*, appendix 12–13.

12. See Sarashina Genzō's history of film in Hokkaido: *Hokkaidō katsudō shashin shōshi* (Sapporo: Kushima Kōgyō, 1960), 43.

13. See, for instance, Article 32 of the 1900 Tokyo Theater Regulations: Takazawa Shofū, *Gendai engeki sōran*, 2nd ed. (Tokyo: Bunseisha, 1919), 211–229.

14. Okudaira, "Eiga to ken'etsu," 306.

15. "Sekai shijō ni taisuru Nihon katsudōkai," *Kinema Record* 12 (June 1914): 5.

16. Cited in "Furyō shōnen: ichi," *Tokyo asahi shinbun*, December 21, 1915, p. 6.

17. See "Katsudō shashin no dageki," *Tokyo asahi shinbun*, August 13, 1913, p. 5.

18. "Furyō shōnen: ichi."

19. "Eiga shikenkan to kōgyōsha," *Kinema Record* 37 (July 1916): 293.

20. "Katsudō shashin no torishimari ga genjū ni natta," *Tokyo nichi nichi shinbun*, June 27, 1913, reprinted in *TNJ*, 1:87.

21. Quoted in "Katsudō shashin no dageki."

22. In August 1913, there were reportedly forty-three movie theaters in Tokyo and twenty-seven applications for new construction: "Katsudō no zō-setsu wa kinshi," *Tokyo nichi nichi shinbun*, July 8, 1913 (*TNJ*, 1:87). The decision by the head of the Public Peace Section may have slowed down the spread of theaters, but did not stop it: there were about sixty-six theaters by 1917.

23. Sarashina, *Hokkaidō katsudō shashin shōshi*, 42.

24. See the reports from the *Osaka mainichi* reproduced in *TNJ*, 2:338–340. Interestingly, the first case that occurred in Okayama involved men in their twenties who had only read Zigomar novels—no mention was made of their connection to film. Popular detective novels were also criticized, but as the hysteria increased, cinema became the main target of reproach.

25. "Heigai ōkii katsudō shashin," *Yorozu chōhō*, August 10, 1916 (*SST*, 5:266).

26. For the case of Sapporo, where the prohibition took place in 1917; see Sarashina, *Hokkaidō katsudō shashin shōshi*, 44.

27. Such was the argument of the school principal Takaoka Ryūho: "Kodomo to katsudō shashin," *Yomiuri shinbun*, April 28, 1916 (*SST*, 5:145).

28. "Kodomo ni wa yūekina katsudō shashin," *Yomiuri shinbun*, March 8, 1915 (*SST*, 4:95).

29. See, for instance, an article written by one Suikō: "Tōzen kaitakusaru beki genka no waga kinema-kai ni tsuite," *Kinema Record* 40 (October 1916): 429.

30. According to Tanaka Jun'ichirō, the Educational Moving Picture Society (Kyōiku Katsudō Shashinkai) seemed at first just to use the word *education* as a way to reassure parents, since the films shown were not any different from the actualities shown at other theaters. Afterward, Sugita formed the Nihon Firumu Kyōkai (Japan Film Association), in 1903 (though production started years later), to create health and educational films. See Tanaka, *Nihon kyōiku eiga hattatsushi* (Tokyo: Kagyūsha, 1979), 28.

31. Reported by Oka Shikei, "Katsudō shashin no zen'yō," *Kinema Record* 35 (May 1916): 196.

32. For an analysis of these regulations, as well as for a history of the Ministry of Education's involvement in the cinema, see Nishimoto Hajime, "Eiga to Monbushō: (jō)," *Hokkaidō Daigaku Kyōiku Gakubu kiyō* 67 (1995): 259–292. See also Makino Mamoru, "On the Conditions of Film Censorship in Japan before Its Systematization," in *In Praise of Film Studies*, ed. Aaron Gerow and Abé Mark Nornes (Yokohama: Kinema Club, 2001), 46–67; and Tanaka, *Nihon kyōiku eiga hattatsushi*, 29–31.

33. For a copy of the 1913 provisions, see *TNJ*, vol. 1, appendix 75.

34. Reported in "Katsudō shashin torishimari," *Miyako shinbun*, May 10, 1914 (*SST*, 2:150).

35. *Kyōiku to katsudōshashin* (Tokyo: Monbushō Futsū Gakumukyoku, 1918).

36. "Kodomo to katsudō shashin," *Yomiuri shinbun*, March 12, 1914 (*SST*, 2:87).

37. "Heigai ōkii katsudō shashin," *Yorozu chōhō*, August 10, 1916.

38. Listed by Oka, "Katsudō shashin no zen'yō," 196.

39. Sandaya Hiraku, *Katsudō shashin ni kansuru chōsa* (n.p., privately published, [1915?]), 20.

40. Ibid., 16, 19.

41. One copy of the resolution is reproduced in Terakawa, *Eiga oyobi eigageki*, 251–252. A slightly different version of the resolution is reported in "Katsudō shashin no torishimari," *Kokumin shinbun*, March 1, 1917 (*SST*, 5:79).

42. Gonda used the same survey results to offer a slightly different analysis, titled "Katsudō shashin to tōkeiteki kansatsu," in the June and July 1918 issues of *Tōkei shūshi* (Statistical Anthology). Both surveys were published in book form in Gonda's *Minshū goraku mondai* (Tokyo: Dōjinsha Shoten, 1921).

43. Ide Tetsujo, the editor of *Katsudō no sekai*, cites the general opinion that the Imperial Education Association's resolution and corresponding research was one of the main impetuses behind the regulations: "Teikoku Kyōiku Kaichō Sawayanagi Masatarō-shi ni teisu," *Katsudō no sekai* 2.11 (November 1917): 4.

44. Ibid., 6.

45. Gonda reiterated in *Katsudō no sekai* that the benefits of film out-weighed its harm, and that he feared that too strict censorship would lead to fundamental errors: "Ken'etsu no kenzen," *Katsudō no sekai* 2.10 (October 1917): 13.

46. Sawayanagi Masatarō, "Dōzo hanshō o shimesazaro," *Katsudō no sekai* 2.11 (November 1917): 9.

47. "Keishichō demo katsudō shashin no torishimari," *Tokyo asahi shinbun*, December 6, 1916, p. 5.

48. "Chikaku kuru katsudō torishimari kisoku," *Yorozu chōhō*, December 7, 1916 (*SST*, 4:429).

49. "Keishichō demo katsudō shashin no torishimari."

50. "Katsudō shashin no shin torishimarihō," *Hōchi shinbun*, December 15, 1916 (*SST*, 4:450).

51. "Chikaku kuru katsudō torishimari kisoku."

52. "Katsudō shashin no shin torishimarihō."

53. See an editorial note at the beginning of an essay by Numata in *Katsudō gahō* 1.5 (May 1917): 170. For more on Numata and early censorship, see Makino Mamoru, "Ken'etsu to Nihon eiga no modanizumu," in *Nihon eiga to modanizumu: 1920–1930* (Tokyo: Riburopōto, 1991), 142–149.

54. "Katsudō shashin wa shakaiteki koji," *Katsdō shashin zasshi* 3.2 (February 1917): 4–11.

55. "Katsudō torishimari iyoiyo kōfu," *Tokyo asahi shinbun*, July 12, 1917, p. 5.

56. A copy of the regulations can be found in Terakawa, *Eiga oyobi eigageki*, 232–245. In his version, it is titled "Katsudō Shashin Torishimari Kisoku" (Moving Picture Regulations), while other sources such as Okudaira call it "Katsudō Shashin Kōgyō Torishimari Kisoku" (Moving Picture Exhibition Regulations).

57. "Katsudō shashin kōgyō torishimari kisoku," *Jiji shinpō*, July 13, 1917 (*TNJ*, 3:85). Asakusa's Sixth District (Rokku) at times had more than ten theaters in a several-hundred-meter section of its main avenue during the Taishō era. Okamura Shihō, editor of *Katsudō shashin zasshi*, complained that the restrictions were insufficient and urged the police to shorten the limit on program times even more: "Katsudō shashin gyōsha hogo hōan," *Katsudō shashin zasshi* 4.1 (January 1918): 4. Gonda reports that, with Asakusa theaters doing an average of three shows a day on weekdays, four hours was the practical limit on program length. On weekends, however, programs would often be shortened to two and a half hours to enable four showings, either by cutting out a film or upping the projection speed *GYC*, 1:82–85. Of course not all theaters were the same: the Denkikan, for example, featured four showings of a three-hour-and-five-minute program every day during the week of April 7, 1916.

58. So said a Tenkatsu official in "Katsudō shashin kōgyō torishimari kisoku."

59. The lawyer Suzuki Seibi, for instance, pointed out these inconsistencies in his "Shinchōrei wa fugōri da," *Katsudō shashin zasshi* 3.11 (November

1917): 29. Another observer, the novelist Iwaya Sazanami, mentioned that contemporary "high-collar" theaters were as dark as movie theaters: "Osshu eiga ni tsuite," *Katsudō gahō* 1.10 (October 1917): 3.

60. "Fukei dōhansha no nyūjō o kyokaseyo," *Katsudō shashin zasshi* 3.10 (October 1917): 21; or Suzuki, "Shinchōrei wa fugōri da," 29.

61. See "Katsudō shashin zutsū hachimaki," *Tokyo asahi shinbun*, August 7, 1917, p. 5.

62. Tanaka Jun'ichirō, in his history of Japanese cinema, described police officials as treating cinema like prostitution: *Nihon eiga hattatsushi* (Tokyo: Chūō Kōronsha, 1980), 1:405.

63. See "Goraku no ninkimono daga, eigakan wa fueisei," *Jiji shinpō,* June 30, 1913 (*TNJ*, 1:87).

64. So claimed a representative of Tokiwa Kōgyō: "Kōgyōkai no ichidai haran," *Yomiuri shinbun,* May 31, 1917 (*SST*, 5:184).

65. *GYC*, 1:77–86. Even though Sandaya questionably interprets the problem of child viewing represented by his data, the figures themselves do not show minors forming the majority of theater audiences, except in one theater in Okayama and one in Nagoya, and only on Sunday. For the rest of the week, children composed about 20–25 percent of the audience in Nagoya, 42–47 percent in Okayama, and 30–35 percent in Kanazawa. (Since he did not obtain his results from directly polling the audience, but rather used police statistics and questionnaires given to theater owners, he admits to the fact that these sources offered different definitions of "children," the upper limit ranging from twelve to sixteen years of age.) One reality his figures seem to show is that most theaters did more than two or three times as much business on Sundays and holidays than on regular days. That one day, when children did occupy more of the seats, could account for nearly 40 percent of weekly attendance. See Sandaya, *Katsudō shashin ni kansuru chōsa,* 5–9.

66. There is the issue of how much income was actually earned from child customers. Some theaters did have a reduced-price policy for children, which would have lessened the economic blow caused by their absence, but others featured a price schedule divided by class of seating, and some used both price schedules. At the very least, it seems the industry suffered financially as much from the loss of family business and other "respectable" adult customers scared away by the commotion as from the loss of child customers.

67. See "Shinken o mushishita hōrei," *Katsudō shashin zasshi* 3.11 (November 1917): 26–27.

68. *Nikkatsu shijūnenshi* (Tokyo: Nikkatsu Kabushiki Kaisha, 1952), 45.

69. This was the public comment by two industry officials: "Asakusa wa tachiikanu to, Kukai ga tatsu," *Miyako shinbun,* September 4, 1917, p. 5 (reprinted in Yano Seiichi, ed., *Miyako shinbun geinō shiryō shūsei: Taishō hen* [Tokyo: Hakusuisha, 1991], 177, hereafter referred to as *MSGS*).

70. The quote was repeated in a *Katsudō shashin zasshi* article: "Shinken o mushishita hōrei," 27.

71. The standards were never made public at the time. Nishimoto lists some of the guidelines that were later reported by Sekino Yoshio in 1942, and remarks, "It is certain only that the content of grade B films was severely slanted more toward 'education' than 'entertainment'": "Eiga to Monbushō: (jō)," 267. According to Sekino, authorities were watching out for films that: (1) dealt with romance; (2) prevented children from studying; (3) obstructed school education and caused disrespect for teachers, (4) went against a good home life; (5) invited mischief; and (6) damaged the intelligence of children. Clearly, these were very broad and vague standards. *Eiga kyōiku no riron* (Tokyo: Shōgakkan, 1942), 253.

72. Many complained that censorship's "no-harm policy" ignored the entertainment value of the film and thus resulted in boring movies. See, for instance, a statement by the industry group Katsudō Shashin Dōshikai, "Shin ni sonbō no toki," *Katsudō no sekai* 2.10 (October 1917): 10. See also the complaints of a lower school principal, Katō Susumu, in a collection of comments by school officials: "Jidō firumu ni tsuite: Jidō kyōikuka no jissaidan," *Katsudō no sekai* 2.11 (November 1917): 19.

73. Not a few commentators, protesting this policy, felt the need to argue that children needed to be shown evil events and individuals if they were to learn the difference between good and bad. See Suzuki, "Shinchōrei wa fugōri da," 29; or Mori Tomita, "Katsudō shashin nomi tokushu no kensoku o nasu ka," *Katsudō hyōron* 2.1 (January 1919): 2.

74. Such was the fate of a film called *Debu-san* ("Fatty"): "Hiradoma o fūfu seki ni," *Hōchi shinbun*, August 1, 1917 (*SST*, 5:266).

75. "Shinken o mushishita hōrei," 26.

76. One exhibitor cited audiences of children paying only half the admission fee as justification for raising prices in April 1918: "Asakusa kōgyōjō no neage," April 22, 1918, *Hōchi shinbun* (*SST*, 6:138–139).

77. This is a point made by the Home Ministry film censor Yanai Yoshio in explaining how the 1917 regulations placed an undue economic burden on the film industry: *Katsudō shashin no hogo to torishimari* (Tokyo: Yūhikaku, 1929), 870–871. Hiroshima apparently instituted its own A/B system in 1920 *after* the Tokyo experiment had ended.

78. The industry apparently tried its luck with bosses from the Seiyūkai and other political organizations: "Katsudō shashin zutsū hachimaki," 5.

79. See "Asakusa wa tachiikanu to, Kukai ga tatsu," *Miyako shinbun*, September 4, 1917. The Ward Council was particularly concerned about the decline in revenue from business taxes and the loss of customers for the other establishments in Asakusa, such as restaurants and bars.

80. The only theater, it seems, that immediately began showing grade B films was Tokyo Kurabu, a theater not owned by any of the film companies but by Negishi Kōgyō, a theatrical company which ran a unique exhibition system in Asakusa's sixth ward: for one price, one could enter any of Negishi's three adjoining theaters and, using the hall joining the three, move from one to the

other. Beyond the movie house Tokyo Kurabu, there was also the Kinryūkan, which presented Asakusa Opera, and the Tokiwaza, which specialized in *shinpa* theater and *rensageki*. This policy underlined the irony that children, who were banned from seeing love stories in the movie theater across the street, could enter Tokyo Kurabu and move to the Kinryūkan to watch the half-naked legs of opera revue girls. This example was specifically cited by some in arguing that the A/B grading system was a failure: Yanai, *Katsudō shashin no hogo to torishimari*, 866.

81. This is related in the Tokyo police department's own history: *Keishichō-shi: Taishō-hen* (Tokyo: Keishichōshi Hensan Iinkai, 1960), 663.

82. For a summary of the incident and its relation to D.W. Griffith's works, see Tom Gunning, *D.W. Griffith and the Origins of American Narrative Film* (Urbana: University of Illinois Press, 1991), 151–156.

83. Yanai, *Katsudō shashin no hogo to torishimari*, 870–871.

84. The numbers are taken from a list printed in *Katsudō no sekai* 2.9 (September 1917): 60–62. The national total excludes the twenty-two theaters listed for the Japanese colonies of Korea, Taiwan, and so on. The editors appended a proviso warning that the theaters which had not responded to the survey were not included in the list. As a comparison, note that the Friends of the Moving Pictures listed sixty-six theater members, and that Gonda counted sixty-nine theaters in Tokyo at the end of March 1917, out of which only fifty-six were film-only theaters, the rest featuring *rensageki* (*GYC*, 1:75).

85. For an elaboration of this issue, see my "One Print in the Age of Mechanical Reproduction: Culture and Industry in 1910s Japan," *Screening the Past* 11 (2000), www.latrobe.edu.au/screeningthepast/firstrelease/fr1100/agfr11e.htm.

86. The police repealed the A/B system in part because they admitted that it caused undue harm to exhibitors: "Kubetsu teppai," *Tokyo asahi shinbun*, November 16, 1919, p. 5.

87. "Shinkisoku go no katsudō shashin," *Miyako shinbun*, August 5, 1917, p. 3 (*MSGS*, 172).

88. Ōhata, "Mushiro shigyō no tame," *Katsudō no sekai:* 2.10 (October 1917): 9–10.

89. Quoted in "Katsudō shashin zutsū hachimaki," 5.

90. Ironically, one of the few to argue that strict censorship might retard the growth of film was the former minister of education Takata Sanae. He approved of the A/B grading system, but feared the overzealous censorship of adult films would hurt not only film but literature as well: "Geijitsujō no sonshitsu," *Katsudō no sekai* 2.10 (October 1917): 17.

91. "Fukei dōhansha no nyūjō o kyokaseyo," 22.

92. Ide Tetsujo, "Hō ni arazushite hito ni sonsu," *Katsudō no sekai* 2.10 (October 1917): 2–8.

93. See Okamoto Kidō, "Tōjisha no funki," *Katsudō no sekai* 2.10 (October 1917): 15.

94. Iwaya, "Osshu eiga ni tsuite," 3.

95. "Shinchōrei tai tōgyōsha mondai," *Kinema Record* 50 (October 1917): 3.

96. Okamura Shihō, "Ken'etsu kaishi dai-ichinen no kan," *Katsudō shashin zasshi* 4.9 (September 1918): 34–37.

97. For more on Tanaka at Nikkatsu, see Okada Susumu, *Nihon eiga no rekishi* (Tokyo: Daviddosha, 1967), 128–131. Okamura Shihō praised *Nogi Shōgun* in his review of the grade B system: "Osshu kōgyō no fushin o tanzu," *Katsudō shashin zasshi* 4.11 (November 1918): 34–37. By 1918, cinema was already tame enough—and its power sufficiently recognized—that producers could begin making films on the life of General Nogi for children.

98. I have done the same thing elsewhere with the 1939 Film Law. For my discussion of the debates on this law, see: "Eigahō to iu eigaron," in *Eigahō kaisetsu/Dai 74-kai Teikoku Gikai eiga hōan giji gaiyō*, Nihon eigaron gensetsu taikei, dai 1-ki: Senjika no eigatoseiki, vol. 8, ed. Makino Mamoru (Tokyo: Yumani Shobo, 2003), 589–607.

99. Okudaira, "Eiga to ken'etsu," 308.

100. Numata used this logic in the interview recorded in "Keishichō demo katsudō shashin no torishimari."

101. See Komatsu Hiroshi, "Tennenshoku kara jun'eigageki e—Nihon eigashi ni okeru Tenkatsu no igi," *Geijutsugaku kenkyū* 5 (1995): 30–31.

102. See an introduction to one of these actresses, Miho Matsuko, in *Kinema Record* 22 (April 1915): 15.

103. "Katsudō shashingeki kyakushokujō no kenkyū: dai ikkai," *Kinema Record* 27 (September 1915): 3.

104. Okamoto Kidō, "Katsudō shashingeki no kyakuhon," *Katsudō no sekai* 2.7 (July 1917): 13.

105. "Katsudō shashin kōgyō torishimari kisoku."

106. "Shinkisoku ni taisuru eigyōsha no iken," *Miyako shinbun*, July 13, 1917, p. 5 (*MSGS*, 168). J. L. Anderson claims that *rensageki* were "outlawed" in 1917 by the government, but he is incorrect on this point ("Spoken Silents in the Japanese Cinema; or, Talking to Pictures: Essaying the *Katsuben*, Contextualizing the Texts," *Reframing Japanese Cinema*, ed. Arthur Noletti Jr. and David Desser [Bloomington: Indiana University Press, 1992], 271). Komatsu states that Kobayashi Shōkai eventually went under because of the blow to *rensageki*: Komatsu, "Tennenshoku kara jun'eigageki e," 32.

107. "Katsudō shashin no atarashii torishimari kisoku," *Miyako shinbun*, February 27, 1917, p. 5 (*MSGS*, 149).

108. "Katsudō shashin kōgyō torishimari kisoku."

109. Okamura, "Katsudō shashin gyōsha hogo hōan," 3.

110. This is the description of the billboards for theaters specializing in Japanese films found in Gonda's report: "The colors are so garish one cannot recognize any sort of aesthetic sense. It seems that the unnatural composition, which exaggerates the content of the picture, cannot help but intimidate the viewer." *GYC*, 1:88. It is interesting to note that two years earlier, the garishly colorful illustrations in children's magazines and picture books had also become a problem, both for being overstimulating and for having adverse

effects on young minds. See "Kodomomuke no zasshi," *Kokumin shinbun,* January 28, 1915 (*SST,* 3:42); and "Zokuaku kiwamaru ezōshirui," *Yomiuri shinbun,* February 25, 1915 (*SST,* 3:83–84). This kind of critical discourse on popular visual style serves as one background for the construction of the sleek, modern, and mass commercial style of the 1920s and 1930s. (The popularity of children's story *manga* would come later, with *Nonkina tōsan* in 1921 and *Norakuro* in 1931.)

111. American theaters also apparently eliminated "garish posters" and "noisy barkers" in an effort to upgrade the industry, though their effort was in most instances voluntary: Eileen Bowser, *The Transformation of Cinema: 1907–1915,* History of the American Cinema, vol. 2. (Berkeley: University of California Press, 1990), 39.

112. "Katsudōya no hikyō," *Miyako shinbun,* August 18, 1917, p. 5 (*MSGS,* 174).

113. The comments are part of a mock conversation on the regulations written by Shinoyama Gin'yō: "Shukuhai," *Katsudō gahō* 1.10 (October 1917): 40.

114. Hase Masato, "Ken'etsu no tanjō: Taishō-ki no keisatsu to katsudō shashin," *Eizōgaku* 53 (1994): 133.

115. See Kayano Yatsuka, *Kindai Nihon no dezain bunkashi: 1868–1926* (Tokyo: Firumu Ātosha, 1992), 380–382.

116. Hatsuda Tōru, in his history of modern space in Tokyo, emphasizes how the shift from early movie theater design—which had spectators either sit on tatami mats just like in a traditional theater or stand on a dirt floor—to elaborate Western-style buildings starting with the Fujikan in 1911, not only helped distinguish the structures from the barracklike shacks of their *misemono* counterparts, but it also produced a more respectable atmosphere capable of attracting the middle class: *Modan toshi no kūkan hakubutsukan—Tōkyō* (Tokyo: Shōkokusha, 1995), 109–113. The trend toward smart and clean design continued with high-class Konparukan in the fashionable Ginza in 1920 and post-1923 theaters such as the truly modern Aoikan (designed in part by Murayama Tomoyoshi), the Shinema Parasu, and Shinjuku's Musashinokan. For more on Murayama and the Aoikan, see Iwamoto Kenji, "Kikai jidai no bigaku to eiga," in *Nihon eiga to modanizumu* (Tokyo: Riburopōto, 1991), 200–205.

117. "Katsudō shashin no shinkisoku," *Yomiuri shinbun,* July 13, 1917 (*SST,* 5:238).

118. It is interesting to note that censorship screenings in police headquarters were conducted with a benshi. The assumption was still that benshi's performances, involving the reading of an approved benshi script, did not differ from place to place or from individual to individual.

119. Hase, "Ken'etsu no tanjō," 130.

120. A *Katsudō gahō* reporter offered the example that, while children were prohibited from seeing a filmed biography of Sakura Sōgorō, the leader of an Edo-era peasant rebellion, they could view the theater piece on the same subject playing in the city: "Rokku no katsudōgai yori," *Katsudō gahō* 1.10 (October 1917): 37–38.

121. Mori Tomita, the editor of *Katsudō hyōron*, promised to devote his journal to the elimination of such "misunderstandings": "Katsudō shashin nomi tokushu no kensoku o nasu ka," 2.

122. Such were the words of a *Jiji shinpō* reporter: "Goraku no ninkimono daga, eigakan wa fueisei."

123. Ōhata quoted in "Shinken o mushishita hōrei," 24.

124. "Katsudō shashin no kyōikujō ni riyōseyo," *Yomiuri shinbun*, March 2, 1917 (*SST,* 5:81). Dr. Sandaya, it seems, was not too expert on the length of films at the time: features were already much longer than he describes.

125. "Katsudō shashin shakai kyōiku ōyō: dai-go kai," *Kinema Record* 46 (April 1917): 167.

126. Tom Gunning, "'Now You See It, Now You Don't': The Temporality of the Cinema of Attractions," *Velvet Light Trap* 32 (Fall 1993): 6.

127. Ibid., 11.

128. Article 42 of the 1900 Tokyo Theater Regulations is devoted to audience behavior, but only insofar as it bans spectators from creating their own obscenity. There is no hint in the regulations of how obscenity in the play might work on the audience.

129. Akashi Takaichirō, "Katsudō shashin no riyō narabi ni torishimari ni tsuite," *Katsudō no sekai* 2.6 (June 1917): 2.

130. "Gendai no fujin no mitaru katsudō shashin: dai-ni kai," *Kinema Record* 48 (June 1917): 279.

131. Ibid.

132. Ide, "Hō ni arazushite hito ni sonsu," 5–6.

133. "Shinchōrei tai tōgyōsha mondai," 2.

134. See an interview with Kuroda in "Rataiga kinshi wa bōkyō to keisatsu o hihan," *Jiji shinpō,* December 12, 1897, reprinted in *Meiji nyūsu jiten* (Tokyo: Mainichi Komyunikēshonzu, 1985–1986), 5:139 (hereafter referred to as *MNJ*).

135. As far as I can determine, the separate room was not set up at the 1896 exhibition, but was in place by at least 1903 for that year's Shirabakai Exhibition. See Seomu, "Shirabakai mangen," *Kokumin shinbun,* October 11, 1903 (*MNJ,* 7:629–630).

136. Ōhata, the head of the Public Peace Section who issued the film regulations, told the papers he would never consider Western standards in evaluating Japanese works, "because they are completely different from our national polity." Nude works, he asserted, would "destroy the nation" and affronted Japanese common sense: nudity, either in person or in a painting, is impermissible. Ohata's comments reveal that he at least refused to distinguish between painting and reality in determining obscenity: obscenity was obscenity. See "Rataiga wa rataiga," *Yomiuri shinbun,* June 6, 1917 (*SST,* 5:192–193).

137. Karatani Kōjin, *Origins of Modern Japanese Literature,* ed. and trans. Brett de Bary (Durham, NC: Duke University Press, 1993), 28–29.

138. Hase, "Ken'etsu no tanjō," 133–134. Hase describes filmgoing by the working class, fundamentally physical in its emphasis on eating, drinking, and

talking, as a kind of "obscene atmosphere"—or, at least, that is how contemporary reformers tended to characterize it (p. 132).

139. Compare the motion picture regulations quoted above with, for instance, Article 35 of the 1900 Theater Regulations, which were the relevant statutes for theater in Tokyo up until 1921: "From before sunset and until audiences disperse, lights should be placed during performances so that the seats and the aisles will not be in darkness."

140. Hase, "Ken'etsu no tanjō," 134.

141. Hansen distinguishes between a public sphere, where the audience operates through a mode of collective experience that mediates between individual perceptions, and the concept of the spectator, who is singular, homogenized, and molded on the pattern of the individual consumer. Miriam Hansen, *Babel and Babylon: Spectatorship and American Silent Film* (Cambridge, MA: Harvard University Press, 1991), 8–15, 84–86.

142. Miriam Silverberg, "Constructing a New Cultural History of Prewar Japan," in *Japan in the World*, ed. Masao Miyoshi and H. D. Harootunian (Durham, NC: Duke University Press, 1993), 127.

143. Furukawa Roppa reports this as an obstacle to efforts by reformers to eliminate the benshi: "Setsumeisha no kenkyū: yon," *Katsudō gahō* 5.12 (December 1921): 95.

144. Reported in Okamura, "Osshu kōgyō no fushin o tanzu," 35–36.

145. Matsui Shōyō, "Katsudō shashin ni tsuite," *Katsudō gahō* 1.10 (October 1917): 5.

146. Hiruta mentioned this in his response to the survey of Tokyo lower school principals conducted by *Katsudō no sekai*: "Jidō firumu ni tsuite: Jidō kyōikuka no jitsurokudan," 15–16.

147. Hansen, *Babel and Babylon*, 96. See also Tom Gunning, *D. W. Griffith and the Origins of American Narrative Film*, 91–94.

148. Hiroshi Komatsu and Charles Musser, "Benshi Search," *Wide Angle* 9.2 (1987): 72–90.

149. See the book published under Tachibana's pen name: Tachibana Takashirō, *Eigadō mandan* (Tokyo: Mumei Shuppansha, 1926), 302–303.

150. The test questions are reproduced in ibid., 295–296.

151. See, for instance, Kishirō, "Benshi no shakaiteki kachi," *Kinema Record* 49 (July 1917): 324: "When explaining in front of the eyes of less intelligent classes, the benshi must be at least one step above their level of intelligence."

152. Ibid. The same analogy was offered by Tachibana Takahiro, *Katsudōkyō no techō* (Tokyo: Kōbunsha, 1924), 90; and Yume Sōbei, *Eiga setsumei no kenkyū* (Tokyo: Chōyōsha, 1923), 60.

153. "Katsudō benshi ninka," *Miyako shinbun*, August 11, 1917, p. 3 (*MSGS*, 173).

154. The *Miyako shinbun* reported that good benshi would be selected through the "principle of character" (*jinkakushugi*): "Genjūna eiga no kensa to danjoseki no kubetsu," *Miyako shinbun*, July 13, 1917, p. 5 (*MSGS*, 167).

155. Article 20 of the 1920 Ehime Amusement Regulations specified who could not be allowed to become a benshi. These regulations can be found in Monbushō Futsū Gakumukyoku, *Zenkoku ni okeru katsudō shashin jōkyō chōsa*, 17–21.

156. Sugawara Kyōzō, "Setsumeisha to kōshū," in *Dai ikkai katsudō shashin setsumeisha kōshūkai kōshūroku*, ed. Takaoka Kokugan (Tokyo: Dai Nippon Setsumeisha Kyōkai, 1921), 245–247.

157. Hase has criticized me on this point, countering that, in the panopticon, prisoners ideally do not know when they are being watched: "Ken'etsu no tanjō," 138. However, I think it is important to stress that technologies of film censorship coupled with the reforms of the Pure Film Movement did much to suppress the audience's consciousness of the space of the theater and its watchmen. As I argued in the previous chapter, the benshi, while maintaining his public role, was constructed as an invisible sentry who could watch without being seen.

158. Carol Gluck has written in detail on the construction of an ideology of the family-state. See *Japan's Modern Myths: Ideology in the Late Meiji Period* (Princeton, NJ: Princeton University Press, 1985), particularly 257–262.

159. In conversations with me, Omuka Toshiharu has likened the benshi to the ideal Japanese father who read the newspaper to his family.

160. I thank Dudley Andrew for helping me clarify this point.

161. It would be interesting to relate this disembodied voice to that of Emperor Hirohito, whom most Japanese heard for the first time precisely as a disembodied voice in that famous radio announcement on August 15, 1945, proclaiming the end of the war.

162. Kitada Akihiro, *"Imi" e no aragai: Mediēshon no bunka seijigaku* (Tokyo: Serika Shobō, 2004), 237–275.

163. Jeffery A. Dym, *Benshi, Japanese Silent Film Narrators, and Their Forgotten Narrative Art of Setsumei: A History of Japanese Silent Film Narration* (Lewiston, NY: Edwin Mellen Press, 2003), 140.

164. Kitada, *"Imi" e no aragai*, 238–275.

165. See my "Word before the Image: Criticism, the Screenplay, and the Regulation of Meaning in Prewar Japanese Film Culture," in *Word and Image in Japanese Cinema*, ed. Carole Cavanaugh and Dennis Washburn (Cambridge: Cambridge University Press, 2000), 3–35.

166. See the comments by an Asakusa lower school principal, Sasai Kazue, in "Jidō firumu ni tsuite: Jidō kyōikuka no jitsurokudan," 12; and the statement by an Uwajima theater owner, Takahashi Yutaka, "Katsudō shashin torishimari shinrei o mite," *Katsudō shashin zasshi* 3.11 (November 1917): 30.

167. "Shinken o mushishita hōrei," 24.

168. See Terada Yukichi's survey response in "Jidō firumu ni tsuite: Jidō kyōikuka no jitsurokudan," 11.

169. See Komagine's response in ibid., 19.

170. One of the common forms of resistance to this education in proper spectatorship was for children to sneak into theaters on their own. The

screenwriter Hirosawa Ei offers a particularly entertaining account of his late-1930s secret film viewing in his *Watashi no Shōwa eigashi* (Tokyo: Iwanami Shoten, 1989). Still, he recalls that one of the films that most profoundly affected him was Tasaka Tomotaka's *Robō no ishi* ("A Pebble by the Wayside," 1938), which he saw on a school outing with his teacher.

171. Akashi, "Katsudō shashin no riyō narabini torishimari ni tsuite," 4.

172. Nishimoto, "Eiga to Monbushō: (jō)," 265.

173. Kaeriyama Norimasa, "Katsudō shashin no shakaiteki chii oyobi sekinin: dai-ni," *Kinema Record* 42 (December 1916): 537.

174. Kaeriyama Norimasa, *Katsudō shashingeki no sōsaku to satsueihō* (Tokyo: Hikōsha, 1917), appendix 35.

175. See my "Wrestling with Godzilla: Manga Monsters, Puroresu, and the National Body," in *In Godzilla's Footsteps*, ed. William Tsutsui and Michiko Ito (New York: Palgrave Macmillan, 2006), 63–81.

176. Akashi, for instance, in pointing out that it was difficult for only the state to restrict children's film viewing, hoped that exhibitors would progress on their own in this direction: "Eiga no sentei to benshi no yōsei," *Yomiuri shinbun*, June 23, 1917 (*SST*, 5:213).

177. Okudaira, "Eiga to ken'etsu," 303–304.

178. For more on wartime attitudes toward film spectatorship, see my "Tatakau kankyaku: Dai Tōa Kyōeiken no Nihon eiga to juyō no mondai," *Gendai shisō* 30.9 (July 2002): 139–149.

179. Yanai, *Katsudō shashin no hogo to torishimari*, 867.

CONCLUSION

1. See David Bordwell, "A Cinema of Flourishes: Japanese Decorative Classicism of the Prewar Era," in *Reframing Japanese Cinema: Authorship, Genre, History*, ed. Arthur Noletti Jr. and David Desser (Bloomington: University of Indiana Press, 1992); as well as his *Ozu and the Poetics of Cinema* (Princeton: Princeton University Press, 1988).

2. In other words, instead of censoring one print of a film title as a representative of the meaning inherent in all the prints (and produced prior to the text in the space of production), censors viewed every single print of every single film and affixed a seal to each print. It was the print that was the text—the celluloid that was to be shown in the theater—not the meaning inherent in its representation. Such a procedure could be pursued because there was still a small number of prints for each film, but conversely one could also argue that this process encouraged the production of few prints.

3. Bordwell, "A Cinema of Flourishes," 334.

4. See my "Eigahō to iu eigaron," in the reprint *Eigahō kaisetsu/Dai 74-kai Teikoku Gikai eiga hōan giji gaiyō*, Nihon eigaron gensetsu taikei, dai 1-ki: Senjika no eigatōseiki, vol. 8, ed. Makino Mamoru (Tokyo: Yumani Shobō, 2003), 589–607.

5. There is no library in the world that has a complete run of that and many other early Japanese film journals. Researchers must shuttle between different archives, and even then they sometimes cannot find a particular issue. Partial reprints of some journals have helped, but have not solved the problem. For more on the difficulties of researching Japanese cinema, see my introduction to the book I cowrote with Abé Mark Nornes: *Research Guide to Japanese Film Studies* (Ann Arbor: Center for Japanese Studies, University of Michigan, 2009).

6. See, for instance, Marshall Berman, *All That Is Solid Melts into Air: The Experience of Modernity* (New York: Simon and Schuster, 1982), 34–35.

7. Even complaints of an overly local basis to film culture were nonetheless generalized because they never cited the specific local elements as the problem, but rather localism itself.

8. See Jeffrey A. Dym, *Benshi, Japanese Silent Film Narrators, and Their Forgotten Narrative Art of Setsumei: A History of Japanese Silent Film Narration* (Lewiston, NY: Edwin Mellen Press, 2003); or Komatsu Hiroshi, "Hisutoriogurafi to gainen no fukusūsei: Taikatsu o rekishikasuru tame ni," *Eigagaku* 13 (1999): 2–11.

9. Tom Gunning, "The Scene of Speaking: Two Decades of Discovering the Film Lecturer," *Iris* 27 (Spring 1999): 76.

10. Dick Hebdige, *Subculture: The Meaning of Style* (London: Methuen, 1979).

11. Slavoj Žižek, "Eastern Europe's Republics of Gilead," *New Left Review* 183 (1990): 60.

12. See Abé Mark Nornes, *Japanese Documentary Film: The Meiji Era through Hiroshima* (Minneapolis: University of Minnesota Press, 2003); Peter B. High, *The Imperial Screen: Japanese Film Culture in the Fifteen Years' War, 1931–1945* (Madison: University of Wisconsin Press, 2003); and Mitsuyo Wada-Marciano, *Nippon Modern: Japanese Cinema of the 1920s and 1930s* (Honolulu: University of Hawai'i Press, 2008).

13. For a copy of the "Eigahō" (Film Law) and related statutes, see Fuwa Yūshun, *Eigahō kaisetsu* (Tokyo: Dai Nippon Eiga Kyōkai, 1941), furoku 1–15.

14. Gregory J. Kasza, *The State and the Mass Media in Japan, 1918–1945* (Berkeley: University of California Press, 1988): 241.

15. Although he does not locate this phenomenon in the prewar era, as I have tried to, Burch does note a similar play of sameness and difference in postwar Japanese film. While he leaves a great deal of room for exceptions for directors like Kurosawa, he particularly laments how a master of the prewar film like Mizoguchi, for example, "discovered that his systemics were perfectly compatible with one of the dominant tendencies in Hollywood at the time: the long take *à la* Wyler." To him, the Japanese cinema as a whole, while retaining surface differences, is little different from the classical mode. See *To the Distant Observer: Form and Meaning in the Japanese Cinema* (Berkeley: University of California Press, 1979).

16. Thus it is important to see the formation of a more "Americanized" Japanese cinema as a result not of the Occupation (which is Burch's contention) but of wartime mobilization. This should advise us not to construct 1945 as breaking point between inherently different prewar and postwar structures; rather, the postwar should be theorized in partial continuity with pre-1945 developments.

17. See my "*Miyamoto Musashi* to senjichū no kankyaku," in *Eiga kantoku Mizoguchi Kenji*, ed. Yomota Inuhiko (Tokyo: Shin'yōsha, 1999), 226–250; and "Tatakau kankyaku: Dai Tōa Kyōeiken no Nihon eiga to juyō no mondai," *Gendai shisō* 30.9 (July 2002): 139–149.

18. The Sun Tribe, or *taiyōzoku*, films, such as Nakahira Kō's *Kurutta kajitsu* (Crazed Fruit, 1956), were films about alienated and delinquent youth that, as Michael Raine argues, constituted a threatening trend in late-1950s cinema centered crucially on the new, Westernized body. See his "Ishihara Yujirō: Youth, Celebrity, and the Male Body in Late-1950s Japan," in *Word and Image in Japanese Cinema*, ed. Dennis Washburn and Carole Cavanaugh (Cambridge: Cambridge University Press, 2001): 202–225. Pink films were the soft-core adult films that became not only a major center of film production from the 1960s on but also a crucial training ground for new directors in the poststudio era and a site of political and cinematic experimentation, often centered on issues of the body and sexuality.

19. That, at least, is how Aoyama Shinji, director of such films as *Helpless* (1996) and *Eureka* (2000), defined his own cinema. See my "Aoyama Shinji," in *Fifty Contemporary Filmmakers*, ed. Yvonne Tasker (London: Routledge, 2002), 16–25.

Selected Bibliography

JOURNALS

Film Record/Kinema Record (1913–1917)
Katsudō gahō (1917–1923)
Katsudō hyōron/Katsudō kurabu (1918–1924)
Katsudō no sekai (1916–1918)
Katsudō shashinkai (1909–1911)
Katsudō shashin zasshi (1915–1918)
Kinema junpō (1919–1924)

NEWSPAPERS AND NEWSPAPER COLLECTIONS

Meiji nyūsu jiten [Directory of Meiji News]. 9 vols. Tokyo: Mainichi Komyunikēshonzu, 1985–1986.
Shinbun shūroku Taishō-shi [A History of Taishō in Collected Newspapers]. 15 vols. Tokyo: Taishō Shuppan, 1978.
Taishō nyūsu jiten [Directory of Taishō News]. 8 vols. Tokyo: Mainichi Komyunikēshonzu, 1988.
Tokyo asahi shinbun (1912–1920).
Yano Seiichi, ed. *Miyako shinbun geinō shiryō shūsei: Taishō hen* [A Compilation of Materials on Entertainment in the *Miyako shinbun:* Taishō Edition]. Tokyo: Hakusuisha, 1991.

BOOKS AND ARTICLES

Abel, Richard. "The 'Blank Screen of Reception' in Early French Cinema." *Iris* 11 (Summer 1990): 27–47.
———. "Booming the Business: The Historical Specificity of Early French Cinema." In *Silent Film,* edited by Richard Abel, 109–124. New Brunswick, NJ: Rutgers University Press, 1996.

————. *Encyclopedia of Early Cinema.* London: Routledge, 2005.

————, ed. *Silent Film.* New Brunswick, NJ: Rutgers University Press, 1996.

Anderson, Benedict. *Imagined Communities: Reflections on the Origin and the Spread of Nationalism.* London: Verso, 1983.

Anderson, Joseph L. "Spoken Silents in the Japanese Cinema; or, Talking to Pictures: Essaying the *Katsuben,* Contextualizing the Texts." In *Reframing Japanese Cinema,* edited by Arthur Noletti Jr. and David Desser, 259–311. Bloomington: Indiana University Press, 1992.

Anderson, Joseph L., and Donald Richie. *The Japanese Film: Art and Industry.* Expanded ed. Princeton, NJ: Princeton University Press, 1982.

Bauman, Zygmunt. *Liquid Modernity.* Cambridge, U.K.: Polity Press, 2000.

Bean, Jennifer M., and Diane Negra, eds. *A Feminist Reader in Early Cinema.* Durham, NC: Duke University Press, 2002.

Berman, Art. *Preface to Modernism.* Urbana: University of Illinois Press, 1994.

Berman, Marshall. *All That Is Solid Melts into Air: The Experience of Modernity.* New York: Simon and Schuster, 1982.

Bernardi, Joanne. *Writing in Light: The Silent Scenario and the Japanese Pure Film Movement.* Detroit: Wayne State University Press, 2001.

Bhabha, Homi K. "DissemiNation: Time, Narrative, and the Margins of the Modern Nation." In *Nation and Narration,* edited by Homi Bhabha, 291–322. London: Routledge, 1990.

Bordwell, David. "A Cinema of Flourishes: Japanese Decorative Classicism of the Prewar Era." In *Reframing Japanese Cinema,* edited by Arthur Noletti Jr. and David Desser, 328–346. Bloomington: Indiana University Press, 1992.

————. *Ozu and the Poetics of Cinema.* Princeton, NJ: Princeton University Press, 1988.

Bourdieu, Pierre. "The Field of Cultural Production, or: The Economic World Reversed." *Poetics* 12 (1983): 311–356.

Bowser, Eileen. *The Transformation of Cinema: 1907–1915.* History of the American Cinema, vol. 2. Berkeley: University of California Press, 1990.

Burch, Noël. *Life to Those Shadows.* Edited and translated by Ben Brewster. Berkeley: University of California Press, 1990.

————. "Primitivism and the Avant-Gardes: A Dialectical Approach." In *Narrative, Apparatus, Ideology,* edited by Philip Rosen, 483–506. New York: Columbia University Press, 1986.

————. *To the Distant Observer: Form and Meaning in the Japanese Cinema.* Edited by Annette Michelson. Berkeley: University of California Press, 1979.

Calinescu, Matei. *Five Faces of Modernity.* Durham, NC: Duke University Press, 1987.

Cazdyn, Eric. *The Flash of Capital: Film and Geopolitics in Japan.* Durham, NC: Duke University Press, 2002.

Charney, Leo, and Vanessa R. Schwartz, eds. *Cinema and the Invention of Modern Life.* Berkeley: University of California Press, 1995.

Chiba Nobuo. *Eiga to Tanizaki* [Cinema and Tanizaki]. Tokyo: Seiabō, 1989.

————. "Eiga yōgo no hassei to rufu no shiteki purosesu" [The Historical Process of the Development and Spread of Film Terminology]. *Eigashi kenkyū* 1 (1973): 40–48.

————. "Modanaizēshon jokyoku: eigaron 1914–1918" [Prelude to Modernism: Film Theory, 1914–1918]. In *Nihon eiga to modanizumu 1920–1930* [Japanese Cinema and Modernism, 1920–1930], edited by Iwamoto Kenji, 32–49. Tokyo: Riburopōto, 1991.

Chow, Rey. *Primitive Passions: Visuality, Sexuality, Ethnography, and Contemporary Chinese Cinema*. New York: Columbia University Press, 1995.

Deguchi Takehito. "Nani ga hakujin konpurekkusu o umidashita ka" [What Gave Birth to the Caucasian Complex?]. In *Nihon eiga to modanizumu: 1920–1930* [Japanese Cinema and Modernism, 1920–1930], edited by Iwamoto Kenji, 104–123. Tokyo: Riburopōto, 1991.

Deleuze, Gilles. *Foucault*. Translated by Sean Hand. Minneapolis: University of Minnesota Press, 1986.

Dōjin Shiin. *Katsudō shashinjutsu jizai* [All about Moving Picture Craft]. Tokyo: Daigakukan, 1903.

Dym, Jeffery A. *Benshi, Japanese Silent Film Narrators, and Their Forgotten Narrative Art of Setsumei: A History of Japanese Silent Film Narration*. Lewiston, NY: Edwin Mellen Press, 2003.

Elsaesser, Thomas, and Adam Baker, eds. *Early Cinema: Space, Frame, Narrative*. London: British Film Institute, 1990.

Foucault, Michel. *The Archaeology of Knowledge and the Discourse on Language*. Translated by A. M. Sheridan Smith. New York: Pantheon, 1972.

————. *Discipline and Punish: The Birth of the Prison*. Translated by Alan Sheridan. New York: Vintage Books, 1979.

Frisby, David. *Fragments of Modernity: Theories of Modernity in the Work of Simmel, Kracauer, and Benjamin*. Cambridge, U.K.: Polity Press, 1985.

Fujiki Hideaki. "The Advent of the Star System in Japanese Cinema Distribution." *Jōhō bunka kenkyū* 15 (2002): 1–22.

————. "Benshi as Stars: The Irony of the Popularity and Respectability of Voice Performers in Japanese Cinema." *Cinema Journal* 45.2 (Winter 2006): 68–84.

Fujita Motohiko. *Gendai eiga no kiten* [Starting Points for Contemporary Film]. Tokyo: Kinokuniya Shoten, 1965.

Fullerton, John. "Spatial and Temporal Articulation of Pre-classical Swedish Film." In *Early Cinema: Space, Frame, Narrative*, edited by Thomas Elsaesser and Adam Baker, 375–388. London: British Film Institute, 1990.

Fuwa Yūshun. *Eigahō kaisetsu* [Commentary on the Film Law]. Tokyo: Dai Nippon Eiga Kyōkai, 1941.

Gaonkar, Dilip Parameshwar, ed. *Alternative Modernities*. Durham, NC: Duke University Press, 2001.

Gardner, William O. *Advertising Tower: Japanese Modernism and Modernity in the 1920s*. Cambridge, MA: Harvard University Asia Center, 2006.

Gerow, Aaron. "The Benshi's New Face: Defining Cinema in Taishō Japan." *Iconics* 3 (1994): 69–86.

———. "Celluloid Masks: The Cinematic Image and the Image of Japan." *Iris* 16 (Spring 1993): 23–36.

———. "Eigahō to iu eigaron" [The Film Law as Film Theory]. In *Eigahō kaisetsu/Dai 74-kai Teikoku Gikai eiga hōan giji gaiyō* [Commentary on the Film Law/Summary of the 74th Imperial Diet Debates on the Film Law], Nihon eigaron gensetsu taikei, dai 1-ki: Senjika no eigatōseiki, vol. 8, edited by Makino Mamoru, 589–607. Tokyo: Yumani Shobō, 2003.

———. "Gonda Yasunosuke ga sōzōshita eiga bunmei gensetsu" [The Discourse of Film Civilization Imagined by Gonda Yasunosuke]. In *Katsudō shashin no genri oyobi ōyō* [The Principles and Applications of the Moving Pictures], by Gonda Yasunosuke, Nihon eigaron gensetsu taikei, vol. 24, edited by Makino Mamoru. Tokyo: Yumani Shobō, 2006.

———. "*Miyamoto Musashi* to senjichū no kankyaku" (*Miyamoto Musashi* and Wartime Spectators). In *Eiga kantoku Mizoguchi Kenji* (Film Director Mizoguchi Kenji), edited by Yomota Inuhiko, 226–250. Tokyo: Shin'yōsha, 1999.

———. "Narrating the Nation-ality of a Cinema: The Case of Japanese Prewar Film." In *The Culture of Japanese Fascism,* edited by Alan Tansman, 185–211. Durham, NC: Duke University Press, 2009.

———. "Nation, Citizenship, and Cinema." In *A Companion to the Anthropology of Japan,* edited by Jennifer Robertson, 400–414. Malden, MA: Blackwell Publishers, 2005.

———. "Nichijō toshite no Hariuddo to sekai kankyaku no shihai" [Vernacular Hollywood and the Control of World Audiences]. *Gendai shisō* [Modern Thought] rinji zōkan 31.1 (June 2003): 124–131.

———. "'Nihonjin' Kitano Takeshi: *Hana-Bi* to nashonaru shinema no keisei" [The "Japanese" Kitano Takeshi: *Hana-Bi* and the Formation of a National Cinema]. *Yuriika* [Eureka] rinji zōkan 30.3 (February 1998): 42–51.

———. "One Print in the Age of Mechanical Reproduction: Culture and Industry in 1910s Japan." *Screening the Past* 11 (2000), www.latrobe.edu.au/screeningthepast/firstrelease/fr1100/agfr11e.htm.

———. *A Page of Madness: Cinema and Modernity in 1920s Japan.* Ann Arbor: Center for Japanese Studies, University of Michigan, 2008.

———. "The Self Seen as Other: Akutagawa and Film," *Literature/Film Quarterly* 23.3 (1995): 197–203.

———. "Tatakau kankyaku: Dai Tōa Kyōeiken no Nihon eiga to juyō no mondai" [Fighting for Viewers: Wartime Japanese Film and the Asian Audience]. *Gendai shisō* [Modern Thought] 30.9 (July 2002): 139–149.

———. "The Word before the Image: Criticism, the Screenplay, and the Regulation of Meaning in Prewar Japanese Film Culture." In *Word and Image in Japanese Cinema,* edited by Carole Cavanaugh and Dennis Washburn, 3–35. Cambridge: Cambridge University Press, 2000.

———. "Wrestling with Godzilla: Manga Monsters, Puroresu, and the National Body." In *In Godzilla's Footsteps*, edited by William Tsutsui and Michiko Ito, 63–81. New York: Palgrave Macmillan, 2006.

Gluck, Carol. *Japan's Modern Myths: Ideology in the Late Meiji Period*. Princeton, NJ: Princeton University Press, 1985.

Gonda Yasunosuke. *Gonda Yasunosuke chosakushū* [Selected Works of Gonda Yasunosuke]. 4 vols. Tokyo: Bunwa Shobō, 1974.

———. *Katsudō shashin no genri oyobi ōyō* [The Principles and Applications of the Moving Pictures]. Tokyo: Uchida Rokakuho, 1914.

Grieveson, Lee. *Policing Cinema: Movies and Censorship in Early-Twentieth-Century America*. Berkeley: University of California Press, 2004.

Grieveson, Lee, and Peter Krämer, eds. *The Silent Cinema Reader*. London: Routledge, 2004.

Gunning, Tom. "Attractions, Detection, Disguise: Zigomar, Jasset, and the History of Film Genres." *Griffithiana* 47 (May 1993): 137–156.

———. "The Cinema of Attractions: Early Film, Its Spectators, and the Avant-Garde." In *Early Cinema: Space, Frame, Narrative*, edited by Thomas Elsaesser and Adam Baker, 56–62. London: British Film Institute, 1990.

———. *D. W. Griffith and the Origins of American Narrative Film*. Urbana: University of Illinois Press, 1991.

———. "'Now You See It, Now You Don't': The Temporality of the Cinema of Attractions." *Velvet Light Trap* 32 (Fall 1993): 3–12.

———. "The Scene of Speaking: Two Decades of Discovering the Film Lecturer." *Iris* 27 (Spring 1999): 67–79.

———. "Tracing the Individual Body: Photography, Detectives, and Early Cinema." In *Cinema and the Invention of Modern Life*, edited by Leo Charney and Vanessa R. Schwartz, 15–45. Berkeley: University of California Press, 1995.

Hall, Stuart. "Notes on Deconstructing the Popular." In *Cultural Theory and Popular Culture*, edited by John Storey. 2nd ed. Athens: University of Georgia Press, 1998.

Hansen, Miriam. *Babel and Babylon: Spectatorship and American Silent Film*. Cambridge, MA: Harvard University Press, 1991.

———. "Fallen Women, Rising Stars, New Horizons: Shanghai Silent Film as Vernacular Modernism." *Film Quarterly* 54.1 (Fall 2000): 10–22

———. "The Mass Production of the Senses: Classical Cinema as Vernacular Modernism." In *Reinventing Film Studies*, edited by Linda Williams and Christine Gledhill. London: Edward Arnold, 2000.

Harootunian, Harry D. "Introduction: A Sense of an Ending and the Problem of Taishō," In *Japan in Crisis: Essays on Taishō Democracy*, edited by Bernard S. Silberman and Harootunian, 3–28. Princeton, NJ: Princeton University Press, 1974.

———. *Overcome by Modernity: History, Culture, and Community in Interwar Japan*. Princeton, NJ: Princeton University Press, 2000.

Hase Masato. "Cinemaphobia in Taisho Japan: Zigomar, Delinquent Boys, and Somnambulism." *Iconics* 4 (1998): 87–100.

———. "Ken'etsu no tanjō: Taishō-ki no keisatsu to katsudō shashin" [The Birth of Censorship: The Police and the Moving Pictures in the Taishō Era]. *Eizōgaku* 53 (1994): 124–138.

Hatsuda Tōru. *Modan toshi no kūkan hakubutsukan—Tōkyō* [A Modern City's Museum of Space—Tokyo]. Tokyo: Shōkokusha, 1995.

Hazumi Tsuneo. "Asakusa no eigakan" [Asakusa's Movie Theaters]. In *Asakusa: Sono ōgon jidai no hanashi* [Asakusa: Stories of Its Golden Age], edited by Takami Jun, 127–136. Tokyo: Shinpyōsha, 1978.

Hebdige, Dick. *Subculture: The Meaning of Style.* London: Methuen, 1979.

High, Peter B. "The *Ancien Régime* of Japanese Film and the Revolt of the Fans: 1911–1918." *Gengo bunka ronshū* 10.2 (1989): 121–148.

———. *The Imperial Screen: Japanese Film Culture in the Fifteen Years' War, 1931–1945.* Madison: University of Wisconsin Press, 2003.

Hirosawa Ei. *Watashi no Shōwa eigashi* [My Shōwa Film History]. Tokyo: Iwanami Shoten, 1989.

Hobsbawm, E.J. *Nations and Nationalism since 1780: Programme, Myth, Reality.* Cambridge: Cambridge University Press, 1990.

Hunt, Leon. "The Student of Prague." In *Early Cinema: Space, Frame, Narrative,* edited by Thomas Elsaesser and Adam Baker, 389–401. London: British Film Institute, 1990.

Ichikawa Aya, ed. *Nihon eiga hōki ruishū* [Anthology of Japanese Film Laws and Regulations]. Tokyo: Ginza Shobō, 1928.

Iijima Tadashi. *Boku no Meiji, Taishō, Shōwa* [My Meiji, Taishō, and Shōwa]. Tokyo: Seiabō, 1991.

———. "Nihon eiga no reimei: Jun'eigageki no shūhen" [The Dawn of Japanese Film: The Context of Pure Films]. In *Kōza Nihon eiga* [Lectures on Japanese Cinema], edited by Imamura Shōhei et al., 1:104–126. Tokyo: Iwanami Shoten, 1985.

———. *Nihon eigashi* [Japanese Film History]. 2 vols. Tokyo: Hakusuisha, 1955.

———. "Shinario bungakuron josetsu" [Introduction to a Theory of Scenario Literature]. In *Shinario bungaku zenshū 1: Shinario taikei* [Complete Works of Scenario Literature 1: Outline of the Scenario], 1–26. Tokyo: Kawade Shobō, 1937.

Imamura Kanae. *Eiga sangyō* [The Film Industry]. Tokyo: Yūhikaku, 1960.

Imamura Miyoo. *Nihon eiga bunkenshi* [A History of Japanese Film Publications]. Tokyo: Kagamiura Shobō, 1967.

Imamura Shōhei et al., eds. *Kōza Nihon eiga* [Lectures on Japanese Cinema]. 8 vols. Tokyo: Iwanami Shoten, 1985.

Imamura Taihei. *Eiga geijutsu no seikaku* [The Quality of Film Art]. 2nd ed. Kyoto: Dai-ichi Geibunsha, 1941.

Inagaki Hiroshi. *Nihon eiga no wakaki hibi* [The Youthful Days of Japanese Cinema]. Tokyo: Mainichi Shinbunsha, 1978.

Inagaki Taruho. *Taruho eigaron* [Taruho's Film Theory]. Tokyo: Firumu Āto-sha, 1995.

Irokawa Daikichi. *The Culture of the Meiji Period*. Translated by Marius B. Jansen. Princeton, NJ: Princeton University Press, 1985.

Ishii Bunsaku, ed. *Nihon eiga jigyō sōran: 1925-nen han* [Complete View of the Japanese Film Industry: 1925 Edition]. 2nd ed. Tokyo: Kokusai Eiga Tsū-shinsha, 1926.

Itō Hideo. *Taishō no tantei shōsetsu* [Taishō Detective Novels]. Tokyo: San'ichi Shobō, 1991.

Iwabuchi, Koichi. *Recentering Globalization: Popular Culture and Japanese Transnationalism*. Durham, NC: Duke University Press, 2002.

Iwamoto Kenji. "Film Criticism and the Study of Cinema in Japan: A Historical Survey." *Iconics* 1 (1987): 129–149.

———. *Gentō no seiki: Eiga zen'ya no shikaku bunkashi* [The Magic Lantern Century: A History of Visual Culture before Cinema]. Tokyo: Shinwasha, 2002.

———. "Kikai jidai no bigaku to eiga" [Film and Art in the Machine Age]. In *Nihon eiga to modanizumu: 1920–1930* [Japanese Cinema and Modernism: 1920–1930], edited by Iwamoto Kenji, 200–213. Tokyo: Riburopōto, 1991.

———, ed. *Nihon eiga to modanizumu 1920–1930* [Japanese Cinema and Modernism, 1920–1930]. Tokyo: Riburopōto, 1991.

———. "Osanai Kaoru to eiga" [Osanai Kaoru and Cinema]. *Waseda Daigaku Daigakuin Bungaku Kenkyūka kiyō* 32 (1986): 139–153.

———. "Senkuteki eiga kenkyūsha Gonda Yasunosuke" [Gonda Yasunosuke, a Pioneering Film Scholar]. *Waseda Daigaku Daigakuin Bungaku Ken-kyūka kiyō* 30 (1984): 191–201.

Iwamoto Kenji and Makino Mamoru, eds. *"Kinema junpō" fukkokuban* [Reprint of *Kinema junpō*]. 19 vols. Tokyo: Yūshōdō, 1993–1995.

Iwasaki Akira. *Eigashi* [Film History]. Tokyo: Tōyō Keizai Shinpōsha, 1961.

Kaeriyama Norimasa. *Katsudō shashingeki no sōsaku to satsueihō* [The Production and Photography of Moving Picture Drama]. Tokyo: Hikōsha, 1917.

Kakimoto Akihito. "Bokujin = shisai to shite no Kon Wajirō" [Kon Wajirō as a Priest/Parson] *Gendai shisō* 21.7 (July 1993): 74–87.

Karatani Kōjin. "One Sprit, Two Nineteenth Centuries." In *Postmodernism and Japan*, edited by Masao Miyoshi and H.D. Harootunian, 259–272. Durham, NC: Duke University Press, 1989.

———. *Origins of Modern Japanese Literature*. Edited and translated by Brett de Bary. Durham, NC: Duke University Press, 1993.

———. *"Senzen" no shikō* ["Prewar" Thought]. Tokyo: Bungei Shunjū, 1994.

Kashiwagi Hiroshi. *Dezain senryaku: Yokubō wa tsukurareru* [Design Strategies: Desire Is Constructed]. Tokyo: Kōdansha, 1987.

Kasza, Gregory J. *The State and the Mass Media in Japan, 1918–1945*. Berkeley: University of California Press, 1988.

Katō Atsuko. *Sōdōin taisei to eiga* [Film and the National Mobilization System]. Tokyo: Shin'yōsha, 2003.

Katō Hidetoshi. *Misemono kara terebi e* [From *Misemono* to Television]. Tokyo: Iwanami Shoten, 1965.

Kayano Yatsuka. *Kindai Nihon no dezain bunkashi: 1868–1926* [A Cultural History of Modern Japanese Design: 1868–1926]. Tokyo: Film Ātosha, 1992.

Keishichō-shi: Taishō-hen [A History of the Tokyo Metropolitan Police: Taishō Edition]. Tokyo: Keishichōshi Hensan Iinkai, 1960.

Kinoshita Naoyuki. *Bijutsu to iu misemono* [The *Misemono* Called Art]. Tokyo: Heibonsha, 1993.

———. "Egakareta 'Meiji no Nihon': Nihon e no/Nihon kara no manazashi" ["Meiji Japan" Depicted: The Gaze at/from Japan]. In *Eiga denrai: Shinematogurafu to "Meiji no Nihon"* [The Introduction of Film: The Cinématograph and "Meiji" Japan], edited by Yoshida Yoshishige et al., 124–188. Tokyo: Iwanami Shoten, 1995.

Kinugasa Teinosuke. *Waga eiga no seishun* [My Youth in Films]. Tokyo: Chūō Kōronsha, 1977.

Kirby, Lynn. "The Urban Spectator and the Crowd in Early American Train Films." *Iris* 11 (Summer 1990): 49–62.

Kirihara, Donald. "A Reconsideration of the Institution of the Benshi." *Film Reader* 6 (1985): 41–53.

Kitada Akihiro. *"Imi" e no aragai: Mediēshon no bunka seijigaku* (The Fight against "Meaning": Studying the Cultural Politics of Mediation). Tokyo: Serika Shobō, 2004.

Komatsu Hiroshi. "The Fundamental Change: Japanese Cinema before and after the Earthquake of 1923." *Griffithiana* 13.38–39 (October 1990): 186–93.

———. "Hisutoriogurafi to gainen no fukusūsei: Taikatsu o rekishikasuru tame ni" [Historiography and Conceptual Multiplicity: To Historicize Taikatsu] *Eigagaku* 13 (1999): 2–11.

———. "Shinematogurafu to wa nan datta no ka—Ideorogī sōchi to shite no eiga" [What Was the Cinématograph?—Cinema as an Ideological Apparatus]. In *Eiga denrai: Shinematogurafu to "Meiji no Nihon"* [The Introduction of Film: The Cinématograph and "Meiji" Japan], edited by Yoshida Yoshishige et al., 103–123. Tokyo: Iwanami Shoten, 1995.

———. "Some Characteristics of Japanese Cinema before World War I." In *Reframing Japanese Cinema*, edited by Arthur Noletti Jr. and David Desser, 229–258. Bloomington: Indiana University Press, 1992.

———. "Tennenshoku kara jun'eigageki e—Nihon eigashi ni okeru Tenkatsu no igi" [From Color to Pure Film—the Significance of Tenkatsu in Japanese Film History]. *Geijutsugaku kenkyū* 5 (1995): 25–37.

———. "Transformations in Film as Reality (Part One): Questions Regarding the Genesis of Nonfiction Film." Translated by A.A. Gerow. *Documentary Box* (English edition) 5 (1994): 1–5.

Komatsu, Hiroshi, and Frances Loden. "Mastering the Mute Image: The Role of the Benshi in Japanese Cinema." *Iris* 22 (Autumn 1996): 33–52.

Komatsu, Hiroshi, and Charles Musser. "Benshi Search." *Wide Angle* 9.2 (1987): 72–90.

Kurata Yoshihiro. *Meiji, Taishō no minshū goraku* [Popular Entertainment in Meiji and Taishō]. Tokyo: Iwanami Shoten, 1980.

———. *Kyōiku to katsudō shashin* [Education and the Moving Pictures]. Tokyo: Monbushō Futsū Gakumukyoku, 1918.

LaMarre, Thomas. *Shadows on the Screen: Tanizaki Jun'ichirō on Cinema and "Oriental" Aesthetics*. Ann Arbor: Center for Japanese Studies, University of Michigan, 2005.

Lehman, Peter. "The Mysterious Orient, the Crystal Clear Orient, the Non-Existent Orient." *Journal of Film and Video* 39.1 (Winter 1987): 5–15.

Lippit, Akira Mizuta. *Atomic Light (Shadow Optics)*. Minneapolis: University of Minnesota Press, 2005.

Maeda Ai. "Sakariba ni eigakan ga dekita" [A Movie Theater Was Built in an Entertainment District]. In *Kōza Nihon eiga* [Lectures on Japanese Cinema], edited by Imamura Shōhei et al., 1:338–358. Tokyo: Iwanami Shoten, 1985.

Makino Mamoru. "Katsudō shashinban: 'Ametsuchi no majiwarishi koro'" [Moving Picture Edition: "The Age of Relations with Heaven"]. In *Nihon eiga shoki shiryō shūsei 1: "Katsudō shashin zasshi"* [Collection of Research Materials Pertaining to Early Japanese Cinema: *Katsudō shashin zasshi*], 1:1–15. Tokyo: San'ichi Shobō, 1990.

———. "Ken'etsu to Nihon eiga no modanizumu" [Censorship and Modernism in Japanese Cinema]. In *Nihon eiga to modanizumu: 1920–1930* [Japanese Cinema and Modernism, 1920–1930], edited by Iwamoto Kenji, 142–149. Tokyo: Riburopōto, 1991.

———. "*Kinema junpō* to eiga hihyō no seiritsu" [*Kinema junpō* and the Formation of Criticism]. "*Kinema junpō*" *fukkokuban* [Reprint of *Kinema junpō*], 13:19–37. Tokyo: Yūshōdō, 1993–1995.

———, ed., *Nihon eiga bunken shoshi* [Bibliography of Japanese Film Publications]. Tokyo: Yūshōdō, 2003.

———. *Nihon eiga ken'etsushi*. Tokyo: Pandora, 2003.

———. "On the Conditions of Film Censorship in Japan before Its Systematization." In *In Praise of Film Studies*, edited by Aaron Gerow and Abé Mark Nornes, 46–67. Yokohama: Kinema Club, 2001.

———. "Shoki *Kinema junpō* shōshi" [A Short History of the Early *Kinema junpō*]. "*Kinema junpō*" *fukkokuban* [Reprint of *Kinema junpō*], 1:19–38. Tokyo: Yūshōdō, 1993–1995.

———. "Sōsōki no eiga bigaku ni kansuru shoshiteki kenkyū—Nakagawa Shigeaki-cho *Shokuhai bigaku* ni tsuite" [Bibliographical Research on the Pioneer Days of Film Aesthetics—on Nakagawa Shigeaki's *Aesthetics of Detached Contact*]. *Eizōgaku* 54 (1995): 65–79.

Malcomson, Scott L. "The Pure Land beyond the Seas: Barthes, Burch, and the Uses of Japan." *Screen* 26.3–4 (May–August 1985): 23–33.

Mast, Gerald. *A Short History of the Movies*. 3rd ed. Indianapolis, IN: ITT Bobbs-Merrill Educational Publishing, 1981.

Miller, Roy Andrew. *Japan's Modern Myth: The Language and Beyond.* New York: Weatherhill, 1982.

Minichello, Sharon, ed. *Japan's Competing Modernities: Issues in Culture and Democracy, 1900–1930.* Honolulu: University of Hawai'i Press, 1998.

Misono Kyōhei. *Katsuben jidai* [The Age of the *Katsuben*]. Tokyo: Iwanami Shoten, 1990.

Miyao, Daisuke. *Sessue Hayakawa: Silent Cinema and Transnational Stardom.* Durham, NC: Duke University Press, 2007.

Monbushō Futsū Gakumukyoku. *Zenkoku ni okeru katsudō shashin jōkyō chōsa* [National Survey of the State of the Moving Pictures]. Tokyo: Monbushō, 1921.

Morris-Suzuki, Tessa. *Re-inventing Japan: Time, Space, Nation.* Armonk, NY: M. E. Sharpe, 1998.

Murakami Okaji. *Jitchi ōyō kinsei shinkijutsu* [Practical Uses of New Modern Magic]. 2nd ed. Osaka: Hakuchikan, 1897.

Musser, Charles. *The Emergence of Cinema: The American Screen to 1907.* History of the American Cinema, vol. 1. Berkeley: University of California Press, 1990.

———. "Rethinking Early Cinema: Cinema of Attractions and Narrativity." *Yale Journal of Criticism* 7.2 (1994): 203–232.

Nagamine Shigetoshi. *Kaitō Jigoma to katsudō shashin no jidai* [Zigomar the Thief and the Age of the Moving Pictures]. Tokyo: Shinchōsha, 2006.

Nakagawa Shigeaki. *Shokuhai bigaku: Keiji shin'in* [An Aesthetics of Detached Contact: Metaphysical Sublime]. Tokyo: Hakubunkan, 1911.

Nihon eiga kantoku zenshū [Comprehensive Collection of Japanese Film Directors]. Tokyo: Kinema Junpōsha, 1976.

Nikkatsu shijūnenshi [A Forty-Year History of Nikkatsu]. Tokyo: Nikkatsu Kabushiki Kaisha, 1952.

Nishimoto Hajime. "Eiga to Monbushō: (jō)" [Film and the Ministry of Education: Part I]. *Hokkaidō Daigaku Kyōiku Gakubu kiyō* 67 (1995): 259–292.

Noletti, Arthur, Jr., and David Desser, eds. *Reframing Japanese Cinema: Authorship, Genre, History.* Bloomington: Indiana University Press, 1992.

Nornes, Abé Mark. *Japanese Documentary Film: The Meiji Era through Hiroshima.* Minneapolis: University of Minnesota Press, 2003.

Okabe Ryū, ed. "Shiryō: Kaeriyama Norimasa to Tōmasu Kurihara no gyōseki" [Documents: The Achievements of Kaeriyama Norimasa and Thomas Kurihara]. *Nihon eiga sōkō* no. 8. Tokyo: Film Library Council, 1973.

Okada Susumu. *Nihon eiga no rekishi* [The History of Japanese Cinema]. Tokyo: Daviddosha, 1967.

———. *Nihonjin no imēji kōzō* [The Image Structure of the Japanese]. Tokyo: Chūō Kōronsha, 1972.

Okano Toshiyuki, ed. *Eiga 100 monogatari: Nihon eiga hen, 1921–1995* [The Story of Cinema 100: Japanese Cinema Edition, 1921–1995]. Tokyo: Yomiuri Shinbunsha, 1995.

Ōkubo Ryō. "Kinodorama to kineorama: Ryojun Kaisen to kindaiteki chikaku" [Kinodrama and Kineorama: The Port Arthur Sea Battle and Modern Perception]. *Eizōgaku* 80 (2008): 5–22.

Okudaira Yasuhiro. "Eiga to ken'etsu" [Film Censorship]. In *Kōza Nihon eiga* [Lectures on Japanese Cinema], edited by Imamura Shōhei et al., 2:302–318. Tokyo: Iwanami Shoten, 1985.

Randall, Richard S. *Censorship of the Movies: The Social and Political Control of a Mass Medium*. Madison: University of Wisconsin Press, 1968.

Sakai, Naoki. "Modernity and Its Critique: The Problem of Universalism and Particularism." In *Postmodernism and Japan*, edited by Masao Miyoshi and H. D. Harootunian, 93–122. Durham, NC: Duke University Press, 1989.

Sakamoto Kitarō. *Jitchi ōyō butsuri kikan* [Practical Uses of Strange Sights]. 2nd ed. Tokyo: Hakubunkan, 1891.

Sandaya Hiraku, *Katsudō shashin ni kansuru chōsa*. N.p., privately published, [1915?].

Sarashina Genzō. *Hokkaidō katsudō shashin shōshi* [A Short History of the Moving Pictures in Hokkaidō]. Sapporo: Kushima Kōgyō, 1960.

Satō Tadao. "Nihon eiga o seiritsushita dodai: Nihon eigashi 1" [The Basis for Establishing Japanese Cinema: Japanese Film History 1]. In *Kōza Nihon eiga* [Lectures on Japanese Cinema], edited by Imamura Shōhei et al., 1:33–34. Tokyo: Iwanami Shoten, 1985.

———. *Nihon eiga rironshi* [A History of Japanese Film Theory]. Tokyo: Hyōronsha, 1977.

———. *Nihon eigashi* [Japanese Film History]. Zōhoban. 4 vols. Tokyo: Iwanami Shoten, 2006–2007.

Schlüpmann, Heidi. "Cinema as Anti-Theater: Actresses and Female Audiences in Wilhelminian Germany." *Iris* 11 (Summer 1990): 77–93.

Sekai no eiga sakka 31: Nihon eigashi [The World's Filmmakers, 31: Japanese Film History]. Tokyo: Kinema Junpōsha, 1976.

Sekino Yoshio. *Eiga kyōiku no riron* [Theory of Film Education]. Tokyo: Shōgakkan, 1942.

Shōchiku kyūjū nenshi [A Ninety-Year History of Shōchiku]. Tokyo: Shōchiku Kabushiki Kaisha, 1985.

Silverberg, Miriam. "Constructing a New Cultural History of Prewar Japan." In *Japan in the World*, edited by Masao Miyoshi and H. D. Harootunian, 115–143. Durham, NC: Duke University Press, 1993.

———. "Constructing the Japanese Ethnography of Modernity." *Journal of Asian Studies* 51.1 (1992): 30–54.

———. *Erotic Grotesque Nonsense: The Mass Culture of Japanese Modern Times*. Berkeley: University of California Press, 2006.

Staiger, Janet. *Interpreting Films: Studies in the Historical Reception of American Cinema*. Princeton, NJ: Princeton University Press, 1992.

Standish, Isolde. *A New History of Japanese Cinema: A Century of Narrative Film*. New York: Continuum, 2005.

Tachibana Takahiro. *Kage'e no kuni* [Land of Shadow Plays]. Tokyo: Shūhō-kaku, 1925.

———. *Katsudōkyō no techō* [Notebook of a Movie Fanatic]. Tokyo: Kōbunsha, 1924.

———. *Minshū goraku no kenkyū* [A Study of Popular Entertainment]. Tokyo: Keigansha, 1920.

Tachibana Takashirō. *Eigadō mandan* [Idle Talk on Filmic Ways]. Tokyo: Mumei Shuppansha, 1926.

Tajima Ryōichi. "Kōgyōshi Kobayashi Kisaburō ron" [On the Exhibitor Kobayashi Kisaburō]. *Nihon Daigaku Geijutsu Gakubu kiyō* 24 (1994): 27–40.

Takaoka Kokugan, ed. *Dai ikkai katsudō shashin setsumeisha kōshūkai kōshūroku* [Class Record of the First Training Course for Moving Picture Benshi]. Tokyo: Dai Nippon Setsumeisha Kyōkai, 1921.

Takazawa Shofū. *Gendai engeki sōran.* 2nd ed. Tokyo: Bunseisha, 1919.

Takemura Tamio. *Taishō bunka* [Taishō Culture]. Tokyo: Kōdansha, 1980.

Takinami Yūki. "Masumura Yasuzō kara Jun'eigageki Undō e: *Intoreransu* kōkai" [From Masumura Yasuzō to the Pure Film Movement: The Release of *Intolerance*]. In *Eizō hyōgen no orutanativ* [Alternative Cinematic Expressions], edited by Nishijima Norio, 275–298. Tokyo: Shinwasha, 2006.

Tanaka Jun'ichirō. "Eigakan nyūjōryō" [Film Theater Admission Prices]. In *Nedan no Meiji, Taishō, Shōwa fūzokushi* [Popular History of Meiji, Taishō, and Shōwa Prices], 163–167. Tokyo: Asahi Shinbunsha, 1981.

———. *Nihon eiga hattatsushi* [History of the Development of Japanese Film]. 5 vols. Tokyo: Chūō Kōronsha, 1980.

———. *Nihon kyōiku eiga hattatsushi* [History of the Development of Japanese Educational Film]. Tokyo: Kagyūsha, 1979.

Tanaka, Stefan. "Imaging History: Inscribing Belief in the Nation." *Journal of Asian Studies* 53.1 (February 1994): 24–44.

Tanizaki Jun'ichirō. *In Praise of Shadows.* Translated by Thomas J. Harper and Edward Seidensticker. New Haven, CT: Leete's Island Books, 1977.

———. *Tanizaki Jun'ichirō zenshū* [Complete Works of Tanizaki Jun'ichirō]. Tokyo: Chūō Kōronsha, 1968.

Terakawa Shin. *Eiga oyobi eigageki* [Film and the Photoplay]. Osaka: Ōsaka Mainichi shinbunsha, 1925.

Tsivian, Yuri. "Russia, 1913: Cinema in the Cultural Landscape." In *Silent Film,* edited by Richard Abel, 194–214. New Brunswick, NJ: Rutgers University Press, 1996.

Tsukada Yoshinobu. *Nihon eigashi no kenkyū* [A Study of Japanese Film History]. Tokyo: Gendai Shokan, 1980.

Turner, Brian S., ed. *Theories of Modernity and Postmodernity.* London: Sage Publications, 1990.

Ueda Manabu. "Kankyaku no tomadoi: Eiga sōsōki ni okeru shinematekku no kōgyō o megutte" [The Audience's Confusion: On the Exhibition of the Cinematheque in the Formative Period of Cinema]. *Āto risāchi* 7 (2007): 129–139.

Wada-Marciano, Mitsuyo. *Nippon Modern: Japanese Cinema of the 1920s and 1930s*. Honolulu: University of Hawai'i Press, 2008.

Washburn, Dennis C. *The Dilemma of the Modern in Japanese Fiction*. New Haven, CT: Yale University Press, 1995.

Yamaguchi Masao. "Jo: eiga izen" [Introduction: Before Cinema]. In *Eiga denrai: Shinematogurafu to "Meiji no Nihon"* [The Introduction of Film: The Cinématograph and "Meiji" Japan], edited by Yoshida Yoshishige et al., 1–12. Tokyo: Iwanami Shoten, 1995.

Yamamoto Kajirō. *Katsudōya jitaden* [Memoirs of a Movie Man]. Tokyo: Shōbunsha, 1972.

Yamamoto Kikuo. *Nihon eiga in okeru gaikoku eiga no eikyō—hikaku eigashi kenkyū* [The Influence of Foreign Cinema on Japanese Film—a Study in Comparative Film History]. Tokyo: Waseda Daigaku Shuppanbu, 1983.

Yanai Yoshio. *Katsudō shashin no hogo to torishimari* [Protection and Regulation of the Moving Pictures]. Tokyo: Yūhikaku, 1929.

Yoshida Chieo. "Kaeriyama Norimasa to *Sei no kagayaki* no shuppatsu made" [Kaeriyama Norimasa until the Starting Point of *The Glow of Life*]. In *Kōza Nihon eiga* [Lectures on Japanese Cinema], edited by Imamura Shōhei et al., 1:236–249. Tokyo: Iwanami Shoten, 1985.

———. *Mō hitotsu no eigashi* [One More Film History]. Tokyo: Jiji Tsūshinsha, 1978.

Yoshida Yoshishige et al., eds. *Eiga denrai: Shinematogurafu to "Meiji no Nihon"* [The Introduction of Film: The Cinématograph and "Meiji" Japan]. Tokyo: Iwanami Shoten, 1995.

Yoshimi Shun'ya. *Toshi no doramaturugī: Tōkyō sakariba no shakaishi* [The Dramaturgy of the City: A Social History of Tokyo Amusement Centers]. Tokyo: Kōbundō, 1987.

Yoshimoto, Mitsuhiro. "Melodrama, Postmodernism, and Japanese Cinema." In *Melodrama and Asian Cinema*, edited by Wimal Dissanayake, 101–26. Cambridge: Cambridge University Press, 1993.

Yoshimura Fuyuhiko. *Zoku Fuyuhiko shū* [A Fuyuhiko Collection Continued]. Tokyo: Iwanami Shoten, 1932.

Yoshioka Hiroshi. "Samurai and Self-Colonization in Japan." *The Decolonization of Imagination*, edited by Jan Nederveen Pieterse and Bhikhu Parekh, 99–112. London: Zed Books, 1995.

Yoshiyama Kyokkō. *Nihon eigakai jibutsu kigen* [Origin of Affairs in the Japanese Film World]. Tokyo: Shinema to Engeisha, 1933.

Yume Sōbei. *Eiga setsumei no kenkyū* [A Study of Film Explanation]. Tokyo: Chōyōsha, 1923.

Zhang, Zhen. *An Amorous History of the Silver Screen: Shanghai Cinema, 1896–1937*. Chicago: University of Chicago Press, 2005.

Žižek, Slavoj. "Eastern Europe's Republics of Gilead." *New Left Review* 183 (1990): 50–62.

Index

Abe Isoo, 72

Abel, Richard, 247n49

Abe Yutaka, 224

actors, Japanese: production of
meaning, 156; in Pure Film
Movement, 110, 114; quality of,
96; in *rensageki*, 193; theatrical,
258n21. *See also* stars, Japanese

actresses, foreign, 102, 158

actresses, Japanese, 3; publicity
for, 160; in *rensageki*, 192–93;
replacement of *onnagata*, 224

aesthetics: in accounts of cinema,
69–70; class-based, 194; Gonda's, 81,
85–86; Heian, 29, 99; in modernism,
215; of Pure Film Movement, 36

aikatsuka (movie lovers), 118*fig.*,
200, 222; apoliticalness of, 263n94;
demands of, 124; knowledgeability
of, 127; pride among, 122; reception
issues of, 129; textual issues of,
129–30; the vulgar and, 117–32. *See
also* spectators, cinematic

Akashi Takaichirō, 200, 217, 286n176

Akiyama Teruji, 70

Akutagawa Ryūnosuke, 84

Amateur Club (film, 1920), 260n38

Anderson, Benedict, 20, 196

Anderson, Joseph L., 17–18, 19,
155; on *benshi*, 104, 134, 135,
139, 265n4, 266n24; on cost of

admission, 263n99; on film industry,
167; on *rensageki*, 281n106

Aoikan (theater), 195, 282n116

Aomori Prefecture, Moving Picture
Regulations of, 176–77, 275n11

Aoyama Shinji, 243n102, 288n19

Arnheim, Rudolf, 79–80, 254n29

arts, Japanese: commingled media in,
134; obscenity in, 203–4; popular
and bourgeois, 75; pre-Meiji, 20;
role in nation building, 20, 240n46;
Western standards for, 283n136

Asahara Ryūzō, 172

Asakura Fumio, nude sculptures by, 204

Asakusa (Toyko): audiences of, 73,
127, 183; effect of Toyko regulations
on, 188; hybridity in, 127, 227;
misemono in, 46; modernity of, 91;
movie theaters of, 54, 56–57, 57*fig.*,
164, 166, 167, 168*fig.*, 185–86, 194–
95, 277n57, 279n80; obscene space
of, 106; theme park in, 53; Ward
Council, 188, 279n79

Asakusa Opera, 101

authenticity, in cinematic reception, 49

authors, cinematic, 161–62; audience
evaluation of, 270n87. *See also*
directors, Japanese

Bandō Tsumasaburō, 160, 224

Baudelaire, Charles, 30, 36

survival of, 7, 97; of Taishō era, 54, 230, 238n31; technical problems of, 113; technological determinism and, 239n37; terminology for, 1–2, 74, 119, 122, 235n2; text-reader relationship in, 131, 134; textual construction of, 134, 148; theatricality in, 3, 11, 66, 85, 97–98, 99, 100–102, 140; traditional culture and, 29; tragedies, 257n9; uncinematic, 8, 10, 12, 226; universalities in, 106, 243n102; vernacularization of, 22; visuality of, 60–61, 63–65, 148, 214–16; Western influence on, 12, 18–19, 239n42; working-class culture and, 78–79, 83–84, 90, 128; during World War I, 18, 109–10; x-ray technology and, 44–45, 47; *Zigomar* imitations in, 54. See also *eiga*; modernism; specific types of cinema

cinema, Japanese sound, 173, 214, 215; Americanized, 288n16; monster movies, 219; of 1960s, 243n102; of 1990s, 243n102; pink, 232; of poststudio era, 288n18; postwar, 219, 232, 287n15, 288n16; in service of state, 219; during World War II, 215, 231–32

cinema, Western: availability of literature on, 112, 260n42; *benshi* for, 140, 146, 264n1; censorship of, 180, 183, 188–89; copyright for, 51, 247n50; effect on Japanese nationalism, 21; embourgeoisement of, 128; French, 51, 247n50; frequency of showing, 163, 271n97; German, 238n29; Japanese domestication of, 22; Japanese titles for, 266n23; lecturers in, 135, 209, 267nn44,50, 268n65, 272n111; modernism of, 215–16; set in Japan, 20, 113–14, 171; standards set by, 96. *See also* cinema, American; Hollywood

cinema culture: impure, 227–29; particularity of, 16; public spheres of, 227

cinema culture, Japanese: *benshi* in, 213–14, 273n112; cultural context of, 4–5; discursive formation of, 4, 5; of domination, 15; embourgeoisement of, 131; forces shaping, 223; in global sphere, 233; hybridity in, 223; local, 115, 233, 287n7; middle class in, 63; mixtures in, 104, 222, 229; polyvocal, 15; power relations in, 26; resistance in, 227–29; storytelling in, 14; textuality in, 131; Western influences on, 11

Cinématographe, 25, 32, 41; in Japanese journalism, 244n4; at Japanese theaters, 42, 43

civilization, cinematic, 76, 77, 84, 86

class: in American cinema, 129; among spectators, 97, 125–29, 200, 224, 228; children as markers of, 186; in cinema reform, 128; in cinematic censorship, 60–61; in film study, 97; geographical definition of, 127; issues for film industry, 123, 125; in Japanese cinema, 7, 14, 26, 63, 117, 125–29, 200, 224, 228; in Japanese culture, 78–79, 83–84, 90, 128; in Pure Film Movement, 122; role in modernity, 30, 31, 38, 131; in Taishō period, 127; women as markers of, 186

classification, cinematic, 185, 187–88; abolition of, 217, 220; children under, 186, 196, 279n71; effect on film industry, 184–87, 188–89, 279nn77,79; in Hiroshima, 279n77; inconsistency of, 196; repeal of, 280n86

class struggle, discursive history of, 23

code-switching: in Japanese cinema, 148; in Japanese culture, 38, 104–5

commercial sample research, Japanese, 256n50

Comolli, Jean-Louis, 239n37

consumption: capitalist, 78; Japanese, 10, 37

Copyright Law, 50–51, 247n49, 248n51, 270n86

Schrader, Paul, 29
science: in cinematic discourse,
    48; *misemono* and, 47; in social
    organization, 90; Western discourse
    on, 43
screenplays, Japanese: censorship
    of, 230, 268n50; discourse of, 10;
    quality of, 113, 224; from theatrical
    productions, 270n89. *See also* texts,
    cinematic
Sei no kagayaki (film, 1918), 1, 2*fig.*,
    107, 110; go-ahead for, 191; release
    of, 266n21; reviews of, 239n43;
    screenings of, 119
Seiyō megane (looking glass), 46
Sekine Tappatsu, 156
Sekino Yoshio, 279n71
Sendai hagi (film, 1915), 97
sesōshi (history of social conditions), 4
Shibata Tsunekichi, 100*fig.*
Shigeno Yukiyoshi, 70, 95, 109,
    111–13; with *Kinema Record*,
    259n32; and Pure Film Movement,
    107
Shizuoka Prefecture, Moving Picture
    Regulations of, 176, 275n10
Shimamura Hōgetsu, 101
Shimazaki Tōson, 49, 50
Shimizu Hikaru, 77
Shinema Parasu (theater), 282n116
Shingeki (realist theater), 101, 110,
    172, 239n41; influence on cinema
    reform, 110
Shin Jigoma daitantei (film, 1912), 54
Shinkankaku school, 37
Shinkokugeki (sword drama), 101
Shinkyōgoku Mototōkō (theater,
    Kyoto), Cinématographe at, 43
shinpa film, 18, 95, 97, 99, 101, 161,
    189, 191, 239n41; benshi for, 265n9;
    fans of, 228; *kowairo* in, 136–37,
    145–46; origins of, 239n41; stars of,
    156; style of, 114
Shirai Matsujirō, 172
Shirai Shintarō, 172
Shōchiku (studio), 19, 110, 162,
    171–72, 224, 231, 273n126; actresses

of, 160; Hollywood methods of,
    260n38; theater chain of, 271n98
Shumi (journal), 49, 94
shunga (erotic prints), 203
signification: discourse of, 7; iconic
    forms of, 154; by images, 224
signification, cinematic, 26;
    centralization of, 173; reformers
    and, 153–54; universality of, 160.
    See also meaning, cinematic
Silverberg, Miriam, 38, 92, 254n23; on
    code-switching, 104; on consumers,
    208; on Gonda, 73, 77; on montage,
    104, 258n26
Smith, Albert, 109
Smith, Anthony, 29–30
social control, role of cinema in, 84,
    217, 218–21
society, Japanese: Meiji, 213;
    modernization of, 10; role of
    cinema in, 4, 12, 86, 192; scientific
    organization of, 90. *See also* cinema,
    Japanese: as social problem; culture,
    Japanese
Sōma Gyofū, 95–96
Somei Saburō, 145
Somei Tenrai, 257n9
Spanish American War, films on,
    247n42
spectators, cinematic, 3; American,
    208; appropriation by, 23, 79, 87, 91;
    approved forms of, 192; class issues
    among, 97, 125–29, 200, 224, 228;
    demographics of, 58–59; desires
    of, 19; discerning, 116, 118, 205,
    220; education of, 203; emotional
    responses of, 80, 81; errors in
    understanding, 139; evaluation of
    authors, 270n87; in filmic space,
    80–81; flexibility of, 104; frequency
    of attendance, 271n101; gender
    segregation of, 185, 186, 193, 197–
    98, 204, 205, 206; historical context
    of, 199; ideal, 223–24; impure, 224;
    inferior, 202–3, 209; interiority
    of, 192, 204, 205, 212; interpretive
    processes of, 60, 88, 134, 139, 149,

Text: 10/13 Aldus
Display: Aldus
Compositor: BookComp, Inc.
Indexer: Roberta Engleman
Printer and binder: Maple-Vail Book Manufacturing Group